The Vietnam Trauma in American Foreign Policy, 1945-75

The Vietnam Trauma in American Foreign Policy, 1945-75

Paul M. Kattenburg

Transaction Books
New Brunswick (U.S.A.) and London (U.K.)

Fifth Printing 1986

Copyright © 1980 by Transaction, Inc.
New Brunswick, New Jersey 08903

Library of Congress Catalog Number: 79-66437
ISBN: 0-87855-378-9
Printed in the United States of America

Library of Congress Cataloging in Publication Data
Kattenburg, Paul M
     The Vietnam trauma in American foreign policy, 1945-75.

     Includes bibliographical references and index.
     1. United States—Foreign relations—Vietnam.
2. Vietnam—Foreign relations—United States.   3. Vietnamese Conflict, 1961-1975—United States.   I. Title.
E183.8.V5K36   327.73'0597   79-66437
ISBN 0-87855-378-9

To my children—Clark, John, Richard, Jeanne, Charles—

And to the young Americans of their generation who helped
   extricate us from our folly, or who suffered or
   perished in it.

Contents

Foreword

Time has not healed the wounds of Earl and Maegene Pittman in Beallsville, Ohio. They lost their only son, Jack, 30,
in the war. He was one of seven young men from the southern Ohio hamlet, all graduates of the same high school, who
died in Vietnam. It was a high price for a town of little more
than 400 people to pay. Mrs. Pittman, 55, is still bitter.
"That's one thing you never forget about," she says. "He's
on our minds all the time. Vietnam wasn't worth anybody's
life. What did they gain by it? The way I feel about it, my
boy gave his life for nothing."

Ed Mechenbier, 35, was a prisoner of war for nearly six
years who returned to civilian life near Springfield, Ohio. He
says perhaps the war should be forgotten. "I don't know that
it's touched anyone good. I just can't see benefits, real or
imagined, out of the whole affair. Personally, it's just a great
big void for me now. I just look at the years I personally
spent there as a void. They just have no meaning. I would
really say wasted."

From "Haunting Memories—Three Years Ago, Vietnam Guns Fell Silent" by
Associated Press writer George Esper, published in *The State*, Columbia, S.C.,
Sunday, April 30, 1978, p. 10-B.

As this is written, more than four years have passed since the final
debacle of April 1975, in Indochina; more than six years have passed
since the last American soldiers, the POWs, came home. For a while,
we wanted to forget. Invitations to lecture on the war, to explain how
and why we got into it and what it meant, which had been frequent in
the early seventies for those of us who claimed some expertise on the
subject, tapered off after 1975. Student interest in my classes seemed to

wane. Adults fell into a sort of collective amnesia. Almost anyone interested had read David Halberstam's masterful *The Best And The Brightest,* which had appeared in paper in 1973, and everything seemed to have been said. We silently nursed the wounds of war, aggravated by those of Watergate. An entire generation of students went through college between 1975 and 1979 largely ignorant of our Vietnam experience.

At present, there is a revival of interest. The subject is no longer taboo. Gen. William Westmoreland, who some years ago suggested in a *Firing Line* interview with William Buckley that the subject best be left for distant future historians to examine in its entirety once all the records had been opened and all the passions had died out, has been waging a one-man campaign to rehabilitate the war, or at least America's engagement in it. He recently told the editors of a new military history of the war, to be published in London and for which he is writing a preface, that here at last was a book of which the children and grandchildren of Vietnam veterans could be proud because it essentially showed that instead of having lost, we had won *(New York Times,* April 22, 1979, p. 59). Westmoreland was first among "the principals" to break a sort of tacit gentlemen's agreement between them that they would not scar each other through the post-war publication of recriminations. Adm. Ulysses Grant Sharp, Pacific Theater Commander during the war, has also recently published on the subject; and the publication of Henry Kissinger's memoirs is imminent.

In the past two years, important new works by non-participants have been published, such as Galluci's *Neither Peace Nor Honor;* Lewy's *America in Vietnam* and Ravenal's *Never Again.* Two significant works, Shawcross's *Sideshow* and Gelb and Bett's *The Irony of Vietnam: The System Worked,* appeared after my own manuscript had been substantially completed. These books complement such important earlier works as Halberstam's, Fitzgerald's *Fire in the Lake,* Barnet's *Roots of War,* Ellsberg's *Papers on the War* and Gloria Emmerson's *Winners and Losers.* A splendid war story, *Dispatches* by Michael Herr, vividly brought home to those who read it the horror and futility of Vietnam from the standpoint of the GI. A spate of Vietnam-related movies are now showing, of which *Coming Home, The Deer Hunter, Friendly Fire* and *Apocalypse Now* are only an early sampling. A major series on the history of the war is being prepared for the Public Broadcasting System. The Congressional Research Service is preparing a detailed historical analysis of Congress's role in U.S. Indochina policy. One gathers that a new and far more detailed documentary history of the war than the *Pentagon Papers* of the early seventies is being readied by specialists in the Pentagon and related think tanks.

The reflowering of interest in the war and its meaning responds to a real need, which is why I have no hesitation in offering still another new book. Recurring and searching questions, especially by the young, deserve the best possible interim answers that can be provided before wholly dispassionate history reexamines the questions in full knowledge of all the available evidence some years, perhaps decades, hence. After all, over 50,000 Americans died in Vietnam, and millions of war veterans, widows, parents, and children of combatants in Southeast Asia live among us. A small number of Americans who fought in the war is still unaccounted for. Hundreds of thousands if not millions of Vietnamese, Laotian, Cambodian, and Montagnard peoples of Indochina, civilians as well as military, died as a result of the war. The exact number of these sad victims depends on how one counts and from when. The ethnic Chinese "boat people" and other refugees, vainly seeking havens on unfriendly shores, are almost daily reminders of the Indochina tragedy.

Our economy has not yet recovered from dislocations of which the root causes are generally and correctly attributed to the war and its costs. An entire generation of younger Americans, now beginning to seize the reins of leadership in the United States, was profoundly affected by the war. A substantial number of its members, whether consciously or unconsciously, blames what it regards as the evil of that war on aspects of the American system itself. Selective Service went with the war. No one can be sure in America today whether or not young Americans would again respond to a military draft. That alone is a fact of enormous potential significance.

Other consequences of the lost war in Indochina have long been apparent in our reduced international posture and prestige; the uncertainties and hesitations of our allies; the renewed truculence of some potential enemies; the virtual equation of the term Third World with anti-Americanism; the weakened structures of our intelligence and policy-making communities; the loss of the domestic consensus on foreign policy which prevailed for so long during the post-World War II decades. The Congress now strongly asserts its role in foreign policy in competition with the Executive. The media, which were responsible for coining the expression and uncovering the fact of a credibility gap during the Vietnam War, have not ceased ever since to cast the sharpest glare of which they are capable upon the probity of every official action. As I attempt to demonstrate in this book, we can regard Watergate, the severest constitutional crisis in the United States since the Civil War, as a natural and direct consequence of Vietnam.

Moreover, the war was extraordinarily important in terms of international and historical perspective. With its conclusion, preceded by the

U.S. rapprochement with the People's Republic of China after 1972, the cold war of the American and Soviet superpowers which had dominated world history during the some thirty years following the end of World War II in 1945 assumed an entirely different and far less threatening character. As leadership generations would shortly change all over the world, so perspectives and perceptions which had controlled the thought and behavior of leaders for the previous three decades would undergo major transformation.

I have tried in this book to begin answering some of the questions, particularly of young and unknowing Americans who are asking: "What happened there and how was it possible? Why did we get so deeply involved and where did we go wrong? How did we manage to contribute to so much tragedy and why does it appear to have been so futile?" I not only consider such questions legitimate, but capable of now being answered with a substantial measure of accuracy. Moreover, I feel that those of us who had some special role in or knowledge of the questions owe some answers to ourselves as well as to the young, and that we should provide these while the war is still relatively fresh in our minds.

In my view, the key to understanding the tragedy that was Indochina for the United States lies in studying, recounting, and analyzing our engagement there not as an issue separate and divorced from the rest of American foreign policy, but rather as an intrinsic and inseparable part of our whole approach to the world in the post-World War II period. This book, therefore, is less concerned with Vietnam or Indochina *per se* than with the whole of American foreign policy between 1945, when Vietnam really started, and 1975 when it ended insofar as the United States is concerned. I realize that there is fighting again today in that benighted Indochinese peninsula, between Vietnamese and Cambodians and between Vietnamese and Chinese. But I have not written about the present or the future, or about Southeast Asia and its role in world politics. I have written about American foreign policy in the recent past, the past ending in 1975, for Americans who shared or were too young to share it. As readers who follow the book through to its conclusions will note, I am not one of those who believe that history, always selective and distorted, offers appropriate prescriptions to help us choose in the present among the many paths opening into the future. But I do believe that as detailed as possible an explanation of the past is essential in order to understand why we are where we are now, and therefore to understand ourselves.

This book then is about American foreign policy during the cold war and what I have called the high cold war. It seeks to analyze and explain why Indochina and Vietnam became so crucial in American foreign policy, ending in 1968 by becoming its very centerpiece and its almost exclusive concern. It seeks to explain why we went about our enterprise the way we did, and why we failed. And it seeks to account for our disengagement over four long years after 1968, what precipitated it, and what results and effects it brought. My method has been narrative and interpretative rather than quantitative or empirical, and I hope that such impressionistic passages as may be found in the book will be tolerated. For any lapses into jargon or flights of perhaps abstruse conceptualizing, I apologize.

I do not apologize, however, for my interpretations. I am eager to have those who would dispute them come forward with their own versions. This is still a great debate, to which I invite with relish those of my former colleagues in the policy-making community as well as all scholars, commentators, and others who are willing and interested. I hope they will join it without vituperation, in the same spirit of rancorless, though certainly not dispassionate, analysis in which I have tried to engage.

It goes without saying that I am solely accountable for every statement made in this book. The list of names and institutions that follows implies nothing but my gratitude, and imputes no responsibility or even a hint that they share my points of view.

Paul M. Kattenburg
Columbia, S.C. and Rapid River, Mich.
August, 1979

Acknowledgments

I am profoundly grateful to Richard L. Walker, director of the Institute of International Studies at the University of South Carolina, for encouragement, guidance, comments, and generous material support. Since he will probably disagree with much that is in this book, it is particularly gratifying that, under his direction, the Institute once more chose "to make a thousand flowers bloom." I am most grateful also to other colleagues at the Institute, in particular James Holland, for assistance, inspiration, and advice.

Sincere thanks to James Kuhlman, Dean Chester Bain, Provosts Davis and Borkowski, and President James Holderman, all of the University of South Carolina, for providing me with sabbatical leave and research and secretarial assistance which enabled the completion of this work.

My deepest gratitude to the following institutions and people who hosted me during the writing phases: Hoover Institution for the Study of War, Revolution, and Peace, Stanford University, which also provided a small grant; Prof. Sheldon W. Simon and his colleagues, Department of Political Science, Arizona State University; Bellagio Study Program of the Rockefeller Foundation, Bellagio-Como, Italy, whose administrator, Roberto Celli, together with his gracious wife Gianna, spared no efforts to ensure the comforts of visiting guest scholars.

Special thanks are due to Robert Wirsing, Donald Weatherbee, and Kendrick Clements, all of the University of South Carolina, for reading my drafts and providing sharply critical and helpful comments for which I am sincerely grateful, even if I did not always follow their advice. I am indebted for inspiration and ideas also to Gerold Guensberg of Washington, D.C., and to other colleagues at South Carolina, particularly Morris Blachman, Lee Jane Hevener, Charles Kegley, William Kreml, James Roherty and Blease Graham and John Stolarek, who provided important information.

My research assistant, Elizabeth L. Normany, did an outstanding and indispensable job in helping me with documentation; she must share fully whatever credit may be given to this book. I am grateful also to Maj. John Cole, Kennedy Center for Military Assistance, Fort Bragg, and to Lt. Col. Michael Eiland and Ms. Louise McNutt, Regional Affairs Officers in the East Asia Bureau of the Department of State, for valuable inputs.

My sincere thanks to Barbara Anderson, Sally Buice, Judy Cain, Lynn Terelle, and especially Sandra Hall, who helped with the typing, photocopying, and administrative chores. My editor, Kerry Kern, provided unstinting assistance, as did James D'Amato in helping construct the index.

I want to express my appreciation for having had faith in me to Edwin Fedder, University of Missouri/St. Louis; Alexander George, Stanford University; Robert H. Johnson, Colgate University; George Kahin, Cornell University; Raymond Moore, University of South Carolina; Richard Ware, Earhart Foundation; Evelyn Colbert, William Hamilton, and Richard Holbrooke, Department of State; and to Irving Horowitz of Rutgers University. David Halberstam was a constant source of inspiration.

Finally, I owe special debts of gratitude to Harold and Marie Miller of Columbia, S.C., who share memories with me of the late Paul Blackstock and Bernard Fall; and to my most patient and altogether admirable wife Mary for helping produce the bibliography and assisting and sustaining me through the agonies and joys of composition.

I should reiterate that I bear the sole responsibility for all the contents of this book.

Chapter I

The United States in Postwar East and Southeast Asia, 1945-54

1. The United States in Postwar East Asia

At the end of World War II, the United States found itself deployed over vast areas of East Asia. It occupied Japan and Japan's former island dependencies in the Ryukyus (including Okinawa) and in the Central Pacific with very sizeable contingents of Army, Navy, Air Force and Marines. It also occupied the southern half of Korea, where the United States maintained a minor military presence until the outbreak of the Korean War in June, 1950. U.S. military forces and advisors remained on the mainland of China to assist the Chiang Kai-shek regime in its civil war against the Chinese Communists until after the failure of Gen. George C. Marshall's efforts in 1946-47 to establish a coalition government between the Nationalists and Communists in China. When the Nationalists finally collapsed on the mainland in the fall of 1949, the remaining Nationalist forces retreated to Taiwan where the United States thereafter retained a strong offshore posture, reinforced after the outbreak of the Korean War by the interposition of the U.S. Seventh (Pacific) Fleet in the Taiwan Straits. In the Philippines, the United States as a result of the war was militarily significantly stronger in the postwar period than it had been before the war.

Our strong postwar military presence in East Asia was a new factor in American diplomacy. The Philippines, China, and Japan had been the only significant exceptions to a prolonged American policy of essentially ignoring East Asia before World War II. Even in these three countries our role had been modest. While we occupied and ran the Philippines after 1898, we promised them eventual independence as early as 1916, and began to implement our withdrawal when we estab-

1

lished commonwealth status for the islands in 1934 and failed thereafter to fortify or prepare to defend them against the likelihood of
Japanese aggression.

In China, Secretary Hay's Open Door notes of 1899 and 1900 had
not prevented the domination of the country by the imperialist powers,
although they facilitated the protection and enhancement of America's
modest trading interests. Our concern before World War II in China
was in essence more sentimental than strategic and was focussed on the
presence of American missionaries. The volume of U.S.–China trade,
despite its vaunted possibilities, remained quite small while U.S. strategic interest in the territorial integrity of China remained a matter for
rhetorical affirmation rather than for interventionary action.

Even in Japan, the U.S. presence and the U.S. role remained relatively small, compared, for example, to our interest in and relations
with the major European powers before World War II. After the negotiations leading to the Washington naval arms limitations agreements
of 1922, we tended to rest content in the belief that Japan, despite her
economic explosion in the thirties and the reiteration of her designs on
the Asian mainland, would neither succeed in fully conquering China
nor seek to expand further into the realms of greater East Asia.

The entire mainland of Southeast Asia was virtually virgin territory
as far as U.S. foreign and strategic policy before World War II was
concerned, with only a minimal concern shown for the colonies of
France in Indochina, the Netherlands in the East Indies, and of Britain
in Burma, Malaya, Borneo, and Singapore. Only in Thailand did the
United States maintain, from about the middle of the nineteenth century onwards, a somewhat esoteric interest, focussed mainly on the
presence of U.S. missionaries and a modicum of trade.

It is significant that the United States never felt the need to intervene
in East Asia before World War II. Despite its historic aversion to alliance policies, it ultimately did not hesitate to come to the assistance of
France and Britain in World War I, particularly after American ship-
ping lanes and interests had been directly affected; nor did the United
States hesitate to intervene repeatedly in Latin American affairs when
its strategic, political, or economic interests seemed directly threatened.
But even after Japan's expansionism started in earnest with the inva-
sion of Manchuria in 1931 and of China proper in 1937, the United
States kept its role one of purely rhetorical opposition. It was only after
Germany had occupied France in 1940 and signed the Axis Treaty with
Italy and Japan that U.S. policy began to change. The change was
precipitated when Japan demonstrated her aggressive intent toward
Southeast Asia by occupying substantial portions of Indochina after the
fall of France in Europe.

At the end of World War II in 1945, the picture had changed drastically. The war had brought U.S. presence to East Asia in great, in fact overwhelming strength. The western portions of the Pacific, including the vast realm of the southwest Pacific and New Guinea, the Philippines, the Ryukyus, and finally Japan and Korea had all been part of the huge theater of operations commanded by Gen. Douglas MacArthur during the war. From their headquarters in Washington and Hawaii, Admirals Chester Nimitz and William Halsey had spread U.S. naval power throughout the whole southern and western Pacific basins. From the China-Burma-India Theater, first Gen. Joseph Stillwell and later Gen. Albert Wedemeyer had extended U.S. military presence into southern, later central and northern China until U.S. Marines reached the Manchurian borders with the Soviet Union. Finally, from British-commanded headquarters of the Southeast Asia Command at Kandy, Sri Lanka (Ceylon), the American OSS (later to become CIA) had extended a feeble but progressively more perceptible presence to the mainland of Southeast Asia.

Thus while the United States had relatively little contact with East Asia before World War II, it found itself at the end of that war occupying a commanding, in fact, an overwhelming position in that region. With U.S. presence, and given the existing conditions and circumstances of the European colonial powers and of Japan, all of which had been fatally or near fatally weakened by the war, there went an ever-increasing extension of American influence.

Asia was no longer, as previously, remote from the American experience; World War II had brought us in, and for the ensuing three decades Asia was to become a major part of the American experience in world affairs. As we shall see, Indochina in a very real sense came to be the crunch-point, the symbolic nub, of this American experience. Symbolizing most of Asia, we had had only remote contact with its peoples and countries before World War II. The war brought us much closer to Indochina. The postwar period saw us exert growing influence and ultimately command over its destinies.

Lack of Wartime Planning

It is appropriate to signal the lack of systematic political planning with which our operations in the Far Pacific and East Asia proceeded during World War II. Although many concepts for the postwar future of Asia were discussed in the United States during the war, none came to real fruition. We entered Asia as conquering military heroes, as liberators of peoples from the Japanese yoke, but without serious concept as to the political organization and future of this vast realm of land and ocean, comprising such a high percent of the world's population. One exception was the Philippines, to which the United States extended independence with alacrity and without afterthought on July 4, 1946.

In Japan and Okinawa, the purposes and methods of Gen. Douglas MacArthur's occupation were also clear: to institute the constitutional, social, economic, and political reforms destined to establish in Japan the type of polity that never again would be capable of aggression against its neighbors in Asia, or of threatening the now extended security interests of the United States in Asia. Japan was first demolished, then disarmed, then democratized; in 1951 the United States signed the peace treaty with the Japanese Empire which was to enable the latter in due course to restore its economic greatness without reestablishing its military predominance. This peace was also to give the United States a permanent military presence in Japan and Okinawa through the network of U.S. military bases which survives to this day.

In China, however, the United States followed an ambiguous policy in the hesitant period of great power confrontation which ensued at the end of World War II and lasted until the outbreak of the Korean War in June 1950. Our policy was a combination of displeasure at the corruption and neglect of the popular will demonstrated by Chiang Kai-shek's U.S.-assisted Chinese Nationalists, and of distrust and fear of the possible threat to U.S. interests represented by the ever-growing and more triumphant forces of Chinese communism led by Mao Tse-tung. In the end, the United States bowed to the realities of the Chinese Civil War, accepted Chiang's retreat from the mainland, and set out to protect him in Taiwan. Two decades of hostile confrontation with Communist China were initiated after the rebuff of initial American attempts to come to terms with Mao. These attempts ended with the Korean War.

Our lack of planning for postwar Asia was most pronounced in Southeast Asia. It applied particularly in Indochina, where President Franklin Roosevelt's strongly expressed and deeply felt distaste for French colonialism seemed destined to induce changes in the postwar period. If Roosevelt can be said to have had a special phobia during the war, it was his revulsion at the French collapse in Europe and at the post-1940 French role in territories like Indochina, which neither rallied to the Free French under Gen. Charles de Gaulle nor supported the Allies in their great war effort against the Axis powers. What had upset Roosevelt most was the willingness of the local French wartime commander, Adm. Jean Decoux, to allow Indochina to be used by the Japanese as a springboard for the penetration and later invasion of peninsular Southeast Asia. Roosevelt seemed determined that never again should France return to Indochina.[1]

Hence it was with Roosevelt's approbation that elements of the OSS, operating from both the China-Burma-India and the Southeast Asia Commands, began to establish liaison with the anti-Japanese guerrilla leader Ho Chi Minh and his followers in the Viet Minh resistance movement during the late stages of the war. At war's end, U.S. diplomacy was at best cool and at worst hostile to French efforts, this time mounted by de Gaulle's government in Paris (1944-45) to regain control over their former rich possession in East Asia. Indochina was divided at the 16th parallel. British forces occupied the southern region with headquarters in Saigon and Chinese Nationalist forces responding to Chiang Kai-shek in Nanking occupied the north, with headquarters in Hanoi. As these operations proceeded after Roosevelt's death in April 1945, no real effort was made by Roosevelt's successors or former principal deputies to give effect to the anti-colonialist sentiments that he had so repeatedly voiced during the war. Efforts by Ho Chi Minh at this time to establish serious contacts with the United States were either rebuffed or ignored.[2]

After Ho's revolution succeeded in Hanoi and briefly in Saigon in August-September 1945, bringing about a rallying of all Nationalist forces under his banner, Ho Chi Minh and his Viet Minh movement were soon forced to retreat to their mountainous "secure rear bases" in Northwest Tonkin. Their southern followers were expelled from Saigon by the occupation authorities and their French hangers-on. After a period of relatively low terroristic activity, the Viet Minh rebellion began to resort to guerrilla war on a larger scale. The French gradually rebuilt their forces in-country, first under the repressive and authoritarian Adm. Thierry d'Argenlieu and later under the more reasonable Gen. Leclerc. By mid-1946, both the British and Chinese Nationalist forces of occupation were withdrawn, leaving the field clear for the French. The latter had, by early 1946, initialed agreements looking toward a peaceful settlement with the Viet Minh, which would have given the latter a key voice in an autonomous government. But the French themselves started to violate these agreements almost as soon as their ink was dry.[3] The United States stood by.

A good argument can certainly be made that the first significant mistake in our postwar Indochina policy occurred as the result of our lack of systematic planning for the Southeast Asian region during World War II and our failure to give effect with force, occupation forces if necessary, to our anti-colonialist rhetoric of the war. If the French had not been allowed to reestablish their presence in Vietnam, Laos, and Cambodia during the year following the end of the war against the Japanese, the ensuing history of Southeast Asia and of the

United States would surely have been very different. And this would have been the case whether or not we had immediately recognized independent regimes under the anti-Japanese partisan leadership of these countries, such as the Viet Minh in Vietnam.

The days of European colonialism in Southeast Asia were to be numbered; and yet the United States had neither prepared itself to fill the vacuum, nor did it appear ready to accept the native nationalisms of various political hues which were emerging in the region. As a result, the British easily regained control of their colonies; the Dutch, though with considerable difficulty, did so for a number of years; and the French slowly crept back into Indochina in a troubled atmosphere which shortly led to the first Indochina War. The latter began in December 1946 with the shelling of Haiphong harbor by French warships and did not end until the debacle at Dien Bien Phu eight years later and the conclusion of the Geneva Armistice Accords on July 20, 1954.

The Importance of Presence

The sheer fact of our overwhelming presence would become a decisive element in the future of East Asia. It induced us to adopt many of the policies that were subsequently followed, policies frequently manufactured in almost *ad hoc* response to the pressures of the moment, and requiring our ever-willing and ever-growing presence for their successful implementation.

U.S. military forces and the accompanying capacity for rapid movement of these forces from one part of East Asia to another, rather than any systematic plan or concept, became a major causal factor for the extended role which the United States began to play after 1945, and especially after 1950, in that part of the world.

Our presence resulted rather rapidly in the acquisition of military bases and positions in postwar Asia, including Southeast Asia. The first such bases were acquired in 1945 by right of conquest in Japan, Okinawa, Central Pacific, and Korea, and later formalized in the peace and security pacts of 1951, 1961, and 1969 with Japan and the 1954 pact with Korea; as well as by bilateral agreement with the Philippines as early as 1947, perpetuating the prewar military presence of the United States in that archipelago.

The outbreak of the Korean War in June 1950 caused the reinforcement and ultimately the solid anchoring of the extended U.S. role and military position throughout East Asia for at least the following two decades. The war confirmed for a long period (1950-72) an American perception of manifest destiny in East Asia and of a major role as emancipator and protector of the peoples of that region.

There followed the interposition of the U.S. Navy in the Taiwan Straits after the onset of the Korean War, and in quick succession thereafter security agreements and U.S. forces positioning on a quasi-permanent basis in Australia-New Zealand (ANZUS Pact, 1951), the Philippines (bilateral security pact, 1951), Republic of China on Taiwan (bilateral security pact, 1954), as well as the SEATO multilateral pact of 1954. The latter extended U.S. protection against "Communist aggression" directly to Thailand and in much more questionable and indirect fashion to the newly independent SEATO protocol states of South Vietnam, Cambodia, and Laos.

2. The Departure of Colonial Powers and the Emergence of Communism in Southeast Asia

The decade following World War II in Southeast Asia was marked by one factor of overwhelming importance, namely the departure of the colonial powers from the region. With the exception of Thailand, all of prewar Southeast Asia had been entirely dominated by Western metropolitan powers: the British in Burma, Malaysia (Malaya and British Borneo), and Singapore; the French in Indochina (Vietnam, Laos, Cambodia); the Dutch in Indonesia (formerly the Netherlands East Indies); the United States in the Philippines.

In a very swift military movement, beginning with their penetration of Indochina in the summer of 1940 and continuing after their attack on Pearl Harbor and Singapore in December 1941, the Japanese had occupied the entire region and expelled all the colonial powers except the collaborationist French in Indochina. Even Australia had been expelled from its mandated territory in Papua-New Guinea. The Japanese held all of Southeast Asia from mid-1942 until their defeat at the hands of the United States, with minimal assistance from other Allied powers, in August 1945.

In the Philippines, despite the establishment of a pro-Japanese puppet government, the population generally and strongly resisted the Japanese, kept faith in MacArthur's famous promise that "I shall return," and effectively supported U.S.-led and organized anti-Japanese guerrilla activity. The returning Americans were acclaimed as heroes in 1944-45 as MacArthur, accompanied by the Philippines' first post-independence president, Sergio Osmena Sr., returned triumphantly to Manila. Independence was achieved smoothly and peacefully in July 1946, but surviving U.S. presence in the form of military bases, substantial economic interests, and indirect exertion of political control gradually led to increasing bitterness in postwar U.S.-Philippine relations.

In Indonesia, the under-strength Dutch, returning for the most part from exile in Australia and later to be reinforced by contingents from the Netherlands proper, immediately ran into an Indonesian national revolution, symbolized by the government of a new Republic of Indonesia. Led by the prewar Nationalist hero Sukarno, who had unabashedly collaborated with the Japanese during the occupation in order to serve his own nationalistic ends, the Republic, centered on Jogjakarta in Central Java, fought the Dutch in Djakarta. A bitter war, called a "police action" by the Dutch, followed (1946-49) during which the Republic, with the support of world opinion expressed primarily in a series of United Nations resolutions and the intervention of U.N. peace-making groups, gradually expanded its base of control around Jogjakarta. It eventually established its full control of the country, taking over the capital of Djakarta in December 1949, as the Dutch slowly withdrew. By mid-1950, as the Korean War broke out, the Republic of Indonesia had become fully independent.

In Burma, the British conferred independence in 1948-49, once they had decided on a similar course for India (1947), and Burma had therefore ceased to play a significant role for Britain as buffer between India and China. Along with India, Pakistan, and Ceylon in the subcontinent, Burma emerged as a fully independent state. But the British were not as eager to release dominion in Malaya and Singapore. The crown colony of Singapore remained firmly in British hands until the end of the decade of the fifties, when it too became an independent republic. As to Malaya, a significant pro-Communist rebellion, led and conducted mainly by ethnic Chinese and known as "The Emergency," had to be put down (1949-55) by British arms supported by a majority of the ethnic Malay population before "Malaysia" (a combination of Malaya and former British North Borneo) too emerged as a full-fledged independent state.

The most complicated situation in Southeast Asia arose in the five former countries controlled by the French in Indochina: the colony of Cochinchina (southernmost Vietnam); and the protectorates of Annam (central Vietnam); Tonkin (northern Vietnam); Laos; and Cambodia. Here—contrary to developments during the occupation of Indonesia, Burma, and Malaysia—a strongly anti-Japanese resistance movement had developed centered around the Communist-led Nationalist "Viet Minh" front, headed by Ho Chi Minh and his close collaborators Pham van Dong (administrator), Truong Chinh and Le Duan (political advisors), and Vo Nguyen Giap (military leader). This movement, an outgrowth of and directly controlled by the Indochinese Communist Party founded in 1930 and led by Ho Chi Minh from that period onward, had been sufficiently well organized to seize Japanese arms and gain control of Hanoi and even briefly of Saigon in the waning days of the war against Japan (August-September 1945). As we can now document from official sources of the period, it had made efforts through OSS to secure American support. But French presence, at first very small, grew during the interim year of British-Chinese occupation of Vietnam (1945-46) and culminated with the war fought by the French beginning in December 1946 to regain control over all of Indochina.

Negotiating efforts between Ho Chi Minh and the French government, which led to the tentative agreements of early 1946, proved unsuccessful once Gen. de Gaulle, who had set them in motion, retreated from the scene in Paris in January 1946 not to return to power for twelve long years. Despite the French decision (1948-49), supported by the United States, to provide constrained and limited independence to the so-called "Associated States of Indochina" (associated in the then existing "French Union"), the three Associated States of Vietnam, Laos, and Cambodia never acquired more than puppet status before the end of the first, or French, Indochina War (1954). They were, however, recognized by the United States and a number of other powers in February 1950 before the outbreak of the Korean War. French forces, which had by the mid-fifties grown to some 500,000 in total manpower, including native auxiliary forces, did not finally withdraw from their former colony until 1955. Accordingly, the end of colonialism was most tortured of all in Indochina.

The decade of decolonization in Southeast Asia is essential to understand as background against which much of what is said in this book rests. We can summarize it as follows: first, the Americans left the Philippines (1946); next the British left India and Burma (1947-49); then the Dutch left Indonesia (1950); finally the French left Indochina (1954-55); and ultimately the small remaining British contingents departed from Malaysia and Singapore (1958-59). This vast region of the world, in which lived about 150 million people of infinitely varied cultural, ethnic, and linguistic backgrounds,[4] had in the period of about ten years following upon the short occupation by Japan thoroughly liberated itself from the colonial yoke.

But who was to be in charge of this new independent region of vast potential and resources? Who would control Philippine sugar and copra; Indonesian oil, rubber, and spices; Malaysian ports, rubber, and tin; Indochinese forests and rice-producing fields? Who would stand athwart the strategic shipping lanes of the Philippines, the Straits of Malacca, the great harbor of Singapore, the natural bays and coves of

Vietnam, the northern routes to China, and the natural barriers between China and her southern neighbors? Who would control the fates of the millions of people within Southeast Asia? And how safe was an independent Southeast Asia for the United States, now engaged in Eastern Asia as never before?

To respond to such questions and to understand the development of U.S. policies, we must first turn briefly to the emergence of communism, mixed with nationalism, in Southeast Asia. It was especially in Indochina, and more particularly in Vietnam, that the emergence of communism came to play a key role in explaining the subsequent lengthy and deep involvement of the United States.

The Emergence of Communism

The significant thing about the emergence of communism in Southeast Asia in the decade following the end of the World War II was that it seemed to appear, and for varying periods to gain dominance over nationalism, in many places all at the same time. U.S. leaders during the war, or for that matter the leaders of Britain, the Netherlands, or France (in the latter two cases, in exile in London, Algiers, or Australia), had never doubted that nationalism, perhaps in virulent form, would be a dominant force in the emerging postwar period. Nationalism had indeed existed and been strongly repressed in the prewar East Indies and in Indochina, as well as in India, Burma, and to a lesser degree in Malaysia and Singapore. In the Philippines, it had existed openly since before the War with Spain of 1898, the establishment of the short-lived and first independent government in Southeast Asia (the Katipunan, 1898-1902), and the expressively nationalistic as well as oligarchic leadership exercised over the Philippine Commonwealth in 1934-44 by Manuel Quezon and his associates.

Thus, nationalism was expected, and the colonial powers, at least initially, thought they could cope with it. Everywhere in this region the colonial governments had denounced prewar nationalism as Communist-inclined and sometimes Communist-led, but only in Indochina was this in fact the case. Nationalism, not communism, was the main concern of the colonial powers as they returned and as the national movements, which had benefited from Japan's occupation and the mortal blow to white European control it had signaled, emerged. For about three years (1945-48), it was largely a matter of nationalism only. Even in Indochina, Ho Chi Minh's movement, quickly going into retreat and engaging in low forms of guerrilla warfare, was not regarded as primarily a Communist problem, but a Nationalist one.

Then, in 1948, several Communist rebellions broke out all at once, or so it seemed, throughout Southeast Asia. The first of these, the so-called "Madiun Rebellion" in Indonesia was crushed by Sukarno in short order. He survived as leader of the Republic and the contending Communist leaders, Musso and Tanmalaka, were eliminated. At about the same time, Communist-led rebellions broke out in Burma just as the latter was on the verge of obtaining independence. The composition of the Communist groups was confused: there were "white flags," "red flags," and tribal Communist groups. They too were subdued as Aung San and later U Nu assumed the leadership of the independent Burmese Republic.

Sometime between 1948 and 1949 Communist-led rebellions broke out in Malaysia and the Philippines. In the former, Chinese ethnic elements led by Chin Peng conducted intense guerrilla war against the British. "The Emergency" was not finally subdued until 1958. In the Philippines, the Hukbalahap rebellion broke out in full force in Central Luzon in 1949. Led by Luis Taruc and supported by American Communists like William Pomeroy (who did not return to the United States from detention in the Philippines until the early seventies), this was clearly an agrarian-based rebellion, resting on the poverty, deprivation, and land-hunger of the peasants of central Luzon. Energetic socio-economic measures on the part of the Roxas and later the Magsaysay administrations, fully supported by the United States, as well as effective counter-guerrilla warfare, brought about the end of the Huk rebellion and the arrest of Taruc by 1953-54.

Finally, in about 1948-49, the Viet Minh rebellion in Vietnam began to gain significant momentum. After Gen. Leclerc's untimely death (1948), France placed its Indochina command in the hands of its greatest wartime leader, Gen. Jean De Lattre de Tassigny. It also began to make political concessions to the small surviving non-Communist, Nationalist forces, such concessions leading to the eventual formation of the Associated States of Vietnam, Laos, and Cambodia (1950).

Nonetheless, Viet Minh strength continued to grow and in 1949-50 these forces inflicted a number of serious military defeats on the French forces in the Vietnam-China border area. By expanding its secure rear bases in northwest Tonkin and northernmost Vietnam, the Viet Minh was able to lay the groundwork for its eventual semi-conventional descents on the Tonkin Delta (1952-53) and its surprisingly strong military posture along the mountain trails and narrow coastal plains of central Vietnam (1953-54); and even to hem-in the Mekong Delta in constantly more bloody and dangerous terrorist and guerrilla warfare, thereby siphoning French forces off the main northern battlefields. The basis was being laid for the eventual culminating conventional confrontation at the battle of Dien Bien Phu on the northwest Tonkin-Laos border (1954).

Thus, in Indochina, contrary to the other countries of Southeast Asia, communism was not defeated or quashed but continued to solidify and fortify its long-standing ascent over all nationalist forces in the country.

The ascent of nationalism in Southeast Asia had begun during a time (1945-48) when the superpowers (United States and Soviet Union) in Europe still carried to a degree the momentum of their collaboration during World War II. It was on sustaining this collaboration that the best hopes for firmly anchoring peace in the postwar period had rested. The entire United Nations structure had been conceived and built in the belief that U.S.-U.S.S.R. collaboration and understanding would continue after the war.

It is true that superpower confrontation did, in a sense, begin as early as the spring and summer of 1945, with U.S.-Soviet disputes over economic and reconstruction assistance to the Soviet Union in the postwar period, and with the severe post-Yalta dispute over the future of Poland. It is also true that the rift grew apace during 1945-46 with dissensions over the occupations of Germany and Japan; over the U.S. possession of a nuclear weapons monopoly; and over the future of Iran, Turkey, and especially Eastern Europe. Moreover, there were severe strains in U.S.-Soviet relations at the Paris Peace Conferences over the Balkans and Italy (1946). The tense year of 1947 witnessed U.S. fears of Soviet advances in Greece and Turkey, the enunciation of the Truman Doctrine, and the dislocation of the original postwar agreements over Germany.

Yet it cannot really be said that what we shall here and later term the "high cold war" began in true earnest in Europe until 1948. The two superpowers, still somewhat hesitantly measuring and sizing each other up, did not reach their final break until after the proclamation of the Marshall Plan and its rejection by the Soviet Union in 1947, and after the initiation by the Soviets of the blockade in Berlin, the counter-U.S. initiative of the Berlin airlift, and the Stalinist coup in Czechoslovakia in 1948. All this put an end to earlier hopes of postwar superpower collaboration. By 1949, the Soviet Union had detonated its own nuclear device and the Chinese Communists had won control of the Chinese mainland. The world seemed fated for major confrontation. It erupted in 1950 in the Korean War.

Before the eruption of the Korean War in June 1950 there was still doubt in the minds of U.S. leaders as to the real nature of the separate Communist rebellions in Southeast Asia, and as to their possible link to a master-minding Communist control center in Moscow and/or Peking. After 1950, such doubts evaporated. The Korean War was initially perceived by the American leadership to have been initiated by the Soviets and Chinese, a judgment now believed to have been erroneous.[5] Similarly, the Communist efforts to gain control over the Nationalist regimes in Southeast Asia or to dominate those anti-colonialist movements where non-Communist Nationalists were weak, as in Indochina, now began increasingly to be regarded by the United States as manifestations of a single and malevolent Sino-Soviet threat to the region.

Since communism erupted in Southeast Asia just as the cold war in Europe was reaching new heights of intensity it is not too surprising that U.S. perceptions of emerging nationalism and especially emergent communism in Southeast Asia changed greatly between 1945-48 and 1948-50. In many ways, this helps explain the profound difference in U.S. attitudes toward the Indonesian Nationalist and the Indochinese Nationalist-Communist revolutions. In Indonesia, we not only tolerated but encouraged the emergence of an independent republic, albeit led by a mercurial statesman who soon proved to be a thorn in our side. The Soviets looked benevolently on and in fact supported the moderate U.N. Security Council resolutions which enabled the Indonesian revolution to triumph and forced the departure of the Dutch.

In Indochina by contrast, the Franco-Viet Minh conflict was never brought to the U.N., owing not only to the French possession of the veto but also to continued U.S. opposition to such a step. Ho Chi Minh's long-standing Communist background, never in any way concealed, came clearly into focus at about the time the other Communist outbreaks in Southeast Asia erupted in 1948-49. American elite and mass media perceptions soon began to range him, his followers, and the Viet Minh movement among the evil forces which, in Asia as in Europe, seemed to stand in the way of Western hopes and plans for progress and peace. This perception would most probably have emerged in the context of the events discussed above even if another major consideration, that of the primacy of Europe in U.S. foreign policy, had not also been present.

The Primacy of Europe

The primacy which Europe and France were taking over Southeast Asia and Indochina in the worldwide foreign policy of the United States during the emerging period of the high cold war led us first to refuse Ho's entreaties for American support and later to oppose him actively by supporting the French. The importance of Europe in the context of the worldwide superpower balance, rendered more acute by the relative weakness and vulnerability of France in the postwar period, reinforced U.S. unwillingness to support a Communist-led Nationalist guerrilla movement opposing France in Southeast Asia. It also strongly reinforced U.S. willingness to support France with money and arms in Indochina, once the Korean War had broken out and the high cold war had swung into full gear.

It is easy to recount these apparent considerations in U.S. policy, but more difficult to follow their logic. Was it in fact logical, given the importance of a strong France in Europe, to support her embroilment in an apparently endless anti-guerrilla engagement in the far reaches of Southeast Asia? The war in Indochina was draining French strength away from Europe into an ultimately lost cause, for which the United States was in fact paying twice—once to strengthen France in Europe and once to strengthen her in Indochina.

The U.S. theater commanders in Asia during the war, American diplomats and military leaders in Asia after the war, and Asianists in the United States both during and after the war, had long chafed at what they viewed as the primacy of Europe over Asia in our foreign policy. The deep resentment of men like MacArthur at America's continued treatment of Asia as remote compared to Europe was in significant measure responsible for some of their excesses of zeal in Asia in later periods. It even had a direct domestic bearing in the United States where the bitter "China Lobby," formed after the fall of mainland China in late 1949, whipped up the notion that we had lost China at least partly out of inattention to Asia and exaggerated concern for Europe. This in turn led to more ready public acceptability of Senator Joseph McCarthy's accusations that the United States was being sold out to communism from the inside, and to the nefarious domestic political purges of the early fifties, to which we shall later return.

Nonetheless, it was in Europe during 1945-50 that the Soviet challenge was being primarily perceived by the United States and that the Soviet threat was predominantly felt. In consonance with this perception, the first permanent alliance in which the United States ever engaged itself outside the Western Hemisphere was the North Atlantic Treaty Organization (NATO), ushered in by the Vandenberg Resolution of 1948 in the Senate and overwhelmingly ratified in July 1949. It was in Europe also that, with the exception of the surviving U.S. bases in Cuba and Panama and the reacquired prewar military bases in the Philippines, we deployed U.S. forces abroad on a quasi-permanent basis for the first time in American history. The U.S. forces which went to NATO Europe as soon as the Korean War broke out are still there.

In this context, and in the tense atmosphere of high cold war breaking out in earnest in Europe after 1948, it is certainly understandable, though perhaps less easily excusable, that the United States lost sight of the Nationalist component and came instead to focus almost exclusively on the Communist component of the Indochinese revolution after the outbreak of the Korean War in 1950.

3. The Soviet Union, China, and the United States in Postwar Southeast Asia

Was the United States correct in its essential overall appraisal that the Communist movements merging with, into, and sometimes dominating the national movements of the Southeast Asia region during the immediate postwar period were basically responsive to commands emanating from Moscow, or from Peking, or from both?

An Objective Look at the Threat

Prior to 1949, only the Soviet Union existed as a major Communist power center capable of exerting influence in the world. The Eastern European Communist regimes, beset with their own difficulties, could hardly have been expected to radiate as far outwards as Southeast Asia. After 1948, however, Yugoslavia under Tito emerged on the scene in an independent capacity. Coincident with this emergence, the Soviets reinstituted a world Communist organization patterned after but weaker than the prewar *Comintern*, which had been allowed to wither. The new organization was called *Cominform*.

The postwar Soviet Union was preoccupied with urgent and massive problems of domestic reconstruction and nuclear defense. Its immediate foreign policy interests were heavily concentrated on Europe (specifically Eastern Europe and Germany), the Middle East, and to a lesser degree Japan. It appears to have had little stomach for an activist world Communist policy, that is for governing and controlling a militant world Communist movement seeking actively to spread communism throughout the world. The *Comiform* proved anything but actively militant.[6]

The emergence of an independent communism in Yugoslavia had two major effects on the problem of reconciling the world revolutionary gospel of the Soviet Union with that nation's overwhelming postwar priority on reestablishing its domestic position and furthering its own specifically Soviet international interests. (1) The Titoist phenomenon made it vital that the Soviet Union find means to restrain the activities of Communist leaders, parties, and groups outside the Soviet Union which might run counter to the major priorities and lines of action in

Soviet foreign policy. (2) The emergence of Tito demonstrated to Soviet leaders, Stalin in particular, that certain foreign communisms had lives of their own which the Soviet leadership would not, in all likelihood, be able to govern and control as it had, at considerable cost, been able to control most foreign communisms before and during World War II.

It must have been evident to Soviet leaders after the Tito break that self-reliant communisms, particularly those which had managed to gain local power through their own exertions rather than through direct and/or indirect Soviet assistance, would be extremely difficult to control. This suggests that the *Cominform,* rather than signifying the revival of a type of *Comintern* organization seeking actively to spread communism, was instead used as a Soviet means to restrain such spread and to bring the tempo of world revolutionary activity in consonance and harmony with the primary objectives of Soviet foreign policy.

These considerations became even more valid from the Soviet point of view after the rise, growth, and ultimately, the victory of the Chinese Communist Party, which established in China a Socialist but hardly Soviet-dominated People's Republic. The Chinese Communists, it is true, received Soviet assistance and in 1950 signed with the Soviets a treaty of friendship, alliance, and mutual assistance under which much more assistance was promised and would, for some years, be forthcoming. But it is clear that the Soviet leaders exercised only a limited and in several respects unreal measure of control over them, particularly after the outbreak of the Korean War.[7]

Mao had not, through his long prewar history, been a really close ally of the top Soviet leaders, and the same was true for a substantial portion of the top Chinese Communist leadership. Moreover, Mao and the Red Chinese Army had gained their victory predominantly on their own, after years of fighting both the Japanese and the Chinese Nationalists against very great odds, including the strong opposition of the United States. They had benefited in limited fashion from the Soviet turnover to them of Japanese war material captured in Manchuria; but they were also bitter at the large amount of booty (Japanese and Chinese) that the Soviets had carted off from Manchuria after temporarily occupying it at the end of the war. Whether deliberately or not, the Soviets had thereby aggravated and delayed the problems of Chinese domestic reconstruction.

We can therefore broadly conclude that there existed three quite separate centers of communism after 1949: the Soviet Union, preoccupied domestically and in Europe; Yugoslavia, presenting a possible model for those self-reliant Communist movements which had resisted the occupying great powers in their regions as partisan Yugoslavia had resisted Nazi Germany, but Yugoslavia was small, distant, and hardly capable of providing much assistance to revolutionary movements in far-off Asia; and China, another model of self-reliance and one perhaps more applicable to Southeast Asian movements, owing to propinquity, history, and the more fundamentally agrarian nature of its revolution.

Which of these three centers would have set in motion the Southeast Asian Communist eruptions of 1948-49? From what if any central planning did they emerge? Some of the literature covering Southeast Asia during this period touches on a Socialist youth conference held in Calcutta sometime in 1948, from which directives presumably emanated leading to the various militant Communist manifestations which have been described in the previous section.[8] But the documentation for such an assertion is rather feeble; to this day it is unclear what if anything of a binding nature was decided in Calcutta, by whom and with what threat of sanction. In any event, it is not really established that this conference had much if any impact in Vietnam or on the leadership of the Viet Minh.

When one looks at the available record with reasonable objectivity, one is struck most of all at the unexpected direction and one-dimensionality of the relationship between international or world communism and Southeast Asia during the immediate postwar years. With the possible exception of Tito, who early on showed a lively interest in the formation of an Indian(Nehru)-led non-aligned bloc in South and Southeast Asia, the relationship seems otherwise to have been almost entirely one-way: not from Moscow or Peking toward Southeast Asia; but from the newly independent Southeast Asian leaderships, associated with Nehru and India, toward Moscow and Peking.

It is reasonable to suppose that either pro-Marxist-Leninist or pro-Soviet or Chinese Communist leanings on the part of Southeast Asian Nationalist leaders would tend to be concealed at the outset, or at least so long as the United States, as the major external power active in postwar East Asia, appeared willing and capable of providing assistance and support in the struggle against colonialism. Such leanings probably frequently existed, owing to the importance of the Leninist theses on imperialism in world Communist doctrine and the persistence of the Leninist anti-imperialist line in Soviet and world Communist policy virtually from 1920 onwards. The doctrine and the line drew many Nationalists from the Asian as well as all other colonial countries strongly to Moscow. But their attachment was at least in part always opportunistic; when conditions began to change after World War II and U.S. ascent in Asia became clearly evident, most Asian Nationalist leaders, including even Ho Chi Minh, were unwilling to sacrifice opportunities of U.S. support on the altar of Soviet theology.

Moreover, aside from the support given Communist China by the Soviets during the Chinese civil war, and except also for whatever assistance Communist China may have provided the ethnic Chinese revolutionaries in Malaysia during their rebellion, there is little evidence that anything other than moral and rhetorical support was provided from Moscow or Peking to the early anti-colonialist struggles in Southeast Asia.[9] On balance, when the whole period 1945-54 is reviewed, neither Stalin, nor Tito, nor Mao played a very significant role in Southeast Asia during its period of emancipation from colonialism. As we shall note later, we would have to except the material assistance provided by China to the Viet Minh during the last years of the first Indochina war. But otherwise it is safe to conclude that there did not exist substantial Sino-Soviet influence in the region during that period, even if one chose to regard Moscow and Peking as still closely tied to each other at the time.

The Korean War significantly affected American perceptions of the situation, probably largely because our role in that conflict so substantially increased the American involvement in all of East Asia. But by the early fifties, insofar as Southeast Asia was concerned, Burma had regained an acceptable measure of stability; Indonesia was proceeding according to its own path toward Sukarno's often proclaimed goals of "Pancha Sila" (neutralism and non-alignment); and the Philippines, by its own American-supported efforts, had managed to rid itself of a Communist insurgency which at no time bears evidence of having received outside material support. Thailand too had remained relatively stable under its monarchy and its revolving, largely undifferentiated, military dictators.

Thus only Malaysia and Indochina could objectively justify an American perception of Sino-Soviet threat, that is, could be seen as possible objects of serious external Communist interest. But in Malaysia, although the "Emergency" continued for several more years, it was eventually subdued and independence in both Malaya-Borneo and Singapore was achieved without a marked external Communist role of any kind. This was evidence perhaps that if Peking supported the ethnic Chinese rebels it did not at the time judge them or their country worth risking enough to stave off their defeat.

In Indochina, the story was different; but even here one is hard put to trace significant external assistance to the Viet Minh until the last stages, at most the last two years, of the French (or first) Indochina

War.[10] Furthermore, such assistance did not extend to the rebel movements then already germinating in Laos and Cambodia: the Pathet Lao were allies, perhaps simple extensions, of the Viet Minh and received Ho Chi Minh's assistance; Sihanouk in Cambodia sought or received no assistance from either Moscow, Peking, or Hanoi; and the Khmer Rouge, with cadre nuclei then being trained in Paris or Hanoi, existed in only rudimentary form. Accordingly, one has to find the Sino-Soviet threat perceived by the United States primarily, if not only, in Vietnam.

The Viet Minh movement as early as 1949 openly admitted the governing and central role within it of the Lao Dong (Vietnam Workers') Party, successor to the original Communist Party of Indochina, and made no bones at any time of its Marxist-Leninist character, leadership, or goals. It abided no opposition from the extreme left, and mercilessly crushed the burgeoning Trotskyite elements in Vietnam during and immediately after the war. It was willing, however, during the periods of national unity (1945-46) and national war of liberation (1946-54) to accept social democratic and even centrist and Catholic groups in its coalitions and fronts, provided the latter allowed all power to reside exclusively in the Communist core of the Viet Minh. Accordingly, the non-Communist groups within the Viet Minh were ineffectual and practically meaningless.

After the Democratic Republic of Vietnam (DRV) was established in Hanoi and Saigon in August 1945 with Ho Chin Minh as president and Pham van Dong as prime minister, its government openly sought Soviet and Chinese Communist support. Moral and propaganda support were received in ample fashion from 1946 onwards. Diplomatic support, particularly from the Soviet Union, had its ups and downs after both Moscow and Peking recognized the DRV in January 1950, as we shall note in later chapters. But insofar as material support was concerned, economic and especially military aid started to flow into the DRV from its major allies in significant quantities only after about 1953. Reasonably reliable statistics show that the Soviets and Chinese provided a total of about $400 million in economic and military assistance between 1945 and 1954.[11] It should be clearly noted, however, that without China's arms assistance in 1953-54, the battle at Dien Bien Phu could probably not have been won when and in the manner that it was.

Would the Soviet Union and People's Republic of China have acquiesced in the destruction of the DRV during 1946-54 if the will and means for such an outcome been in the possession of the French, or the French and the Americans? The answer is, of course, a matter of sheer speculation, but it might be surmised that the People's Republic of China would have intervened militarily in Vietnam had the DRV, at least after 1953, been threatened with imminent destruction, as it had intervened earlier in Korea under like circumstances. The imminent destruction of the DRV never seemed probable, however, particularly after the United States had decided not to enter the war in support of the French in the spring of 1954—so the question is really a moot one. On the other hand, would Moscow or Peking have stepped in simply to ensure the DRV's victory if the stalemate in the French Indochina war had continued beyond 1954? The answer to this is, of course, equally speculative, but it may be surmised that they would not have done so; that they were no more willing than the United States during its own Indochina war later to ensure the victory of what some chose to call their clients, and concerned only with staving off these clients' defeat. This too, of course, is a moot question.

On balance, we may conclude with the hindsight of the late seventies that there existed no serious objective Sino-Soviet threat in Southeast Asia in either 1945-50 or, for that matter, in 1950-55. This in no way vitiates the fact that American leaders *perceived* such a threat. But in support of our proposition, it is important to note that during 1950-55 Peking was enormously preoccupied with the Korean War and subsequently with the beginnings of domestic reconstruction. As to the Soviet Union, it was embroiled at least from 1953-55 in an enormous internal political struggle of succession following Stalin's death, not to mention its other severe domestic and international problems.

The period 1953-55 was in fact marked by an interesting lapse in the high cold war insofar as the Soviet Union was concerned. During this period, which lasted roughly from Stalin's death at the beginning of 1953 to Khrushchev's firm assumption of the reins of power at the Twentieth Party Congress in February 1956, the Soviets (initially under Malenkov) actually made some efforts to resume a dialogue with the West.[12] By mid-1955, the Soviets were amenable to President Eisenhower's calls for a summit meeting, which took place in Geneva in July of that year and at which Eisenhower propounded his "Open Skies" proposals.

It is accordingly not very surprising that the Soviets in 1950-55 paid little attention to the distant realm of Southeast Asia, which they then (and, to a degree, later as well) tended to relegate to an oceanic type, proto-American sphere of influence. Nonetheless, this in no sense prevented the Soviets, as indicated, from supporting the DRV fully in their propaganda. Their continued virulent calls for the destruction of colonialism in Indochina as elsewhere could only help them with the world

Communist movement and the burgeoning worldwide "movements of colonial peoples against imperialism." We shall return in the next chapter to the question of specific Soviet interest in Indochina, particularly in relation to the question of Vietnam's partition, which arose acutely in 1955-56.

After 1950, the United States harbored an intense hostility for China, compounded from communism's mainland victory, China's intervention in Korea, and domestic McCarthyism in the United States. Chou En-lai's famed visit to the first conference of the non-aligned powers at Bandung in 1955 was regarded with particular suspicion and as a particularly hostile gesture by Secretary of State Dulles. Yet it was Nehru and Sukarno among other South and Southeast Asian leaders whom Chou greeted at Bandung. Why should the presence of the Chinese Communist foreign minister at a conference of Asian Nationalist leaders, who were convening for the expressed purpose of announcing they wished no truck with either Moscow or Washington, have aroused such hostility in the United States? Why was China regarded, as was Moscow, as evil incarnate rather than as a war-weakened Communist power, perhaps seeking the support as well as the leadership of other newly independent Asian states in what might have to become an eventual stand against Moscow as well as Washington?

Factors in U.S. Perceptions

As already indicated, the initially benevolent U.S. posture toward anti-colonialism in Southeast Asia had shifted from a focus on nationalism to a strong focus on communism sometime after the outbreak of the various Communist-led local uprisings of 1948-49. This started a period during which ideology predominated over all other factors in the making of our foreign policies toward that region of the world. Whether Moscow and Peking concerted to induce the uprisings in Southeast Asia, or either of these two powers induced them alone, or neither of them had anything to do with it, the relevant fact is that key U.S. policy-makers believed in both such inducement and the existence of a real Sino-Soviet threat to the integrity of the Southeast Asian states. Among the principal considerations which gave rise to such perceptions in U.S. policy, the following seem most relevant:

First, the appraisal of a highly aggressive and potentially extremely threatening Soviet posture toward Western Europe and the Balkans after 1946 led to the elaboration of the U.S. doctrine of containment and the enunciation of the Truman Doctrine in 1947. Containment in turn provided the conceptual parameters for the perception of spreading Moscow/Peking-directed communism in Southeast Asia. We shall return in the next chapter to the effects of the containment doctrine on U.S. policies in Southeast Asia.

Second, the Korean War further bolstered the American perception of a Sino-Soviet threat to our extended role in East Asia and of aggressive communism on the move in Southeast Asia. This occurred not only because the Soviets and Chinese were perceived in Washington as having at least sanctioned and at worst incited their client state of North Korea to aggression; an equally strong reason was that Peking, always presumed to be underwritten by Moscow, was seen in Korea as surprisingly possessing both the will and the means to give the American superpower in East Asia quite a bloody nose.

Third, by 1950-55 the United States was domestically conditioned, in fact predisposed, to the perception of a threat from its central enemies, the Soviet Union and China, arising anywhere in the world. It was during this period that the United States engaged its clandestine apparatus, the CIA, in a successful effort to overthrow the legal government of Iran (1953) and in an equally successful operation to overthrow the left-leaning regime of Guatemala and replace it with one more responsive to U.S. wishes in the Central American region (1954).

This domestic predisposition was ultimately the result of a troubling and prolonged transformation of the U.S. Congress and eventually of U.S. public opinion from a relatively relaxed postwar stance of hope in superpower collaboration to one of extreme bellicosity toward the Soviet Union. It has been said, and to a degree demonstrated, that overreaching rhetoric had to be used by American leaders to mobilize and later to galvanize our public and Congress into taking "an internationalist" stance in world affairs.[13] This was allegedly necessary for the Executive to obtain the means with which to implement the Marshall Plan for European reconstruction and to conclude alliances such as NATO and our later bilateral and multilateral pacts with which the worldwide wall of containment around the Soviet periphery was built. But such galvanization of public opinion through overreaching rhetoric tends to become a Frankenstein monster; it makes statesmen and diplomats prisoners of their own rhetoric, unable to maneuver flexibly through the complex shoals of world political waters, and mesmerizes them into faulty perceptions of reality.

Finally, we may advance the proposition that the United States, unable to accommodate itself to Communist-led nationalism in Southeast Asia even though the communism involved appears to have been largely automomous in inspiration, needed the perception of a Sino-Soviet threat in order to mobilize itself for intervention in the region;

and that once such a threat materialized in Europe and Northeast Asia, the U.S. entered into a self-fulfilling prophecy by easily extending its perception of it to a region where, basically, it did not exist.

The specific U.S. role in Southeast Asia, especially during 1950-54, can be summarized in a few sentences. In the Philippines, things continued to go in a manner generally acceptable to the United States. In Burma, as U Nhu's non-alignment became more perceptible, the U.S. washed its hands of the situation (much as in India) and observed from the sidelines. In Thailand, we began in this period to extend at first minimal assistance to the existing oligarchic, military-led regimes. In Malaysia, we encouraged the British, whom we had assisted in Europe, to carry the burdens and costs involved in curbing the "Emergency." In Indonesia, despite our increasing annoyance at Sukarno's excesses and growing lack of amenability to our wishes, we basically continued a standoff posture and refrained, at least until 1958, from any direct intervention.

In Indochina, the United States began after the initial hesitation of 1945-48 to see the Communist handwriting on the wall and to turn increasingly to support of the French, who in any case appeared absolutely essential to its position in Europe. The United States did not raise and answer for itself the question: Would France have provided a stronger bulwark in Europe without the drain from its Indochina involvement? This question was, in effect, pre-empted by the post-Korean War perception that a Communist threat to Southeast Asia could not be allowed to develop further. In the absence of the French, there would have existed no force save that of the United States itself that could have coped with the threat. France had a special veto over our position so long as the United States believed that a European defense community, led by France and Britain, was essential to complement if not eventually to substitute for the slowly elaborating NATO defense structure in Europe. In 1953-54 it was by no means obvious that the Congress would forever allow U.S. forces to remain in Europe.

We recognized the three Associated States of Vietnam, Laos, and Cambodia in early 1950, although they had no real independence, and we ended up by extending them very substantial economic and military support through France between 1950 and mid-1954. In toto, over these four years, U.S. aid to Indochina reached the staggering total of some $3.5 billion in economic and military assistance.[14]

Thereafter, to all intents and purposes, the United States was "in" Southeast Asia.

Notes

1. *The Pentagon Papers: The Defense Department History of U.S. Decision-Making on Vietnam* Senator Gravel Edition (Boston: Beacon Press, 1971), 1: p. 1.
2. *Ibid.,* p. 17
3. Ellen J. Hammer, *The Struggle for Indochina* (Stanford: Stanford Univ. Press, 1954), pp. 181-87.
4. George B. Cressey, *Asia's Lands and Peoples,* 2nd ed. (New York: McGraw Hill, 1951). The population of Southeast Asia today is estimated at about 300 million.
5. *See,* for example, Robert R. Simmons, *The Strained Alliance: Peking, Pyongyang, Moscow, and the Politics of the Korean Civil War.* (New York: Free Press, 1975). *See also,* by the same author, "The Communist Side: An Exploratory Sketch," in *The Korean War: A 25-Year Perspective* ed. Francis H. Heller (Lawrence, Kan.: The Regents Press of Kansas, 1977), pp. 197-208.
6. Adam B. Ulam, *The Rivals: America and Russia Since World War II* (New York: Viking Press, 1971), pp. 131-33.
7. David J. Dallin, *Soviet Foreign Policy After Stalin.* (New York: J.P. Lippincott, 1961), pp. 83-94; Ulam, *The Rivals,* pp. 170-83.
8. John F. Cady, *History of Post War Southeast Asia* (Athens, Ohio: Ohio University Press, 1974), pp. 62 ff.
9. Bernard Morris, "Communist Strategy in India and Southeast Asia," in *Political Change in Underdeveloped Countries: Nationalism and Communism* ed. John H. Kautsky (New York: J. Wiley & Sons, 1962), p. 295.
10. Evelyn Colbert, *Southeast Asia in International Politics, 1941-56* (Ithaca: Cornell University Press, 1977), p. 213.
11. Extrapolated from King C. Chen, *Vietnam and China, 1938-54* (Princeton, N.J.: Princeton University Press, 1969). Chen uses a wide variety of sources to deduce these statistics. *See also* Jay Taylor, *China and Southeast Asia* (New York: Praeger, 1974, 1976), p. 9; George K. Tanham, *Communist Revolutionary Warfare: The Viet Minh in Indochina* (New York: Praeger, 1961).
12. Adam Ulam, *The Rivals,* Chapter 7.
13. John Spanier, *American Foreign Policy Since World War II,* 6th ed. (New York: Praeger, 1973), p. 43.
14. John D. Montgomery, *The Politics of Foreign Aid: American Experience in Southeast Asia* (New York: Praeger, 1962), pp. 22 ff and Appendix I-A, pp. 281-84. Montgomery's sources include congressional reports and reports of the International Cooperation Administration.

Chapter II

The Effects of Containment on U.S. Policies, 1945-59

1. Political and Ideological Aspects of Containment

"Containment" was the name of the foreign policy doctrine adopted by the United States in the post-World War II period to counter Soviet moves which the United States regarded as hostile and threatening to its security interests. Perceptions of Soviet policy which led to U.S. containment included the following:

1. That the Soviet Union harbored hegemonious designs over the entire region of Eastern Europe, which it had in effect annexed as a sphere of influence after World War II, and helped to install and maintain in each of the countries involved regimes willing to do its bidding.
2. That the Soviet Union might threaten to extend its influence over areas of Western Europe and the Balkans (Greece and Turkey in particular) that it did not yet control.
3. That, similarly, Soviet influence might spill over into regions of the "northern tier" of Middle Asia (specifically Iran, Afghanistan, Pakistan) into certain countries of the Middle East (Syria, Lebanon, and Iraq were the obvious targets, but Egypt and others offered possibilities), and might even extend into India.
4. That the ideology of international communism compelled the spread of Soviet influence into "every nook and cranny" of the non-Communist, soon-to-be-dubbed "Free" World where it was not firmly resisted. U.S. Foreign Service officer George F. Kennan had used this colorful expression in his famous and anonymous article "The Sources of Soviet Conduct" by "X," which appeared in the July 1947 issue of *Foreign Affairs,* the quarterly publication of the U.S. Council of Foreign Relations. The article was based on a lengthy telegram Kennan had dispatched from the U.S. embassy in Moscow to the Department of State in February 1946.
5. That by firmly resisting Soviet pressures "at every point," as suggested by Kennan, the United States might be able to thwart Soviet designs and thus

to preserve a climate conducive to the plans and policies of the United States for a free, stable and accessible world political order.

Kennan, one of the foremost diplomats and thinkers on international affairs which the United States has produced in the period since World War II, has repeatedly and unsuccessfully tried since the early fifties to erase a number of erroneous interpretations to which he feels his famous message gave rise. It is not to the heart of the containment doctrine itself that Kennan objects, or to the infinitely subtle and complex analysis of immediate postwar Soviet policy on which it is premised and which he himself in large part authored. Kennan objects to what he feels were misinterpretations of his message of "containment" by top policy-makers in the United States, and to the politics which led to the enunciation of a doctrine of containment in President Truman's statement of March 1947, which became known as the "Truman Doctrine." The doctrine's consequence was the conception and implementation, largely through military means, of U.S. foreign policies which Kennan considers to have been both faulty and in some respects threatening to the peace of the world.[1]

Soviet and World Communist Positions

We shall look first at the Soviet and world Communist positions in the immediate postwar period; and then in greater length at the American position. The Soviet Union emerged from the war terribly weakened and shattered in the essential fabrics of its society. Hundreds of plants and factories lay idle, destroyed, or in disrepair, although new and relatively productive industrial complexes had emerged unscathed from the war in the more distant eastern regions. The transport system was, generally speaking, in shambles; agricultural production at an all-time low. Millions of men and women returning from war had to be reabsorbed into the labor force or the collective farms, while an increasingly intolerant and unbearable tyranny by the aging dictator Stalin trusted no one and nothing, but disposed of unlimited means of repression. Above all, the Soviet Union had suffered some 20 to 25 million dead, directly or indirectly, as the result of the terrible war that had raged throughout all of Western Russia.

The extent of the consequent internal popular unrest and discontent, even dissidence of very significant proportions, cannot be doubted and was in fact demonstrated by the indiscriminate reign of terror, so well described later by Solzhenitsyn, in which literally millions of people were deported to Siberian labor camps. The existence of significant dissidence among the Soviet people had been demonstrated even during the war, when hundreds of thousands of Soviet soldiers and prisoners of war defected to the Germans and then to Gen. Vlasov's army, which fought on the Nazi German side against the regime of their own nation.[2]

Although the Soviet leadership proudly insisted on the "superpower" status it had gained as a result of its size, scope, visibility in the world, and its triumph in World War II, it could not afford to open Russia for outsiders to gauge the extent of the internal ravages and weaknesses. This desire to maintain a closed society dovetailed nicely with the traditional distrust of the Russian people for foreigners and foreign powers. After all, the memories of the Soviet masses, and particularly of the Soviet leadership, were long: memories of anti-Bolshevik, anti-revolutionary occupation by Western, including U.S., military forces in 1918-19; of obdurate world capitalist anti-Bolshevism in the twenties and thirties; of failure on the part of Britain and France to join the Soviets in the mid and late thirties in constructing an anti-Axis alliance; and above all memories of the repeated depradation caused on Russian soil throughout modern history by both Eastern European powers and Germany, the former often pushed by their stronger Western partners [3]—as in the French "Little Entente" policies of the interwar period.

This last memory in particular, may explain Soviet obduracy in controlling Eastern Europe in 1945-46. As far as the Soviets leaders were concerned, all regimes on the western borderlands of the Soviet Union would be pro-Soviet. This was only in a minor degree a matter of ideological concern; it was rather a capital question of the survival and security of the Soviet state.

The status of world communism on the morrow of the war does not strike one, when considered today, as substantially stronger than that of the Soviet Union itself. In the East, communism was rising, but was still far from triumphant in China; virtually non-existent in occupied Japan; merged with uncertain nationalisms and focussed strictly on anti-colonialism in Southeast Asia, where in any case it was inherently weak except in Vietnam. India was moving toward democratic socialism, not Marxism-Leninism; and throughout the entire Middle East well-ensconced traditionalist-oligarchic regimes, or the presence of Western powers, or the influence of Islam, offered formidable barriers to communism. In Latin America, communism right after the war was virtually moribund.

Only East and West Europe offered possibilities; but while the Soviet Union held a tight grip on the former, Western-type capitalist democracy seemed to be regaining an equally firm footing in the latter. In

France, despite the wartime influence of Marxist-Leninist-led partisan forces, the democratic center proved solid in the postwar period, even after de Gaulle left power in January 1946. In West Germany, the Communist Party was wholly unable to revive its pre-Hitler strength while the Social Democrats increasingly opted for gradual, non-revolutionary progress, and all elements in the population profoundly feared and distrusted a Soviet Union which was regarded as basically responsible for the postwar division of the country and the unlikelihood that reunification could ever again be achieved. Indeed, by opting early for a satellite East Germany, the Soviet Union had sacrificed whatever hopes it may have held to detach West Germany from the West. But this decision was not entirely made by the Soviets alone; it can be argued, on the contrary, that it was at least in part forced upon them by Western policies in West Germany.[4] Only in Italy and Greece might the Soviet Union have held some legitimate hopes for future Communist growth.

None of the above helps much in explaining rising postwar American and Western perceptions of an aggressive Soviet Union and a worldwide Communist movement on the march. In fact—despite Soviet internal repressiveness, justly decried everywhere; despite Soviet harshness in Eastern Europe; despite the immediate postwar Soviet grab for and annexation of the Baltic states and East Prussia (territories of special threat to Russia throughout its modern history); and despite the imposition of an effective veto on Finland's foreign policies—nowhere outside Eastern Europe did the Soviet Union move firmly or inflexibly to acquire control. In Azerbaijan and Northern Iran, the Soviets retreated as soon as the West made clear in the U.N. that their actions would not be tolerated (early 1946). In Greece, the ELAS revolutionary movement was directly supported, not by the Soviets, but by the Yugoslav government under Tito—a Communist government which broke with the Soviet Union as early as 1947-48, thereby signaling the weakness, not the strength or cohesion, of the world Communist movement.[5]

The only region in which the Soviet Union showed itself aggressive, inflexible, and truculent, the region not only of its prime but it could accurately be said of its only non-domestic immediate postwar concern, was Eastern Europe. It was in the cauldron of turbulent East European politics, the resistance of democratic leaders in the region to the exercise of Soviet hegemony, and the servile attitudes of its local Communists, that the Soviet threat and the high cold war were, in the main, born.

With over thirty years' hindsight, one is today naturally and obligatorily led to ponder why considerations such as these did not seem to weigh more heavily in the analyses of the Western powers, particularly the United States, at the time containment was conceived. In part, the answer is that they did play an important role as long as Roosevelt and Harry Hopkins were alive and in charge of U.S. foreign policy. There is much reason to believe that Roosevelt did indeed understand Stalin at Yalta, where one of his major concerns was to obtain Soviet entry, despite Soviet war-weariness and fatigue, into the war against Japan. The Soviets did enter that war at its very end; by shifting badly exhausted forces from one to another distant front, they gained a handle on Manchuria and on the subsequent political evolution of both Korea and China.[6]

It is possible that the deal at Yalta would not have been struck if the United States had been more aware of Japanese military weakness after the apparent capture of most of the vaunted Japanese Kwantung (Manchurian) Army in the Philippines. The United States seems also to have taken into little, if any, account at Yalta the overwhelming predominance of power it would shortly acquire as a result of its detonation of nuclear weapons. But these are the "ifs" of which history is replete. We contend here that the United States (and Britain) at least in spirit acquiesced at Yalta and earlier to Soviet demands for absolute security in Eastern Europe, and to the consequent political moves in that region which Stalin undertook.[7]

What then were some of the main factors that led to such a disproportionate U.S. appraisal of the Soviet threat so soon after the end of the war, and at a time when U.S. forces were eagerly demobilizing and the U.S. public was so clearly demanding rest, tranquillity, and the domestic prosperity of which it had been deprived during the long years of the Depression and the subsequent years of war?

A host of answers suggest themselves, some of which we shall next attempt to examine. We shall group what we consider the main factors under two headings: those bearing primarily on events and developments external to the United States; and those stemming in the first instance from domestic sources. But all these external and domestic factors are important, none are primary, and all are intertwined.

External Factors Underlying Containment

The rapidity and scope of the Soviet imposition of hegemony in Eastern Europe was undoubtedly a shock to Congress and the American public, as well as to the leadership around President Harry S Truman, which succeeded to high office when President Roosevelt died two months after Yalta. Perhaps Roosevelt, Hopkins, Averell Harriman (as ambassador to the Soviet Union), and others in the immediate Roosevelt circle might have acted differently in response to Soviet actions in Eastern Europe throughout 1945, had Roosevelt lived. After his death, however, Truman almost immediately became bellicose toward the Soviets, partly no doubt to convey to the Congress an impression of his toughness and capacity to handle the extremely complex international situation.[8] New personalities, such as James F. Byrnes as secretary of state and James Forrestal as secretary of defense, soon emerged in key decision-making roles. Harriman himself did little to ensure a smooth transition in Soviet relations; on the contrary he rapidly became a spokesman for a tougher and eventually a hard line toward the Soviet Union. Only Henry Wallace remained in the Truman administration to express the old hopes for postwar superpower collaboration and a policy of meeting Soviet security needs, translated in practice as hegemonic aspirations in Eastern Europe, outright; but Wallace was soon derided and discredited. In the case of Eastern Europe it is probably fair to state that the Soviet Union behaved generally as it should have been expected to behave; but a number of domestic factors, on which we shall dwell later, combined with Truman's need to demonstrate assertive leadership to produce unexpectedly strong U.S. responses.

The bluntness, inflexibility, and obdurateness of the Soviet occupation policy in Germany, and of Soviet policy in Berlin, reinforced U.S. government and subsequently U.S. public perceptions of an aggressive Soviet leadership, bent on having its way wherever it was not met with equal rigidity and with the use of threats. "Deterrence," which began to be conceived in the immediate postwar period, consisted after all of a threat: If you do this and that (which we don't like) to us, we shall do this and that (which you won't like) to you; therefore don't do it. This was quite the opposite of the traditional diplomatic approach founded on inducement: If you behave at least partly the way we want you to, we shall make it worth your while. We shall explore deterrence in much greater detail in a subsequent chapter; here let us note that from the outset of its application by the United States and the Western allies in Europe it took on the character of a "zero-sum game" (either you win and I lose, or I win and you lose). In respect to Soviet policy in Germany, it is probably fair to state that the United States responded appropriately to truculent and militant Soviet behavior in Berlin and on its side of the now rapidly falling iron curtain in Central Europe; but it is also possible to surmise that if the United States had been more receptive to policies of inducement (such as acceptance of the status quo in Eastern Europe), it might have found the Soviet Union more amenable to perpetuating reasonably conflict-free quadripartite rule over Germany. It is consequently possible that the high cold war might have been mitigated, if not averted.

While the likelihood of threatening Soviet moves toward Western Europe, the English Channel, and the Atlantic was exaggerated out of all proportion in the immediate postwar period, the potential for Soviet moves in the Balkans (Greece and Turkey) was not. This was frightening because the imminent departure of British power from the Eastern Mediterranean and Near East threatened a power vacuum in a strategically vital corner of the world. While not eager, and in fact hardly capable, to fill this potential vacuum itself, the United States was certainly unwilling to see it become an area of major Soviet influence. Accordingly, it is probably fair to state that the United States met the specific situation in the Eastern Mediterranean with appropriate countermeasures, as it did in the proclamation of the Truman Doctrine. However, as we shall observe later, the Truman Doctrine went far beyond the Eastern Mediterranean in proclaiming American obligations of assistance and protection.

In East Asia, Yalta had given the Soviets an entry; their occupation of the Kuriles, of Sakhalin, and of other small islands north of Japan (which continues to this day) gave them further extended position; their relatively brief occupation of North Korea and their role in Manchuria were perceived as directly benefiting Maoist prospects in the then brewing Chinese civil war. Thus, in East Asia too, the Soviets appeared threatening. Their behavior and actions were to a degree assimilated with and perceived as indistinguishable from those of the Chinese Communists who were already a significant element in Asia. This lack of distinction in U.S. perception was erroneous.

Finally, in Western Europe, there was at least doubt on the U.S. side that the restored democratic capitalist regimes could survive. Until the Marshall Plan for European reconstruction began operating in 1948, such doubts had considerable justification. It is easy with hindsight to perceive today the weakness of Western European communism then; but in the context of the times, it should not have been weak. Rising as the phoenix from the ashes and ruins of European wars, the Communist parties of Western Europe, which had in large measure led and inspired the anti-Nazi resistance movements, should have become leading contenders for monopolistic power in their countries. Had not Karl Marx, Friedrich Engels, and V.I. Lenin predicted that revolutions would be born in the inevitable wars that the inner contradictions of capitalism forced upon the working masses of the world? Moreover, the postwar Western European Communist leaders were not then Eurocommunists as we call them today; men like Maurice Thorez in France had never wavered, even in the crucial days after the Nazi-Soviet pact of 1939, in their true allegiance to the Soviet Union, and the Soviet Union only.

Accordingly, it is fair to state that there were substantial immediate postwar external threats justifying the developing U.S. doctrine of containment. It is useless to argue that these threats were not and did not convert themselves into real security dangers for the United States and the West; the reason they were not, and did not so become, may be due as much to the policies conceived and implemented under containment as to the possible weaknesses inherent in the concept of containment in the first place. It is, in fact, impossible to resolve the following "iffy" dilemmas of history: Had the United States analyzed differently and responded less aggressively and with more inducements to the perceived Soviet threats, would these have evaporated and would Europe and the world still have emerged substantially as we know them now? Would European leaders like Alcide De Gasperi in Italy, Maurice Schuman in France, and Konrad Adenauer in West Germany have arisen at least partially to unify West Europe and to give it the spirit without which the NATO structure could not have been elaborated, had containment not been conceived and implemented by the United States?

Domestic Factors

The role of immigrant European ethnic groups in the development of the U.S. containment policy must be stressed. These groups maintained in the United States during 1945-55 a veritable barrage of opposition to Soviet moves in Eastern Europe, deeply influencing the Congress and all domestic elections of the late forties and early fifties. Well-organized Polish, Baltic, Czech, Hungarian, and other ethnic lobby groups of Eastern or Central European origin were especially outraged at the communization they saw occurring in Eastern Europe along with communism's offensive against the Catholic Church there. Moreover, they and German ethnic groups in the United States were inflamed by the problem of displaced persons, that is the 10 million or more ethnic Germans and others expelled or chosing to depart from the portions of greater Germany seized by Russia or recovered by Poland and Czechoslovakia in compensation for territories taken by Russia in their eastern sectors. Most of these D.P.'s, as they were called, sought initial refuge in West Germany whence, over the course of time, hundreds of thousands of them immigrated into the United States and swelled the ranks of the anti-Soviet ethnic lobbies. It is in our view doubtful that an active U.S. policy of Soviet containment would have gained the rapid support it obtained in the Congress, or that subsequently McCarthyism would have gained its very high visibility (1949-54), without the role that these lobbies played in postwar American foreign policy.[9]

The explosion of our first atomic device at Los Alamos in July 1945, the subsequent use of two A-bombs (Hiroshima and Nagasaki) to end the war against Japan, and the U.S. possession of an atomic monopoly until 1949 have been treated in some revisionist literature as demonstrating that we employed our military superiority to force the Soviet Union, as early as the summer of 1945, to bow to the supremacy of U.S. power and accordingly to accept the creation of a postwar world political order patterned on U.S. terms.[10] This reasoning may have gained a degree of credibility as a long ex post facto explanation of events; but it does not hold up well when critically reviewed in the light of perceptions existing in U.S. policy in mid-1945.

In the first place we perceived ourselves as an extremely strong power at the end of the war in Europe, even before the A-bomb, and as ready to and capable of playing a major role in support of world order and peace everywhere. In the second place, Truman interposed no obstacles to Russia's entry into the Japanese war which, along with the atomic bomb, he and the rest of the top leadership in Washington continued to regard as essential to bring about the desired unconditional surrender of Japan. The Japanese were still viewed in mid-1945 as possessing great military power in their homeland. Third, while it is likely that the U.S. leadership did not accurately represent to itself the weakness and exhaustion of the Soviet Union at the end of the European war, the reason for this was at least in part that the Soviet leadership was showing itself highly truculent in Eastern and Central Europe, hardly cause to believe that it would have readily bowed to even an awesome demonstration of U.S. military power.

It is undeniable that Secretary of War Henry Stimson opposed the use of the A-bomb against Japan, but he did so principally on moral grounds and based on a more acute perception of the willingness of the Japanese to surrender than that held by other key policy-makers in mid-1945. Moreover, if use of the bomb was indeed viewed by Truman, even if only in part, as a means to influence Soviet behavior, it seems to have been a singularly unsuccessful ploy in bringing about the desired result. It is possible that our monopolistic possession and use of this "absolute weapon" increased Truman's already mounting propensity for a tough stance toward the Soviets.[11] But the United States certainly did not convert its use against Japan into any real diplomatic advantage: the Soviet Union did not retreat from Northern Japan, North Korea, or Manchuria; it did not diminish the virulence of its hegemonic policies in Eastern Europe; it did not cease its anti-U.S. or anti-imperialist propaganda; and it did not cave in to Allied desires in Germany, or cease opposition to U.S. and Western policies in Western Europe or elsewhere. Moreover, never during the period of its atomic weapons monopoly (1945-49) or its hydrogen weapons monopoly (1949-53), did the United States use or seriously threaten to use nuclear weapons in a preventive or preemptive mode.

Accordingly, the monopolistic possession of the absolute weapon, though perhaps providing the United States with a cushion of comfort or margin of safety as it was engaging itself in containment and devising the doctrines of nuclear and conventional deterrence, cannot be regarded as a major factor *per se* in inducing U.S. rigidity toward Soviet policy, or its role in the initiation of what, after 1950, became the high cold war.

Truman's personality is quite another matter. Truman came to the Senate from modest beginnings in Independence, Mo., and acquitted himself creditably of his investigative tasks as chairman during the war of a Senate committee overseeing war production and the war effort. He did not, however, expect to be nominated for vice-president when a split between Byrnes and Wallace developed at the 1944 Democratic convention and Roosevelt chose him over the others. Much less did he expect that Roosevelt would die two short months after his fourth inauguration and that he, Truman, would so suddenly and at such a difficult moment in U.S. and world history, be catapulted into the presidency of the most powerful nation on earth. There is little doubt, looking back, that Truman lacked self-confidence in the vast and dangerous field of foreign and national security affairs when he entered the White House.[12] Whether consciously or unconsciously, he quickly gathered how vital it was for him to demonstrate a leadership capacity if he was to gain the respect of such giant figures of world affairs as Winston Churchill and Joseph Stalin, with whom he would immediately have to deal. Further, it was equally essential that he establish his credibility in and a measure of control over the Congress, particularly the Senate, where he was of course well known and respected but not regarded as a towering figure.

Truman's manifestations of leadership came quickly and occasionally in the form of muscle-flexing or macho demonstrations, as when he berated Soviet Foreign Minister Vyacheslav Molotov without much reason in the White House just before the start of the San Francisco Conference on the United Nations Charter (April 1945), forcing Molotov to complain bitterly about his treatment by Truman.[13] Truman, of course, saw to it that the incident was duly recounted in the Senate cloakrooms, where his prestige immediately rose. Other demonstrations that he was in full command followed rapidly: lecturing both Stalin and Churchill at Potsdam; unhesitatingly ordering the nuclear blows on Japan against Stimson's opposition; "guiding" Senator Tom Connally and other prominent congressional insiders into the complexities of the forthcoming U.S. international role; removing Secretary of State Edward Stettinius and in due course, White House advisor Harry Hopkins and replacing them with hard-liner Byrnes; navigating the perilous waters of the Paris Peace Conference and the break-up of four-power unity over Germany; inspiring Churchill to build him up to act as "leader of the free world" in Churchill's famous Westminster College, Mo., "Iron Curtain" speech.

Later demonstrations of leadership by Truman included: presiding over the standing interpretation of Kennan's telegram and the birth of containment policies; facing the Greek and Balkan threats; enunciating in 1947 the doctrine that permanently bore his name; obtaining from Congress later in 1947 the National Security Act, which completely reorganized the Executive's foreign policy and national security components, created the Defense Department, the CIA, and the National Security Council; obtaining N.S.C. Resolution 68 in 1949-50 which gave the U.S. foreign affairs and national security bureaucracies the marching orders of containment and became their inflexible guide for the ensuing quarter century.[14]

It is intriguing, difficult, and yet essential to sort out the role domestic economic factors played in the elaboration of the U.S. doctrine of containment and the implementation of policies taken in its name. There may be possible merits in a Marxist analysis of a postwar United States incapable of reabsorbing its demobilized military manpower into the labor force and therefore facing a huge threat of unemployment; or of a decrepit and dying capitalism for which the need to export and consequently to imperialize the world under U.S. hegemony was an essential and last possible survival mechanism. But the facts, as well as we can now discern them, do not bear out such an analysis. The United States easily reabsorbed its manpower; domestic demand after the war was more than ample to ensure growth in American industry and a potential for economic prosperity in the postwar period surpassing all expectations. All this came to pass with a minimum of economic dependence on foreign raw materials, foreign export markets, or foreign fields for U.S. capital investment. This was the case at least until after the Korean War. By economic indicators alone, one cannot seriously begin to talk of U.S. economic dependence on foreign markets, raw materials, or investment opportunities until the late fifties, by which time U.S. capital as had been its custom in the past had begun heavily to follow the flag abroad.[15]

This being acknowledged, it is also correct to state that the postwar period saw a very rapid expansion of U.S. markets and economic influence abroad, and that after the first decade (1945-55), the ground had been laid for a literal explosion of American foreign trade, and especially American investment abroad. The period 1955-70 saw a capital outflow of such proportions that it led in the seventies to the most severe dislocations due to foreign factors that the American economy has ever experienced: profound trade and payments imbalances; a dollar crisis of major proportions; and a now structural dependence on certain vital raw materials like petroleum. All this developed in the seventies to a degree which previously would have seemed scarcely conceivable.

Was it all planned? Did the American capitalist leadership, secretly concerting or not (who could ever know that?), plan via the political means of containment, deterrence, and related foreign political policies for which it would presumably have constructed the necessary climate, to engage in an unprecedented economic conquest of the world—one of such vast scope that it would end up out of control, turning against the interests of its own original creators? It is indeed most doubtful that the capacity for such long-range planning existed at all in the rather plodding and unimaginative chambers of America's corporate leadership. It is more plausible to argue that the U.S. elites, perhaps quite unconsciously but nonetheless effectively, sought a world climate propitious to access for U.S. trade, U.S. acquisition of essential raw materials, and later for U.S. investments. America sought, to use Robert W. Tucker's term, a world "congenial" to America's capitalist economic values as well as to its own democratic political ideals, which were felt to make the spread of its economic values more possible.[16] This was not done for evil motives, or a desire to interfere anywhere or everywhere; but simply, as we shall suggest in greater detail in Chapter III, out of conviction that we had the best, that others not only could but would wish to have it too, and that in the flowering of our own destiny, we had a lot to offer to the then quite miserable but expectant world.

Democratic capitalism, U.S. style, would provide bounty and progress for mankind; communism, or even socialism, by contrast would inhibit, arrest, or prevent progress and freedom; consequently, these evil doctrines had to be impeded; and to do so the United States would need a world congenial to American values. A congenial world need not have been a world coequal with American values. Yet we proceeded shortly under the policies of containment to equate American security with the acceptance almost everywhere of a world order based on our own value structure.[17]

We turn last to domestic anti-communism as a moral and ideological force, and to the fundamental role it came to play in our foreign policies virtually from the end of World War II to the end of our Vietnam involvement. No single factor is more important in understanding the shaping of our postwar and later foreign policies of containment; none more responsible for both their successes and failures, the latter including our tragic involvement in Indochina.

Our tendency to mass hysteria toward communism as an ideology, or Marxism-Leninism as a system of thought, stems fundamentally from ignorance. There is in it also, at least in latent phase, a dimly sensed perception that the goals pursued by Communists in the abstract—equality of opportunity and of status, the abolition of class and caste—are similar to and therefore seriously rival those sought in the ideals of democratic capitalism. Communism seeks the achievement of such goals on behalf of individuals through the improvement of the collective and collective institutions. It therefore places the collective, rather than the individual, at the center of all considerations. This naturally leads to its having a centralist or totalist character in state practice, and to the loss of individual freedom.

But it is not only the loss of individual freedoms or the atheism of communism that Americans seem to fear. It is also communism's threat of abolishing the possession of private property. In our psyche, all rights accrue to the individual, even if this impedes the collective (i.e., government) in the dispensation of social justice. Depriving the individual of his right of possession in favor of the collective, even in the name of social justice as communism in the abstract would do, seems inherently wrong to Americans—and this is understandable, given the American experience. That it does not seem wrong to millions of human beings in the world who have not shared the American bounty or the American experience and have never owned property or anything else, does not obviously strike many Americans.

We shall adduce in the first section of the next chapter reasons why the American people find it so difficult, in fact inconceivable, to believe that men of goodwill and who have escaped from the fate of status-, rank-, and class-conscious society could seek sociopolitical solutions different from those devised under the fundamental American "rules of rule"—the Declaration of Independence; the Constitution; the Bill of Rights. What we wish to consider here in slightly greater detail is the ease with which the United States, government and public alike, equated communism (and even socialism, despite its democratic nature in Western Europe) with expansionist totalitarianism and hence with evil. There can of course be no question regarding the extreme totalitarian nature of the Soviet Union as a state system. But why is it that the state practice of the Soviet Union could, and can still, be so easily equated in the U.S. view with expansionism, with the practice of communism by other, non-Soviet Russian states, and with the ideology of communism in the abstract?

The equation between expansionism and the totalitarian Soviet Union, and thence with communism in the abstract, was easy for the insufficiently tutored American masses to accomplish immediately after the war. The greatest war in history, against one major totalitarianism (Nazism) and several minor ones (Italian fascism, Japanese militarism) had just been won by the Allies, in the minds of most Americans mainly by the United States itself, at very great cost. No sooner was this war won when another repugnant totalitarianism, the Soviet Union, appeared to be misbehaving expansionistically, seeking—or so it was perceived—to fill the vacuums left by the defeat of Hitler and Japan. The equation of the Soviet system with the Nazi one, and with evil, presented alluring possibilities and was not all that far off, considering the devastatingly evil internal nature of the Stalinist dictatorship, particularly immediately after the war. Yet as we have seen, the Soviet Union was not militantly expansionist, either in Europe or in Asia. More than the evil nature of Stalinism was needed to erase distinctions in the American mind between the Soviet Union and communism as an ideology *per se,* and to launch us on the great crusade against communism, not just the Soviet Union, which resulted from the erroneous interpretations of George Kennan's doctrine of containment, which he deplored.

The instrument which accomplished this, whether or not by design (though certainly by the design of some elements of the American leadership), was the Communist victory on the mainland of China. It could quite plausibly be argued that the Soviets, who had little if any control over the Chinese Communists during their civil war with the Nationalists, suffered not one, but two devastating blows by the Chinese Communist victory on the mainland in 1949. First, China rose as a power rivaling them for leadership and command of the world Socialist movement. Second, China's rise to power would so upset the United States as to lead the latter almost indiscriminately to identify it with the Soviet Union because of the name of the ideology they shared in common, thereby setting in motion an enormously hostile confrontation which was to last for almost a quarter century.

The sentimental attachment for China in the United States played no small role in this development; it was vexing, crushing, and humiliating to see China, which Americans had so long admired and so strongly supported against Japan, "go down the drain to Moscow" almost immediately after the Japanese defeat. As a consequence, one of the most unthinking and blind phenomenon in recent American history set itself on course: the search for the pro-Communist American culprits who must have connived to lose China to communism. Without this irrational and tragic search for non-existent American scapegoats—for after all, if anything was clear under the sun it was that China had lost itself to communism—postwar and later American history might indeed have been very different. Containment, though well in motion before 1949, might never have reached the scope it attained in the Third World in the fifties; the high cold war ushered in after 1948 and Korea might have been mitigated or averted through a series of diplomatic settlements; and it is even possible that our Indochina engagement would not have been undertaken at all, or that we would not have sustained it so long and at such cost.

But scapegoats for this unwelcome blow involving one quarter of mankind lost to communism had to be found. The first victims of the witch hunt were America's finest Asia experts, in the Department of State, and elsewhere throughout the American polity—a story which has been told many times and need not again be repeated here, though we shall from time to time allude to it in forthcoming chapters of this book.

The Anti-Communist Climate and Indochina

McCarthyism (1949-54) was the technique of denouncing as soft on communism, and thus as suspect of betrayal, anyone not stridently or at least positively [18] disposed to militant, immediate, and sustained denunciation of the Soviet Union and of Communist China as expansionist, and of communism in the abstract as evil. It spread a net of purges in the American polity and society far wider than the Chinese or Asian experts in the State Department or the U.S. government, of whom, incidentally, not one was ever found to be a *bona fide* Communist or Soviet agent. For example, the movie and publishing industries were purged; positive loyalty oaths were administered in the military forces, many U.S. government-connected businesses and institutions, and in some state governments; academic freedom was infringed in some of our universities. But the problem we must address here is not so much who Sen. Joseph McCarthy and his acolytes, or the Senate Internal Security Committee under such figures as Senators William Jenner and Thomas Dodd, or the House Committee on Un-American Activities (both committees are now defunct), or the FBI, managed to smear, or force to testify or confess to irrelevant and frequently imaginary sins. In the end, once President Eisenhower and the traditional American establishment, restoring the Constitution's guarantees of freedom of expression, had found the means in the Army v. McCarthy hearings (1954) to bring the demagogue McCarthy to a halt, the purges themselves were of relatively little consequence for national policy—though not of course for the many people who had been their direct targets.

What was most serious was the general climate of opinion which this period of anti-Communist hysteria created in the United States and which continued to linger in American society for at least two decades. In such a climate, those who spoke for diplomatic accommodation with the Soviet Union, or even for seeking to understand the mass appeals of Marxism-Leninism or of Maoism to Chinese or other Asian peasants, or for objectively analyzing the strategies of Asian Nationalist anti-colonial movements, could no longer be heard. Those American diplomats, for example, who had dared report what they sensed, heard, and understood when they stated that the Chinese masses and not external powers had brought Mao to power, would no longer dare to speak. Thus, men of responsibility and goodwill would cease telling the truth as they saw it and begin instead to tell it as they thought the country wanted it heard. Few if any policy practitioners in Washington or among American representatives in Asia would dare say in 1950, for example, when Ho Chi Minh was beginning to defeat the French: "Ho is certainly a Communist, but he has great appeal; he is regarded as a champion of nationalism and of anti-colonialism; he is forging an unbreakable bond with his people; he will win his revolutionary struggle regardless of the odds, for we can see, hear, and sense that the masses of the people support him and not the French or their puppets."

Stilling or silencing voices such as these, and hearing instead only those who said: "Ho is a Communist, therefore, he cannot really represent the aspirations of his people, and moreover they regard him as a tool of Russia or China," led American leaders and people as well into an anti-Communist climate of deafness and blindness which after 1949 became one of the most important factors in American foreign policy. It was one of the most dangerous, in fact potentially suicidal, things a great nation could do in world affairs: to cut off its eyes and ears, to castrate its analytic capacity, to shut itself off from the truth because of blind prejudice and a misjudged dispensation of good and evil.

2. Dominoes and Geneva; SEATO and the Support of Diem

Almost imperceptibly between 1950 and 1955 the United States slipped into Indochina and Vietnam. In 1950, before the Korean War broke out, we were still hesitant, though our Southeast Asian focus had shifted from nationalism to communism in 1948-49 after the eruption of the simultaneous uprisings discussed in Chapter I. Once we had recognized the Associated States of Indochina in February 1950 we established in Vietnam and shortly thereafter, though initially at a less elevated status, in Cambodia and Laos U.S. diplomatic missions which rapidly began to acquire a considerable say in U.S. policies. They provided the outlets for vigorous advocacy of positions presumably held by leaders of the governments in these countries, but frequently placed in the minds of these leaders by our own ambassadors.

It must be observed that this was truer in Vietnam than in Cambodia and Laos. In Phnom Penh, Cambodia, U.S. representatives dealt with the mercurial and unpredictable Prince Norodom Sihanouk, whose basic affinity lay with France and who would not allow us the operational latitude we desired. In Vientiane, Laos, our representatives could not help but be aware of the artificial nature and precarious existence of the country, really a congeries of tribes, with which we dealt. The astute Laotian leader Prince Souvanna Phouma, a half-brother of his Communist opponent Prince Souphanouvong, the leader of the pro-Communist "Pathet Lao," also tended to keep us at arms' length.

In Vietnam, however, Ambassador Donald Heath quickly saw a chance to promote himself in the good graces of Washington and to maintain the primacy of European and French considerations in U.S. policy by broadcasting to Washington and the world the presumed reality of the wholly fictional independence conferred by the French upon the Vietnamese emperor, Bao Dai. The latter's playboy proclivities, which had become a legend on the French Riviera, and the deep corruption and essential artificiality of the so-called independent political structure in Saigon, were not lost on many members of the U.S. mission in Vietnam.[19] In the end, however, it turned out that everyone played out a game clearly conditioned by the containment policy atmosphere which we have described in the previous section. This game was one in which the leaders of the Fourth French Republic in Paris, despite their frequently acrimonious differences, and the successive French supreme commanders in Saigon (Gen. De Lattre de Tassigny, 1950-52; Gen. Salan, 1952-53; Gen Navarre, 1953-54) called the shots; the United States payed most of the bill; and the succession of mediocre Vietnamese prime and other ministers under Bao Dai, several of whom returned later in the post-Diem governments of the sixties and early seventies, played a charade with both the French and the Americans. In it the Vietnamese puppet ministers of the French were at one and the same time the apparent masters, the obedient servants, and the self-conscious victims of the Viet Minh, which was growing in strength by the month and year.

There were many crises during the first (or French) Indochina war, before, during, and after the epic battle at Dien Bien Phu (March to May 1954) which led to the Geneva Armistice Accords of July 20, 1954, and to the end of the French presence in Indochina (1955). Most of these crises have now been consigned to the dustbin of history, where we may safely leave them for the purposes of this book. Before we do so, however, some points relating to U.S. policy deserve brief mention.

First, the Korean War, breaking out in June 1950, provided strong confirmation for the perception of U.S. leaders that by assisting the French in Indochina they were in effect helping to arrest the spread of a worldwide Sino-Soviet menace. This perception was directly related to the containment concepts discussed earlier. It reinforced the concepts' already powerful role as American policy doctrine, whether or not George Kennan agreed with the transformation of his theory of politically containing Soviet power in Europe into a doctrine of encirclement of both the Soviet Union and China by primarily U.S. military means in such distant places of doubtful U.S. security value as Indochina. Southeast Asia began after Korea to rank quite as high on the U.S. list of vulnerable areas where the threat must be contained as Western Europe, the Near East, or Northeast Asia. Soon the United States was to view all threats virtually anywhere, including those perceived in such areas as Pakistan, Iraq, Lebanon, and Latin America, in virtually the same vein.

A small U.S. military mission began to establish itself in Vietnam after 1950 to assist in the administration of U.S. military assistance to what now began to be euphemistically called "the Franco-Vietnamese forces." However, at no time before Dien Bien Phu did Vietnamese contingents constitute more then auxiliary elements, termed *suppletifs* by the French, in these forces. The Vietnamese contingents played an extremely minor, purely supportive role for the French. By the time of the Geneva Conference in July 1954, our military mission had reached a size of about 400 men.

Second, the struggles against the multiple Communist insurgencies elsewhere in Southeast Asia (Philippines, Burma, Malaysia) confirmed and strengthened U.S. resolve in 1950-54 to maintain its course of firmness against the Communists in Indochina. However, in contrast to the Philippines for example, where the United States directly assisted the Filipinos, the French colonial power remained the main instrument whereby U.S. aims were to be achieved in Indochina, even after the cease-fire (1951) and the Panmunjon Armistice (1953) in Korea had released at least some U.S. material assets for possible use in Southeast Asia. There was initially no thought in Washington or among Americans in Saigon of replacing the French by American or Vietnamese forces, only of supporting them with military and economic assistance and cajoling and persuading them into being more responsive to the restlessness of the Vietnamese with their puppet or quasi-puppet political structure.

Finally, when the situation ultimately turned from critical to desperate for the French in Vietnam, and when it became increasingly apparent that French domestic opinion would no longer sustain the casualties and the financial drain of this remote imperial war, the U.S. government set about finding new doctrines and rhetoric to buttress the credibility of its position of supporting the French with the Congress and with the American public. This was done toward the end of the first and the beginning of the second year of the Eisenhower-Nixon administration (1953-54).

Dominoes and the "Domino Theory"

It remains unclear just who conceived the domino idea, but it is likely that Secretary of State John Foster Dulles' briefings provided President Eisenhower with this rather simple and superficially logical game analogy. Southeast Asia, not just Indochina, was compared to a row of dominoes: Thailand, Malaya, Singapore, Indonesia, Burma, and the Philippines—gateways, respectively, to India in the west and to the whole Pacific basin in the east. The first of these dominoes was Indochina: if Vietnam fell, then surely Laos and Cambodia (then still truly infant states) would fall; whereupon the whole row of dominoes in Southeast Asia would tumble. All of these countries were already involved in various phases of internal unrest.

It was this hurriedly conceived and barely examined outgrowth of containment thinking, baptized "the domino theory," which Eisenhower took to the American public, Congress, and to foreign governments to justify his policies in Indochina in 1954 and even 1955.[20] The theory was hardly valid because of the many divergences in almost every aspect of social, political, and economic life among the many countries and multitude of peoples in Southeast Asia. Even in Indochina proper, there was hardly anything in common between culturally

Sinified and Frenchified Vietnam, also containing a large Catholic population in both the North and South; fiercely identity-conscious and anti-Vietnamese Cambodia, made up of the Buddhist descendents of the great Khmer empires of the 10th to 14th centuries; and the vague, overlapping, diffuse, and distant tribes in Laos who related to Thailand in the South and Center, and to China, Burma, and Northwest Tonkin in the North.

As the saying goes, facts and knowledge are never a match for a good theory, as we shall note again in subsequent chapters. This "substantive theory of history" [21] was conjured up from reasoning by historical analogy, in this particular case that aggression must be stopped before its perpetrators can extend it from one to another contiguous area, as Hitler had done in the thirties. It was also derived from the mood of the present, from the containment and Truman doctrines, as well as from the domestic climate of anti-communism in the United States. Interlinking all Communist threats, whether or not the Soviets or Chinese were directly involved, the United States would counter them with the vigorous interposition of its influence, of U.S. assistance to the victims of aggression, and if ultimately necessary, with U.S. arms in their defense.

The U.S. executive, in charge of a superpower with worldwide interests and a major role to play in East Asia, now saw itself challenged by small and mysterious but externally supported local communisms. Their momentum had apparently slowed itself in Burma and Indonesia by the early fifties; it was being arrested by a judicious mix of Philippine and U.S. activity in the Philippines, and by smart Anglo-Malayan police and intelligence work and programs in Malaysia. What would keep the United States and the French from succeeding in arresting them in Indochina and Vietnam as well?

But by 1954, after the "eight years arduous struggle" as it called the war it had waged, the Viet Minh, still united under Ho Chi Minh, Pham Van Dong, Truong Chinh, Le Duan, and Gen. Vo Nguyen Giap, was about to expel the French expeditionary forces with heavy losses from Vietnam. The French people at home had turned decisively against continuing what they dubbed "the dirty war" in Indochina.

In the spring and early summer of 1954, the domino theory was to be given a real test: would the United States accede to demands from elements in the French military and government that it intervene militarily to save France in Vietnam? The French had had serious differences over the years with the Americans about the conduct of the war, and before 1954 had not believed direct U.S. intervention to be at all desirable. As the battle of Dien Bien Phu reached its climax and the

Viet Minh finally broke the French fortress on May 7, 1954, the French still did not believe it likely. The post-Dien Bien Phu commander in Indochina, former French Chief of Staff Gen. Paul Ely, had been surprised to hear from the American chairman of the Joint Chiefs of Staff, Admiral Arthur Radford, during a visit to Washington in March 1954, that under certain circumstances the United States might be prepared to intervene.[22] What Ely had in fact obtained was an incorrect signal from one of the several key players in a major political battle which had begun to absorb the top decision-makers in Washington. It is not our purpose here to describe or analyze this particular decision-making battle in detail; only to signal highlights which help explain the later course of events.

Secretary of State Dulles desired the formation of a European Defense Community (EDC), including the Germans, in Europe; and he was willing to go far for the support of the French in its creation and effective establishment. In the end, however, the French National Assembly defeated the EDC, perhaps in part in return for the exercise of Soviet influence upon the leaders in Hanoi to settle the Indochina war on better terms for the French. The two issues may not have been unconnected in the mind of French Prime Minister Pierre Mendes-France; for at Geneva in July 1954, the Democratic Republic of Vietnam (DRV) ultimately settled for a line of demarcation giving South Vietnam far more territory in the center of Vietnam than the French position on the battlefield could have led it to expect.[23] But whether or not there was such an understanding, the facts on the French side were pretty clear after Dien Bien Phu: if the United States would not come in and save them by direct intervention, then the French would settle for the best they could obtain. Like it or not, the United States and the Vietnamese who had collaborated with France would have to swallow the result.

As we have suggested, direct U.S. military intervention in support of the beleaguered French was indeed favored by some elements at the top of the U.S. leadership (Admiral Radford and, at a critical moment, Vice President Richard Nixon); in addition, intervention was definitely considered and studied by all the key U.S. leaders involved: President Eisenhower, Secretary of State John Foster Dulles, CIA Director Allen Dulles, the other members of the Joint Chiefs, Secretary of Defense Charles E. Wilson, and leaders of the principal foreign affairs and defense committees in the Congress. The decision was ultimately negative, therefore in a sense denying the validity of the domino theory. Were or were not these dominoes vital to the security and the national interest of the United States? Although the chairman of the Joint

Chiefs of Staff thought they were, and that U.S. intervention by air strikes from carriers conceivably coupled with a nuclear threat could have signaled Franco-U.S. intent to continue fighting in Indochina until victory, President Eisenhower, receiving strongly contrary advice, thought otherwise.

General Matthew Ridgway, former commander of our Korean and Far Eastern forces and now the Army member of the Joint Chiefs of Staff, to his credit advised Eisenhower against a move he felt certain would lead to the entry of U.S. ground forces into another land war in Asia which would most likely end unsuccessfully in stalemate, as in Korea. Never again, Ridgway advised, should the United States engage itself in a limited ground war on the mainland of Asia. He thereby became the founding member of what in the fifties came to be known as the "Never Again Club" in the U.S. Army, a movement which crumbled later under the assault of new ideas of "counterinsurgency" and "subliminal war."

But Eisenhower also wisely consulted the British; and Foreign Minister Eden counseled him against involvement. Moreover, by shrewdly playing on certain members of the Congress, including democratic leaders of the Republican-controlled Senate such as Senators Mike Mansfield, Edwin Johnson, and John Stennis, President Eisenhower was able to forge a coalition inside the U.S. government (including the British ambassador to Washington) strong enough to overcome the Nixon-Radford axis, which was equivocally supported by Secretary of State Dulles. One could wish that such a coalition of non-interventionists, possibly under the leadership of then Undersecretary of State George Ball, had been forged again ten years later, in 1964! But as we shall see, this was not to be.[24]

The U.S. failure to intervene by direct military means in support of the French during and immediately after the battle of Dien Bien Phu did not signal that the domino theory had died. It was indeed destined to be revived again in later years. But after the battle of Dien Bien Phu, it became chiefly a rationale for U.S. policies seeking the perpetuation of a type of stalemate between the United States and communism in Indochina and Southeast Asia. If such a stalemate could be continued, it would avoid the domestic political repercussions on the U.S. leadership for losing another round to communism anywhere.

Put another way, by not engaging ourselves militarily against communism in Southeast Asia in 1954, we indicated that we could live with it in stalemate in this area as well as in Europe, Korea, or the Taiwan Straits. But we also ensured, by means shortly to be described, that the *appearance* of stalemate would continue; and that the *appearance* of

total communist victory or of complete U.S. withdrawal would be prevented. We find here the origins of the "stalemate machine" explanation of the U.S. role in Indochina so persuasively argued by Daniel
Ellsberg,[25] and to which we shall later return. The United States, according to Ellsberg, did not walk into a quagmire in Southeast Asia
from which it could not extricate itself. Rather, it walked into a quagmire from which it would not extricate itself because of the domestic
opprobrium perceived by American leadership to attach to an administration losing to communism. Accordingly, the United States managed to transform the Southeast Asian quagmire into a stalemate
machine. The first U.S. president to help conceive and manage this
transformation was the Republican president, Dwight Eisenhower, who
like his then vice president and later successor, Richard Nixon, some
fifteen years later (1969) could have, had he wanted, walked out of the
Indochina quagmire.

We next address the question of how the appearance of stalemate
was preserved in Southeast Asia after the French defeat.

Geneva and SEATO

At the Geneva Conference of 1954, and whether or not by way of a
deal on the European Defense Community, France was able to obtain
from the leadership of the Democratic Republic of Vietnam the latter's
agreement to the temporary division of Vietnam between "two zones"
(north and south) at the 17th and not a lower parallel, as the battleground situation might have easily justified.

The Geneva Agreements of July 20, 1954, left the DRV in control of
the northern region from the 17th parallel to the China border, with
the French evacuating that zone completely. French presence was to
continue for a period south of the 17th parallel, but administrative
control in the southern zone was to be assumed by Bao Dai's "State of
Vietnam." Laos and Cambodia, like both zones of Vietnam, were to be
demilitarized, neutralized, and not subject to foreign interference. In a
political provision which was all-important to the DRV, the Geneva
conferees agreed in their unsigned final declaration that "consultations
between the two zones" of Vietnam were to begin on July 20, 1955,
(one year later) with a view to holding "general elections by secret
ballot" in July 1956 to decide upon the reunification of Vietnam. Another important provision of the accords stated that persons (refugees)
desiring to leave either zone for the other could do so within a stipulated time-frame, under the auspices of the International Control
Commission (ICC) established for the purpose of supervising and
monitoring compliance with the battleground armistice. This commis-

sion, composed of India (chairman), Poland, and Canada, eventually supervised the movement of about 800,000 Catholic refugees from North to South Vietnam as well as the exodus from South to North Vietnam of about 300,000 Communist cadres and elements of the DRV armed forces.[26]

* Bao Dai's foreign minister, Tran Van Do, expressed his government's total dissatisfaction with and reservation on these accords, which it can therefore be considered to have accepted only under duress; South Vietnam was in fact soon to demonstrate its non-compliance with them. The United States on the other hand, in the person of our chief delegate, Gen. Walter Bedell Smith, expressed specific reservations on portions of the accords but in doing so stated explicitly that it would do nothing to upset them by the use or threat of use of force. Looking at the matter in retrospect, the exception that the United States placed on its reservations turned out to be more important than the reservations themselves. For while the Eisenhower administration did not like these accords, it substantially lived with them during the remainder of its term. It was the successor Kennedy administration which violated the U.S. promise not to upset them by raising the numbers of men in the American military mission in Vietnam. Of course, as we shall see later, the Kennedy administration thought that it had good cause for its actions.

With Geneva, a chapter closed on U.S. policy in Indochina, but certainly not the book—for a few weeks after the conference, which Secretary Dulles had pointedly snubbed partly because of the presence of Chou En-lai, Dulles persuaded Eisenhower to support him in carrying out in Southeast Asia one of the most dubious diplomatic operations of all time. This was the holding of the Manila Conference of September 1954 and the signing of the Southeast Asia Treaty of Mutual Security and Defense, known as SEATO. This vague and imprecisely-drawn document, later to obtain Senate ratification and an organizational superstructure headquartered at Bangkok, obligated eight very divergent states to come to each other's assistance in the treaty area if any member were the victim of unprovoked "Communist" subversion or external attack. The sources of a Communist external attack were not otherwise defined; the meaning of "subversion" was not otherwise spelled out.

The eight powers which the United States had managed to congregate in Manila were France, the United Kingdom, Pakistan, Thailand, the Philippines, Australia, New Zealand, and of course the United States itself. We must note immediately the strange character of this alignment: two former colonial powers in Southeast Asia, European allies of the United States whose continuing presence in the region was to be of only short duration and whose interests there were soon to dwindle to insignificance; a South Asian rival of India and ally of the United States (Pakistan) in no way engaged or concerned with Southeast Asia; a Southeast Asian ally of the United States (Philippines), lying offshore and with virtually no history or tradition of involvement in or cooperation with the mainland Southeast Asian countries; two Southwest Pacific allies of the United States (Australia/New Zealand), previously remote from the region's core, but both with an obvious interest in its evolution; finally, a single *bona fide* Southeast Asian state (Thailand), which was never before a formal ally of the United States, and was distinct from all the other Southeast Asian states at the time by virtue of its military-led autocratic regime and, like the Philippines, a willingness appreciated by the United States to become aligned against communism.

Note the absence of India, Burma, Indonesia, Malaysia (not then independent, however), and above all, the states of Indochina. The latter were of course to be non-aligned under the provisions of the Geneva accords. But despite this, and without their direct participation, SEATO at Manila decided to extend them protection under its umbrella. This protection against Communist external attack and internal insurgency, if it materialized, was spelled-out in a special protocol of the Manila treaty. It was this thin reed to which the Johnson administration clung in the later sixties to justify legally what was called the U.S. commitment to South Vietnam—a matter which we shall explore in greater detail below.

SEATO was a paper tiger, an empty gesture, from its creation in 1954 to its final official demise as an organization twenty years later (1974), after the United States had withdrawn all its forces from Indochina. The treaty, vague in the commitments obligating its members, in the area it covered, and in the procedures under which collective sanctions might be undertaken, served only one general and two specific purposes. Specifically, it provided a forum for annual consideration by the member states of developments in the Southeast Asian region, as well as a virtually negligible though controversial arena for the promotion of regional collaboration. In a more general way, it supplied, as already suggested, an excuse ratified by the U.S. Senate for a variety of U.S. interventionary moves in Indochina. Even so, the treaty was systematically invoked only quite late by the United States (1966, by Secretary Rusk) and never with great conviction.

Ultimately, however, SEATO's most important role, and the only reason we have dwelt on it in this detail here, was that it provided the required appearance of ongoing momentum to America's continuing policy of containment in Southeast Asia, and to its continued expressions of belief in the domino theory. The question whether Southeast Asia was a region of vital U.S. interest and concern, ultimately justifying U.S. military intervention on behalf of these interests, was answered negatively by the Eisenhower administration at Dien Bien Phu and at Geneva. But under the aegis of Dulles' SEATO brain-child, the policy of containment and anti-communism in Southeast Asia kept its momentum, the domino theory appeared intact, and the stalemate machine—inspired by the apparent necessities of domestic anti-communism—continued. All this was to be further demonstrated in 1955 when the United States decided to support the Ngo Dinh Diem regime in South Vietnam.

The Problem of South Vietnamese Leadership

During 1950-54, after the United States had recognized Vietnam as an Associated State in the French Union, the continuing weakest spot of its policy in Southeast Asia was its support, through the French but increasingly more direct, of a regime led by a playboy emperor. The regime was lacking serious political roots of any kind, governed by a series of farcical and untutored prime ministers, not possessed even of an army worthy of the name, and operating through the remnants of a colonial bureaucracy rife with traditionalism, lassitude, incompetence, and corruption. When we reflect upon it now, the similarities between South Vietnam under Bao Dai and under the presidencies of Khanh, Ky, and Thieu, after the 1963 coup that ended the Diem regime, are striking.

Moral and political corruption pervaded the numerous governments that succeeded Diem, whether their effective heads were civilian or military. In no significant way was a regime led by a Prime Minister Hung, Quat, or Oanh, or by a President Khanh or Ky, better than one fifteen years previously, led by a Prime Minister Tam. In some respects, the post-Diem cabinets were inferior to their pre-Diem predecessors, because men like Tran Van Anh, minister of information in both pre- and post-Diem regimes and who at least possessed some understanding of their country, increasingly tended to flee it. The South Vietnamese leaders, before and after Diem, were mediocre men of the same basic mold: small absentee landlords; traders; small businessmen or semi-professionals with a predominance of pharmacists; minor journalists; former noncoms in the Vietnamese auxiliaries of the French Army, now risen to the exalted ranks of colonel or general. Most of them were French or French-colonial educated; until the later sixties they spoke only French along with their native Vietnamese dialects; they thought mainly of themselves, of their positions, and of their class and personal privileges in the society. They were harried always by their knowledge of the very short term they would have in power, forever cognizant of a reality few would admit even to themselves, much less to others: that the enemy, the dreaded Viet Minh or Viet Cong, had the mandate, the legitimacy, the righteous cause. Worse yet, they always knew deep inside that there was no tomorrow, that the enemy would inevitably triumph.

In each of his enemies, fighting above or underground for the triumph of Nationalist communism under Ho's banner, each South Vietnamese leader, politician, or bureaucrat before and after Diem recognized a classmate or colleague of old, who had early on cast the die for nationalism and, at his peril, abandoned the comforts of urban life for the rigors of guerrilla existence and guerrilla war. In each of his associates against the Communists, each anti-Communist Vietnamese leader, perhaps subconsciously but nonetheless really, recognized a man fundamentally like himself: with rare exceptions, a man lacking courage, tainted by colonialism and destined always to remain so; a man who had chosen urban comfort over the rigors of resistance to foreign imperialism; a man in a position to profit and steal and finding it irresistible not to do so since he doubted there was a tomorrow. Not trusting each other since they could not trust themselves, the anti-Communist Vietnamese could never, as the Americans wanted it, "get together to fight this thing." The explanation for the later torments of Ambassadors Henry Cabot Lodge and Maxwell Taylor—for they at least were tormented and not frozen onlookers like Ambassador Bunker or do-it-ourselves operators like pacification chief Robert Komer—was as simple as that.

This apparently blanket condemnation of South Vietnamese leaders will bring protests from many who sincerely liked and admired some Vietnamese. It need not be extended to younger generation Vietnamese who served in lesser positions in the Vietnamese armed forces or bureaucracy from the mid-sixties on; or to the Nationalist-neutralist Buddhist monks who mobilized themselves for a brief period (1963-66) to attempt to rescue South Vietnam from the evils of imperialism and of communism and war. But with a few possible exceptions, the condemnation does apply in blanket fashion to almost everyone who served in leadership capacities in civilian or military governments in South Vietnam between 1950-54 and 1964-75.

It does not apply to Ngo Dinh Diem, who despite his many and major faults was the only leadership figure to appear between 1945 and

1975 in South Vietnam even remotely capable of thinking disinterestedly of his country and its future, of building a political structure, or of challenging the Communist leadership on something approaching legitimate grounds. A case might be made for the monk Tri Quang, or for General Duong Van ("Big") Minh and those who shared power at the top with him for only two and a half months after the November 1, 1963, coup that toppled Ngo Dinh Diem. But the case would be weak and carry special overtones in that both Tri Quang and Minh's junta, who mutually supported each other, were in essence ready to find a "Vietnamese solution"—that is, to form a coalition regime with the Communists.

The Support of Diem

When Ngo Dinh Diem emerged in 1954, it was with enormous relief and a heavy dose of wishful thinking that the U.S. government—though not immediately, it took almost a year—greeted and accepted him as the only potential hero on the bleak Vietnamese political and moral landscape. Diem was indeed unique among post-World War II non-Communist Vietnamese. In his person he represented not only the best of ancient, elitist, Confucian, mandarin, and traditional Vietnam; but also of modern political man, attuned to Western, especially Catholic, theories of the state, such as Thomism, Maritainism, welfare Catholicism. Whether this mix of the traditional Vietnamese with the modern Catholic social reformist was at all applicable to the masses of poverty-stricken peasants in rural Vietnam, or to urban dwellers yearning for material welfare, or to older elites longing for tranquility and opposing social reform was a question that Washington never paused very long to ponder.

What attracted the U.S. government were Diem's reputation as an incorruptible, strong personality and the nationalist purity he had shown in refusing in 1948-49 to sanction the French Halong Bay Proposals under which Bao Dai had accepted the semblance of sovereignty. In the late forties, Diem went into exile to France and then, almost uniquely among Vietnamese of the period, to the United States in the early fifties rather than accept to serve or live under the constrained Bao Dai regime. Even more important were Diem's unimpeachable anti-Communist credentials. He had not only refused in 1945-46 to collaborate with or to serve the Viet Minh, which had been responsible for the murder of one of his many brothers, but he had strongly expressed himself as an anti-Communist on every possible occasion, both in Vietnam and in exile.

Moreover, U.S. government analysts reported from both Vietnam and Washington that Diem had a measure of popularity and was well-regarded in all three regions of Vietnam (North, Center and South). Some analysts conveyed that Diem was viewed by a variety of Vietnamese sources in the early fifties as the only possible non-Communist Nationalist savior in sight.[27]

In addition, Diem was more or less a U.S. discovery and this increased his potential in U.S. official eyes. There were few, if any, Vietnamese in the United States during the first Indochina war, but Ngo Dinh Diem was in exile at a Lakewood, New Jersey, Catholic seminary and being introduced to selected audiences and people in the United States by a respectable professor of political science at Michigan State, Dr. Wesley R. Fishel. This specialist in Japanese and Southeast Asian politics had first encountered Diem through contacts in Japan. Through Fishel, Diem met some people in the State Department as early as March 1953.[28]

Contrary to oft-expressed opinion, however, it was *not* the U.S. government that put Diem in power in Saigon, although it enshrined him during the following nine years (1954-63) before contributing to his downfall in the November 1, 1963, coup. The French had long been aware that Diem had some popular following in Vietnam, but since he was far too independent to have served their purposes, they were content to leave him in quiet exile in the United States. When Diem departed the United States for France in the early spring of 1954, shrewdly sensing the direction of events and apparently hoping to save at least a vestige of non-Communist Vietnam, the French held him in reserve for the post-armistice period. This was not long in coming, and after the Geneva Conference it was France, not the U.S. government, which persuaded Bao Dai to call on Diem to form what the French probably thought would constitute the last non-Communist government of Vietnam. For neither in France, nor in the United States itself, was there much serious hope after the Geneva agreements that a non-Communist South Vietnam could survive for very long, whether elections for reunification as called for by the agreements were held or not.

Diem accepted the mission, on condition that Bao Dai not return and give him a completely free hand. Within limits, Bao Dai accepted this role in 1954-55 and began slowly to fade from the scene. His few loyal subordinates in South Vietnam, such as Gen. Nguyen Van Hinh, were gradually purged by Diem. When the latter returned to Saigon in mid-1954, he found an incredibly uncertain and troubled situation there. Without assistance of any kind—for, with reason, he trusted virtually no one—he set about to become a sort of one-man government, a single and lonely figure symbolizing what was left and what might be built of an independent, non-Communist Vietnamese state.

Opposition to Diem abounded in 1954-55: among the so-called political-religious sects (the Cao Dai, Hoa Hao, and Binh Xuyen, the latter really an organized theft syndicate along the Saigon waterfront); within the slowly forming Vietnamese Army; and among what was called the Saigon "cafe politicians." [29] He found his strongest support among the Catholic refugees from North Vietnam around whom, with the later assistance of his brothers Ngo Dinh Nhu and Ngo Dinh Canh (the latter operating mainly in Central Vietnam), he set about to build his personal support organization, which became known as the Can Lao Party.

During this difficult period (mid-1954 to spring 1955), Diem received the political advice and support of a number of American diplomatic and intelligence officers whose influence clearly rose in Vietnam. Among them was Brig. Gen. Edward Lansdale, USAF, who had successfully assisted Philippine President Ramon Magsaysay in his victorious struggle against the Communist-led Huk rebels in Luzon. Lansdale set in place the beginnings of an effective anti-Communist intelligence network in South Vietnam and advised Diem on building up both a military capability and political support. Working in tandem with Lansdale was Diem's old friend, Prof. Fishel. Gradually, Diem built up domestic American support, particularly in Catholic circles and especially through Cardinal Francis Spellman. His struggle was noted and supported in the Congress by Senators John F. Kennedy and Mike Mansfield, both Catholics and both interested in Southeast Asia. As Diem's stature grew, so did support for him on the part of U.S. Ambassador to Saigon Donald Heath, who had earlier so strongly supported Bao Dai.

The only strong criticism of Diem to reach Washington came from General J. Lawton Collins, whom President Eisenhower sent to Saigon late in 1954 to review the entire situation. Neither Gen. Collins nor his French counterpart, Gen. Paul Ely, thought that Diem had the charisma or the organizational ability required to build a political and administrative structure in South Vietnam capable of stemming the Communist tide. But by the time Gen. Collins returned to Washington in May 1955 to bring his views to the president, the situation in Vietnam had taken a decisive turn in Diem's favor.[30]

Realizing that Diem was making progress in 1954-55, and that Viet Minh exhaustion after the eight years' war and the necessities of reconstruction in North Vietnam would give Diem a further breathing spell,

Diem's opposition in South Vietnam united long enough in the spring of 1955 to mount what it believed would be a successful assault against his rule. With some illicit support from remnants of the local French colonial establishment, and with the surreptitious assistance of disaffected army leaders still loyal to Bao Dai, the political-religious sects united at that time to challenge Diem's authority. In the "Battle of the Sects" waged through the streets of Saigon in late May 1955 Diem, with the support of loyalist army leaders, was able to completely rout the Binh Xuyen, then the strongest armed of the sects, and to exterminate its leader, the thug Bay Vien. Moreover, Diem simply refused to share any measure of authority with the Cao Dai and Hoa Hao leaders. Shared authority was, and remained throughout the ensuing nine years, a concept completely alien to him.

By the late spring of 1955, Diem had largely obtained what he wanted in Saigon: total and complete authority and power in the hands of the Ngo family. The family included his brother Ngo Dinh Nhu, soon to become his chief political lieutenant, and Nhu's wife; brother Ngo Dinh Canh, soon to become political and governmental plenipotentiary in Central Vietman (based in Hue); and brother Ngo Dinh Thuc, a Catholic archbishop of Vietnam who was to help him maintain support in Rome and among his natural following in the Catholic population of South Vietnam, including the North Vietnamese refugees. After the battle of the sects, the Cao Dai and Hoa Hao retreated slowly into the Mekong Delta background and never again threatened Diem's rule. But they never completely disappeared either, for they reemerged later in the sixties and seem to survive even under Communist rule today.

We should note here the absence of an active Buddhist political movement in Vietnam until much later—1963, in fact, the year of Diem's end. At the time of Diem's accession to power, 1954-55, there was in South Vietnam no discernible independent Buddhist force to be reckoned with; nor had such a force existed in the previous decade. Experts on religion in Vietnam regarded Buddhist rites and ceremonies there as eclectic and decaying, fatally mingled with Confucian and even animistic elements, and as extremely weak and impure compared with the lively, organic, popular Buddhism manifest in neighboring Laos and Cambodia.[31]

By the time Washington officially reviewed its policies toward Vietnam in the late spring of 1955, the battle of the sects had been won and Diem seemed in command. The new U.S. ambassador, Frederick Reinhardt, was instructed to provide him assistance and full support. The United States started thinking seriously of its role in training Vietnam's military forces, and committed significant economic assistance. It also decided to support Diem in his obdurate resistance to holding consultations with the North on the question of the all-Vietnam elections of 1956 stipulated by the Geneva accords. We shall cover this key issue in the next section of this chapter.

In the fall of 1955, Diem brought to the fore the matter of the future structure of the Vietnamese state. In two referenda held late in 1955, he first permanently eliminated Bao Dai as chief of state, substituting himself; and then obtained popular assent for the institution of a constitutional republic of Vietnam, of which he became the first president. We need not go into the methods used by Diem and his advisors to obtain the popular support which he represented as virtually unanimous, nor into how he himself wrote and imposed the constitution under which he legitimized his rule. The important point is that, by manner foul or fair, Diem had placed himself firmly in the saddle in South Vietnam by the beginning of 1956; and the United States stood fully behind him.

Quiet in Indochina

As soon as he was legitimately in full control, Diem began, somewhat surreptitiously at first, to extirpate and eradicate the remnants of those Communist cadres and pro-Communist elements in South Vietnam on which his supporters and services could lay their hands. This last element in the situation was perhaps insufficiently reported and appreciated in Washington as South Vietnam began to emerge in U.S. perception as a really independent non-Communist state. The U.S. government's attention [32] was perhaps too strongly riveted on questions of North-South Vietnamese relations and performance under the Geneva accords, and not sufficiently on Diem's secret internal campaign against the Communists, including as well all other elements opposing him. This campaign was bound, sooner or later, to bring about Vietnamese Communist counteraction.

The United States, with some reason, looked upon Vietnam and Indochina with considerable satisfaction in 1956. The advance of communism, which had seemed so threatening in early and mid-1954, had apparently been halted. Washington chose to believe that this had occurred through the success of Diem in South Vietnam, the emergence of apparently united and reasonably independent entities under Sihanouk in Cambodia and Souvanna Phouma in Laos, and the creation of SEATO, with its rhetorical pledges of mutual security assistance in Southeast Asia. Moreover, as we shall note in the next section, the partition of Vietnam appeared in 1956 as if it would in fact hold fast for at least a number of years.

New dangers, new threats, were emerging to preoccupy the United

States in its containment policies on other horizons: Africa would soon become a serious arena of superpower confrontation; even earlier, the Middle East, galvanized by Nasser, would explode in the Suez crisis and the second Arab-Israeli War of October-November 1956. This would bring about tensions of major proportions between the United States and its oldest European partners, Britain and France. In Europe, anti-Soviet rebellion suppressed in East Germany in 1953 was about to break out again, this time in Hungary (October-November 1956), leaving the United States confronted with a major dilemma at the moment of its national elections. No wonder that, as 1957 approached, the United States was more than willing to pay what seemed a small price for continued calm in Indochina, a region which, though remote from its major concerns on the globe, had nonetheless once already (1954) brought it to the edge of war.

The price for continued quiet in Vietnam was indeed rather low: economic and security assistance to Diem's Vietnam in the amount of about $300 million per year starting in fiscal year 1956; the presence there of specified individuals desired by Diem, such as Lansdale and Fishel; as well as of a military training and assistance mission which remained at about 400 men until the end of 1956 when it was roughly doubled in number.[33] In the United States, Leo Cherne, an expert in refugee resettlement and in consequence thereof interested in Vietnam, founded "The American Friends of Vietnam" which, with the support of Cardinal Spellman and Senators Kennedy and Mansfield, began to constitute Diem's small lobby group in Washington.

As imperceptibly as the United States had crept into Vietnam in 1950-55, Vietnam now began to creep out as a major topic on the Washington policy agenda, which it had been for so long. As Diem took things in hand and as the Communist forces, exhausted by their eight-year arduous struggle, recouped in their northern lair, the United States relaxed in Indochina. But this would not have been possible without the partition of Vietnam and the growth of U.S. military power in Asia in the late fifties, subjects to which we now turn. Moreover, many of those analyzing the issue for the U.S. government in late 1956 knew very well that only a short-time card, at most, had been secured in Indochina.[34]

3. The Partition of Vietnam and the Crest of American Power in East Asia

There existed relatively stable, independent and non-Communist states in South Vietnam, Cambodia, and Laos during 1956-59, which must have been the result of a minor miracle, because in mid-1954 such a prospect would have appeared almost inconceivable. On the morrow of Dien Bien Phu, the Viet Minh (DRV) appeared triumphant and invincible throughout Vietnam. In Laos, the Viet Minh's satellite Pathet Lao movement had swiftly developed during the years 1949-54 and occupied the two northern provinces of Sam Neua and Phong Saly, to which it held fast after the Geneva Conference. In Cambodia, Sihanouk held the reins of official power, but Communist influence was emergent and the presence of Viet Minh forces along the remote borders with Vietnam was already felt. Moreover, Sihanouk had little use for the South Vietnamese, for Diem, or the Americans. Politics and geopolitics seemed almost certain to move him slowly toward the Communist orbit.

Laos and Cambodia

Neither Cambodia nor Laos fell. Two main reasons account for their survival after 1954 and well into the period of the deep American engagement in Indochina in the sixties. First, the DRV's post-1954 priority clearly remained Vietnam; and even there its own state of exhaustion and disrepair was such that its capabilities for waging further war were severely limited. Second, both Sihanouk in Cambodia and Souvanna Phouma in Laos made shrewd use of external influences—Soviet, Chinese, French, Indian, and even American—to dissuade the Vietnamese Communists from further advances. Sihanouk managed to control his local Communists until well into the sixties. In Laos, however, their momentum had so grown by 1959-61 that President Kennedy noted shortly after his inauguration: "Ike never even mentioned Vietnam. Laos was all Ike ever talked to me about." [35]

One of the probable reasons for the growing momentum of the Pathet Lao supported by the DRV in the late fifties was the growth of a Laotian anti-Communist army, surreptitiously armed and trained by the United States. Parts of this army turned against their own government in 1958 and Souvanna Phouma left power. The Laos government fell in the hands of a tool of the U.S. military and CIA, General Phoumi Nosavan. Rebellion against Phoumi in turn broke out in Laotian Army ranks in 1960, bringing about the emergence of a neutralist force led by Capt. Kong Le. The latter threatened alliance with the Pathet Lao who were by then receiving substantial and direct Soviet material support.

In the midst of the Laotian confusion of 1961, the United States seriously studied and actively considered direct military intervention in that benighted land. Although the Joint Chiefs of Staff favored it under certain conditions, cooler and wiser heads prevailed.[36] After the Kennedy administration took office, Ambassador Harriman negotiated a second Geneva Agreement (1962) with the Soviets and Chinese, which returned the shrewd and accommodation-prone Souvanna Phouma to office and once more reaffirmed the status of Laos as a non-aligned state. Phoumi Nosavan, in turn, took the road of exile to Bangkok. The Pathet Lao subsided, and an uncomfortable peace continued in Laos until the early seventies, when once again U.S. military intervention— the so-called "secret war in Laos"—precipitated Pathet Lao onslaughts that finally brought the Laotian Communists into Souvanna Phouma's coalition regime of 1973, and ultimately to full power (1975).

The 1962 Geneva Accord on Laos, which restored the neutrality that both the United States and the Soviet Union had breached there, was attained only after the United States had demonstrated the seriousness of its intentions in Southeast Asia by a major display of its military strength in the region. In 1962, the United States sent nearly 10,000 Marines on a staging operation to Thailand whence they could have been rapidly moved into Laos. This move contributed in a major way to Thailand's alignment with the United States, which was ratified later in 1962 by the signing of the Rusk-Thanat Agreement.[37]

Thus, through the Laos crisis of 1959-62, foundations were laid for a major U.S. military commitment in the heart of mainland Southeast Asia—a commitment more serious than the one made in SEATO, and one which would eventually contribute to our increasing descent into the Vietnam snakepit.

Vietnam

In Vietnam, U.S. expectations after Geneva were that the DRV would exploit its momentum, press its advantage, and conclude as rapidly as possible the victory of the then ten-year-old Vietnamese revolution. The reasons the Communist revolution did not break out in a major way again until 1959 need to be briefly examined.

The first reason was exhaustion of the DRV. The DRV's victory of 1954 was not a victory in the full sense of the word.[38] The entire eight years' war, and especially the concluding battle at Dien Bien Phu, had demanded all the sacrifices in lives, treasure, and energy that a small, technologically backward Asian peasant population was capable of making, even with high morale and superb military and civilian leadership. At least some years of respite were essential. Communist cadres, whether northern or southern in origin, that had been operating in the southern regions during the war and had been repatriated under the provisions of the 1954 accords, were regrouped and retrained in the North. The economy of the North regained priority in the allocation of the DRV's scarce resources, and the North was at least partially rebuilt and economically refloated in 1954-59. While building strength in the northern fatherland of socialism was the clear goal during this period, the ideal of extending freedom and socialism to the southern regions of Vietnam was of course never for an instant abandoned.[39]

A second reason why a Communist revolution did not occur until 1959 was the success of the Diem regime. With heavy U.S. economic and military assistance and U.S. moral support, the Diem regime did not do badly in 1956-59. Hundreds of thousands of Catholic refugees from the North were absorbed. Communists, proto-Communists, suspected Communists, and anyone suspected even of sympathies with the Communists were jailed, exiled, or otherwise confined. Anti-Communist Nationalists not wholly loyal to the Ngo family or regime were rendered virtually powerless. The political-religious sects were suppressed. The economy was improved, though on a very patchwork basis. Great schemes of land reform under the aegis of U.S. technical assistance programs were promulgated, but not many peasants obtained actual title to the land they were tilling.[40]

Diem's success reached its peak in 1959, at just about the time the DRV itself had recovered from its exhaustion; 1959 was therefore an important turning point. Had the DRV not then set its revolution in motion again in the south, what remained of its assets there might have been totally lost. That was one reason why the southern cadres regrouped in the North were strongly urging the DRV leadership to allow national liberation to regain top priority in DRV policy.

The Soviet Position and the Partition of Vietnam

A third reason why the Indochina revolution remained dormant until 1959 derives from Soviet policy and the lack of support the DRV could hope to obtain from the Soviet Union until Soviet policy began to change in 1959. Soviet policy in Vietnam and in Indochina as a whole during the period 1954-59 showed a marked lack of militancy or activism. As already suggested earlier, the Soviets had done little for the DRV when it was struggling against the returning colonial French in 1945-48; and except for moral and propaganda support, they did not do much more for Vietnam during the first years of the high cold war (1948-54). As we noted, material assistance provided to the DRV in 1953-54 came from the People's Republic of China, though the Soviets had no doubt supplied much of this equipment to China originally, and underwritten its passage to Vietnam.

The Soviet Union also approached the diplomatic settlement at Geneva in 1954 with a remarkably detached attitude. As we suggested,

French Prime Minister Pierre Mendes-France may have obtained from the Soviets in advance an advantageous deal in Vietnam in return for the defeat of the European Defense Community in the French National Assembly. If that was in fact the case, it indicated the primacy that the Soviets, like the United States, placed on the European theater of confrontation and the secondary place to which they relegated Southeast Asia in their world policy. It must however be recalled that the period 1954-55 was a difficult one for the Soviet Union. This was the period of the Stalin succession, during which first Beria, then Malenkov and Molotov, were shunted aside by Khrushchev, who later also reduced Bulganin's influence. We have previously called 1953-55 a period of remission in the high cold war; it happened to coincide with the victory of the DRV against the French in the first Indochina war.

Nonetheless, despite internal instability in the Soviet Union, the relaxed Soviet stance toward Indochina probably signified a more profound calculation which may well have held sway in Soviet foreign policy during the entire high cold war and which in turn tended to condition U.S. attitudes toward Southeast Asia. This was that the distant and oceanic zone of Southeast Asia lay outside the area of top or immediate Soviet priority and concern. The chief Soviet interest in the area, which began to be manifest only in 1959 with the appearance of Soviet activity and personnel on the side of the Pathet Lao and neutralists in Laos, was to keep Chinese Communist influence to a minimum in Southeast Asia, and certainly below that of the Soviets themselves.

It is useful to recall that Communist China, by 1954 only some five years in control of its own mainland and barely rid of its Korean War involvement, was then by any measure still a minor actor on the Asian and world stage, with only minimal influence in Southeast Asia (mainly in Malaysia). China, preoccupied with domestic reconstruction and with the problem of Taiwan, fell in with the Soviet position at Geneva and played no independent role on behalf of the DRV there.

Soviet preoccupation with the future of Southeast Asia and that of the Vietnamese Communist state appeared to be minimal at the Geneva Conference of 1954. What the Soviets did, or sanctioned, at Geneva included the following:

1. They probably [41] influenced the DRV to settle for a line of demarcation (17th parallel) inferior to that justified by its on-the-ground military position.
2. They probably [42] influenced the DRV to accept ambiguous provisions for political settlement in the conference's final declaration. These did not spell out the type of institutions "general elections by secret ballot" were to establish in Vietnam, nor the procedures to be followed to bring about the

pre-electoral, interzonal consultations planned for 1955 or the elections of 1956 themselves.
3. The Soviets agreed to preside over the future of the Geneva accords by sharing the permanent co-chairmanship of the Geneva Conference with the British, thereby making it more difficult for the DRV to protest internationally if principal provisions of the accords were allowed to lapse, as indeed they were.

It is therefore clear that the Soviet Union provided a relatively easy way out for the French, and the Americans, at Geneva. But the Soviets in fact did more to ease the French way out of, and the American way into, Vietnam. Reviewing it some twenty-five years later, one is almost compelled to suspect that Khrushchev deliberately maneuvered to render the entry of the "imperialist camp" into the Indochina quagmire as easy as possible. The next Soviet move took place at the foreign ministers conference held at Geneva in November 1955 in sequel to the 1955 summer summit meeting at Geneva at which Khrushchev had presented abortive German proposals, while Eisenhower had pressed his abortive scheme for "open skies" inspection of the superpowers' mutual nuclear capabilities.

This item is so instructive that it is worth recounting it here in some detail.[43] As co-chairmen of the continuing but never reassembled Geneva Conference on Vietnam, the Soviets by late 1955 were in receipt of at least a dozen formal notes from the DRV protesting the failure of South Vietnam (and the United States) to engage in the interzonal consultations called for by the 1954 accords. These notes, regardless of the degree of DRV supplication that accompanied them, were invariably forwarded to the British Geneva co-chairman. From the British Foreign Office, they would float unhurriedly to the U.S. State Department, which duly filed and forgot them.[44]

Finally, in late October or early November 1955, all the DRV's notes of protest having remained without consequence, the Indian chairman of the International Control Commission for Vietnam, displaying great concern about violations of the Geneva accords, persuaded the Indian government to bring the matter to the British co-chairman's attention with the urgent request that "Indochina" be placed as an item on the agenda of the forthcoming foreign ministers sequel to the Geneva summer summit. As chairman of the I.C.C., established for all three Indochina countries by the 1954 accords, India was charged not only with the enforcement of the armistice in Vietnam but also with supervision of the implementation of the political provisions of the accords.

Moved by India's insistence, the United Kingdom for the first time raised the matter at high levels in Washington, and pressed it strongly enough that the United States, albeit reluctantly, agreed to place the issue of Indochina on the agenda of the forthcoming Geneva meeting.[45] When the item "Indochina" was finally reached on the foreign ministers' agenda on the last day of the meeting at Geneva in November 1955, Molotov arose to request that it be deleted. The United Stated and United Kingdom were delighted to comply.[46]

Never again thereafter was an international conference held on the issue of Vietnam. This seems remarkable to say the least, considering the international tensions and anguish the Vietnam issue was subsequently to cause. Moreover, Molotov's gesture at Geneva in November 1955 permanently ended efforts to enforce the political provisions of the Geneva accords of 1954, and provided confirmation for those in the U.S. government who believed that the Soviets, and indeed the world, intended the Vietnam partition to continue into the indefinite future. Those in the U.S. government who favored application of the Geneva political provisions in Vietnam thereafter saw the game taken away by the advocates of partition. Diem's refusal to hold consultations as required in July 1955, which had been at first hesitantly and later more confidently supported by Secretary Dulles, now looked like wisdom of the first order. It was thenceforth clear that there would be no all-Vietnam elections in July of 1956.

Aside from having in effect diplomatically abandoned the DRV at Geneva in 1954, the Soviets in 1955 thus took (or failed to take) steps of momentuous consequence for the future of Vietnam—whether the Soviets recognized this or not, whether they did so deliberately or not. As the world entered 1956, the *de facto* partition of Vietnam was an accomplished fact as far as the U.S. government was concerned, and the perception grew apace in Washington of *two countries in Vietnam*, the southern (as in Korea) subject to the threatening challenge of its northern counterpart. In January 1957, Khrushchev gave further ballast to the concept of *two Vietnams* by proposing them both for membership in the U.N., a strange entreaty to which the United States remained strangely unresponsive.[47]

From 1956 on, the perception grew among U.S. policy-makers that the Soviets held a relaxed view of Indochina. This perception had become virtually fixed in the minds of key U.S. leaders by the mid-sixties and helps explain why they seem repeatedly to have found it so easy in 1965-73 to go to this ally of our enemies to attempt to help the cause of our friends. This bizarre U.S.-Soviet bilateralism, transcending on-the-ground Indochinese considerations, may have been a factor in U.S. thinking later that it could bomb North Vietnam with impunity even while Prime Minister Alexei Kosygin was in Hanoi (February 1965), and that it could repeatedly ask Leonid Brezhnev and/or Kosygin, directly or through intermediaries, to intervene on American behalf with Hanoi. But more of this in later portions of this book.

The Crest of American Power in Asia

Between 1954 and 1959, the United States reached the crest of its military and political power in postwar East Asia. It was heavily deployed in Korea, Okinawa, and Japan; possessed of major rear bases in the Philippines and Guam; buttressed by willing Australia-New Zealand military and diplomatic support in the Southwest Pacific; in command, together with its Chinese allies on Taiwan, of the waters in and the air over the Taiwan Straits. The latter was demonstrated in the proxy air battles fought by the U.S.-armed Chinese Nationalist forces in the Taiwan Straits in 1958. The United States was also extended significantly into mainland Southeast Asia by the provision of considerable military and economic support to Vietnam, to Laos, and even to Thailand. The latter was now fast drifting away from its traditional diplomacy of equilibrium to one of pro-U.S. alignment. Presiding over the SEATO multilateral treaty and over an ever-spreading network of CIA agents and CIA collaborators throughout East Asia, the United States which had even intervened covertly though unsuccessfully in support of anti-Sukarno Indonesian Army plotters in 1958, seemed unassailably *the* superpower in East and Southeast Asia.

The Senate had ratified the security commitments to the Philippines (1951), Japan (1951), Anzus (1951), Republic of China (1954), Korea (1954), to which would later be added the Rusk-Thanat Executive Agreement of 1962 providing Thailand with a similar though less formal commitment. Military basing rights acquired throughout East Asia for the performance of U.S. commitments and obligations were contained in a host of executive agreements, as were the terms for the provision of economic and security assistance. The latter increasingly acquired the character of direct U.S. budgetary support for the weak treasuries of East Asia. Such support was extended by the dubious process of concessional commercial import programs in the host countries, which in turn generated the local currencies required for the financing of U.S.-inspired military enhancement and economic development programs.

There also began during this period a significant movement of private American capital from the United States to East Asia, particularly to Taiwan, Korea, Hong Kong, the Philippines, and later to Japan, Australia, New Zealand, and to Southeast Asian mainland countries such as Thailand and Singapore. The inflow of U.S. private investment buttressed the general sense of U.S. presence and power in the region.

Not only did the United States seem supreme in East and Southeast Asia during 1954-59, it also seemed unchallenged, except in the Taiwan Straits. While it is true that India, Indonesia, and Cambodia's non-aligned policies occasionally pricked the sensitive skin of U.S. diplomacy and strategy, these were really not serious challenges. Even the course that India had undertaken under Nehru and Khrishna Menon after 1948 and until about 1955-56 to influence political developments in Southeast Asia seemed to recede into passivity with the growth and spread of U.S. influence. After 1955, the French were gone; and after 1958-59, the British. From Communist China, then in the full throes of the reconstruction program which was to lead in 1958 to the disasters of the "Great Leap Forward," the only serious challenge arose in the Taiwan Straits and this was beaten back quite successfully in 1955-58 and in the minor confrontations over Quemoy-Matsu in 1959-61. As already indicated, until 1959 at least, when Khrushchev's truculence became acute not only in Europe but in Africa, the Western Hemisphere, and Asia as well, the Soviet stance was relaxed.

Basking in its superpower status and in the benefits of its new-found role as major actor in East Asia, as well as facing its problems there, the United States had almost imperceptibly begun to build a major stake in the region. The stake was not merely that attendant to the policies of containment against Soviet power begun in Europe, and against Sino-Soviet and Communist power begun in Asia and elsewhere. It consisted also of positive interests of a magnitude and scale the United States had never before held in Asia. These interests were political, strategic, economic, and human as well; for thousands of American citizens had joined the growing civilian and military bureaucracies the U.S. government was now deploying throughout the region. Following the manifest destiny which had begun in North America over a century earlier, the United States by 1960 had spread fully westward across the Pacific to its latest, and perhaps last, frontier.

Notes

1. For a discussion of containment, of Kennan's original thesis, and a summation of his views regarding the "X" article and its consequences, *see Foreign Policy Quarterly* 7 (Summer 1972): pp. 5-53. *See also,* Charles Gati, ed., *Caging The Bear: Containment and the Cold War* (Indianapolis: Bobbs-Merrill, 1974), pp. 3-53; Martin F. Herz, ed., *Decline of the West? George Kennan and His Critics* (Washington, D.C.: Ethics and Public Policy Center, Georgetown University, 1978).
2. Alexander Dallin, *German Rule in Russia, 1941-45: A Study of Occupation*

Politics (London: Macmillan, 1957), esp. Chs. XIX, pp. 409-27, and XXVI, pp. 553-81. *See also,* George Fisher, *Soviet Opposition to Stalin* (Cambridge: Harvard University Press, 1952).

3. Alvin Z. Rubinstein, ed., *The Foreign Policy of the Soviet Union,* 2nd ed. (New York: Random House,1966), pp. 86-87.
4. John L. Gaddis, *The U.S. and The Origins of the Cold War, 1941-47* (New York: Columbia University Press, 1972). See esp. Ch. 10.
5. *Ibid.*
6. *Ibid.,* Ch. 3, pp. 78 ff.
7. *Ibid.,* Ch. 5, pp. 135-39.
8. *Ibid.,* Ch. 7, pp. 203 ff.
9. *Ibid.,* Ch. 5, pp. 139 ff.
10. Gar Alperowitz, *Atomic Diplomacy: Hiroshima and Potsdam* (New York: Random House, 1965).
11. Walter LaFeber, *America, Russia and the Cold War, 1945-1971,* 1972 ed. (New York: Wiley & Sons, 1972), p. 35.
12. Cabell Phillips, *The Truman Presidency: The History of a Triumphant Succession* (New York: Macmillan, 1966), p. 52.
13. Gaddis, *Origins of the Cold War,* pp. 204-05.
14. Daniel Yergin, *The Shattered Peace: Origins of the Cold War and the National Security State* (Boston: Houghton Mifflin, 1977), p. 401.
15. For a discussion of economic factors and motives in America's postwar world policies, *see* R.W. Tucker, *The Radical Left in American Foreign Policy* (Baltimore: Johns Hopkins University Press, 1971).
16. R.W. Tucker, *Nation or Empire: The Debate Over American Foreign Policy* (Baltimore: Johns Hopkins University Press, 1968).
17. *Ibid.,* particularly pp. 138-60.
18. During McCarthyism, a government employee, for example, had to demonstrate "positive" anti-communism, by way of statements or cooperation in investigations of colleagues, if he was to overcome suspicions of being pro-Communist. This can be documented from the proceedings of the State Department Loyalty Review Board, 1950-56, for instance.
19. A good account of the atmosphere in the U.S. mission in Saigon in the early fifties can be found in Robert Shaplen, *A Forest of Tigers* (New York: A.A. Knopf, 1956).
20. Eisenhower defined what he called the "falling domino principle" as follows during his press conference of April 7, 1954: "You have a row of dominoes set up, you knock over the first one, and what will happen to the last one is the certainty that it will go over very quickly. So you could have a beginning of a disintegration that would have the most profound influences." *The New York Times,* April 8, 1954, p. 18.
21. A substantive theory of history, as distinguished from the epistemological conceptions usually termed "theories of international relations"—such theories as realism, integration, system, etc.—is a conceptual framework held by and acted upon by statemen and political leaders. The domino theory, in this sense, was a real theory of international relations, as was appeasement theory, and the theory of national wars of liberation to which we turn in Chapter III.
22. Peter Poole, *The United States and Indochina from FDR to Nixon* (Hinsdale, Ill: Dryden Press, 1973), p. 27.

23. On the Geneva settlement and its relation to Europe, *see* Colbert, *Southeast Asia,* Ch. 10; and F.R. Randle, *Geneva 1954* (Princeton, N.J.: Princeton University Press, 1969). On the defeat of the EDC in France, see F. Roy Willis, *France, Germany, and the New Europe* (New York: Oxford University Press. 1968 ed.), pp. 178 ff.
24. The 1954 U.S. debate concerning intervention in Indochina is covered in *Pentagon Papers* 1: pp. 88-94; Melvin Gurtov, *The First Vietnam Crisis* (New York: Columbia Univ. Press, 1967), pp. 92-110; and Bernard B. Fall, *The Two Vietnams: A Political and Military Analysis,* 2nd ed. (New York: Praeger, 1967), pp. 224-33.
25. Daniel Ellsberg, *Papers on the War* (New York: Simon and Schuster, 1972).
26. Bernard B. Fall, *Vietnam Witness 1953-66* (London:Pall Mall Press, 1966), pp. 73-83; B.B. Fall, *Two Vietnams,* pp. 152-55.
27. Memorandum by J.W. Lydman and P.M. Kattenburg, INR/State to Philip Bonsal, director of Southeast Asian Affairs/State, October 1952. (Personal recollection.)
28. Ngo Dinh Diem first visited the State Department in March 1953 to discuss the then ongoing Viet Minh invasion of Laos. He met the director of Southeast Asian Affairs and various other lower echelon officials. He did not meet, on this or subsequent occasions before mid-1954, with officials at the assistant secretary level or higher. (Personal recollection.)
29. See Chapter V, Section 3.
30. *Pentagon Papers,* 1:pp. 231-39; Poole, *The United States and Indochina,* pp. 45-46.
31. Kenneth Landon, *Southeast Asia: Crossroads of Religion* (Chicago: University of Chicago Press, 1949).
32. Including my own attention as desk officer, the official principally involved on a day-to-day basis in the State Department.
33. See Chapter III, Section 3.
34. *Pentagon Papers,* 1: pp. 106-07.
35. *NBC News White Paper: Vietnam Hindsight, Part I,* Broadcast on Tuesday, December 21, 1971; Transcript, p. 10.
36. Roger Hilsman, *To Move A Nation* (New York: Doubleday, 1967), pp. 127 ff.
37. See below.
38. P.M. Kattenburg, "Vietnam and U.S. Diplomacy 1940-1970," *Orbis* XV (Fall 1971): pp. 818-41.
39. B.B. Fall, *Two Vietnams,* pp. 308-12. *See also* Carlyle A. Thayer, "Southern Vietnamese Revolutionary Organization and the Vietnam Workers' Party: 1954-1974," in *Communism in Indochina: New Perspectives,* ed. J.J. Zasloff and MacAllister Brown (Lexington, Mass: D.C. Heath, 1975), p. 33.
40. Wolf I. Ladejinsky, "Agrarian Reform in the Republic of Vietnam," in *Vietnam: Anatomy of a Conflict,* ed. W.R. Fishel (Itasca, Ill.: F.E. Peacock, 1968), pp. 517-538.
41. Conjectural by necessity until Soviet archives become available. However, see Colbert, *Southeast Asia.* Randle, *Geneva 1954.*
42. *Ibid.*
43. I am recounting this item from personal knowledge and memory; so far as

I know, it has not been previously divulged. Messages documenting the episode should become available when the State Department's *Foreign Relations of the U.S.* for 1955 are released.
44. The Soviet transmission of these notes was not, so far as I can best recall, accompanied by any commentary. I was then the desk officer at State responsible for filing these notes received via the British Embassy in Washington, D.C.
45. From personal knowledge and recollection.
46. *Ibid.*
47. *U.S. Participation in the U.N.—Report by the President to Congress for 1957.* Issued by U.S. Department of State, June 19, 1958.

Chapter III

The Pitfalls of Global Approaches, 1959-62

1. The United States as Superpower

The role of superpower was not thrust upon an unwilling United States by some combination of powers or circumstances beyond our control at the end of World War II. The United States assumed what its people almost unanimously regarded, after the experience of that enormous war as their manifest role and obligation, pointed to by a destiny which the vast majority felt had been theirs for the past several decades.

American Values and the World

Are there salient features central to the American tradition and experience which have made the United States perform its superpower role in what we might term a particularlistic way? In other words, are there specially distinctive American traits which would not have emerged if the superpower had been France or the United Kingdom, and which do not characterize the Soviet Union or China in the performance of that role?

The one certainly salient and distinctive trait of the United States is that its people are of many and highly diverse traditions and racial and ethnic origins, who have lived together on the American land for only a very short period of time as history goes. Today's Britons, though also of diverse origins, have peopled the United Kingdom for at least 1,000 years; French, though equally diverse, have been on the soil of France even longer; and so on their lands have lived Italians, Iberians, Greeks, the Slavic, and many other peoples of Russia, the Han Chinese, or the ethno-linguistically diverse people of India. But not over a tiny fraction of "American people" descend from those who have been on this continent only some three hundred years; a few look back to families that have been on this soil two hundred years. The overwhelming majority of those who form the American nation today have been here a mere one hundred years or less. A hundred years or less is a very short time to form mutual bonds between diverse peoples, and bonds between peoples and their land. The United States is not a generic "people-land" country in the sense that England, France, China, or Japan are; or even in the sense that the Soviet Union, through its dominant White Russian people, is. U.S. people are not yet held together predominantly by a sense of belonging together as descendants of generational patrimony, by a bond to land. What holds the United States together is saliently a set of principles and ideals. Thus, the United States is an "idea" country, rather than a "people-land" one.

Accordingly, principles and ideals hold a cardinal place in the U.S. national ethos and crucially distinguish U.S. performance in the superpower role. The American principles and ideas, the "value structure" to use more refined language, were in part: (1) inherited from an Anglo-Saxon tradition and adopted; (2) inherited from a continental, including French, German, and Hispanic, tradition and incorporated; (3) laid down by the founding fathers, those pure geniuses of detached contemplation; (4) refined by subsequent leading figures of thought and action, among whom John and John Quincy Adams, Abraham Lincoln, Theodore Roosevelt, Woodrow Wilson, and Franklin Roosevelt are just a very few among the many who stand out; and (5) tested and retested in the process of settling the continent, healing the North-South breach, developing the economy from the wilderness in the spirit of free enterprise, and fighting World Wars I and II, not so much for interests as for the survival of the very principles by which most Americans were guiding their lives.

This entire process of binding the diverse American people to land still in the process of being settled, of forging the American nation-state, took place very rapidly and in cramped circumstances. The 1890 immigrant could not know much of his country of vast spaces and abundant resources. Absorbed in the factories and sweatshops of the East or Midwest, the farms of the South or ranches of the Western plains, he knew that the United States meant freedom of assembly, speech, person, and enterprise; equality and the absence of oppression based on class, caste, or social ostracism; opportunity for education, self-improvement, horizontal or upward mobility—at least for most Americans.

Values and principles, beliefs and ideology, came not only to occupy a central place in the American popular psyche; but in fact to symbolize it altogether. To be American meant to be free, to see the world as open and progressive, to be optimistic as to the future and the fate of man. And to be optimistic, progressive, and free meant to be "American." In the isolated confines of the American continent, these values quickly came to be seen as virtually the only ones worthy of pursuit by mankind. By a strange psychological twist, those excluded from the pursuit and achievement of such values, that is, most of the world outside America, came in the eyes of many Americans to be regarded as deprived of genuine humanity. In a very real sense, Americans began to equate America with the world much as our grunts in Vietnam during the 1960s spoke of two universes, "Nam" and "the world." Hence, Texas buildings were not just the tallest in the United States but "in the world"; the American baseball championships were "World Series"; good American things were, in general, "the finest in the world," "richest in the world," etc.

Together with the tendency to equate America and the world there also grew in the United States, in direct function of the U.S. value structure, a rather unique perception of linear progress. Since each successive generation in America, particularly after about 1865, was doing better than the previous one on a test of at least material possessions, there was no perceptible reason why this process of improvement could not go on indefinitely into the future. We need not dwell on just how much such a linear notion of progress from generation to generation differs from the cultural perception of, say, Javanese, Peruvian, or French peasants who have seen—in de Gaulle's marvellous words [1]—"decline and renewal" move cyclically over the centuries. Graphically, one could represent the distinction as a continuous series of curves for most of the resigned world; and upward sloping line for the American perception of the generational progress of mankind. To the American people, a linear concept of progress must and did seem a universal quest. Progress, then, was centrally what America would bring to the world because of the principles it symbolized and upheld.

These images and concepts were sincerely held by the overwhelming preponderance of Americans as they assumed the superpower role. They provide a basic reason why this role was so easily assumed by Americans, why such "manifest destiny," not thrust upon them or unwillingly shouldered and not taken as a burden, was eagerly grasped as inevitable fate.

America as Emancipator

The national ethos and outlook of Americans brought with it a cultural ethnocentricism of the first order, perhaps rarely equaled in the history of the world. Russians knew when they conquered Poles that the latter were neither Russian nor anxious to emulate most Russian values or qualities, great as some of these may have been. French knew when they colonized Africa and Indochina that the undoubted benefits of their *mission civilisatrice* must be imposed before they could become accepted and eventually desired. Han Chinese were in their own eyes civilizing, to be sure, but they were civilizing barbarians who must be made to accept civilization. Britons, like those others, never doubted the superiority of British culture, ideas, enterprise, and technique over that of any other people, but they never deluded themselves into thinking that Hindis, Afghans, or Boers shared their point of view. The Japanese, successful in every war but their last, devised the "Greater Coprosperity Sphere" to legitimize their military conquest of Asia, but never doubted that ostensibly cooperating puppets like Sukarno in Indonesia or Jose Laurel in the Philippines did not fully share their assertions of its benefits to them.

However, Americans in the superpower role have never seemed to doubt, or conceivably never knew, that the schemes they devised for the assistance, reconstruction, regeneration, development, and regional integration—in short, the progress—of others could be regarded by the latter as conceived in any other way than wholly for their benefit. American post-World War II policy is in this respect devoid of artifice or deception. The American mind set, the minds of our leaders or of the people, was entirely the mind set of an emancipator. In such a mind set, one need not feel or act superior, or believe one is imposing one's ethos or values on others, since one senses naturally that others cannot doubt the emancipator's righteous cause anymore than his capacities. In this respect, the American role as superpower, particularly in the early postwar years, is very analogous to the role that can be attributed to a professor, mentor, or other type of emancipator.

Postwar American statesmen, in fact, remind one much more of professors than of, say, missionaries or evangelists with whom they have sometimes been identified.[2] The professor is obviously capable, or he would not be teaching in the first place and trusted with the job of mentoring the unknowing and the young. He is clearly disinterested, since his students do not pay him directly for his task of emancipation. He is also clearly needed, or there would be no students in his classes; and his message is accepted by others, as it is by him, as not only relevant but right. Moreover, like the American superpower, the professor does not control the lives or destinies of his students; they remain free to come or go. If they remain, he will dispense more wisdom, in the measure they have earned it. If they leave, the professor's assumption is that emancipation will pass them by, as China passed the United States by and therefore seemed, under communism, irredeemably lost to Americans for a very long time.

It will help us understand America's performance and psychology as a superpower, and the whys and wherefores of its Indochina involvement, if we bear in mind this analogy of the American performance in the superpower role with that of the benevolent but clearly egocentric professor, dispensing emancipation through knowledge of both righteousness and the right way to the deprived students of the world.

The Role of Power

Some observers have reflected on the muscle flexing syndrome in American politics and, by extension, American diplomacy and foreign policy.[3] There is too much evidence of it to deny the machismo factor in American leadership or the physical way in which American society tends to approach problems of conflict, power distribution, war, and peace in the world.

The United States ended World War II and ushered in the postwar period by the two atomic explosions at Hiroshima and Nagasaki. The fundamental motivations for this action were themselves physical: to end the war by crushing blows, much as the surrounding circumstances and secondary diplomatic motivations may remain in doubt.[4] It is true that the immediate postwar period of hope in sustained Soviet-American collaboration and consequent hesitancy on the part of the United States to commit itself, along with the rapid and almost total demobilization of U.S. military forces, resulted in a period of respite during which diplomatic settlements were unsuccessfully attempted.

But at the first serious indication of renewed trouble on the world stage, the U.S. response turned heavily to strategic and military means. Our thinking in the early, as well as the later, stages of the high cold war was far more military-strategic than diplomatic-political; and the procurement, deployment, and maintenance of bases and of weapon systems came to preoccupy us much more than the traditional means of inducement, persuasion, bargaining, negotiations, and accommodation.

There are several important questions to pose with respect to this ascent of strategy over diplomacy in American foreign policy during the high cold war, the answers to which we will attempt to supply throughout this book. First, why was the national interest interpreted in such largely physical and geostrategic terms? Second, if we were so powerful a superpower, and getting stronger as the years passed, and if our strategic and conventional arms were multiplying, why were we so constantly fearful? Why was our security apparently always threatened, instead of the sense of threat diminishing as we increased our military strength to cope with the challenges posed by our rivals? And why did only a shift of method, but not a fundamental change in the overwhelming role that strategy and muscle continued to play as against diplomacy and negotiations in our policy, occur when the cast of leaders changed significantly in 1961 and the "New Frontier" under Kennedy came into office?

With respect to geostrategic perceptions of the national interest, it is oversimplified but correct to state that the postwar and cold war periods manifested the real revenge of realism over idealism in the conduct and formulation of American foreign policy.[5] Pre-World War II perceptions of our national interest had been profoundly affected, and both complemented and constrained, by idealism—the high moral tone, ethical upbringing, and profoundly felt sense of world order through law which had dominated virtually a whole generation of American scholars and foreign policy-makers before World War II.[6]

After World War II, there appeared a new school of policy-makers and commentators entirely opposed to the moralism of the prewar American idealists. The new postwar realistic appraisals of world history, politics, and economics took their root in the *raison d'état* theories of such continental historians as Meinecke and Ranke, and geopoliticians like Mackinder and Haushofer. These newer, more sophisticated views were predicated on the assumption that the United States could be secure only if the rimlands of Asia and Europe were not controlled by a single hegemonious power, possessed of a central position in the heartland of Eurasia from which it could shift its military power west or east at will.[7]

The Soviet Union fitted the model of the potentially threatening heartland power almost too well. From 1945 on, first in germ and then in full eruption, quasi-geopolitical notions of our national interest dominated the conceptual and intellectual baggage which the rising generation of American leadership obtained in school and carried into politics and public life. Moreover, almost all such men—examples are almost too numerous to offer [8]— had been affected in their most important formative years by participation during World War II in our now suddenly prestigious military forces. The small U.S. military establishment of the pre-World War II period, virtually meaningless on the world scene, had given rise to an unequaled, marvelously efficient military machine of great thrust, mobility and power.

After World War II, the U.S. Navy commanded the seas; the Air Force patrolled the world's skies; our armies were ubiquitously deployed from Japan and Korea to Germany and France, from Alaska to

Panama. This machinery was there to be used; many careers were being built on sustaining and enhancing it; and the conceptual model for its employment had been provided by the emergence of the realism or *realpolitik* of Hans Morgenthau, Robert Strausz-Hupé, and Henry Kissinger among so many others.[9] Realism was now the prevailing doctrine in the schools training the leaders of tommorow. And power in American foreign policy, previously shunned in favor of ideals, had come of age.

The Role of Ideology

Yet geostrategic thinking and the mere existence of highly developed military instruments would not by themselves have been sufficient to set the enormous machinery of postwar U.S. foreign policy in motion. The American people, for all the reasons we adduced earlier, were too avid for ideals and a sense of purpose and the American leadership was too fundamentally motivated by an urge to serve mankind for a doctrine and a machinery to have been utilized without basic moral or ethical purpose.

The moral purpose of post-World War II American foreign policy, the inevitable ideology within its realism, became anti-communism. The combination of three essential ingredients constituted the heart of our postwar perception of the national interest: geostrategic doctrine and *realpolitik;* instruments of coercion in the form of the first demobilized, then reconstructed and optimized U.S. military machine; and moral-ideological purpose in halting the spread of communism.

Without moral-ideological purpose, without anti-communism, the American military and later our "nation-building" machineries could not have been mobilized. Their mobilization was achieved through the anti-Communist rhetoric of the Truman Doctrine (1947), the Marshall Plan for Europe (1947), the adoption of the NATO Resolution in the Senate (1948) and later the ratification of the NATO Treaty (1950), and finally through the effects of the loss of China. Without the anti-Communist lubricant, the geostrategic doctrine would have remained a dormant conceptual framework, and American troops would not have been permanently deployed overseas as they were for the first time in American history [10] after the Korean War had frozen our perception of an aggressive and worldwide Sino-Soviet threat.

U.S. leadership and the public in general during the high cold war viewed communism, wherever it appeared and in whatever form, as essentially and inherently evil. It made no real difference that the locale was China or Yugoslavia, North Vietnam or France, Italy or Cuba. Since the value pattern itself was evil, the leadership of such societies must be opposed and arrested in their disastrous path. There ensued an anti-Communist crusade of great virulence, in which certain domestic manifestations such as McCarthyism were, as was earlier suggested, even more significant than those abroad.[11]

At the root of the American superpower's crusade was the feeling, or better said, the knowledge that people could not choose communism of their own free will.[12] Not only was the feeling in accord with the mentor propensities of the United States—that it had found the key to human progress and welfare—but America's certainty that communism could not be voluntarily espoused by other peoples was also predicated on its conviction that as a philosophy it could only be alien to and divorced from the mainstream of normal human beliefs. Accordingly, since people could not espouse communism (or socialism) of their own accord, it clearly had to be imposed on them from the outside. If peoples and leaders abroad, whether Frenchmen, Algerians, Indonesians, or for that matter Vietnamese, could not possibly choose evil when their eyes were open, then evil must have been forced or somehow imposed upon them when their eyes were closed.

The American superpower manifested as one of its most significant behavioral characteristics a profound, virtually immutable belief that communism and revolution were both exportable and exported merchandise, imposed upon unwilling peoples. Nowhere that it appeared, included Indochina, could it be truly indigenous either in inspiration or in leadership. The wish being father to the thought, as E.H. Carr so long ago put it,[13] communism everywhere came to be regarded and later documented by the United States as an evil external imposition. World politics came to be seen by the U.S. superpower during the high cold war as an arena in which the Communist forces of darkness forever challenged the American forces of light.

2. Our Appraisal of National Liberation Wars

Wars of National Liberation as Seen by the Communist Powers

The term "wars (or struggles) of national liberation" entered the world political vocabulary in the late fifties, when Khrushchev and other Soviet leaders and commentators began to use it to refer, in a very general and imprecise way, to revolutions in less developed or Third World (neither Communist nor anti-Communist) countries. These revolutions were directed either against the colonial masters that still ruled; or against bourgeois-capitalist regimes that had in some instances gained control of the governments of new countries (i.e., countries just emerging from colonialism); or against military- or autocratic-type regimes that had recently taken hold or had held power in less developed countries for a long time.

In the Soviet usage of the time, for example, Lumumba's movement in the Congo (1960-63) was an example of the first type; the Communist struggle in South Vietnam of the second; and Castro's revolution against the Batista regime in Cuba of the third. It is obvious from these examples that the Soviet usage of the term was very loose; probably deliberately so. For instance, although Col. Nasser in Egypt and Gen. Abdul Kassim in Iraq clearly headed autocratic-type military regimes, the Soviets saw no inconsistency in backing them and their national liberation struggles with propaganda and moral and, in due course, military support. On the other hand, the certainly not dissimilar regime in Pakistan, headed by Gen. Ayub Khan, which was allied in CENTO (Central Treaty Organization consisting of Turkey, Iran, and Pakistan) and SEATO to the United States, was firmly rejected as nefariously pro-imperialistic. Again, Lumumba in the Congo presumably conducted a genuine national liberation struggle, whereas other anti-colonialist leaders in the Congo such as Adula did not; and Diem in Vietnam represented bourgeois capitalism and was a running dog of imperialism, whereas the revolutionary forces in Peru—which would shortly emerge in the leftist-oriented, Velasco-led military dictatorship—represented a genuine movement of national liberation. So did, for example, the crazed Abbé Yulu in Congo/Brazzaville; though of course the crazed Papa Doc Duvalier in Haiti was an imperialist lackey.

There is little point in continuing to illustrate our simple contention that the Soviet Union was rather crudely engaging in propaganda. Those revolutionary movements which declared for Moscow in the titanic bipolar struggle between the superpowers which occupied center stage circa 1959-62, at the period of crest of U.S. world power, were given direct aid whenever possible as representing essential assets in the world resistance to imperialism. Those which refused to support the United States and did not shy away from denouncing Washington's moves on the world stage as maneuvers of imperialism directed against the welfare of peoples were supported as good and beneficial. Those revolutionary or anti-colonial movements or governments in the less developed world which declared for the United States, or provided the United States access or means for penetration, irrespective of their regime character, were denounced as evil and as witting or unwitting instruments or puppets of U.S. imperialism. Thus, in the latter category, we find the democratic governments of India (at least until about 1970), of the Philippines, of Chile under Frey, of Israel, as well as the dictatorship of Suharto, who in 1965 succeeded the mercurial Sukarno as leader of Indonesia. Ben Bella in Algeria was splendid and Boumedienne at least acceptable; Khadaffi of Libya was a hero, but Morocco and Tunisia were western puppets even after their expulsion of U.S. bases; and the leadership of Mexico remained highly suspect even after it had, alone in all Latin America, recognized Castro Cuba.

There was then no great subtlety in Soviet policy in the so-called Third World: if you were not pro-Soviet, the chances were that you were pro-American and therefore suspect; if after examination and time you remained impervious to U.S. entreaties, you might in due course enter Soviet good graces. The policy was applied as suited location, time, and the mood and capacity of Soviet leaders. In the late fifties and early sixties, Soviet leaders meant Khrushchev; for in 1959-62 we reach the period of Khrushchev's greatest and monopolistic power, followed after the Cuban Missile Crisis of 1962 by his downfall (1964).

The term wars (or struggles, or movements) of national liberation was also espoused, and in similarly eclectic fashion, by the lesser communist powers. Tito early designated most non-aligned regimes or revolutionary movements declaring for non-alignment between the superpowers as playing their proper role in the necessary and inevitable struggle to rid the world of imperialism. (This did not prevent him from sustaining good relations with the United States as his counter to excessive Soviet concern with developments in Yugoslavia.) Communist China began strong efforts after 1959, and especially after 1962, to ally itself with and give moral support and even material assistance to movements of national liberation. This effort became more acute as the conflict between the People's Republic of China and the Soviet Union developed apace after 1959. And because this conflict became acute, it caused the Soviets to redouble their efforts to lead the national liberation struggle of oppressed peoples and to provide direct aid or intervention in issues where otherwise such intervention on the part of the Soviets might have remained purely rhetorical. Soviet intervention in Laos in and after 1959, and even perhaps Soviet support for Communist Vietnam after the U.S. had massively entered South Vietnam are cases in point.

It is beyond the scope of our study to examine the causes and nature of the Sino-Soviet conflict, although we shall continue to refer to this conflict in terms of its consequences for U.S. policies. We should stress here its transcendent importance for the subsequent, post-1959, history of world politics; and the severe nature of the competition it engendered between the Soviet Union and the People's Republic of China for leadership of the "world peoples' struggle." The Sino-Soviet conflict soon began and continues even today to have an enormous impact on the sociopolitical evolution of the Indochinese peninsula and, in fact, of all Southeast Asia.

Fidel Castro, assuming command of Cuba in 1959 on the morrow of a national liberation struggle in which, regardless of the earlier sacrifices by the small group of leaders involved, hardly a shot was fired, was next on the list of entrants and competitors for a leadership role in the world struggle for national liberation. But at least until the mid to late sixties, the constraints on Castro owing to U.S. animosity and propinquity were great and ultimately decisive in lining him up with the Soviet Union. Somewhat relieved of Soviet constraints by the mid-seventies, Castro Cuba today looms as large as China and perhaps as the Soviet Union itself in leading the national liberation struggle, this time on the African continent.

Before we turn to the American reaction, we shall examine briefly the basic nature of wars, struggles, and movements of national liberation, an issue in which the United States would begin, with the advent of the Kennedy administration, to immerse itself so thoroughly.

Ingredients of Third World Revolutionary Movements

We can distinguish several preponderant ingredients in the revolutionary or, as the U.S. came regrettably (because of the pejorative connotation of the term) to call them, "insurgent" movements that developed after about the mid-fifties in what is so loosely termed the Third, or less developed, World.

Ethno-Linguistic-Cultural Factors. In a historic movement continuing without interruption to this day, and more recently aggravated and complexed by the consequences of world population movements and migration patterns, smaller and smaller ethno-linguistic groups were and are searching for recognition of their identity or "self." Thus a movement like the Kurdish rebellion against Iraqi, Iranian, or Soviet rule (wherever Kurds live, in other words) is every bit as much a national liberation movement as the most sanctified revolutions espoused by the Soviets, say the Cuban revolt against Batista or the Vietnamese anti-colonial (1946-54) and anti-imperialist (1959-73) revolutions. In the Philippines, the Moslem populations in the mountainous southern parts of the archipelago have been uninterruptedly rebelling against rule by lowland Christian Filipinos since about 1900. In Belgium, Flemings have long struggled for recognition against the French-speaking minority; and in Spain, Catalan and Basque rebellions well antedate even the Spanish Civil War (1936-39). Such movements, continuously erupting all over the world during the fifties and sixties, were less perceived during the momentous events of those years than they are today when even the Soviet Union on occasion admits to difficulties with its rebellious nationalities, and the United States wrestles with the identity-recognition problems of Black, Hispanic, and American Indian minorities.

Nationalism. Nationalism pushes the revolt of ethno-linguistic-cultural groups seeking identity recognition one step further into the acceptance by such groups of a single leadership elite which seeks not just recognition of identity but acceptance by other states of its status at the head of a new independent state. The Nationalist elite seeks recognition even if several minorities are to be contained in a new state and even if the elite itself is composed largely or exclusively of members of a minority within the new state. For example, although Hausa and groups allied with them did not constitute a majority in Nigeria, they secured the support of the large and compact Ibo group during the independence struggle and the Ibos initially accepted Hausa leadership of the new state. Only later did Hausa domination become so unbearable to the Ibos that they revolted in the Biafra War, which resulted in their being crushed by the Hausa's possession of superior education, technology, and force.

There is absolutely no ethnic homogeneity in India, or in Indonesia, or in the Philippines, where there is not even a single numerically dominant ethnic majority like the Javanese in Indonesia. Yet the force of nationalism—the passion of *wanting* to be bound to others in recognized, independent status—is such that for at least a period it holds ethnic minorities and other groups such as those based on class, region, sex, or occupation together on behalf of the symbols and ideals of the "nation state." No force in twentieth century history has been comparable to the force of nationalism in binding people and committing them to causes and struggles. The principal cause nationalism has served has been liberation from colonial control, leading to independent statehood. Throughout the thirty-year history of the Vietnamese Revolution (1945-75), nationalism was the prime ingredient which bound its many varied elements together and enabled its ultimate triumph. But it was not the only factor.

Socioeconomic Elements. This enormous, highly varied, and complex set of factors in national liberation movements and wars involves, reduced to its barest minimum: (a) urbanization of at least part of a traditionally rural population which has been subjected to the incipient beginnings of industrialization; (b) education, part-education, or at least literacy of a population, such education frequently started by

Christian missionary organizations; (c) an increase in expectations on the part of a traditionally agrarian population which becomes aware, largely through the effects of new means of transport and communications, of the possibility of material betterment. Nothing socioeconomic, least of all peasant revolutions in underdeveloped agrarian societies, happens spontaneously or simply by the introduction of external, say Soviet or Chinese, influences. What may occur results from the inter-relationship of the factors just indicated.

Thus, urbanization and the small beginnings under colonialism of industrialization, developing from the existence of colonial trading bases, leads to the creation of a small urban bourgeoisie which can afford education for its children. The latter, second generation urban middle or lower-middle class, frequently turn to professional or semi-professional occupations like teaching, medicine, engineering, or law. Their aspirations being great, and their frustrations greater, the way is then open for radical philosophies and political theories to persuade them; hence the virtually universal appeal of Marxism-Leninism's holistic explanations of the world and of world history to liberators or leaders of national liberation movements in the Third World. The latter in turn seek mobilization of the peasantry, which is extremely difficult to accomplish since the peasantry, through long experience and suffering, finds itself extraordinarily skeptical of change. The aspiring elites must either accomplish their mobilization of the agrarian masses, as they essentially did in Vietnam; or await a time when the native urban bourgeoisie has become strong, numerous and frustrated enough to provide their single main source of support in the struggle to gain power.

Leadership. Finally, a leadership factor of at least equal significance to the others enters into the composition of genuine and victorious movements of national liberation. The leadership, preferably that of a single leader at least initially, must be well trained and educated, fearless, charismatic at least to a degree, and self-abnegating. It must have utter, blind faith in its convictions and a ruthless ambition to drive to their realization. Many incipient national liberation movements and struggles have failed or been perverted for the lack of an outstanding leader like Nasser in Egypt, Castro in Cuba, Mao in China, Tito in Yugoslavia, Sukarno in Indonesia, Nehru in India, or Ho Chi Minh in Vietnam. Like de Gaulle in the liberation of France during World War II, such leaders must be ruthless and restless enough to continue a movement's momentum against all setbacks and defeats.

We see from this very brief analysis of a subject on which there exists a massive literature [14] how complex, infinitely variegated and nuanced is the phenomenon of national liberation movements, revolutions, and wars. But the U.S. government did not pause long in the late fifties or early sixties systematically to study and analyze the phenomenon. Rather, it tended to adopt ready-made answers and assumptions in roughly the same crude way and with roughly the same type of cynicism with which the Soviet Union approached this complicated issue. A main difference emerged in that, perhaps, the Soviet Union chose its national liberation heroes in the sixties in somewhat luckier fashion than the United States chose its own client leaders and states. By the mid-seventies, however, the Soviets had probably equalled if not surpassed the United States in the number of its wrong or unlucky choices, as when it flip-flopped from support of an autocratic Somalian regime to support of an anti-Somalian Ethiopian militarist regime in 1977-78.

In approaching problems of national liberation we deal with ancient, long-standing sociopolitical and socioeconomic phenomena. On the sociopolitical side: with racial problems; ethno-linguistic identity problems; problems of nationalism and statehood; problems of regime character; and finally problems of international involvement or alignment. On the socioeconomic side: with problems of generational, occupational, and regional stratification (principally, agrarian v. industrial); problems of income distribution and redistribution (class); problems of economic organization, degree of technologization, and involvement in or alienation from the existing international economic order. Everywhere, we deal most fundamentally with the problem of the *status quo.* Across all social, economic, and political boundaries, some people accept the status quo and are willing to live their lives under it; others do not and are not. The root question in national liberation struggles and wars is that of the struggle between forces that stand for leaving the existing internal and external order of things intact, and those that stand for changing it, by revolutionary means if necessary.

Passivity of the Eisenhower Administration

What we have just reviewed is relevant to the U.S. government's appraisal of struggles and wars of national liberation, because in essence the United States government at no time during the period of this study (1945-75) appraised such struggles and wars as fundamental efforts to change the status quo or the existing distribution of values in the world. It can be argued that the Soviet Union was similarly oblivious to the real underlying motive of national liberation movements and was, in essence, concerned only with using them on behalf of its interests. Wholly engaged in their mutual struggle for supremacy over an existing world order, neither superpower qualified as a revolutionary force during the high cold war, or later.

Between 1959 and 1961, with the major exception of its intervention in the Congo in 1960, the United States in the Eisenhower administration did little to react to Khrushchev's demonstrative truculence after 1957-58 in the Third World. This may be understood in part by the shock engendered in the United States by the Soviet success (1957) in sending the first satellite, Sputnik, into space and the consequent U.S. perception that its technological lead in nuclear weapon delivery systems may have been lost, forcing a significant and attention-capturing review of U.S. defense systems and doctrine. We shall examine later some of the effects of this review, particularly on U.S. Army missions. In 1959, the United States entered the period of its perceived "missile gap," on which John F. Kennedy capitalized during his 1960 political campaign. This ultimately proved to be a myth, though one not without advantages for the United States since it culminated by placing the U.S. after 1961 enormously ahead of the Soviets in the numbers of its nuclear carriers (missiles), thereby complementing the already overwhelming U.S. lead in total megatonnage.

Another factor was the death of Secretary Dulles and his replacement in 1959 by the relatively unprepared Christian Herter, who focussed his attention with good reason on Europe, where Khrushchev had in 1958 delivered his first ultimatum on Berlin. (Unless the United States dealt with East German authorities on its ground access roads to West Berlin, it would cease to gain access to the city.) Furthermore, President Eisenhower was preoccupied with the domestic economic recession of the later fifties; the first serious recession of the postwar period, as well as with the coming political campaign of 1960, in which he would eventually accept and support the candidacy of Richard M. Nixon.

Probably the most significant factor in the relative absence of preoccupation with national liberation movements at the end of the Eisenhower administration was the U.S. president's desire, in the wake of the unresolved Berlin crisis of 1958, to try once more to come to terms with Khrushchev. This desire was apparently reciprocated by the latter, who was impaled on the dilemma of his own unsuccessful Berlin ultimatum. The Rambouillet summit meeting, actively sponsored by de Gaulle for mid-1960, eventually failed to occur ostensibly because of Khrushchev's ire at the intrusion into Soviet air space of an American U-2 spy plane, which the Soviets shot down. But it is at least arguable that Khrushchev had already changed his mind and, by this time, saw what the Soviets call "the world correlation of forces" moving in a direction the Soviets desired. Perhaps he himself fell victim to the myth of the U.S. missile gap. In any event, he probably accurately noted de Gaulle's then still veiled decision to settle the Algerian national liberation war of 1958-62 in terms of full independence for Algeria; as well as de Gaulle's firm decision to move away from the United States and NATO in the direction of a Third Force Europe, in order, as de Gaulle put it, to relieve France and West Europe of "the twin hegemonies of the giants." These events tended to diminish the need for Soviet-U.S. understanding, from the Soviet point of view.

Nation Building in the New Frontier

The transformation of relative U.S. relaxation toward the Third World into a posture of feverish activity on the part of the United States toward the less developed regions occurred simultaneously with the end of the Eisenhower administration, the growth (then only dimly perceived by U.S. policy-makers) of the Sino-Soviet split, and rising U.S. fear of increased Soviet technological and political capabilities. It is not too surprising that the United States had stood relatively relaxed during the period of its power crest (1959). Containment had after all succeeded in barring the way just about everywhere. It was deployed in great strength along the whole periphery of the Soviet Union and its Chinese ally. It had, it seemed, succeeded in stemming the menace of the Sino-Soviet bloc, still perceived in Washington as essentially manipulated by the Politburo leadership in Moscow alone.

But in 1960, with great suddenness, all this seemed to be changing; the Soviets seemed to have gained a technological lead in the defense area; they were, again, charging in Europe, and Europe's response was becoming doubtful; the status quo was being badly shaken in Algeria and Central Africa (Congo); the Soviets were directly assisting the Laotian rebels; and revolution had broken out again in Vietnam.

Once the 1960 campaign was over and Kennedy had taken office, relaxation came to an abrupt end, to be replaced almost instantaneously by a period of maximum activity and intense involvement in the Third World. We shall return in Chapter V to some of the causal factors for the premium on action with which the New Frontier tried to infuse a now well ensconced and appropriately conservative, as well as huge, national security and foreign policy bureaucracy in Washington. We shall return also to the character of the New Frontier leadership. All these elements of course interrelate. What we next wish to explore in some detail is the Kennedy administration's perhaps unexpectedly strong reaction to Khrushchev's meddling in support of national liberation movements and wars, and some of the reasons that caused our appraisal and reaction to be so profoundly erroneous in so many ways.

When the New Frontier arrived on the scene, it brought to power in Washington, for the first time since the New Deal of the early thirties, highly accredited intellectuals from the nation's very best universities and graduate schools. Many of these men had had frequent, although generally intermittent and brief, experience in and exposure to the problems of the world's so-called less developed regions. They had worked in academic settings, think tanks and research institutes which had multiplied during the fifties owing to the government's generous financial support for "international relations and area studies research." These were the men who conceived "Project Camelot," an ill-fated Defense Department-sponsored research project in Latin America.[15] Despite the briefness of their on-the-spot inspections and research visits to the countries concerned, many of them had formed very clear views as to what was needed in the poor countries and how development could best be advanced and achieved.

In much of Latin America and the Middle East, as well as in large portions of Asia—it was then still too early for deep U.S. involvement in Africa—there existed huge and highly active American Agency for International Development (AID) missions. These were only too ready to perpetuate their functions and anxious to find new rationales for the provision of AID in the models, conceptual schemes, theories, and pre-scriptions of the research intellectuals. Some of the intellectuals, now moving into positions of leadership in the New Frontier, were eager to provide. One of the New Frontier's very first initiatives in foreign pol-icy, antedating even the Bay of Pigs, was to prepare for the convening of a major conference in Latin America which would, it was hoped, inaugurate through the Alliance for Progress a whole decade of sus-tained development throughout that neglected region of the world. The conference took place at Punta Del Este, Chile, in August, 1961 and the Alliance for Progress was launched. The New Frontier was confi-dent it had the answers.

Men of the New Frontier, such as Professor Walt W. Rostow pre-viously of the government-supported Center for International Studies at the Massachusetts Institute of Technology, were perhaps less con-cerned with the new truculence of the Soviets in prompting so-called movements and wars of national liberation than they appeared to be in their pronouncements. Rostow specifically judged the Soviet regime as internally weak and beset by problems, and viewed the Chinese Com-munists, then just beginning to climb out of their disastrous Great Leap Forward program, as hardly a model worthy of emulation. As denoted in the title of the last book he wrote before coming to Washington,

The United States in the World Arena,[16] what most preoccupied Rostow was the United States and the implementation by an energetic American leadership of the conceptual models and schemes for development in the Third World which he and some of his colleagues had helped to author.

It is true that it did appear as if Khrushchev was extending the challenge and as if, in the Third World at least, Eisenhower had allowed the initiative to pass to the hands of the Communists. Even in Vietnam, quiet between 1956 and 1959, the revolution in the South had been restarted in earnest in 1959 and by 1961 seemed to be rapidly gaining ground. Revolution and disorder reigned in Central Africa and Algeria. Moreover, in the propinquous and therefore always special area of the Caribbean, Castro had by 1961 rebuffed early entreaties made to him by the United States after the fall of Batista. (The Chinese Communists had similarly rebuffed U.S. entreaties in 1949-50, before Korea, and probably for about the same reason, namely, the need to keep alive the image of an unrelenting external enemy in order to build unity at home.) Castro was now avowedly declaring his allegiance both to communism and to Moscow.

On the other hand, the overall position of the United States in the world still appeared mighty powerful when Kennedy took office in 1961. Other than Castro, who was presumably shortly to be taken care of by the invasion at the Bay of Pigs (April 1961), nothing seriously threatened U.S. security in the Western Hemisphere. In relation to Europe, the balance, to the extent that it had ever faltered, had been restored by the rapid accumulation of U.S. missile launchers, a firm attitude of opposition to de Gaulle's policies of substituting an independent Europe for one tied to the United States in NATO, and by calling the Soviet bluff on Berlin. The Middle East was then exceptionally tranquil for such a normally disturbed region; nothing of threatening magnitude was to occur on the Arab-Israeli front between the second war of 1956 and the third war of 1967; and the slow growth of Arab oil-money power was then still imperceptible to Western governments. Eastern Europe, though restless, had generally accepted Communist regimes somewhat milder than those that had prevailed during the Stalinist period; and Communist China, repelled in the Taiwan Straits, was rebuilding at home.

This left the uncertain and complex national liberation movements in such Third World places as Algeria, Central Africa, and Indochina for an activist-minded U.S. foreign policy to be concerned about. What in fact Soviet propaganda emphasis on these struggles in the late fifties and early sixties threatened most was not America's security or power, but America's *will* to develop the Third World along the lines of its own models and theories of what the New Frontier now called "nation building." The danger that men like Rostow, U.S. AID Director David Bell, and a bevy of other intellectuals brought in by the New Frontier perceived most was the danger that if we did not proceed quickly and firmly with our own nation-building programs, these might be altogether pre-empted. We would, in effect, be put out of the development business; and with that they feared that the balance of forces in the world would change tremendously. Change and instability of uncertain direction might be introduced; the status quo and the existing world order might be seriously jeopardized.

Analyzing America's Appraisal

Prof. Rostow repeated over and over in at least half a dozen speeches and in a succession of memos and statements to the leadership in the White House, State and Defense Departments that national liberation wars would spread if not arrested and that if they spread successfully, they would contagiously infect the world and turn the balance of power against America.[17] This was the heart of the New Frontier's message and appraisal of Khrushchev's truculence and interventions in the less developed regions between early 1961 and the Cuban Missile Crisis of October 1962. In that short period of less than two years, the United States made major commitments and set in motion enormous forces, both at home and abroad, to maintain the momentum of its own developmental schemes and plans while at the same time seeking to stop the infections and contagions of what its new leaders saw as the Soviet- and Chinese-inspired schemes to export revolution by inciting and supporting national liberation movements and wars. What sort of validity did such an appraisal have?

It is quite understandable that men like Rostow and others saw in Marxist/Leninist-inspired revolutionary movements, even when not obviously or ostentatiously supported by Moscow or Peking, dangerously corrosive movements which, if successful in galvanizing support, might both permanently change the future directions of their countries and severely set back nation building and developmental plans inspired and supported by the United States in these countries.

What is certainly less acceptable is the next step in their appraisal: that if successful in one country, such movements would therefore automatically gain contagious advantage in other countries of the same world region; and if successful in one region of the world, their success would therefore automatically extend to other regions. The common element between countries and regions which this type of appraisal underlined was that the countries involved were colonial, or poor, or underdeveloped—any of these, or all in combination. Thus it did not draw a line between Vietnam on the one hand and Laos, Cambodia, or Thailand on the other, or between Indochina on the one hand and Southeast Asia as a whole, including Indonesia, on the other; or even between Southeast Asia and Latin America, or Africa, or the Middle East. Hence, under the appraisal which held compelling sway in the U.S. government in 1961-62, and even later, if successful in Vietnam a national liberation war not only had a good chance but in fact the strongest likelihood of succeeding throughout Southeast Asia, and thereafter (and therefore) of succeeding also in Colombia or Peru.

The idea that there was anything in common between such diverse lands and peoples other than the poverty they shared, and that therefore the unique set of circumstances and conditions in one would not materially affect the automatism of the spread phenomenon seems difficult to entertain today. Yet Prof. Rostow certainly entertained it compellingly early in the New Frontier, to a point where he flatly refused to listen to "particularistic" briefings on countries like Vietnam or China and would send the briefer away as irrelevant.[18] Even though David Halberstam suggests [19] that Rostow was regarded as an oddity early in the New Frontier, he leaves the correct impression in his book that Rostow was heard and that his policy prescriptions were taken. Rostow was indeed a powerful intellectual and in retrospect he appears as the single most influential thinker in both the Kennedy and Johnson administrations.

Some of the sources for the sort of reasoning we have reviewed are to be found in the globalistic methodologies introduced into the study of political science in the United States in the fifties. "Comparativism" entered the field along with and as a generic ingredient of behavioralism. Borrowed largely from sociology and indirectly from biology, behavioralism presumed to make the study of society more rigorous and scientific, to arrest the trend toward purely normative or utopian studies in political science and, like the *realpolitik* school in the study of international relations which was mentioned earlier, to restore realism to the study of politics. The comparativist pioneers in political science drew their inspiration from the sociologist Talcott Parsons and the political scientist David Easton, one of the first to apply Parson's "system theories" to the study of government. Rejecting the approach by which one simply examines the structure and the spirit of governments and countries one at a time, without necessarily drawing definitive cross-boundary conclusions, comparativists like Gabriel Almond began to introduce often still tentative conceptual models of how politics operate in societies—not some, but all societies. Demands and interests aggregate, producing inputs; governments respond through outputs in order to preserve themselves; if they do not respond appropriately, they will be overthrown.

Transposed on underdeveloped countries, these comparativist methodologies produced globalistic policy prescriptions of a highly static, i.e. status quo oriented, character. They perceived Marxist-Leninist or socialist-inspired programs as system destructive; as contrasted with Western-inspired system inputs which, if properly conceived and implemented, would permit system maintenance. The key function of governments was such system maintenance. We are accordingly dealing with theories of the status quo and upholders of the status quo. Employed in this fashion, the study of politics and society can perhaps become somewhat more scientific in appearance, but it is difficult to see how it can induce desirable change.

That Rostow was a system theorist and globalist in both his economics and his politics can best be seen in his master work, *The Stages of Economic Growth,*[20] which quite clearly lays out the steps, phases, and stages of development from "takeoff" to sustained growth. Because this work had such enormous influence on the mind set of the decision makers who came to power in the New Frontier, mention of it must be made here. Before he entered government, Rostow had discovered how the world economy, particularly that of the underdeveloped regions, could evolve and could be saved. What he did when he entered government was first to analyze, apprehend, and appraise events in the light and context of his discovery, and then to execute his prescriptions. For Rostow, Marxist-Leninist movements, system destroyers, had to extirpated; guerrilla wars of that type had to be contained and fought to their ultimate defeat. Stalemate was not enough; the Marxist guerrillas must in the end be eradicated. Tools of a rival world conceptual model, their presence would upset and eventually defeat the valid model prescribed in *The Stages of Economic Growth.*

Events in history cannot be fully comprehended without some understanding of the intellectual baggage carried by those charged with decision making during the period under consideration. It is especially spurious to wave intellectuals and theorists away on grounds that "they didn't really count." Intellectuals and theorists always count, because they furnish the substantive theories of history which make up the usually meager conceptual baggage of the decision makers.[21]

Some Further Thoughts

U.S. foreign policy makers in the New Frontier regarded struggles and wars of national liberation, by which they meant only those so designated by the Soviets or other communist powers or characterizing themselves as Marxist-Leninist in inspiration, as evil, nefarious, and capable of contagious spread. The results of the contagion would be the transnational rise of anti-Americanism on a world scale, and would signal the doom of American efforts diligently pursued after the success of the Marshall Plan in Europe to build nations through systematic programs of social and economic development, American-style.

There may be some surprise that we have not treated this American reaction to national liberation movements and wars with greater stress on what some observers might regard as determinant economic motives. American capitalism, they might aver, was simply protecting its interests wherever the threatening hand of Marxism-Leninism showed itself. We have not done this because we do not believe that economic considerations stemming from the capitalist order of U.S. society or from capitalist interests provided the chief animus of American leaders and statesmen in the period 1959-62. There were no American economic interests to protect in Indochina when the New Frontier threw itself into the task of stopping the increasingly successful Marxist-Leninist inspired nationalist-revolutionary movement there. To say that the United States had to intervene in Vietnam in order to protect and preserve American economic preponderance in Japan and East Asia generally, as has sometimes been argued, simply will not do. American capitalism would certainly have been blind if it had pushed the U.S. government into Vietnam in order to protect itself, its world order, and its future. American capitalism may have been many things, but it was not that blind. However, some American intellectual and global theorists were; and it was in Vietnam that their developmental theories were being put to the test.

We have discussed above only *some* of the intellectuals of the New Frontier. There were other intellectuals in office at the same time who expressed sincere and severe doubts as to the validity of the U.S. appraisal of national liberation movements and wars.[22]

Moreover, there were also those in the top echelons of the Executive, in the Congress, the press and the public who perceived the advances in Vietnam of what Diem had baptized the "Viet Cong" as the most serious manifestation in a very long time on the world scene of a challenge to American power, leadership, and even security. We turn in the next section to the problem of U.S. commitments throughout the globe as it related to the precipitating developments of the early sixties in Vietnam.

3. Our Appraisal of Commitments and Their Credibility

The Globalization of Commitments

The issue of U.S. security commitments around the world was confronted by the New Frontier simultaneously with its tackling of the issue of national liberation wars. The main policy-makers in this case were not certain New Frontier intellectuals joined by elements of the AID bureaucracy and later, as we shall see, of the U.S. military. They were key officials of the national security and foreign affairs bureaucracies and politicians in the White House, the Executive, and the Congress, supported by major elements in the press and U.S. public opinion.

The United States made roughly three types of commitments during the period of containment and the high cold war. First, it made *formal* security commitments. Second it made *apparent* security commitments in countries where it became deeply involved through the provision of AID, military assistance, PL 480 projects,[23] cultural programs and Peace Corps projects, and where U.S. military bases were located. Third, it made *potential* security commitments in places where it demonstrated significant interest or concern and appeared willing to make a commitment, although it had not yet invested substantial assets or resources in a country.

Stated generally, U.S. policy on all three types of commitments was basically the same: it would uphold all assumed commitments regardless of their nature, and with the graduated use of all the means at its disposal. These means included first diplomatic and rhetorical support to the threatened partner; if that was insufficient, then arms assistance and, to the extent required, covert support [24] would be provided; if still more was needed the United States would face up to the necessity of intervening militarily, but only with the minimum of force required to maintain or restore the status quo; and ultimately, if there was no other choice, it would intervene with all the force at its disposal, even to the extent of considering (or allowing others to feel it was considering) the employment of nuclear weapons.

The underlying yet insufficiently analyzed premise of the U.S. failure to prioritize commitments was that if it failed to uphold a commitment in one given place, it would almost *ipso facto* lose its credibility in all others. In other words, failure to uphold what was perceived as a commitment to one country would, in the view of U.S. policy-makers, make all others disbelieve that it would stand by them if they were threatened. The lack of discrimination in this policy and its underlying assumption is apparent. The problem, in all these cases, should have been addressed as follows: "Have we given, or appear to have given, or may in the future be giving, a commitment to country X? If yes, what response does an external challenge to the integrity of X require, or what response does an internal challenge to the existing regime in X require? Is the response in either case commensurate with our capabilities, and with the overall significance of X in the world power balance and the constellation of U.S. interests, including fundamental U.S. values?" Instead, U.S. policy-makers of the high cold war, including those of the New Frontier, tended to address the issue simply this way: "We are committed to the integrity of X; how do we at this stage and later uphold our commitment?"

Part of the reason for this disconcerting state of affairs lies in the vague nature of the "commitment sense" in which the U.S. executive branch, seriously plunging itself into peacetime world affairs for the first time in American history, allowed itself to slip after 1950 and the Korean War. This phenomenon was fully brought out and aired, though the issue was not necessarily resolved, in the so-called national commitment hearings held by Sen. William Fulbright's Senate Foreign Relations Committee and its subcommittee chaired by Sen. Stuart Symington from 1967 to 1970, when it was all much too late.[25] Once a nation, especially a superpower, makes informal and potential as well as formal commitments which it then regards with the same degree of seriousness, that nation is bound to have problems. (Or perhaps it acts that way because it is a superpower, or its being a superpower compels it to act that way. The Soviet Union has not been too dissimilar from the United States in this general area, and is liable, if it has not already, to reap some of the same consequences.)

The formal treaty commitments undertaken by the United States from 1950 to 1968 and ratified by the Senate as required by the Constitution are the clearest and least questionable cases of commitments. Here, obligations were formally spelled out; the U.S. word was indeed put on the line. Such were the multilateral NATO and ANZUS commitments; the bilateral commitments to the Philippines, Japan, the Republic of China and the Republic of Korea; the commitments under the inter-American system set up by the Rio pact; and, though more debatably, the SEATO commitments. In all these instances except SEATO we deal with external threats to the security of states. Only in the case of SEATO did the United States commit itself to respond to internal challenges as well, and this is why we call it more debatable because it was less enforceable.

Perceived informal and potential U.S. commitments are much more difficult cases to handle. Vietnam can be viewed as falling within the category of an informal commitment; and so today can Israel and Saudi Arabia among others. India can be viewed as an example of the category of potential commitment; the moment did indeed come with the presumed Chinese border attacks upon India in 1962, now believed to have been a response to Indian provocations,[26] when the United States began to uphold this potential commitment through military assistance to India. We will leave potential commitments of this nature out of further discussion, after pointing out that their existence tends to increase the unpredictability and hence instability of the international environment. It leaves outsiders in the dark about the intentions of a major committing world actor such as the United States. For example, it is conceivable that a potential U.S. commitment of this nature is in the offing again today with respect to either the Republic of South Africa, or conversely the black front-line states of Africa that challenge South Africa. Even Americans are uncertain. However, it must be said that in part this uncertainty is clearly inevitable in the kind of world we live in, a world which contains large and ubiquitous superpowers like the United States or the Soviet Union.

We return to the large and complex category of informal commitments, of which Vietnam and Indochina were a part. If an informal commitment, resulting simply from a heavy resource investment on the part of a protector or mentor power, is regarded as a commitment just the same as if a treaty had been signed and duly ratified by the Senate, then obviously the distinction loses meaning. All commitments, whether formal or informal, have about the same force and require about the same gradation in the nature of the response, and are treated about the same in analysis.

Why this informality and ease of commitment, this lack of discrimination from country to country, region to region, zone to zone? The nature of the thinking about U.S. credibility by decision-makers in the Executive branch of the U.S. government which resulted in this approach appears to have resulted chiefly from the growth and development of deterrence doctrines and from reasoning by historical analogy. It led to the perception by the United States of the existence of commitments regardless of the perceptions of the countries to which we were allegedly committed; and it was reinforced by U.S. possession of quasi-universal response capabilities.

Deterrence Doctrines

As already indicated in the previous section of this chapter, the conceptual baggage that practitioners, decision-makers, and statesmen carry with them into office is a factor of great importance in foreign policy. The deterrence doctrines which became such a fashionable part of that baggage after World War II, and which were further refined during the period of the high cold war, are modified descendants of the collective security doctrines of the twenties and thirties.

Although doctrines of collective security failed on application at the crucial turning points of the thirties, and the way was left open for the outbreak of World War II in Asia as well as Europe, this did not diminish the validity of these doctrines in the minds of postwar statesmen. They reasoned that it was precisely because the doctrines were not applied when they should have been that the war broke out. They did not research closely why collective security had failed, or they might have concluded otherwise.[27]

At the heart of collective security doctrines, like deterrence doctrines and all alliance doctrines, lies the following basic set of mechanistic equilibrium-of-power propositions. State A declares that it will attack State B if State B attacks State C. Thus, A is protecting C against B by promising in advance that it will assist it against B. This can lead in two directions. Either B obtains the like assistance from D against A that C obtained from A against B, in which case the system goes into blocs and a balance of power system emerges. Or all states agree, as in collective security doctrine—which must be as universal as possible to function as validly as possible—that they will ensure the entire system against attack on any of its members.

The great powers at the end of World War II—United States, United Kingdom, France, the Soviet Union, the Republic of China—may have in theory established such a system by signing the U.N. Charter in San Francisco, but this depended entirely on their continued cooperation and similarity of outlook, particularly between the two superpowers, the United States and the Soviet Union. The moment these two superpower allies turned to hostile confrontation leading to bitter enmity, postwar collective security through the U.N. proved a dead letter. It was replaced after the Korean War by regional security pacts sanctioned under Article 51 of the U.N. Charter. Pacts such as NATO, the Warsaw Pact, ANZUS, CENTO, SEATO, etc., signaled clearly the end of collective security under the U.N. system and the rise of superpower-directed blocs. It is in the context of the latter that contemporary deterrence theories rose to general acceptance and to their ultimate refinement in the high cold war.

Behind either nuclear or conventional deterrence lies the simple threat: "If, despite my warning, you do what I tell you not to do, I will ensure that it will hurt you and cost you dearly, so if you know your best interests you had better not do it." In the nuclear arena, this meant in effect that a first (preventive or pre-emptive) strike on the part of one superpower upon the other would provoke such a crushing retaliatory blow that neither would ever start the exchange. As long as both superpowers possess invulnerable and credible second-strike retaliatory forces, mutual deterrence—known as "Mutual Assured Destruction (MAD)"—has proved effective in keeping the superpowers from starting the unspeakable devastation of worldwide nuclear war. Much practice with MAD has since 1969 led to rational discourse in SALT between the two superpowers directed in the first instance at maintaining levels of parity in MAD capabilities, and hopefully later at the reduction of such capabilities to levels of "minimum assured deterrence." But the nuclear arena, though complex enough, is relatively simple compared to the enormous range of problems encountered in conventional deterrence.

We should note the threatening and negative nature of deterrence as described above. The approach more likely to be practiced in traditional diplomacy is for a state to approach another through inducement rather than threat: "If you do what I would like you to do, I will ensure that it will benefit you, so you will gain by doing it." The traditional diplomatic approach is positive or "non-zero-sum," meaning that it is possible for both parties to win something and neither to lose anything, while the deterrence approach assumes a view of states' relationships which can be called "zero-sum": there is not room for both of them to win.[28]

In practice, U.S. conventional deterrence during the high cold war was almost entirely zero-sum. After 1959, it complemented U.S. appraisal that national liberation movements and wars would contaminate the world and upset the balance of power against the United States if they were not arrested and ultimately defeated worldwide. Decision makers in Washington felt that wherever the government of a state in which we had made some form of commitment was threatened, the source of the threat must be confronted. Wherever danger to the status quo threatened a place in which we had established a position, this danger must be deterred, i.e. threatened back with fear of greater loss than the gain that a potential opponent might obtain by going forward.

The extension reasoning of deterrence went basically as follows: for deterrence to work, our threat posture must be credible, that is, believable by "the enemy." But how could the enemy believe it if we applied it discriminately; if we threatened him here, but not there; barred his way in Europe, but not in Vietnam? If he was not stopped in Vietnam, what was to make him think that he would be stopped in Western

Europe, or the Middle East, or Korea if he tried there again? As we have already indicated, "the enemy" as perceived during the early sixties remained a single monolithic communist force—a Sino-Soviet bloc manipulated and operated entirely by the leaders of the Soviet Politburo in Moscow.

In Indochina, after 1959, U.S. decision-makers were as much if not more concerned with the credibility of their commitment as with the nature of their response. President Kennedy, Robert Kennedy, Dean Rusk, Robert McNamara, McGeorge Bundy, Maxwell Taylor, Walt Rostow, and later Lyndon Johnson and others, all felt sincerely and without the benefit of very profound analysis that if they failed somehow to deter the enemy in Vietnam, the credibility of the entire worldwide posture of the United States would be endangered in the whole non-Communist or Free World. We will return again later to this important point. But we should note here that one of the cardinal principles of deterrence did not in fact work out in Vietnam: despite our threats, the Vietnamese Communists apparently never accepted the proposition that their best interests would be served by not incurring the costs we threatened if they continued their action. But on this also, more later.

Reasoning by Historical Analogy

We referred earlier to the U.S. tendency in its superpower role to equate communism with evil and as a consequence, to treat various communisms in undifferentiated fashion, that is, to equate the various communisms in the world. We noted that this tendency arose in part out of the experience of confronting evil in the person of Hitler and the power of the German Reich, and of lumping Mussolini's fascism and Tojo's militarism with Hitler's nazism during the titanic struggle of World War II. Along with our allies, and with plenty of justification, we designated World War II as a crusade against the evil of totalitarianism. This equation of enemies by powers at war against them was not only perfectly understandable, but the fact of the Axis Alliance justified the notion that the Axis was evil, and about as evil in its lesser parts as in its major center.

What was justified during war was, however, more difficult to justify during the postwar period, particularly when the slowly growing process of equating the perceived expansionism of the Soviet Union with that of Nazi Germany began to extend in the later forties and fifties to the equation of communisms everywhere, with all of them being regarded as analogues or clones of the Soviet model.

Some of our previous discussion has already touched on the conservatism of Soviet foreign policy under Stalin, despite his internal tyranny, as well as on the topsy-turvy and unpredictable manner by which communism grew in the postwar period in such places as Yugoslavia, China, and Vietnam. Although the utterly tyrannical and totalitarian character of the Soviet regime under Stalin made it equatable domestically with the regime in Germany under Hitler, the foreign policies of the two countries were a different matter. Hitler had used his power largely in order to change the status quo outside as well as within Germany, to restore the greatness of the old Reich, and to expand its sway and that of the Aryan race over what he regarded as lower peoples, such as Slavs and Latins. Stalin, on the other hand, had used his power almost exclusively to consolidate the Bolshevik revolution by his own methods within the Soviet "socialist fatherland." The Trotskyite concepts of simultaneous world revolution had been expressly repudiated by Stalin and his acolytes as early as the twenties; and Stalin had liquidated much of even the subservient, puppet-like Comintern leadership of the thirties in the great purges of these prewar years. As we noted in a previous chapter, the Cominform of the late forties in no way restored the old Comintern, and the world Communist movement of the later forties was, if not leaderless, at least diffuse, disorganized, and incipiently split.

In the postwar forties, Stalin's one great megalomaniac obsession was power at home; as we have seen, only Eastern Europe, including of course East Germany, was of real concern abroad. Basically, Stalin's foreign policy was conservative and routine; neither directly nor indirectly expansionist outside Eastern Europe, except when irresistible targets of opportunity presented themselves—and even then retreat was quickly sounded when a potential Soviet advance was confronted.[29] Korea was no exception to this general proposition; to this day we have no reason to believe that the Soviets did more than sanction Kim Il Sung in a move they might in any case have been unable to prevent, and which resulted at least in part from misperception on the North Korean, Chinese Communist, and Soviet sides of probable U.S. intentions in Northeast Asia.[30]

After Stalin died, there followed a period of remission in the cold war while his succession was being settled at home. Only after the February 1956 speech by Khrushchev to the 20th Party Congress which established his control over the Politburo, after the rise of Nasser in the wake of the Middle Eastern events of 1955-56, and after Sputnik (October 1957), did Soviet foreign policy turn activistic and militant.

Nonetheless, U.S. policy-makers, reasoning largely by historical analogy, continued to compare the Soviet Union's postwar behavior with Hitler's prewar behavior, and that of postwar international communism with that of the prewar Axis. This thinking was often simplistic. Decision-makers tended to personalize the state-units involved: as Hitler had personalized Germany, so Stalin personalized Soviet conduct. Since he was evil, it was easy to syllogize Soviet behavior as evil. Since Hitler had been devious, Soviet behavior would be devious. Since the European leaders of the thirties had failed to stand up to Hitler, U.S. leaders of the fifties would stand up to Stalin. Since Khrushchev also personalized Soviet behavior, and since he also appeared evil, Soviet behavior under him too would be devious, and therefore in the sixties we would stand up to him too, anywhere if necessary, including Vietnam.

Reasoning by historical analogy became a virtual ritual in the United States under Secretaries of State Acheson (1949-52), Dulles (1953-58) and Rusk (1961-68), who very early persuaded themselves that the Soviet Union under Stalin and Khrushchev, the Chinese under Mao, as well as the Vietnamese Communists under Ho, behaved similarly in all important respects of external policy to the Nazi Reich under Hitler, Fascist Italy under Mussolini, and Japan under the militarists. These evil dictatorships had, at what tragic cost, been appeased by the reigning powers of the thirties. To deal diplomatically and on a serious basis with such monsters, the reasoning went, was in fact akin to appeasing them. Rather than being dealt with diplomatically, they must instead be contained and deterred. If the counter threat confronting their threat was sufficient, they would pull back and the status quo could be preserved.

But the analogies did not hold. Aside from the conservatism of Stalin in foreign policy, the rise of polycentrism in world communism with the emergence of Tito, Communist China, and Communist Vietnam, and the Sino-Soviet conflict, were tearing the Sino-Soviet bloc asunder. Communist China, intent upon internal reconstruction after the Korean War, and externally concerned only with the China Straits thereafter, never seriously threatened any of its neighbors in Asia. The triumphant Vietnamese Nationalist Communists of the late fifties and early sixties could not be compared to the weak Nazi puppet states of the forties in Europe. In the global perspective of our decision-makers, however, all issues were interlinked and all our commitments, whether formal or not, had to be indiscriminately upheld or they would be everywhere indiscriminately violated. In our decision-makers' thinking, appeasement at Munich in 1938 figured as the permanent centerpiece.

U.S. Perception of Its Commitments and Response Capabilities: Vietnam

We have noted earlier that by 1959 the United States had reached its crest as a superpower in Europe, Asia, and Latin America. Its line of containment was deployed all along the Sino-Soviet periphery: from Korea, Okinawa, the Philippines, and Japan; through the CENTO partners (Pakistan, Iran, Turkey); the NATO allies (Greece to Iceland and Canada); to southern command in Panama. But it was in 1959 that the world began to change: the Sino-Soviet rift erupted after Khrushchev's Camp David visit to Eisenhower (1959) and grew quickly into a second cold war; Soviet technological advances threatened the onset of parity in strategic nuclear forces after a long period of U.S. predominance; de Gaulle's assault on NATO and U.S. hegemony in the West emerged, to be emulated by Rumania's parallel defection from the Soviets in the East; the non-aligned bloc of states began to founder under the triple pressures of rivaling Soviet, Chinese, and U.S. demands for Third World allegiance; and in Indochina, the Vietnamese Communists had rekindled the revolution that had been placed in remission after the 1954 Geneva Conference.

At the crest of its postwar power, it is really not surprising that the United States considered itself committed almost every place, irrespective of the specific—formal, informal, or potential—nature of its commitment. Thus the United States seems to have considered itself committed in such diverse places as Laos, when the aftermath of the Kong Le neutralist coup threatened the pro-American regime of Phoumi Nosavan; Lebanon, where U.S. Marines had landed in 1958 and a growing amount of assistance was flowing; Israel, America's best friend in the Middle East; and such Latin American nations as Brazil and the Dominican Republic, where regimes flirting with communism, like those of Goulart and Bosch, would not be allowed to retain or come to power. From the differing perspectives of the scholar and the operator, Richard Barnet and Joseph B. Smith [31] have documented the pervasive character of our worldwide covert (CIA) involvements and engagements. So have the intelligence hearings of the Congress in the mid-seventies. Recent literature abounds with studies of our global involvements.[32]

The question arises whether all these countries, in which the United States was now acquiring protective domains in the form of security and economic assistance investments, and beginning in the sixties in the form also of growing inflows of U.S. private capital, always regarded the United States as their protector. Even if they accepted it as mentor, did they in fact consider it *committed* to their defense? It is doubtful that Lebanon so considered it when U.S. forces landed on her shores after the 1958 coup in Iraq, invoking the vague and ambiguous Eisenhower Doctrine of 1957; and that Laos so perceived it when some 10,000 U.S. Marines were landed in Thailand in 1962 presumably to ensure Laos' protection. Laos shortly thereafter changed governments and went to a policy of diplomatic negotiations and non-alignment in which the United States ultimately joined (Geneva, 1962). Furthermore, despite U.S. landing on its soil and the existing terms of SEATO, Thailand itself certainly did not regard the United States as committed since it continued relentlessly to press for formal U.S. security guarantees, which were never provided in treaty form.

Did the Republic of Vietnam regard the United States as committed when Vice President Johnson suggested, during his first visit in the spring of 1961, that U.S. troops might be brought in under the guise of assisting Diem in coping with the virtually annual flooding of the Mekong Delta, but really in order to assist Diem in coping with the Viet Cong? [33] Diem rejected this initial offer in full cognizance of the fact that direct American intervention in the guerrilla war would totally change its character. Diem, in fact, had some difficulty reaching this negative decision, precisely because refusing what appeared as a generous, if at the time inopportune, offer on the part of the United States might result in weakening U.S. resolve to continue to help Vietnam in the way Diem desired. This was not with troops, but with money, material, advice, and a "free hand." What Diem did request, and he did so twice in October 1961, was a formal bilateral security treaty with the United States.[34] The United States did not oblige.

In early 1961, when Kennedy took office, the United States had no more of a formal commitment to the Republic of Vietnam (RVN) than it had had on the morrow of the Geneva accords of 1954. The latter, as a matter of fact, had specified the neutrality of both zones of Vietnam. It is true that U.S. interest in the integrity of the Republic of (South) Vietnam had been additionally expressed in the diplomacy of sponsoring SEATO and backing Diem against the holding of interzonal elections in 1954-56, as well as in an October 1954 Eisenhower letter to Diem,[35] and in the joint statement issued by Presidents Eisenhower and Diem at the conclusion of the latter's state visit to the United States on May 11, 1957.[36] These statements, of which the Senate was barely cognizant, in no sense expressed a formal commitment to the defense of South Vietnam.

Even the informal commitment, in terms of the extent of U.S. presence and security assistance investment in Vietnam, had hardly grown during the 1956-61 interval. In toto, the amount of U.S. economic, military, and budgetary assistance through the commercial import program to Vietnam still stood at slightly over $300 million each fiscal year. The U.S. diplomatic mission in Saigon was not in early 1961 noticeably larger or more importantly staffed than it had been in 1956. The MAAG or military contingent, including the equipment advisors, the TRIM or training group, and remnants of the TERM or equipment recovery mission established in 1956 to recover U.S. military material before the French could ship it to Algeria, stood at the same size—about 800 men—that it had been since Dulles had negotiated with Nehru in 1956 the doubling of the MAAG ceilings imposed by the Geneva Armistice Agreement.[37]

There is little question, however, that U.S. self-perception of this commitment had grown vastly in the interim. In 1954-56, Vietnam had been important, to be sure, in containing the spread of communism in Southeast Asia. But the U.S. government's perception of its role both as mentor and as guarantor, fortified by the apparent Soviet willingness discussed in Chapter II to accept the quasi-permanent partition of Vietnam at the 17th parallel, had grown by quantum leap. Since South Vietnam had not fallen, as so many had expected, and since Diem with U.S. help had succeeded in making it into a going concern, we now regarded the RVN as our ward, an essential cog at the Free World boundary of communism's advance in the Third World.

When Ambassador Frederick Nolting replaced Ambassador Elbridge Durbrow at the beginning of the Kennedy administration, there was in Washington a strong sense of concern that this ward, which had looked so promising in 1959, was again seriously endangered. In fact, Durbrow had been sufficiently encouraged by the situation only two years previously to preside over the departure of some of Diem's most prized American associates—Gen. Lansdale of the CIA and Prof. Fishel of Michigan State, for example—on grounds that they were now no longer needed since Vietnam could stand on its own two feet. But by 1961, the situation had seriously deteriorated; in only two years of relatively low-key terrorism and guerrilla operations, the reinfiltrating cadres and remaining supporters of the Vietnamese Communists in South Vietnam had re-emerged as a major force threatening the viability of the regime in Saigon.

The impression of impending danger in Vietnam had been reinforced by Vice President Johnson's findings on his visit in the spring of 1961. President Kennedy had read a serious report by Lansdale pointing out the increasing gravity of the internal situation.[38] We shall see in detail in the next chapter how Kennedy and the New Frontier responded. What is important to note here is that at this crucial stage, in mid to late 1961, the United States simply assumed a commitment. It once more asked itself: "By what means do we best uphold this commitment?" It did not ask, as it should have, "Do we really have, want, or need a commitment in that particular place at this particular time?"

This brings us to the important point of the existence of U.S. response capabilities. Although the self-perception of a commitment on the part of a protector power is naturally essential to set response machinery in motion, it is perfectly conceivable that the sheer existence and widespread deployment of ready-capable means of response can themselves engender strong reinforcement in the protector power's perception of commitment. This phenomenon involves the near-automatic growth of national interest perceptions on the part of great and superpowers. Thus, the fact that the United States was in Vietnam with some, though in 1961 still insufficient, ready-capable response mechanisms, buttressed by the now enormous and deployed fighting and logistical capabilities of an eager theater commander in the Pacific (CINCPAC), in itself impelled us to regard Vietnam as a national interest, and its availability to our access as being of vital strategic value.

It was not possible, in the Washington of about 1959-65, to get a policy-planning exercise to state what was in fact a vital interest of the United States. It was possible only to get such an exercise to state how best to maintain and enhance a vital interest of the United States, and at what tolerable cost. Policy-planning exercises never defined vital interest positions themselves, but always assumed them. They did so for the simple reason that a vital interest of the United States in this period was any position in the world in which the United States had, however minimally, deployed some investment and shown some concern.[39]

Summary

The threatening and negative nature of U.S. deterrence doctrines; the tendency of U.S. statesmen, top bureaucrats, and top politicians to replay history and perceive the continuous re-emergence of the last war; the overly self-conscious nature of U.S. perception of a wide range of commitments in virtually every portion of the globe; and finally the fact that the United States was in fact equipped to respond almost immediately to almost anything almost anywhere, whether or not what it was to respond to had been precisely or even seriously defined; all these factors combined to make the United States during the heyday of its superpowerdom ultra-prone to perceive, seize, and uphold commitments. The United States continued without much analysis to assume that failure to do so would dangerously jeopardize its credibility along the entire, and exposed, line of containment it had constructed across the globe.

Notes

1. Charles de Gaulle, *Memoires de Guerre* vol 3 (Le Salut, Paris: Plon, 1959). "Vieille France, accablée d'Histoire, meurtrie de guerres et de révolutions,

allant et venant sans relâche de la grandeur au declin, mais redressée, de siècle en siècle, par le génie du renouveau!" p. 337.

2. Dean and David Hiller, *John Foster Dulles: Soldier for Peace* (New York: Holt, Rinehart and Winston, 1960), pp. 91-121. *See also,* Townsend Hoopes, *The Devil and John Foster Dulles* (Boston: Little Brown, 1973).

3. Richard J. Barnet, *Roots of War* (New York: Atheneum, 1972), pp. 13-22.

4. On the controversy surrounding U.S. use of nuclear weapons to end the war with Japan, see G. Alperovitz, *Atomic Diplomacy.; R.J. Barnet, Roots of War,* pp. 16-17.

5. Robert E. Osgood, *Ideals and Self-Interest in America's Foreign Relations* (Chicago: University of Chicago Press, 1953).

6. Consult especially the prewar works of James T. Shotwell, Frank H. Simonds, Russell M. Cooper, Charles Seymour, Hubert Herring. As a statesman, Henry L. Stimson, who occupied the posts of both secretary of state and secretary of war, exemplified this point of view.

7. Edmund A. Walsh, S.J., *Total Power: A Footnote to History* (New York: Doubleday, 1948), esp. ch. XI; *see also,* John E. Kieffer, *Realities of World Power* (New York: David McKay, 1952), pp. 1-7 and 195-210. The classic geopolitical view is expressed by Sir Harold Mackinder in "The Round World and the Winning of the Peace," *Foreign Affairs* 21 (July, 1943): pp. 595-605.

8. Walter Millis, ed., *The Forrestal Diaries* (New York: Viking Press, 1951), pp. 14, 24, 39-41.

9. Hans J. Morgenthau, *Politics Among Nations: The Struggle for Power and Peace* (New York: Knopf, 1948); Robert Strausz-Hupe, *The Balance of Tomorrow: Power and Foreign Policy in the United States* (New York: Putnam's Sons, 1945); Henry A. Kissinger, *The Necessity of Choice: Prospects of American Foreign Policy* (New York: Harper, 1961).

10. With the exception of previous deployments at Guantanamo (Cuba), Panama, and Clark A.F.B. (formerly Fort Stotsenberg), Philippines—all American-occupied territories at the time of our initial force deployments there.

11. On McCarthyism and domestic anti-communism in the late forties and early fifties, *see inter alia* Earl Latham, ed., *The Meaning of McCarthyism* (Boston: D.C. Heath, 1965); Alan D. Harper, *The Politics of Loyalty: The White House and the Communist Issue, 1946-52* (Westport, Conn: Greenwood, 1969); Earl Latham, *The Communist Controversy in Washington: From the New Deal to McCarthy* (Cambridge, Mass: Harvard University Press, 1966).

12. "Individuals yearn to do what will satisfy them, not their masters . . . Only under coercion do they accept a system which repudiates love of family, love of country, love of God, and which treats men as bits of matter." John Foster Dulles, "The Peace We Seek," Department of State (DOS) Bulletin XXXII, No. 813, Jan. 24, 1955, pp. 123-25. "During recent years, the Communist rulers, through their propaganda, have sought to capitalize on love of peace and horror of war as a means of extending their rule over all the human race." John Foster Dulles, "Principles in Foreign Policy," DOS Bulletin XXXII, No. 826, April 26, 1955, p. 671.

13. E.H. Carr, *The Twenty Years Crisis* (London: Macmillan, 1946).

14. *See,* Gabriel Almond and James S. Coleman, *The Politics of the Developing Areas* (Princeton, N.J.: Princeton University Press, 1960); Hannah

Arendt, *On Revolution* (New York: Viking Press, 1963); Henry Bienen, *Violence and Social Change* (Chicago: University of Chicago Press, 1968); David Bell, *Resistance and Revolution* (Boston: Houghton Mifflin, 1973); Harry Eckstein, ed., *Internal War: Problems and Approaches* (New York: Free Press, 1966); Samuel P. Huntington, *Political Order in Changing Societies* (New Haven: Yale University Press, 1968); Chalmers Johnson, *Revolutionary Change* (Boston: Little Brown, 1966); Cyril E. Black, *Communism and Revolution: The Strategic Uses of Political Violence* (Princeton, N.J.: Princeton University Press, 1961).

15. Paul Dickson, *Think Tanks* (New York: Atheneum, 1971). See esp. pp. 65-69; pp. 113-36 on Project Camelot; and pp. 136-71. *See also* Irving L. Horowitz, ed., *The Use and Abuse of Social Science: Behavioral Research and Policy Making* (New Brunswick, N.J.: Transaction, 1975).

16. Walt W. Rostow, *The United States in the World Arena: An Essay in Recent History* (New York: Harper, 1960).

17. Walt W. Rostow, "Guerrilla Warfare in Underdeveloped Areas," in *The Guerrilla and How To Fight Him*. ed. Lt. Col. T.N. Greene (New York: Praeger, 1962), pp. 54-61. For early speeches by Walt Rostow, *see* DOS Bulletin XLVI, No. 1199, June 18, 1962, pp. 967-70; *Ibid.*, XLVI, No. 1190, April 6, 1962, pp. 625-31; *Ibid.*, L, No. 1304, June 22, 1964, pp. 961-66. Later addresses on the same general theme are in DOS Bulletin LII, No. 1345, April 5, 1965, pp. 492-97; *Ibid.*, LIII, No. 1358, July 5, 1965, pp. 21-27; *Ibid.*, LVI, No. 1448, March 27, 1967, pp. 491-504.

18. Told to me by James C. Thomson who, as a National Security Council and State Department China specialist in the early sixties, tried to brief Walt Rostow on China.

19. David Halberstam, *The Best and the Brightest* (Greenwich, Conn: Fawcett Crest Paper, 1972), pp. 192-200; 761-62.

20. Walt W. Rostow, *The Stages of Economic Growth: A Non-Communist Manifesto* (Cambridge: Harvard University Press, 1960).

21. See Note 21, Ch. II.

22. Several New Frontier intellectuals, among them Richard Goodwin, James Thomson, and Arthur M. Schlesinger, Jr., harbored considerable reservations from the time they first came to Washington.

23. Under Public Law 480, the United States generates local currencies in developing countries through the sale of U.S. surplus agricultural commodities. The proceeds are used to administer development assistance projects.

24. "Covert support" means CIA assistance to individuals or organizations abroad, extended through a variety of clandestine techniques.

25. "U.S. Commitments to Foreign Powers," *Hearings Before the Committee on Foreign Relations,* U.S. Senate, 90th Cong., 1st sess., on S.R. 151. (Washington, D.C.: U.S.G.P.O., 1967); "U.S. Security Agreements and Commitments Abroad, Broader Aspects of U.S. Commitments," *Hearings Before Subcommittee on U.S. Security Agreements and Commitments Abroad,* U.S. Senate, 91st Cong. 2nd sess., Nov. 24, 1970.

26. Neville Maxwell, *India's China War* (New York: Pantheon Books, 1970).

27. Arnold Wolfers, *Discord and Collaboration: Essays on International Politics* (Baltimore: Johns Hopkins University Press, 1962), esp. Ch. 16, pp. 253-73.

28. See discussion of aspects of Containment, Ch. II, section 1.

29. Rubinstein, *Foreign Policy of the Soviet Union*, p. 251.
30. Robert Simmons, *Strained Alliance.*
31. Richard J. Barnet, *Intervention and Revolution* (New York: New American Library—Mentor, 1972); Joseph Burkholder Smith, *Portrait of a Cold Warrior* (New York: Putnam, 1976).
32. *See* Raymond Aron, *The Imperial Republic: The United States and the World, 1945-73* (Cambridge: Winthrop, 1974); Richard J. Barnet and Ronald E. Müller, *Global Reach* (New York: Simon and Schuster, 1975); Melvin Gurtov, *The U.S. Against the Third World: Antinationalism and Intervention* (New York: Praeger, 1974); Herbert K. Tillema, *Appeal to Force: American Military Intervention in the Era of Containment* (New York: Crowell, 1973).
33. *Pentagon Papers,* 2: pp. 55 ff.
34. *Ibid.,* Chronology, pp. 12-14.
35. U.S. Senate. Committee on Foreign Relations, *Background Information Relating to Southeast Asia and Vietnam* Sixth rev. ed., June 1970, p. 179. *See also, DOS Bulletin* XXXI, Nov. 15, 1954, pp. 735-736.
36. U.S. Senate. Committee on Foreign Relations. *Background Information,* pp. 184-86.
37. See Chapter IV, Decision 1.
38. *Pentagon Papers,* 2: pp. 25-27.
39. This is the personal impression I brought away from the policy-planning process of this period, in which I participated on occasions.

Chapter IV

Ten Fateful Decisions on Vietnam, 1961-75

In the present chapter, we seek to describe how the United States got itself progressively more involved in Vietnam. Starting with a relatively modest "counterinsurgency" program developed by the New Frontier in 1961 to cope with the local Communist-inspired and led national liberation war, as well as to convey U.S. determination to uphold the credibility of its global power and worldwide commitments, the U.S. moved inexorably to deeper and deeper engagement and to more and more fateful decisions.

This process, which led the United States by the mid-sixties into waging massive warfare in Vietnam, was arrested though not immediately reversed by the Communist Tet offensive of early 1968. Thereafter, the United States slowly disengaged itself from Vietnam; but the war itself continued and was in fact broadened to the whole of Indochina. The direct U.S. combat role in Indochina was finally concluded with the signing of the Paris Peace Accords in January 1973 at the very beginning of the second Nixon administration. Ultimately, in 1975, all of Indochina fell into the hands of Communist forces.

The years 1961-75 were by far the most significant in the long history of our involvement in Indochina. In reviewing and describing below the ten decisions which we regard as the most fateful of all those made by the United States during these years, we seek to apprehend basic and necessary knowledge of the events that occurred. Using that knowledge base, we go on in the last four chapters of this book to a more detailed and systematic examination and evaluation of our Indochina policies of the sixties and early seventies in their domestic and global context.

1. Decision to Break Through Geneva MAAG Ceilings and Engage in Counterinsurgency Programs, 1961-62

Of all the decisions made by the United States in Indochina, especially Vietnam, between 1945 and 1975, we regard those made in 1961-62 as the most fateful because by making them the United States in effect cast aside the Geneva accords of 1954. With that, something intangible but immensely important went out of our Indochina policy. Regardless of all our aid to Diem before 1961-62, Geneva had presented a type of hidden but nonetheless real restraint.

The decision to support France and recognize the Associated States of Indochina in 1949-1950 had been fateful in that it got the United States initially involved; the decision to back Diem against the holding of all-Vietnam elections in 1956, and to support him from 1955 on with considerable U.S. assistance had been even more fateful, but not fatal. The United States could still, had it carefully reviewed and appraised the situation in 1961, have disengaged with honor and a minimum of damage. Even though it had increasingly come to think of Vietnam between 1956 and 1961, as a nation divided between two quasi-permanent states (the RVN and the DRV), and even though as seen in Chapter II the Soviets had given the U.S. government ample justification for this perception, there was nothing inherent in Vietnam or in U.S. policies toward Vietnam before 1961 to compel the United States to fully engage itself. That it did so was the result of superpowerdom, of its appraisal of national liberation wars, and of its appraisal of commitments and their credibility, as suggested in Chapter III.

Before 1961, the United States had been careful in regard to the armistice provisions of the 1954 Geneva agreements. For example, even a relatively minor move such as the doubling in 1956 of the 1954 size of the Vietnam Military Assistance Advisory Group (MAAG), from about 400 men in 1954 to about 800 in late 1956, made in order to accommodate the Temporary Equipment Recovery Mission (TERM), had been preceded by the most careful diplomatic negotiations between Dulles and Nehru. The latter, acting for India in her capacity as chairman of the International Control Commission, gave his assent to Dulles in the spring of 1956 only after Dulles had assured him that the augmentation was temporary. (As noted earlier, it was made to prevent U.S. equipment left in Vietnam from being shipped to Algeria, an objective shared by India.) Moreover, Dulles had persuaded Nehru that, based on the disinterest in Indochina they had demonstrated the previous year, the Soviets would be unlikely to object.[1]

Between the fall of 1956 and the winter-spring of 1962, the size of the U.S. military mission in Vietnam (MAAG, including all its components) remained at the ICC-assented augmented ceiling of about 800. Six years is a long time! But by mid-1962, the US/MAAG in Vietnam had, quite suddenly, risen to a size of over 12,000 men. There is, in fact, an enormous difference in the international significance of an 800-man administrative-type uniformed force and the presence of a body of soldiers, sailors, and airmen approaching division size. The difference may not have appeared so glaring to the ICC or other powers, including even Soviets and Chinese, but to the Vietnamese Communists it could only confirm their worst suspicions of U.S. intent in South Vietnam, that the United States would "imperialize" the South and permanently perpetuate the partition. This perception of course played into the hands of hard liners in Hanoi and is not unrelated to the decision to create the National Liberation Front of South Vietnam in 1961-62. To the United States itself, where its significance was perhaps greatest, it signaled to the foreign affairs and national security bureaucracies the end of Geneva and of restraint — even if the partition had long been regarded as quasi-permanent in these quarters — as well as the beginning of an epoch in which we would really put Communist wars of national liberation to the acid test in Southeast Asia.

This extraordinarily fateful decision stemmed directly from the reports prepared in the summer of 1961 by the economist Eugene Staley and, more significantly, in the fall of 1961 by Gen. Maxwell Taylor and Professor Walt Rostow on their return from a field mission on which President Kennedy had sent them to examine the whole deteriorating situation. But the decision cannot be analyzed separately from the climate of thinking vis-à-vis the Third World which the New Frontier brought to Washington and which was reviewed in the previous chapter. As we noted, this globalistic thinking saw in Soviet sponsorship of national liberation wars a maximal challenge to America's own preferred schemes and models for development and progress in the Third World. In his public statements, Rostow stressed that national liberation wars, if not defeated in a place like Vietnam, would spread infectiously and challenge us victoriously everywhere.[2] What he and those of similar mind-set feared most, however, was that if U.S. schemes and models for development could not succeed in a fertile soil like South Vietnam, where they could obtain all feasible backing from the United States, they might well be defeated everywhere else, and with them all the plans and hopes of the nation builders of the New Frontier.

History works amazing coincidences; but the advent of the intellectual nation builders on the national stage in 1961 occurred simultaneously with the return to authority and power in central national security decision-making roles of U.S. Army leaders long shorn of a mission. If the decade of the forties had been that of the Army in national security policy, that of the fifties, especially after the Korean stalemate, had been that of the Air Force above all other services. The Air Force had the royal slice of the defense budget, the resources of the Strategic Air Command, the Tactical Air Command, the North American Defense Command, and most of the important bases abroad. Now, with the advent of the missile age, it would also obtain control of the new strategic delivery systems. The Navy had fared less well than the Air Force, but it had survived and had continued to deploy. Its three fleets—Atlantic, Pacific and Mediterranean—also stood to gain a major piece of the strategic nuclear forces in the form of submarine-based ballistic missiles (Polaris, later Poseidon).

What, though, of the Army? Retrenched since Korea, inheritor of limited war concepts developed mainly in think tanks and which it at heart neither understood nor cared about, it had been sitting in wait in Europe so long that its very *raison d'être* had come to be in doubt. The Army, to put it succinctly, had been in search of a mission from the mid-fifties on. Such a sense of mission, precisely when it was most desperately needed, was what Gen. Maxwell Taylor supplied in his book, *The Uncertain Trumpet*, published in 1960.[3] The book laid the doctrinal foundations for what was to become the Army's great new crusade of the first half of the sixties: "Counterinsurgency."

Counterinsurgency

If ever a doctrine without serious analytic foundations appeared in the annals of military history, it was the U.S. doctrine of counterinsurgency which made its appearance at the onset of the New Frontier. And lest we exaggerate Gen. Taylor's role in authoring this doctrine, let us hasten to add that there were many other and much more obscure authors than he.[4] Some of these were French, like the military analyst Pierre Galula, who managed to devise from the French defeat in Indochina lessons into how it could have been averted; others were colonial British, for example Brig. Gen. Sir Robert Thompson, whose lessons from the victorious British "Emergency" operations in Malaysia bore—and not for want of trying—little applicability to the revolutionary situation in Vietnam.[5] In fact, there were as many conceptions of what counterinsurgency meant and how it was to be applied operationally as there were counterinsurgency thinkers in the Army, the CIA, the think tanks, and even the State Department in about 1959-63, and these were legion. To this day, we contend, no one either in the military or outside, has ever understood its real meaning; but that is not too surprising for this eclectic doctrine was whatever those who applied it thought it was.

To men like Taylor, highly sophisticated and perhaps over-highly educated, counterinsurgency provided the Army with a mission. The mission was to assist loyalist local military and police forces and political-social elements in the Third World in engaging and defeating revolutions which the authors of the doctrine, including Taylor, did not necessarily fully understand. The elements to be defeated were presumably not revolutionaries, but "insurgents"—otherwise they would have been simply called "revolutionaries" or "rebels." But not only were these latter terms dysfunctional from the U.S. point of view—how could the United States openly and overtly promote counterrevolution?—they were also praiseworthy terms in the Third World where much oppression palpably justified revolution. Accordingly, the United States coined the obfuscating word counterinsurgency, a disingenuous expression conveying the very confusion in which U.S. thinking was floundering.

Insurgents were to be countered through a mix of guerrilla-type operations, including activities by special forces, assaults by airborne and amphibious groups, and a befuddled jumble of psychological warfare and civic action-type operations. These were to include intelligence collection, the dissemination of information, technical assistance to villagers, entertainment and propaganda programs, the promotion of village welfare, etc. But counterinsurgency as applied in the field was fairly simple. The United States would train and equip ready forces for low levels of warfare to help villagers hold their ground against Communist insurgents. These forces would be sent into the field in places like the Mekong Delta of Vietnam; there they would advise, equip, and complement the local army in chasing the guerrillas out of the villages. The general American perception of the guerrillas in the early sixties was extremely vague and largely erroneous, both among our military and our civilians, particularly those who supervised or managed these operations in Washington. The guerrillas were viewed as clearly alien and distinct elements, who intruded suddenly and after long forced marches from secure rear bases equipped by China and Russia upon peaceful rice-growing villages which they would then terrorize mercilessly.

U.S. counterinsurgency did not view the guerrillas as men and women of the villages themselves, or as men from nearby villages, whose requests for food, succor, passage, and above all information were not necessarily spontaneously resisted but, on the contrary, frequently abundantly provided by the peasant masses, whether out of fear, sympathy, compassion, or simply because these men were of their kind—or a combination of these reasons. Few Washington counterinsurgency planners realized that those killed or terrorized in the villages were often those who had misused their authority to plunder the most and to render life in these villages most miserable. Hardly ever did a U.S. counterinsurgency expert conceive that the guerrillas in Vietnam, for all their misbehavior, could be perceived as champions of national independence, whether or not they were also Communists.

Weak doctrine as it was, counterinsurgency fit in well with the needs of New Frontiersmen who were determined to engage the United States in nation building abroad. The Army would now complement and supplement, but hopefully remain subordinate to the AID missions, special economic development groups, technical assistance units, and other elements in the paraphernalia of U.S. nation-building fever.

What Taylor and Rostow reported and recommended when Kennedy, moved by the deteriorating situation in Vietnam in mid-1961 as represented to him by Nolting, Lansdale, and others, sent them on their fact-finding mission and for talks with Diem in the early fall of 1961 was a far cry from the simplistic proposal to despatch U.S. forces under the cover of flood aid made by Vice President Johnson and rejected by Diem earlier that spring. Taylor and Rostow proposed to send as many U.S. Army counterinsurgency specialists and experts to Vietnam as necessary to turn the tide and to retrain the Army of the Republic of Vietnam (ARVN) from the conventional warfare posture in which it had been molded by the U.S. MAAG from 1955 to 1961 to a counterinsurgent posture in which the ARVN could meet the guerrillas at their own level on their own grounds.[6] The recommendations produced a whole new arena for U.S. policy in Vietnam. Henceforth, the U.S. commitment was to be for real, and immense in scope; the United States would not quit until, with its counterinsurgency assistance, Diem's ARVN had surmounted and finished the Viet Cong (VC) once and for all.[7]

By mid-1962, the United States had military advisors throughout South Vietnam and with all major force units. Entrenched in little "Beau Geste" forts along the Cambodian and Laotian borders, U.S. Special Forces were perhaps unknowingly reliving the experience of French Foreign Legionnaires only eight or nine years previously. The Army Special Warfare Training Center at Ft. Bragg, N.C., appropriately renamed the John F. Kennedy School for Special and Counterinsurgency Warfare in 1964, had been greatly expanded. In a major address to some of its first graduates, Professor Rostow had declared, on June 28, 1961: "We are determined to help destroy this international disease. That is, guerrilla war designed, initiated, supplied, and led from outside an independent nation." [8]

Moreover, covert and semi-covert operations in Vietnam had been strongly intensified. From bases deep inside South Vietnam, unmarked U.S. bombers with U.S. crews flying under the cover name of "Operation Farmgate" were systematically endeavoring to eliminate enemy rear bases and infrastructure. In this process, a lot of civilians were bombed and strafed, which according to some U.S. officers and civilians on the ground, only produced more Viet Cong.[9] From Saigon, the CIA was masterminding elaborate intelligence collection nets and, in collaboration with Diem's security services and Ngo Dinh Nhu's political cadres and special forces, endeavoring to uncover and remove recalcitrant elements and to stimulate support for the Diem regime. Heavy use of the notorious Cayson prison cages dates from this period.[10]

In Washington, White House Aide Michael Forrestall and State Department Assistant Secretary Roger Hilsman, both within two years of 1962 to grow quite disenchanted with our whole Vietnam enterprise but then caught up in the fervor of the moment, conceived the "Strategic Hamlet Program" under which scores of Vietnamese villagers were rounded-up and relocated to presumably secure encampments. The program floundered by early 1963.[11] In fact, the whole counterinsurgency program came under scrutiny and criticism when the Viet Cong guerrillas won their first major military victory of the second Indochina war at Ap Bac in February 1963. This victory was duly reported by correspondents like Neil Sheehan and David Halberstam of *The New York Times* but denied by the Saigon MAAG command and Pentagon authorities. Prelude of things to come!

Kennedy and Vietnam

The 1961-62 decisions to send about 15,000 U.S. military men into Vietnam were *the most fateful* ever made by the United States in Vietnam because they closed an era (1950-61) during which honorable disengagement had remained possible, and opened an era (1962-73) during which it became increasingly difficult for the United States to contemplate withdrawal. They therefore mark a real and crucial watershed in the history of U.S. involvement in Vietnam. To understand somewhat better why the top of the U.S. government acceded to these decisions and undertook what became a decade of war in Indochina, we must set the events mentioned above in the perspective of other developments which occurred during the all-important year of 1961.

Consider the blows that befell President Kennedy right after he took office on January 20, 1961. First, an enormous fiasco at the Bay of Pigs in April, for which he assumed full responsibility although both the CIA and the Joint Chiefs of Staff had severely let him down. The credibility of American power and leadership suffered another blow, at least in the perception of key U.S. politicians and officials, when Kennedy met Khrushchev at Vienna in May. It was a bruising confrontation, in which Khruschev did not retreat an inch on Berlin or Soviet actions in the Third World, although he may have been left under the impression (or so Kennedy might have feared) that Kennedy did. While de Gaulle had been courteous and correct, he increasingly seemed to assume a mentor's role with the young president, a role which the latter felt U.S. politicians expected of him, not of foreign leaders.

In the middle of 1961, Khrushchev and the East Germans suddenly precipitated and then ended the Berlin crisis by building the Berlin Wall, as a result of which no East Berliner or East German could go to the West without special permission, although movement in the other direction was permitted and the Soviets rather than East Germans continued to perform their long-assigned role of checking and allowing access by Allied officials into East Berlin. The substance of this decision safeguarded Western interests; but its appearance conveyed Western weakness and Soviet strength. The U.S. reaction was to sit tight and reinforce our forces in Europe. This did not at first sit well with our French and German allies. De Gaulle began to assume a tougher posture with Khrushchev than had Kennedy himself. He also went full speed ahead with plans, frowned on in Washington, to build a strictly independent, if small and crude, French nuclear strike force.

An impression of overall weakness had by this time begun to emerge about the Kennedy administration's foreign policy. We should note that this impression seemed stronger and more significant in the United States itself than it did abroad, where U.S. power was on the whole still perceived to be at the dizzy heights it had reached in 1959 and where the fresh personality of Kennedy held enormous appeal. Nonetheless, the emerging impression of weakness was further aggravated by two other developments in mid-1961. First, American indecision as to policy in the former, now independent, Belgian Congo, where the United States appeared to be straddling the fence between the colonialist-tainted Tshombe and his Katanga diehards on the one hand, and the central authority in Leopoldville (now Kinshasa), which was leaning increasingly leftward, on the other. Second, Kennedy in mid-1961 gave Averell Harriman, then his assistant secretary for East Asian affairs—he was later to become deputy undersecretary—the go-ahead for diplomatic resolution of the Laos problem (see Chapter II). This led the United States slowly to disengage from support of Phoumi Nosavan and his generals and to revert to support of the coalition government-minded Prince Souvanna Phouma, who re-neutralized Laos.

The combined impression of these moves and events on the hard-line anti-Communist U.S. foreign policy-making elite, including members of Congress, was one of increasing fear that the president would prove weak in the face of what was perceived as a mounting worldwide communist challenge. We will further develop in the next chapter the role of toughness and force in U.S. policy, but it may be suggested here that it was largely in order to obviate the growing impression of weakness, and to provide instead an appearance of toughness and strength, that Kennedy so readily fell in with the recommendations of the Taylor-Rostow mission. Vietnam, a place with which Kennedy was somewhat familiar owing to his early support of the Catholic Nationalist Diem and his early opposition to the French (see Chapter II), offered an arena where a Communist challenge to the Free World could be met head-on by a strong and perceptible U.S. response. The response, in the form of investment of some 15,000 U.S. counterinsurgency advisors and special forces, and the initiation of covert operations like Farmgate and other hopefully deniable CIA activities, could be a low-cost one. At least, there was no immediately significant indication that the Soviets or Chinese would step in, or even that the North Vietnamese would at once substantially raise the ante in an area which was already going their way. This proved a short-sighted calculation.

In late 1961 and early 1962, President Kennedy and his closest advisors, including McGeorge Bundy, Robert Kennedy, Dean Rusk and, in an increasingly important capacity, Robert McNamara, decided to take the step. (It is unclear to what degree the experienced and generally wise Averell Harriman, then deeply engaged in the Geneva negotiations on Laos, was a participant in this early but crucial decision.) An additional word is required on Defense Secretary McNamara's role. At least initially (1961-63), McNamara saw in the nation-building efforts and counterinsurgency plans and techniques which were being promoted for Vietnam a great opportunity for quantifiable, direct, cost-effective U.S. defense inputs. This might be the real type of war the United States would have to fight in the future—as Gen. Taylor, shortly to become chairman of the Joint Chiefs of Staff, was telling him—far more realistic and cheap than the costly and unthinkable strategic nuclear scenarios premised on massive retaliation. These were in any case due for review with the approaching condition of parity of the two superpowers in deliverable nuclear power. Moreover, counterinsurgency gave the Army, which was getting increasingly vocal and potentially rebellious in the defense community, a much needed mission to fulfill.

It is unlikely that Kennedy thought that his administration had, this early, made an irrevocable commitment in Vietnam. Some believe that Kennedy continued to his death in 1963 to feel that if the Vietnam involvement went too far, and it looked as if the United States were entering a quagmire, he could still have worked out a disengagement.[12] It seems clear however, that because of its adoption of the Taylor-Rostow proposals, leading it to break the armistice provisions of the 1954 Geneva accords—as the Eisenhower administration had earlier supported the violation of the political provisions of the accords—and to engage itself in counterinsurgency operations in Vietnam, the Kennedy administration bears the *principal responsibility* for involving us in what would become our nightmare of the sixties.

2. Decision to Back ARVN Against the Diem Regime, 1963

The decision, made during the period spanning the months of August through October 1963 to back the Vietnamese Army generals in their coup against the Diem regime followed inexorably from the 1961-62 decisions to engage the United States much more deeply in Vietnam, and from its firm determination to "see it through." (As we shall see in subsequent chapters, just what it was the United States would "see through" always remained quite ambiguous.) The previous decisions and their sequitur meant essentially that henceforth the Vietnam conflict (as it was then still called) would be handled and conducted, fought and solved "the American way," and not "the Vietnamese way."

The United States felt that in counterinsurgency techniques it had found answers that had heretofore eluded the Vietnamese. In 1962-63, there was great emphasis on and study of the methods used by the British and Malays in eradicating the Chinese insurgents in Malaysia during the Emergency there. Brig. Gen. Sir Robert Thompson, one of the chief architects of the Malaysian success and an expert in coordinated intelligence and police work, was brought to Saigon along with staff, to assist our MAAG. Much less attention was paid to the largely sociopolitical methods used by Magsaysay in the Philippines in defeating the Huk rebellion, an "insurgency" much more similar to the Vietnamese in a country and terrain far more comparable to Vietnam. In regard to the U.S. desire henceforth to conduct the war its way, it must be observed that Diem had managed to botch up the job pretty badly by 1963, at least in American eyes; but Diem would have rather been deposed, as he eventually was, than fight the war any other way than his.

The diametrically opposed Diemist and Washington conceptions as to the conduct of anti-guerrilla operations came in direct conflict when Diem and his advisor-brother Nhu seized the political initiative in April-July 1963 in an unexpected arena. They began harshly to repress strong internal Buddhist pressures and demonstrations for reform and change in the character of the Diem-led Vietnam government. As noted in Chapter II, Buddhism had not previously manifested itself as a significant political force in Vietnam, and when it erupted dramatically on the world stage in the spring of 1963 by means of photographs throughout the world press of monks immolating themselves in protest against the Diem regime, the Ngo brothers at once discerned a fine Communist hand behind these demonstrations. The U.S. government, wholly preoccupied with its counterinsurgency and nation-building programs, at first sensed only a hindrance in something so dramatically detracting from the anti-Communist effort as these Buddhist demonstrations. By June-August 1963, however, its view was that Diem and Nhu's repression of the Buddhists could only lead to greater turmoil and thus further delay the adequate—"our way"—conduct of the counterinsurgency and nation-building programs.

Accordingly, at about the time Ambassador Henry Cabot Lodge was despatched to replace Ambassador Frederick Nolting in Vietnam (early July 1963), the United States changed its posture from what had been ultra pro-Diem to doubtful on Diem. When a junta of key generals in the Vietnamese Army, led by Gen. Duong Van ("Big") Minh prepared and, after long delays,[13] finally carried out a coup against Diem on November 1, 1963, the United States had informed it that it would not stand in its way. The United States had in fact encouraged the coup, or "climatized" it, as an accurate designation of the time put it, by a series of more-or-less calculated broadcasts on the Voice of America as well as by a campaign of what was called "salami-slicing" U.S. aid to Diem (September-October 1963). This consisted of slowly drying-up Diem's sources of U.S. support while simultaneously Ambassador Lodge kept his distance from Diem, waiting for Diem to approach him, which Diem finally did only a few days before the coup, far too late for any understanding to be reached. While the United States certainly climatized the coup, i.e., made it possible, there was never in the U.S. government any joy at witnessing the downfall of the only serious anti-Communist nationalist figure ever to have emerged in Vietnam, a leader who, whatever his many faults, had stood staunchly at our side for nine long years. When the generals ordered him and his brother

Nhu to be murdered after their capture, the news was greeted with horror in Washington and nowhere more so than at the White House.[14] But in Saigon, the celebration of the city crowds was enormous after the coup.

The decision to allow and even encourage a change in government after nine long years of Ngo family rule in Vietnam was fateful because: (1) it was not accompanied by careful analysis of why, in the end, Diem had lost all domestic support; (2) it was not accompanied by careful review and reappraisal of the *political* nature of the regime that might succeed Diem under ARVN auspices; (3) it was not accompanied by significant review of the stakes the United States had in Vietnam, and why. With respect to Diem's loss of support, U.S. reasons for promoting a governmental change revolved only around the question of unhindered conduct of the anti-guerrilla war. They took into little or no account the obvious aspirations of the Vietnamese masses for a less oppressive regime, one less distant and aloof from the people. In other words, the efficiency calculations of Americans did not mesh with the *political* aspirations of the Vietnamese.

With respect to the probable nature of a successor regime, had the U.S. government analyzed and considered more carefully the character of the military commanders who would arrange the government of South Vietnam after a coup, it might have discovered several reasons for the most serious doubts about continuing its efforts in Vietnam. As Diem knew only too well, the top ARVN command was, from the point of view of waging sustained anti-Communist guerrilla warfare, unreliable in the extreme. Leaving aside a small group of "gung-ho" non-political generals, like Nguyen Van Thieu (RVN's last president), in whom Diem and others could have confidence, the remainder split into two basic groups. First, those who were largely opportunistic and corrupt, both afraid to fight and cognizant that, as discussed in Chapter II, there was no tomorrow, hence they should grab all they could today. Second, those who far-sightedly might have tried to seek some sort of arrangement with the enemy, selling their skills and their possession of weapons and resources in return for possible moderation of enemy behavior which might have permitted some form of integration of the warring forces in the South. Among the latter generals, it is fair to list Gen. Big Minh who took over the reins of government after the November 1, 1963, coup. (The presidency reverted purely formalistically and only very briefly to the vice president under Diem, Nguyen Ngoc Tho, who had been and remained a non-entity.)

Big Minh's regime lasted barely two and one-half months, after which he was overthrown with only last-minute consultation with

Lodge and Washington by the "gung ho" commander of II Corps, General Nguyen Khanh, the latter soon became the U.S. hero of the day in Vietnam despite his utter incapacity to end Buddhist-led domestic turmoil or to pull either the civilian or military leadership together behind him. Khanh was eventually confronted in early 1965 with then Ambassador Maxwell Taylor's strong displeasure, and later forced to resign in his turn, leading the way to equally unsuccessful civilian regimes and to the eventual accession to power of Air Force Marshal Nguyen Cao Ky. But in the short period of the Minh Regime, tentative feelers toward some form of accommodation with the Viet Cong may have been put out, conceivably with Buddhist connivance. Neither Lodge in Saigon, nor the policy-makers in Washington would have any of this, which they designated as the "neutralist" tendencies of the Minh regime.[15] The latter was soon regarded as unreliable and the Khanh coup was greeted by the United States with relief when it occurred.

We now turn to the third of the three points made earlier, that the decision to allow the anti-Diem coup was fateful in that it was not accompanied by a significant review of U.S. stakes in Vietnam. In fact, the period between the raids of Nhu's special forces on the Buddhist pagodas (July 20, 1963) and the coup that brought down Diem (November 1, 1963), may well have been the last best chance the United States had to examine in a concerted and systematic way whether or not it ought to continue in Vietnam.

A Personal Note

At this point, a personal note in regard to my role in these events is justified, since my role has obtained some notice and is covered both in the *Pentagon Papers* and in some detail in Halberstam's book.[16] When I returned to Washington from a brief visit to Saigon on August 30, 1963, I realized three things, largely as a result of consultations with both Ambassador Lodge and President Diem and of conversations with old acquaintances in Saigon: (1) that Diem's situation was desperate and that the masses, at least in the cities but probably also in the countryside, desired a change and *an end to the war*, (2) that the army was largely incapable and corrupt, although it contained some leading elements who might be willing to work out an arrangement to end the fighting, using the Buddhist leaders in this effort, (3) and this is harder to state, my feeling based on admittedly brief observations both in Saigon and Washington was that our leadership, from the top down, was almost entirely uncomprehending of the nature of the struggle in Vietnam and particularly of the enormous sociopolitical pulling power that the Viet Cong adversary possessed in an area still so recently colonial and sociostructurally so little modified by the nine years of the Diem regime. Reflecting about it on the plane coming home, I decided that counterinsurgency in the U.S. mode and perception was nonsense, and would not work.

The morning after my return, on August 31, 1963, I was hurried without preparation by my old friend and then boss Assistant Secretary Roger Hilsman into a meeting of the executive committee of the National Security Council. I grew increasingly appalled as I listened to speaker after speaker, men at the top of our government like Rusk, McNamara, Taylor, and Robert Kennedy who simply did not know Vietnam, its recent history, or the personalities and forces in contention. I concluded that under such leadership, and given the extremely difficult circumstances in Vietnam, we would never be able to succeed there. I finally and imprudently for such meetings blurted out that I thought we should now consider "withdrawal with honor." Dean Rusk and Lyndon Johnson's responses, cavalier dismissals of this thought, were indicative precisely of what I felt: that these men were leading themselves down a garden path to tragedy. We could not consider thoughts of withdrawal because of our will to "see it through," a euphemism once more hiding the fear of our top leadership that it might look weak—to Congress and the U.S. public even more than to the Soviets.[17]

Missing Our Last Best Chance

Despite the varied and largely undocumented accounts to the effect that Diem through Nhu had sought, before the coup, to engage in some sort of dialogue with the Communists, it is most unlikely that he personally ever entertained such notions—it simply was not in the nature of the man. It is possible, however, that Nhu either held or simulated some meetings with Communist contacts in order to convey scare signals to the United States during the period September-October 1963 when the Ngo regime stock in U.S. policy had sunk to its lowest point.[18]

In retrospect, it is at least somewhat odd that the United States, which had been willing to resume negotiations with the Communist powers over Laos, was not apparently willing to do so in Vietnam. While events in the year 1961, including the decision to negotiate on Laos, had perhaps made it all-important that the United States show toughness in Vietnam, the situation there could still have been reconsidered in 1963, after the detrimental internal balance that had existed in 1961 had at least to some presumed extent been improved. In 1963 we still had a going concern in Vietnam—a weakening asset to be sure, but one which the Communist powers might still have been willing to bargain over. The best moment for any such bargaining would probably have been immediately after the coup that overthrew Ngo Dinh Diem.

In the first place, as already indicated, Diem himself would never have agreed to negotiations with the Communists over South Vietnam, whether within a resumed Geneva conference framework or otherwise. Second, the junta around Big Minh contained men, including Minh himself but principally his foreign affairs counselors Gen. Le Van Kim and former Foreign Minister Tran Van Do, the latter restored to some influence after a period of disgrace under Diem, who saw the task ahead as chiefly political and diplomatic, not military. These men, who also included Gen. Tran Van Don and the pro-Buddhist former Foreign Minister (under Diem) Vu Van Mau, might have made good use in any such enterprise of their surviving and in some respects important contacts with leading French personalities. The French, like the Vatican and Polish (ICC) representatives then in Saigon, would almost certainly have been only too glad to lend good offices. As early as 1961, de Gaulle had counseled Kennedy not to get mired down in Vietnam [19] and in the summer of 1963, as he did again one year later, he had issued a call for compromise and negotiations.

Under these circumstances, had the U.S. government been able and willing properly and calmly to analyze matters in November-December 1963 it might have concluded that its chances for preserving at least a vestige of a neutralized and non-aligned South Vietnam after negotiations with the Communist were probably better than its chances of successfully achieving its counterinsurgency objectives. Observers in the field were telling it that the battle situation was turning sour, while the political situation was chaotic. Even McNamara was pessimistic during the Honolulu Conference held to review the situation on November 20, 1963.[20] As it was, failure of analysis resulted from a host of factors which had already plagued the United States for many years during the high cold war, and which we will examine in much greater detail in Chapter V; but it resulted also from the feverish and near-chaotic atmosphere in which foreign policy was being conducted in Washington toward the end of the Kennedy administration, and from the president's assassination on November 22, 1963. After Vice President Johnson assumed the presidency, the same inexpert but willful men continued their advisory role to the president on Vietnam.

3. Decision to Start "Rolling Thunder," February 1965

The bombing of North Vietnam, which started in sustained fashion in February 1965, was called "Rolling Thunder." This graphic code name for the operation well conveys the fact that although the bombing started in earnest at the end of February, after a brief period of so-called "tit for tat" retaliatory strikes, it was continuously interrupted for pauses to permit cease-fires, negotiation efforts, or other reasons and it was never unlimited in scope. As the code name suggests, the thunder would come and go, mostly south of the 20th parallel at first, later increasingly all over North Vietnam including the boundary zones with Laos and China, and with greater frequency in 1966-68 in the key region of Hanoi-Haiphong.

The decision to start bombing the North, which was over a year (1964) in preparation and has been treated in a considerable amount of literature,[21] followed inexorably from the previous decisions to wage counterinsurgency warfare in South Vietnam and to "see it through our way," continuing this effort after the fall of the Diem regime and without having reviewed or redefined the U.S. stakes in Vietnam. It was an extremely fateful decision because it brought about precisely the opposite of what its authors and proponents had hoped. Rather than bringing the Vietnamese Communists to the conference table to negotiate on U.S. terms it stiffened their resistance as well as their capabilities to fight the United States and the South Vietnamese to a standstill on the ground. Accordingly, this decision in turn inexorably set in motion the later U.S. decision to send ground combat forces to Vietnam.

All during 1964, as both the political and the military situations continued to deteriorate in South Vietnam, the United States contemplated the recommendation of the "graduated escalation" school of thought led—again!—by Professor Walt W. Rostow. This school recommended the start of a systematic but carefully tailored bombing program against North Vietnam. The program was envisaged by its advocates to fulfill three mutually reinforcing aims: First, to inflict damage and pain on North Vietnam, with the hoped-for effect of signaling our determination to the North Vietnamese and demoralizing it to the point where it would perceive the uselessness and cost of continuing its support of the rebellion in the South. (An additional aim in nature of a rationale was subsequently added to this first, namely that bombing the North would similarly signal our determination to the South and greatly reinforce the latter's morale and willingness to fight.) Second, to derogate seriously from the assumed ability of the North Vietnamese to supply their cohorts in the South by cutting off their routes of supply, forcing incessant repairs of trails and roads, and in general harassing and weakening the logistical support capabilities of the North for the South. Third, to "bring North Vietnam to the negotiating table," that is to create conditions conducive to eventual negotiations on U.S. terms. U.S. terms originally were, in essence, the following. "If you agree to leave the South alone, we will stop the bombing." *Ad nauseam,* Secretary Rusk repeated: "All they have to do (to stop the bombing, or end the war), is to leave the South alone." [22] Of these three objectives, the last was probably the most important in the minds of key U.S. planners, if not necessarily of U.S. military commanders. It was this aim that eventually persuaded National Security Advisor McGeorge Bundy and consequently President Johnson to adopt the bombing policy in February 1965.

Graduated Escalation

Thunder starts with a distant soft roll which slowly gives way to a deafening explosive roar. The advocates wanted us to start softly, and, depending on the results obtained, to move (with B-52s) into a deafening roar. This idea of "graduated escalation" requires some detailed analyzing, largely so we can understand why it was so unsuccessful in impressing the Vietnamese Communists in the manner contemplated by its authors. Like "flexible response," which came to replace "massive retaliation" in strategic (nuclear) war doctrine, after Secretary McNamara endorsed it in the early sixties,[23] graduated escalation or pressure was a relatively crude national security policy distillation of complex academic thinking stimulated by economist Thomas Schelling's book *The Strategy of Conflict* (1959), later further refined in Schelling's *Arms and Influence* (1966).

Schelling at Harvard and his colleagues in many think tanks reasoned, briefly put, as follows. The United States has devastating retaliatory capabilities. Threatening to use them massively will weaken deterrence (that is the objective of obviating the need to employ them at all) not only because their massive employment is getting less credible as the enemy gains similar capabilities, but also because it bars the United States from contemplating refined uses of its capabilities, i.e., uses tailored to what may be less than maximal threats. Massive retaliation thus forces planning only in terms of what Schelling and others called "spasm war"—or the massive and continuous ejection of the whole nuclear arsenal. Because of its destructiveness and consequent immorality, this is in reality unthinkable. Therefore, new concepts of "refined deterrence" were needed, under which the United States might be able to utter the threat say of delivering only one nuclear bomb (rather than the whole arsenal) if the threat it was countering or the stakes it was defending were worth only one bomb. If the threat or stakes increased, the United States could gradually escalate the retaliatory blow.

Flexible response as a doctrine for strategic nuclear war was never really popular in Europe or well understood there, although it is certainly still the order of the day. On the other hand, the United States had successfully used refined means of deterrence in connection with the Berlin crisis of 1961. U.S. threats there had not been total; U.S. response had been flexible and tailored, but it had occurred; and the Soviets, having built their wall and dammed-in their East German subjects, had relented. There never again was a serious Soviet-U.S. crisis over Berlin after the confrontation of U.S. and Soviet tanks at "Checkpoint Charlie" in late October 1961. Ten years later, the Quadripartite Agreements of 1971 on Berlin were to be signed by the French, British, Soviets, and United States. They effectively settled an issue that had brought the superpowers into hostile confrontation almost uninterruptedly during the high cold war.

Moreover, and even more significantly, the United States had successfully used "refined deterrence" in the Cuban Missile Crisis of October 1962, the most serious direct Soviet-U.S. confrontation of the entire cold war. Some high-ranking leaders of the National Security Council's executive committee or Excom—which operated only under President Kennedy and included his brother Robert, the attorney general—had advocated bombing against, or militarily invading Cuba after the Soviets had established operational offensive missile launchers in Cuba targeted against U.S. territory. Kennedy and some of his principal advisors, including McNamara, Robert Kennedy, and Adlai Stevenson, had resisted this course of action. They had instead used the refined means of signaling to the Soviet Union through use of the quarantine (or blockade) at sea U.S. determination that no further missiles would be installed in Cuba and that those already there would have to be removed. Simultaneously, the United States had remained in communications with the Soviets, partly through the Kennedy-Khrushchev exchange of "hot line" correspondence, and partly through direct contacts carried out by Robert Kennedy and Soviet Ambassador Dobrynin with the assistance of private parties. The policy of refined deterrence had worked in the Cuban Missile Crisis, providing the president with renewed U.S. public as well as international support. The U.S. national security bureaucracy had thereby been strongly reinforced in the notion that it was a correct approach. The same approach had even been successfully used in devising the "salami-slicing" tactics by which U.S.

aid to Diem had been slowly diminished in September-October 1963, signaling to the potential army coup-makers in Vietnam that the road was open to them.

However, North Vietnam was not the Soviet Union in Berlin, or the Soviet Union in Cuba. The Vietnamese Communist leaders in Hanoi's DRV and in the South's Viet Cong or National Liberation Front (NLFSVN) were men of a mold and mind entirely different from that of the members or leaders of the Politburo in Moscow. The latter, after all, like their counterparts in the United States, operated in the extraordinarily volatile and sophisticated environment of push-button nuclear war. The Communist leaders in Vietnam were rough and primitive in comparison. The refined sophistication of graduated pressure or escalation seemed to elude them completely.

Opposition's Arguments

Those who argued against "Rolling Thunder" and the application of graduated escalation techniques to North Vietnam through bombing strategies reasoned, in the main, that these Vietnamese Communists would be impervious to the type of highly sophisticated war gaming in which it was suggested the United States engage itself. The main points which the opponents of the bombing policy marshalled were as follows, although to recount them here has a certain aura of futility since, in the end, only part of one of them was persuasive to top U.S. policy-makers.

1. North Vietnamese targets were few and not easily replaceable; thus, as more-or-less one-time targets, they were not really subject to sequentially harsher bombing.
2. North Vietnamese support and supply to the Viet Cong in South Vietnam was not essentially of the linear type, at least in the period before a full net of roads and trails could be completed along Vietnam's western borders. This supply operated instead in a seamless webb type system, which U.S. forces (and civilians) had difficulty in apprehending because it was so unique. Small craft marine transport; transport by primitive means such as handcarts and bicycles; massive employment of male, female, and youthful manpower; deception; and the prepositioning of weapons caches played at least as important a role in this system of supply as roads and trails. Moreover, important supplies were being provided through smuggling in commercial sea-going transports landing either in Sihanoukville, Cambodia, or directly in Saigon, where the United States consistently failed to obtain accurate inspection of customs procedures. In any case, this system of supply was essentially impervious to ever more severe bombing runs on the North.
3. Vietnamese Communist morale was unlikely to be adversely affected by U.S. bombing of North Vietnam. On the contrary, and especially given the North Vietnamese population's experience with the previous Indochina

war, support for the Hanoi leadership was likely to be bolstered and consolidated by conditions conducive to the creation of an atmosphere that could be depicted as open imperialist aggression. Hanoi would then ask that this be countered by a no-sacrifice-barred policy of survival and liberation.

4. Leaving aside the legal implications of a U.S. bombing policy against a non-declared enemy, which at this time (February 1965) was not formally at war with the United States or even acknowledging the presence of any of its forces or elements in South Vietnam, world public opinion would not long sanction a spectacle of torture being administered by the world's greatest superpower against a small, distant, backward, and relatively defenseless Asian peasant state. On this last point, it is important to note for the sake of the historical record that the United States had no valid evidence in hand in late 1964 or early 1965 of the presence of any significant numbers of North Vietnamese regular forces—as distinct from the reinfiltrated southern Communist cadres, who had been returning south in growing numbers after 1959—in South Vietnam. It is certainly clear that no formations of the Peoples Army of Vietnam (PAVN) entered South Vietnam as regular units until after sustained bombing started in late February 1965.[24]

5. Finally, opponents of "Rolling Thunder" within the national security and foreign affairs bureaucracies argued that the graduated bombing policy was inherently dangerous when applied to North Vietnam because it would almost certainly lead the Vietnamese Communists to retaliate by the easiest means at their disposal, namely, the despatching of increasingly large and eventually massive combat forces in the South. Further, it would undoubtedly provoke both the Soviet Union and the Chinese Communists. This would be so because of the existence in North Vietnam of a bona fide socialist republic which had long been an acknowledged and valued member of the socialist bloc, and which could not be allowed to go under without severe loss of prestige to both the Soviet Union and China. Moreover, the simple factor of propinquity, of having a long and exposed Sino-Vietnam border zone, would make the policy appear extremely threatening to the security of the People's Republic of China, as well as—from both the Soviet and Chinese points of view—to the existing balance of forces in East Asia.

The Inner Circle

The validity of that part of the opponents' argument which concerned the Soviet Union and China was on the whole accepted by the small inner circle of top decision-makers who were now increasingly, and in near total secrecy, making U.S. Indochina policies. This circle essentially consisted of a more and more tormented President Johnson; a suddenly rather bloodthirsty McGeorge Bundy—he had been exposed first-hand to the horrors of a Viet Cong attack on a U.S. military barracks in Pleiku;[25] an ever-optimistic Walt Rostow—shortly to assume Bundy's position as national security advisor; an ever-cool, cost-conscious, methodical, and self-confident McNamara; an always impassive, sphinx-like Dean Rusk, who had Johnson's entire confidence; and, in the field, an ever-reflective and analytically inclined yet strangely politically uncomprehending Gen. Maxwell Taylor, now the new ambassador to Vietnam. These men were "the principals."

Some steps removed from the inner circle, the players were Gen. William Westmoreland, head of what was now called MACV (Military Assistance Command, Vietnam), who shrewdly foresaw that the bombing policy would inevitably lead to the entry of U.S. ground forces; Admiral Sharp, theater commander of the Pacific at Honolulu, whose thinking, appropriately for a military man, was entirely strategic and whose instincts, again appropriately, pushed him to reject refined escalatory maneuvers; and lesser top officials, men such as William Bundy, assistant secretary of state, and John McNaughton, assistant secretary of defense, whose refined and sophisticated doubts about the refined and sophisticated policy of graduated pressure were simply too complex to be forcefully conveyed to the principals (although McNaughton was later instrumental in slowly changing some of McNamara's preconceptions).

Acceptance by the principals of the constraints which Russia and China imposed explains why the United States never fully went to war or never launched a ground invasion of North Vietnam, whatever contingency plans may have at one time or another existed in the minds or file cabinets of U.S. military commanders during the later stages of the war. But the risks of carefully controlled, tailored bombing of North Vietnam were accepted; and the Russians and Chinese were judged, correctly as it proved, unlikely to intervene in the war at least so long as the survival of the Democratic Republic of Vietnam was not directly threatened. As a result, great care was taken in Washington, most particularly at the White House where President Johnson himself spent hours pouring over lists and maps of North Vietnamese targets, that U.S. intentions not be inadvertently misread in Moscow or Peking.

The off-and-on, tailored air war on North Vietnam was from its adoption in late February 1965 difficult for the U.S. military and the U.S. public to understand. It consequently became an endless source of frustration for the armed forces, misunderstanding for and by the media and the U.S. public, and chagrin for the nervously concerned White House. Many "hawks"[26] would simply ask, and with considerable public support in 1965-68: "Since we're bombing them anyway, why don't we simply let them have it with all we've got?" To that question, crude and simplistic as it may have seemed, civilian sophisticates at the White House, State Department, or Defense Department never had a satisfactory answer. General Curtis Le May may not only have been immoral, deeply unwise, and dead wrong in advocating the bombing of North

Vietnam back into the Stone Age, but given the administration's half-war policy, his position seemed to make common sense. More of that in later chapters of this book.

Tonkin Gulf Resolution and U.S. Politics

The advocates of Rolling Thunder had the upper hand throughout 1964 in the inner councils of the U.S. government, as the situation in Vietnam proper steadily deteriorated. The succession of civilian-led governments appointed by Gen. Nguyen Khanh was getting nowhere in reducing Buddhist-led civil dissent, improving the South Vietnamese economic or social situation, or infusing the ARVN with fighting spirit or proper leadership. Counterinsurgency, U.S.-style, was proving a failure. Even Gen. Maxwell Taylor, appointed in mid-1964 to replace Ambassador Lodge in Saigon when the latter (briefly) entertained notions of obtaining the Republican presidential nomination, found himself almost totally frustrated. In his case, as in that of others who slowly came around to Rostow's well-staffed briefs for escalation in 1964, frustration with the existing situation was as much a reason as any other. At least, the bombing would dramatically relieve the slow, grinding march to the disaster which almost any observer could then forecast just around the corner in South Vietnam. At least, bombing the North would be better than doing nothing. Or would it?

But the advocates of bombing did not show their hand pending the November 1964 U.S. elections. What they were waiting for was some dramatic event which would allow the Congress to support them. Even if they obtained it, as they did in the Tonkin Gulf incidents of the summer of 1964, they still would not move to sustained bombing until the elections were safely behind them. And even then, the initial bombing policy would be one of "tit-for-tat" retaliatory strikes in its first few weeks.

What happened in the Tonkin Gulf in mid-1964 has been the subject of several analyses.[27] In short, there is little doubt that the first attack by North Vietnamese PT boats on U.S. destroyers in the Gulf was provoked by covert (code named "34A") South Vietnamese island-landing assault operations proceeding along the North Vietnamese coast nearby, even though the U.S. destroyers' commanders were unaware of such operations. As to the second attack, it is uncertain whether it ever in fact occurred; but if it did, it was clearly responsive to the presence of U.S. "DeSoto Patrol" destroyers on reconnaissance missions so close to the North Vietnamese coast.

Administration leaders seized on these incidents with alacrity to pull-out a proposed joint congressional resolution, a draft of which had been reposing in Assistant Secretary of State William P. Bundy's drawer for several months in preparation for just such an eventuality.[28] The draft resolution, supporting the president in his determination to take all necessary measures to repel what was depicted as a deliberate and systematic campaign of aggression by the North Vietnamese against their neighbors,[29] was lobbied quickly through both houses and passed with only two dissenting votes (those of Senators Gruening of Alaska and Morse of Oregon, the latter an opponent of the administration's policies in Indochina virtually from their inception). Thereafter, the Tonkin Gulf Resolution became the standard document by which the Johnson administration claimed congressional support for its undeclared war and justified the constitutionality of its subsequent moves and policies toward Vietnam. *The president never went to Congress again, even when a few months later he started despatching U.S. ground combat forces.* But the Congress later turned with great force on the president, as we shall see in subsequent chapters.

Johnson ran his deceitful electoral campaign of the fall of 1964 on the promise not to send American boys to die again in a land war in Asia. He brushed lightly over the desperate internal situation in South Vietnam and held out the promise that it would improve shortly. He did not mention the forthcoming bombing, other than to denounce his opponent, Senator Barry Goldwater of Arizona, for advocating it openly, characterizing him as a wild-eyed warmonger who would land us into war with China. Johnson won overwhelmingly, by one of the biggest landslides ever given to a presidential candidate in U.S. history.

While all this was happening in the open arena, a small group of officials within the State Department was endeavoring behind the scenes to restrain the U.S. government's headlong slide into bombing and, inexorably, into land war in Indochina. Regrettably, several factors worked against this group in terms of bureaucratic-political warfare within the U.S. government. First, with one exception, its members were middle or lower ranking officials—men like William Trueheart, former deputy chief of mission in Saigon; Allen Whiting, deputy director of East Asian Research in State; Robert Johnson, a member of the Policy Planning Council; Carl Salans, of the Legal Advisor's Office— who lacked pulling power against men of the stature of Taylor, the Bundy brothers, Rostow, or Gen. Earle Wheeler, the new chairman of the Joint Chiefs of Staff. Second, they did not constitute a coherent group or force within the bureaucracy but rather worked individually and apart. Third, they failed to move across departmental lines to seek allies in agencies like Defense and CIA or even in the Congress. Finally, they were all just sufficiently career oriented not to dare pit their personal futures on the single issue of stopping the slide toward bombing. Most of them felt that gestures such as press statements or resignations would, in the context of these early times, have proved futile in any case.[30]

The one exception was Undersecretary of State George Ball who not only opposed the policy of escalation but determinedly and vigorously dissented with our policy of deep engagement in Indochina. A summation of Ball's views, which were frequently and honestly expressed directly and privately to President Johnson, who always gave him a hearing, can be found cogently stated in the Ball memorandum of July 1, 1965,[31] which deals principally with the entry of U.S. ground forces and the need for a compromise solution to cut our losses. It was thus written well after Rolling Thunder had started. However, Ball vigorously opposed the bombing policy in 1964 and 1965. But Ball too, was a loner, who conceived his role principally as that of a personal advocate of dissent to the president. He too failed, or did not want to see that the U.S. government's slide to disaster might have been arrested only by the formation of a strong countervailing coalition of bureaucratic-political power to oppose that of the inner circle. A coalition similar, perhaps, to that formed by and under President Eisenhower to resist the Nixon-Radford-Dulles axis favoring U.S. intervention at Dien Bien Phu. Even then, had a comparable coalition been formed in 1964-65, it is by no means certain that the Johnson-led march to deepening involvement could have been stopped.

Effects of Rolling Thunder

Rolling Thunder was a fateful U.S. decision in Vietnam primarily because it brought about what its opponents feared, massive ground retaliation by the North Vietnamese, without bringing what its proponents sought, the DRV to the conference table on terms then acceptable to the United States. Before February 1965, the presence of PAVN units in South Vietnam could not be validly documented, although Communist military, technical, supply, intelligence, and propaganda cadres (both northern and southern in origin) infiltrated from North Vietnam, had certainly been there in sizable numbers since the early sixties. But after February 1965, first regiments and later divisions of PAVN started to come down across the Laos border trails, over the demilitarized zone along the 17th parallel, by sea, and by other circuitous routes such as through Laos and Cambodia. With that, the threat to the continued existence of a non-Communist South Vietnamese regime in Saigon grew even larger than it had loomed throughout 1964. The determination of the DRV not to respond to U.S.

sophistry and accede to the U.S. demand that it leave South Vietnam alone grew even stronger.

The groundwork was thus laid for the coming fateful U.S. decision to send ground combat forces to South Vietnam. But before we turn to that decision we must examine briefly how one final chance for decent exit was missed by the United States in Vietnam.

4. Decision to Discard the DRV Four Points, April-May 1965

The story has been told of U.S. failure to give consequence to an apparently sincere Italian mediation offer in the fall of 1965.[32] This offer, prompted by Prime Minister Amitore Fanfani on the basis of reports by two Italian professors who met DRV leaders in Hanoi, was based on the existence of the so-called "Four Points Program" of the Democratic Republic of Vietnam, on the basis of which a cease-fire and a negotiated settlement of the Vietnam War might presumably have been achieved.

But the DRV Four Points well antedated their discovery by the two Italian professors. They were in fact first officially communicated to the United States as early as April 1965 in the form of an official note from the French government. The note stipulated that the official representative of the Democratic Republic of Vietnam in Paris, Consul General Mai Van Bo, had been authorized by his government to transmit to France (and accordingly, to the United States) a four-point program which the DRV considered formed the basis for a correct solution to the Vietnam problem.[33] The note did not say "formed the *only* basis for a solution," but simply "formed *the basis* for a correct solution"—a distinction which is important since it indicated, if one so wished to consider it, a degree of elasticity in the DRV position. What the DRV was here offering was negotiation on the basis of its Four Points, and not simply a "take it or leave it" or a propaganda statement. If it had been the former, it would have been presented as the "only correct solution"; and if it had been the latter, it would not have been sent officially through the French government with a stipulation which the DRV obviously wanted passed on to the United States.

Moreover, and this is really the important aspect, the DRV Four Points were conveyed in this manner shortly *after* the beginning of the bombing program but shortly *before* the introduction of U.S. ground combat forces, which by April 1965 must have appeared imminent to the DRV. The United States had already deployed Marine units in Danang to defend its Hawk air-defense missile installations there; these units already had permission to patrol aggressively within a wide perimeter outside their bases; and they were manifestly engaged in preparations for the arrival of still more Marine units.

The Four Points themselves called for: (1) withdrawal of U.S. forces from Vietnam and cancellation of U.S.-South Vietnamese military ties; (2) respect for the military provisions of the 1954 Geneva accords pending Vietnam's reunification; (3) settlement of South Vietnam's internal affairs in accordance with the program of the National Liberation Front; (4) no foreign involvement or interference in the reunification of Vietnam. Even a cursory look at these four points indicated that points one, two, and four accorded basically with recently reiterated positions of the United States. Since 1964, as the internal situation in Vietnam had deteriorated steadily while an increasingly desperate United States contemplated escalation, the United States had volunteered in numerous statements by top officials including the president that it sought no bases in or permanent military ties with South Vietnam, and that it was willing to revert to the Geneva accords of 1954 as the basis for a proper solution to the Vietnam War.[34] Therefore, only point three offered significant obstacles. If one looked up the National Liberation Front's program, one found largely a reiteration of the 1954 Geneva political and military provisions, but one also found the National Liberation Front pointedly listed as one of the parties that must be directly involved in settling South Vietnam's internal affairs.

While Washington immediately recoiled at this DRV third point, several questions must be raised in this regard. First, since the conflict in South Vietnam before the introduction of massive U.S. and DRV ground forces was essentially one between the National Liberation Front (Viet Cong) and the government of the Republic of Vietnam, how could one legitimately have expected one of the two fighting parties not to be involved in the settlement? But second, even if that proved unacceptable, why not focus on the DRV's opening for negotiations—i.e., that this program formed *the basis* for a correct solution, not necessarily the solution itself—rather than on the substance of its proposal? After all, serious negotiations always open with gambits and end, if they do at all, with agreements greatly at variance with opening positions. And finally, did Washington fail to realize that this moment in time was a crucial one, that it was the moment after bombing had started and before ground forces had been massively introduced by either party?

Furthermore, why did Washington apparently cavalierly dismiss the fact that the DRV note had been transmitted to it by one of the then highest ranking officials of the French Foreign Office? Washington was cognizant of de Gaulle's displeasure with the U.S. role in Vietnam and of his offers in mid-1963, and in more elaborate fashion in mid-1964, to convene a new Geneva-style international conference on the problem. Moreover, as the United States discovered later (1968), France and Paris were the DRV's preferred conduits to the West.

The DRV was probably well aware of the frustration arising at the top of the U.S. government in the weeks and months immediately following the initiation of Rolling Thunder, when this program showed itself as forecast by its opponents, to have little or no effect.[35] At a minimum, the DRV was probably seizing this opportunity to present the United States with a serious and final chance to halt its bombing in return for a DRV commitment not to send massive ground forces in South Vietnam. At best, from the DRV's point of view, the U.S. would use negotiations to disengage itself altogether from Vietnam on what might have been acceptable, even honorable political terms before it started the introduction of U.S. ground combat forces, thereby confronting the DRV's long-term objectives in South Vietnam with formidable odds.

However, the U.S. inner circle, which had conceived Rolling Thunder largely in order to bring the DRV to the conference table, was unwilling seriously to respond to this DRV offer to engage it in a dialogue on the Four Points. After first ignoring the offer, the United States several months later, and after its ground combat forces build-up had already begun in South Vietnam, embarked on an exploration of the DRV Four Points in the so-called "XYZ Affair." [36] This brought absolutely no results.

The conclusion seems justified that in the late spring of 1965, the United States simply did not want to negotiate in Vietnam—on any terms. The original key objective of Rolling Thunder, to bring the DRV to the conference table, had been at least temporarily abandoned. U.S. terms had never meant a surrender of the DRV, or even its abandonment of the 1954 Geneva provisions as a framework for solution, merely that the DRV should leave the South alone. But now, Washington was spoiling for real war; it was enthralled, and its top officials entirely preoccupied, by new scenarios in the brewing; the war had, in a sense, been taken over by its own momentum; and Washington did not want to talk at all.

By failing to negotiate seriously on the DRV Four Points note of April 1965, the United States made a fateful decision, because it lost its last chance to settle with the Vietnamese Communists before incurring the costs of real war.

5. Decision to Send U.S. Combat Forces to Vietnam, Spring-Summer 1965

This extremely fateful decision followed inexorably from the previous step of initiating the sustained bombing of the North, which had in turn followed inexorably from the failure of counterinsurgency on the ground. It followed inexorably because, as already pointed out, bombing failed to achieve its aims either of bringing the DRV quickly to its knees, or bolstering the situation on the ground in the South to a point where it would at least begin to improve. Instead, bombing brought about the massive, though gradual, introduction of PAVN troops into the South; while in the South itself the politico-military situation was not improving. Neither had it improved a year later, in March 1966 when ARVN in a series of battles in central Vietnam crushed remaining Buddhist dissidence there. In fact, these secondary battles against the virtually unarmed Buddhists had serious splintering effects upon the ARVN and Vietnamese civilian top leadership, and caused the loss or defection of some of the best ARVN commanders, such as Gen. Nguyen Chanh Thi.[37]

By late April 1965, the war situation still looked desperate to U.S. principals gathered for a meeting convened by McNamara in Honolulu, and it was recommended that U.S. forces enter the war directly. President Johnson approved this recommendation so promptly, and Gen. Westmoreland was so quick in responding with very high figures [38] to requests from the Pentagon as to the size of U.S. forces he would require, that Ambassador Taylor was compelled in a series of messages to Washington to urge restraint.[39]

The decision to send ground combat forces was probably reached more quickly and with less staffing, planning, and forethought—except by Gen. Westmoreland and the MACV staff in Saigon—than any comparable fateful decision ever made in U.S. history. While over one year had elapsed before President Johnson had finally and still reluctantly acted on the proposals for Rolling Thunder, and while during this period the Congress had at least had a chance to express itself in the Tonkin Gulf Resolution, nothing comparable occurred in this instance. One reason for this certainly was the much greater sense of political security that President Johnson felt after having been overwhelmingly elected in his own right. Moreover, an atmosphere of inevitability had gradually settled over the Washington national security bureaucracy with respect to the Vietnam War. We have already indicated that Washington at this point no longer wanted to negotiate. If we said that it was spoiling for real war, that was not entirely correct; what it was actually doing was settling for the inevitability of a long, drawn-out war involving U.S. ground forces.

Everything had been tried, everything had failed, and everyone was fatigued. Nonetheless, lassitude in the bureaucracy on the one hand and the president's politically reinforced ebullience on the other could hardly justify the failure to carefully measure the impact on the U.S. armed forces, on our manpower reserve capabilities, on our worldwide strategic posture, and above all on the U.S. economy itself, of plunging headlong into such a ground war.

As already indicated, Marine units first went ashore near Danang in Central Vietnam in March-April 1965 ostensibly to protect ground air-defense installations. (It might be worth noting here in passing the fact that the DRV never introduced air tactical or strategic units into, or penetrated South Vietnamese air space during the entire span of the second Indochina war, 1959-75, whether or not it had the capabilities. On the other hand, North Vietnamese tactical air defenses—both ground and air—proved extremely effective, particularly after 1966, against U.S. bomber and bomber-defense aircraft over North Vietnam.) Additional U.S. ground forces with unspecified roles were shortly added to the first Marines. Most likely, their purpose was to prepare for the arrival of the Marine and airborne divisions which Westmoreland requested and quickly obtained in the spring, summer and fall of 1965. The general objective was set at about 150,000 U.S. ground forces—not counting counterinsurgency elements already in place—by the end of 1965; but the important point is that all this was to occur gradually and in stages, conveying the impression that indeed it had not been intended or systematically planned out.

The ingenious (or disingenious?) mind of our restless and deceptive president considered it vital that the United States and especially the Congress not "go to war," but "find itself at war"—in a situation from which it could neither retrieve its ground forces by withdrawing them, nor fail to support them with every means that fighting men on a dangerous distant battleground required. This scheme was fully accepted by Westmoreland, who played it to the hilt; but not by Taylor, to whom it represented the defeat of sophisticated war and the start of a potentially uncontrollable ascent by military strategists of the all-or-nothing school. It worked almost to perfection.

The initial congressional and public reaction was one of puzzlement at the incremental and gradual nature of the steps being taken. If only a relatively few forces were being dispatched to fight what was now becoming "our war" in Vietnam, it must mean that they would be there for only a very short period. No need, accordingly, to mobilize the reserves, or to take action on the budget or on other defense dispositions. No need either to press the president to "show them all we've got"; he was doing the necessary already. This was precisely the reaction Johnson intended; it gave him a maximum of latitude to pursue both his cherished domestic and his war programs, and it kept Congress off his back. In the summer of 1965, with the transformation of counterinsurgency and graduated escalation into "our war," Ambassador Taylor resigned his post to pass it on, once more, to Ambassador Henry Cabot Lodge, whose incarnation as a major general in the U.S. Army Reserve was coming to life, his incarnation as a potential presidential candidate having been shelved.

The inner circle's decision to make it "our war," most likely made by President Johnson, Secretary McNamara and Secretary Rusk over their "Tuesday Lunch" table,[40] took little if any account of the pessimism with which most U.S. experts—many military as well as civilian—at the second, third or lower echelons of government regarded such a fateful step. *(A personal note:* I was working in State's Policy Planning Council in the spring of 1965 when Chester Cooper, then White House advisor on Southeast Asian Affairs, asked me what I thought the effects would be "in the entirely hypothetical event we were to consider introducing U.S. ground forces." I recall saying, "500,000 men; 10,000 casualties; 5 to 10 years; and then what?" I was entirely too optimistic! 500,000 men; 55,000 casualties [U.S. dead only]; 8 years; and then Communist victory, is how it ended. These input, casualty, and time figures, and their consequence, are strikingly similar to those incurred by the forces of the Fourth French Republic in the first Indochina war.)

Ending Some Fictions

The decision to enter the Vietnam War with U.S. ground combat forces ended the fiction that U.S. intervention in Vietnam was in the nature of assistance only, with the authorities and forces of the RVN conducting the war and responsible for its strategy. In fact, the United States had been running the war for a good many years already, and it had certainly been supervising the government of RVN—whatever there was of it—also. Now that it was directly in the war the fiction that "American don't fire in Vietnam" died once and for all, and with it the fiction that "RVN or ARVN commands." From now on it was clear that MACV, first in the person of Gen. Westmoreland and later Gen. Creighton Abrams, was in command of the war. His chain went through CINCPAC (Admirals Ulysses G. Sharp and later John McCain) to the Joint Chiefs of Staff (JCS) and the White House. An always uneasy relationship was established by the commanders with the American ambassadors in Vietnam—first Taylor, later Lodge on his second tour, then Ellsworth Bunker and finally Graham Martin.

The ambassadors, assisted by numerous high-ranking deputies, were responsible for political liaison with the Vietnamese government, which was shortly to become entirely militarized first under Marshall Nguyen Cao Ky and later Gen. Nguyen Van Thieu, and for the conduct of what came to be known as "pacification" or the "other war." It should be noted here that while MACV possessed more of the power resources in Vietnam (manpower and weapons), he did not control CIA or the resources of "pacification," which were in the hands of the ambassadors. The White House itself continued to control the air war over North Vietnam.

The fact that we had now taken over the war did not keep President Johnson from evoking the role of the Vietnamese leadership whenever he felt it advantageous to do so. When it suited him, he would trundle out Ky or Thieu as the great leaders of our valiant allies who would, or would not, allow certain courses of action which Johnson did, or did not, favor. Nonetheless, as far as the American public was concerned, the Vietnamese tended increasingly to fade out of sight as the United States took over the war and television brought to every U.S. living room the sight of GIs putting the torch to Viet Cong "hooches."

The entry of U.S. ground forces also put an end to the fiction that the DRV was not intervening directly in South Vietnam, but providing only moral and material advice and support to the National Liberation Front. The DRV, no more than the United States, formally admitted after 1965 that it *commanded* Communist operations in the South, and it went well beyond credibility in continuing formally to deny the outright presence of major PAVN units in South Vietnam. But, with the possible exception of some very credulous U.S. anti-war protesters, this fiction fell nonetheless. The DRV at no time after 1965 hesitated to speak for both North and "liberated and struggling" South Vietnam in world forums or in international councils. No serious observer, East or West, doubted its full-fledged military engagement in the South.

Although the U.S. continued after 1965 to respect the line of partition at the 17th parallel *on the ground*—and this for reasons we discussed earlier in terms of the DRV's importance to the Soviet Union and the People's Republic of China—it tended increasingly to blur the distinction between bombing North Vietnam south and north of the 20th parallel. Intermittent bombing pauses for purposes of temporary holiday cease-fires in the South, as well as for occasional U.S. sallies into presumed efforts at negotiations, did continue after 1965 and before 1968; but the frequent bombing of targets in the sensitive Hanoi-

Haiphong area signalled clearly that, for the foreseeable future, the United States was at war with North Vietnam in Indochina.

6. Post-Tet Decision to Seek Honorable Disengagement, 1968

President Johnson's "abdication speech" of March 31, 1968 marked the beginning of the end of our deep involvement in Indochina and the start of our efforts at disengagement. It was a decision cast in the form of a domestic political speech after weeks and months of complicated top-level maneuverings and consultations to bring about the president's ultimately firm but never easy resolve. These maneuvers among top politicians and officials in Washington have been fully described by Townsend Hoopes [41] and others and need no additional recounting here. The president, after three years of the optimism floated into his ear by Gen. Westmoreland and by his national security advisor, Rostow, found it difficult to believe that the Viet Cong could "keep on coming"—as they had demonstrated so powerfully in the Tet offensive of February 1968. During Tet, they had temporarily seized every provincial capital in South Vietnam and much of the city of Saigon and held the ancient capital city of Hue for nearly a month. But by March, Johnson had once again come to believe that Tet was the enemy's last gasp. He therefore found it hard to understand that Secretary McNamara wanted out of office.

Johnson ultimately turned to an *ad hoc* council of outsiders and elder statesmen for advice. The latter—including such luminaries as former Secretary of State Dean Acheson; former Undersecretary of State George Ball; former JCS Chairman Gen. Omar Bradley; former National Security Advisor McGeorge Bundy; former Ambassador Henry Cabot Lodge (replaced in Saigon by Amb. Bunker); former Undersecretary of State Robert Murphy; former Army Chief of Staff Gen. Matthew Ridgway; and former JCS Chairman and Ambassador Maxwell Taylor; among other illustrious persons—firmly counseled him to seek disengagement without victory. They had been briefed by men like former Saigon Embassy Political Counselor Philip Habib, who on this solemn occasion told them honestly that there was no light at the end of the tunnel in Vietnam.

Johnson, who had not failed to notice the symbolic victory of the peace candidate, Senator Eugene McCarthy of Minnesota, in the New Hampshire primary, was especially anguished in the wake of Tet by a new troop request for over 200,000 men from Gen. Westmoreland, strongly supported, in fact prompted by Gen. Earle Wheeler, chairman of the JCS.[42] With this additional increment, Wheeler and Westmoreland felt they could actually win the war rather quickly, since they indeed believed the enemy had gambled his all on Tet. But the new secretary of defense, the shrewd lawyer and Democratic Party advisor Clark Clifford, who had heretofore been a hawk on Vietnam, first discouraged and later opposed a positive response. Rather than an additional 200,000 men, Westmoreland got less than 50,000, coupled with Washington's firm assurance that no more would be sent. At about this same time, Gen. Westmoreland was reassigned by the president to succeed Gen. Wheeler as chairman of the JCS. The "win the war" minded Admiral Sharp at CINCPAC was also replaced. The die had been cast; Johnson had, finally, decided to throw in the towel.

The decision to begin our disengagement by ending the air war against North Vietnam, thereby setting the stage for negotiations with the DRV, and by replacing the chief decision-makers at the top including Johnson himself, who announced that he would not seek or accept renomination, was fateful because it belatedly though courageously reversed the course of no return into never-never land which had been set in motion in 1961. But the new course of returning to reality proceeded extremely slowly. Johnson thought this essential in order to safeguard Democratic chances in the coming presidential elections. He was still by no means convinced the majority of Americans wanted out of the war; he was even less convinced they would tolerate abandoning our Vietnamese allies to the Communists, which almost any form of negotiated settlement seemed to him to make inevitable. Accordingly, though the DRV responded positively and at once to the expressed U.S. presumption that "productive talks" would ensue upon the permanent cessation of the bombing of the North,[43] Johnson delayed for several months the selection of a mutually agreeable site for talks. He finally accepted Paris as such a site in mid-1968.

During this period, and the ensuing one which saw Johnson at odds with Ho Chi Minh over whether the conference table should be two or four-sided—this dilemma being finally resolved by making the table a round one—the United States continued supporting ARVN's war effort in the South. Under new commander Gen. Creighton Abrams, however, U.S. strategy began gradually to change from Westmoreland's search and destroy to a more reserved one of holding major U.S. units to secure cleared areas or enclaves while the ARVN chased the enemy main forces.

Therefore, although Johnson's decision of March 1968 denoted that the United States would invest no more in Vietnam than it already had, and that it would accept a settlement, this did not mean that it would disengage rapidly or give the Viet Cong (NLF) the role in the future government of South Vietnam to which it aspired and for which it had conducted its long war. Vice President Hubert Humphrey, who became the Democratic nominee for 1968, sought on the strong urging of his advisors in August 1968 to move beyond this limited policy into a more active advocacy of rapid withdrawal, accepting the inevitable political costs. Johnson's furious reaction quickly brought Humphrey back into the fold and possibly cost Humphrey the narrow margin of votes with which Nixon won the November 1968 elections.

When Harriman and Cyrus Vance finally started the negotiations with the DRV in Paris which would last four long years, they began in far more difficult circumstances for the United States than if a similar conference had started, had we wanted it to, in May of 1965 on the basis of the original DRV Four Points. (See decison 4.) Nonetheless, they might well have succeeded in ending our involvement in the war by 1969 or 1970 on roughly the same terms the United States ultimately obtained in the Paris Accords of January 1973 had it not been for the change of administrations in the United States which brought Richard Nixon and Henry Kissinger to power.[44]

7. Decision to Disengage Over Four Years—"Vietnamization," 1969

(Note: The following discussion is partly conjectural and less documented than the discussion of previous or later decisions we cover in this chapter. Nonetheless, the writer wishes to present his thesis on the Nixon-Kissinger approach as strongly and directly as possible.)

Nixon, who came into office in 1969 on a promise not otherwise elaborated or detailed to end the war, decided early in his administration to do it very slowly. More committed than any other U.S. politician of the post-World War II period to the ideological and political premises of containment and to anti-communism, he was not about to turn abruptly on what he regarded as the conservative hard-core of the Republican party and of his electorate. Yet he also realized that, perhaps more than any other public figure in American life, and largely because of his previous political stands, he could guide U.S. foreign policy on a path of reversal from the high cold war. Such a reversal seemed indicated not only by the exigencies of the war in Vietnam but also by those of superpower relations in an age of substantial nuclear parity and Sino-Soviet conflict.

Nixon and Kissinger patterned their withdrawal policy closely on that which de Gaulle had pursued in extricating France from Algeria in 1958-62. Just as de Gaulle in 1960 had told the masses assembled on Algiers's main square, in the vaguest of terms, "Je vous ai compris" ("I have understood you"; but who or what had he understood?), so Nixon promised to end the war without ever saying how. Sharing de Gaulle's passion for monumental secrecy followed by dramatic announcements in the full glare of television, he and Kissinger kept their moves veiled from even their closest associates and advisors in the U.S. government. Some of these, but only a very few, inevitably had to be privy to selected tactical moves, but only the two principals themselves ever knew the full plan.

In virtual total secrecy, Kissinger began in the summer of 1969 to narrow down major U.S.-DRV differences in almost two dozen top secret shuttle meetings held in private Paris apartments with the DRV negotiator Le Duc Tho. Simultaneously, the U.S. delegation, headed by the official negotiator, Ambassador William Porter, kept up an obdurate posture of non-concessions at the Paris Peace Conference, as did the DRV delegates in that same forum. Then, all of a sudden, Nixon in mid-1971 revealed Kissinger's meetings with Tho on national television, as well as Kissinger's even more secret preparatory trips to Peking. Nixon then proceeded to travel to the People's Republic of China himself to sign the earthshaking Shanghai Communiqué of February 1972 and to start the process of U.S. reconciliation with Communist China.

Why the gradualness and secrecy about quitting an involvement that had turned into a disaster by 1969? Once more, the U.S. leadership's perception of the likely domestic political consequences of losing or selling-out to communism, proved to be the decisive factor. Let us examine precisely why this factor made the decision to disengage from Vietnam over such a long period of time, four years, such an extremely fateful one.

The Primacy of Domestic Politics

The gradualness of the disengagement process, 1969-72, caused savage fighting to continue for years after the outcome of the war had in fact been decided by the Tet offensive and the declared American resolution to withdraw. We do not mean by this to imply that the decided outcome was one of total Communist control over South Vietnam, as eventually occurred in 1975. But the formal recognition by the United States after March 1968 that the combined Vietnamese-U.S. forces could not perpetuate a stalemate in South Vietnam within the parameters set for the conduct of the war implied, at a minimum, acceptance of the NLF demand for a voice in the government of a postwar South Vietnam. It was of course contended then and after that a Communist role in government was synonymous with complete control. That is what had been contended ever since 1961. Yet it was finally what the

United States accepted in 1973, even if the Thieu government of South Vietnam never really did. It therefore gained nothing, in terms of the provisions of a peace agreement, by continuing to wage war between January 1969 and January 1973. Did it gain anything in other terms?

The fighting in 1969-72 resulted in over 20,000 U.S. war deaths; and it caused hundreds of thousands of Vietnamese civilian and military casualties and literally horrendous damage to both the South and North Vietnamese countrysides, as well as to Laos and Cambodia. Had the 1968 decision to disengage been followed quickly by the signing, in early 1970 for example, of accords basically similar to those eventually signed in early 1973, all this pain and violence—including also the student riots and other conflicts in the United States between 1969 and 1972—might have been averted. It is doubtful that Nixon and Kissinger thought in 1969 that they could have obtained, by waiting until early 1973, better terms than they would have obtained from 1970 on, although this last point can of course not be proven, and Nixon and Kissinger aver otherwise.[45]

However, Nixon and Kissinger were not necessarily seeking better peace terms by prolonging the agony; what they were seeking was simply time. Time for the first Nixon administration to elapse, and Nixon's reelection to be sought without Nixon having lost or abandoned Vietnam. Within these four years, Nixon championed and supported détente in Europe, resulting in some very significant steps such as the success of German *Ostpolitik*, the 1971 Berlin Quadripartite Agreements, and the 1972 SALT I accord. He also pioneered reconciliation with Communist China in Asia, resulting in the Shanghai Communiqué. After this, Nixon reasoned that he could no longer be seriously challenged at home on grounds of softness on communism; for serious and significant efforts at accommodation with the major Communist powers had by 1972 become the order of the day, sanctioned by the Congress, the entire foreign policy-making elite, and the U.S. public at large.

The thesis here is not that Nixon reasoned incorrectly—the 1972 elections demonstrated that he was entirely correct—only that he did so at great cost in U.S. lives and in terms of the fabric of American values and society. As we shall try to demonstrate in a later chapter, his policy if effective was nonetheless immoral by any appropriate standards that may be applied.

Vietnamization

The slow disengagement decision of 1969 was fateful because the entire corresponding process of "Vietnamization," invented by Nixon and Kissinger, assisted by Defense Secretary Melvin Laird and Secretary of State William Rogers along with many others, to cover our gradual withdrawal, was a sham which gave false hopes to the South Vietnamese and to the U.S. bureaucratic and business interest complex in South Vietnam. Although many U.S. officials in the field believed Vietnamization to be our real policy after 1969, the United States in fact achieved very little in terms of improving the internal political fabric of South Vietnam, ameliorating the conditions of the people, or improving the fighting or command capabilities of ARVN. Again, this assertion will be contested; yet subsequent events prove it substantially correct.

Gen. Nguyen Van Thieu, long the real power behind the scenes in the ARVN high command, finally assumed the presidency of Vietnam, with Marshall Ky as his vice president, after the acceptance by a portion of the South Vietnamese electorate in September 1967 of new constitutional provisions which provided a form of legitimacy to the post-Diem South Vietnamese regime. Thieu was reliable and reasonably competent; but also obdurate, obstinate, arrogant, and extremely repressive. Ambassador Bunker had never been able to make him see it "our way," nor had Gens. Westmoreland or Abrams. What was called Vietnamization was in essence the abdication of the self-imposed U.S. task, assumed after 1961 and more so on the morrow of the army coup of 1963 and even more so after 1965 to run things "our way." After mid-1968, we were willing to acknowledge that things might go better if they ran "their way." To enable them to do so, the United States started turning over massive amounts of weapons and equipment of all kinds to the South Vietnamese.

Vietnamization did not keep many officials at the top of the U.S. government and others at lower echelons in the field from feeling that the Vietnamese way—at least with those Vietnamese, but they were "the only Vietnamese we've got!"—was the wrong way. While they would aver, and tell the press, that Vietnamization was working well, they were painfully aware of the corruption reigning in the government and within the ARVN; of the brutality of the military in the villages; the repressiveness of the police and security services against any, even the slightest form of dissidence; the frustrations of the city masses; the distress in the countryside; the failure of land reform; and, worst of all, the tendency of the regular forces to avoid or perform poorly in battle.

Signs of all this kept creeping up: such as the discovery of the prison cages; the traffic in narcotics by high-ranking personnel; the debasing of the Chieu Hoi (prisoner conversion) program by torture or sadism; blackmarketeering; uncontrolled inflation; failure until the early seventies to even prescribe much less enforce conscription of able-bodied youth; above all, the pitiful performance of the ARVN troops that fled helter-skelter back into Vietnam after invading Laos in 1971 at the first sign of enemy resistance. Finally, the NLF/DRV spring offensive of 1972 demonstrated that very little if anything had been achieved. Still, in order to render a fair account, we must note that some ARVN units performed courageously and well during 1969-72 on a relatively few specific occasions.

On Thieu's part, expectations rose with Vietnamization. If the United States left decision-making to him but would facilitate matters by boundless and endless generosity, complemented after its withdrawal from Vietnam by maintenance of a strong military posture in nearby zones of the Asia-Pacific area and the threat to return if things went sour, the war in Vietnam could perhaps remain stalemated permanently. The old fears of the South Vietnamese leaders of a takeover by their thirty-year Communist enemy might still be staved off for at least the remainder of their own lives. Accordingly, Vietnamization created in the minds of the ruling South Vietnamese the false hope that they could survive. This was certainly a major factor in explaining Thieu's obdurate refusal to accept the January 1973 Paris Peace Accords and his refusal to live by their terms in 1973-74. It accordingly helped lay the groundwork for the ultimate collapse of the Republic of Vietnam in April 1975.

Contrary to South Vietnamese elite hopes, and those of the U.S. interest complex in Vietnam—a force of advisors, contractors, adventurers, and men of the Last Frontier which had grown to major proportions during Vietnamization and which will be examined later—Vietnamization was really hogwash. The minimum Nixon and Kissinger required, which is what they obtained, was to gain the necessary years to the next U.S. election. Thereafter, the U.S. could forget South Vietnam.

8. Decision to Invade Cambodia, 1970

This decision, made in such total secrecy that even Secretary of State William Rogers had virtually no input into it,[46] was fateful because of its dramatic domestic consequences and its disastrous impact on the course of events in Cambodia itself.

In terms of domestic effects, it seemed to galvanize at one sudden and certainly unexpected moment, from the White House point of view, all the opposition to the war which had been crystallizing among the nation's youth and even among their elders, most of whom had by now ceased to believe either in our capacity or in our real need to win in Vietnam. This sudden galvanization of opposition was understandable, given the relative quiet that had reigned on the domestic front with respect to the war in Indochina during the first year of the Nixon administration. Now, all of a sudden, instead of terminating, the war was taking an unexpected and expansive surge.

The United States had invaded hitherto neutral Cambodia, where (March 1970) the dubious Gen. Lon Nol had just seized power, overthrowing the deft and neutralist Prince Sihanouk during the latter's absence from the country. Sihanouk had managed to keep the great powers (U.S., China, Soviet Union) at a distance for some twenty years, during which war had raged in neighboring Vietnam and Laos. In the latter, the Pathet Lao, responding to the "secret war"—bombing and covert penetrations—being waged against it by U.S. and South Vietnemese forces after 1969, was again threatening a military takeover of the government in Vientiane. As to Cambodia, the Vietnamese Communists had increasingly used it, since the massive U.S. intervention of 1965 in Vietnam, as a staging, logistical, and sanctuary area for their forces fighting in South Vietnam. Sihanouk had not only tolerated this but even turned it to personal and national advantage. The new regime of Lon Nol would not do so, and was disposed instead toward alignment with the United States and South Vietnam, thus turning Cambodia into a battleground.

The Nixon administration's explanations that the U.S. military probe into Cambodia was limited to the objective of destroying DRV logistical support bases for South Vietnam were of little avail as the feeling grew within the United States that the war was being extended, not curtailed. Moreover the Cambodian expedition proved militarily abortive—U.S. forces apparently could not pinpoint their presumed targets, and when South Vietnamese forces were sent in to replace them, they suffered extremely heavy casualties. As all this occurred, opponents of the war in the United States were obtaining increasing hearing for their claims that the United States was also extending itself into what later came to be known as the secret war in Laos, involving saturation bombing of trails, rear bases, and logistical camps in that country. They further obtained anti-war support by their assertions that the United States was indiscriminately and savagely bombing civilian population centers in Cambodia—this last claim proving to have much basis in fact.[47]

The belief that we were broadening instead of tapering-off what was now being increasingly tagged in the United States as a lost, wrong, and immoral war grew domestically to such proportions that the Congress, rising from its long lethargy, now felt justified in finding methods of limiting Executive war actions. The Cambodian invasion and its adverse domestic political consequences led directly to a series of measures enacted by the Congress over the next three years, which strictly limited the Executive in conducting further warfare in Indochina. In turn, these measures became the basis on which the War Powers Act was enacted in 1973. The act signaled clearly to U.S. presidents of the seventies and beyond, that henceforth Congress would be involved, in the words of Senator Fulbright repeating an earlier aphorism attributed to Senator Arthur Vandenberg,[48] at the launching as well as at the crash-landings of U.S. war-waging operations abroad. This indeed represented the intentions of the Constitution's framers.[49]

As to the internal effects of the U.S. action on Cambodia, they were similarly fateful. From the moment we entered Cambodia, in what was perceived as an effort to bolster Lon Nol's weakening forces against a growing threat from the Cambodian Communists or Khmer Rouge, the Vietnamese Communists lost any of their earlier compunctions against unleashing their somewhat unreliable Khmer Communist allies to attack the U.S.-aligned Phnom Penh regime. In some two to three years of intense and often savage fighting, in which DRV forces supported the Rouge and U.S. bombing unabashedly hit every possible target in sight, much of the hitherto lush and, by Southeast Asian standards, fairly prosperous country was laid to waste. By early 1975, the Phnom Penh regime collapsed completely, opening the door to the vicious dictatorship of the Peking-aligned, anti-Vietnamese Khmer Rouge leader Pol Pot. Similarly in Laos, and despite the secret war, the Communist Pathet Lao in 1974-75 gained decisive assent and obtained control of the previously neutralist government.

9. Decision to Sign the Paris Accords, January 1973

Whatever pretenses may have been made at the time, the entirely expected decision to sign the January 1973 Paris Accords, laboriously negotiated between Henry Kissinger and Le Duc Tho between mid-1969 and October 1972, with a further brief negotiating interlude after Nixon had been safely, in fact overwhelmingly, re-elected in November 1972, represented the logical culmination of the policy decision made early in 1969—to disengage over a period of four years of so-called "Vietnamization."

By January 1973, exactly four years had elapsed, and the November 1972 elections were behind. Nixon, though gradually withdrawing U.S. forces from Vietnam, had intensified the war during 1969-72 by engaging U.S. and South Vietnamese forces in severe if useless fighting throughout Indochina. He had thereby, and through the device of Vietnamization, kept the U.S. "hawk" elements safely in his political fold. At the same time, by allowing Henry Kissinger to initial the draft Paris accord of October 14, 1972, and to publicize it on U.S. television just three weeks before the elections as in effect representing the accomplished conclusion of an honorable and worthy peace, Nixon secured sufficient lethargy and defection among U.S. "dove" elements to ensure Senator George McGovern's overwhelming defeat. (Shades of Lyndon Johnson in 1964!)

We shall never know how different the electoral picture might have been had Henry Kissinger told the truth in October 1972, that Gen. Thieu of South Vietnam would have none of his accord with Le Duc Tho; and had Nixon revealed that he shortly intended to place North Vietnam under the most intense civilian target-directed bombing of the entire war, and perhaps the most intense brief bombing period ever sustained by any civilian population in any war. But even had the U.S. elections of November 1972 not been affected by any of this, the profound cynicism of Nixon's late 1972 actions stands for history to behold.

(Conjecturally, but interestingly, it is even possible to speculate that Nixon's pre-electoral cynicism and dishonesty with respect to his Vietnam plans for late 1972 played a role in inducing the campaign nervousness and overkill by Nixon cohorts which resulted in the break-in at Watergate and associated illigitimate covert political activities in the United States in 1972.)

Nixon's cynicism in delaying the Paris signing until January 1973, after he had won the elections and instituted the intensive bombing of North Vietnam, also had fateful consequences in South Vietnam. Thieu continued firmly to resist a peace accord which gave the Vietnamese Communists their demand for a voice in the Saigon government. There was now to be a tripartite transitional regime, made up of followers of the Thieu government (though not Thieu himself); members of the so-called and by now virtually non-existent, because so severely repressed, "Third Force" of anti-Thieu but also non-Communist neutralists in South Vietnam; and leaders of the National Liberation Front, who had finally—and very late indeed—declared themselves as "The Provisional Revolutionary Government of South Vietnam" (PRG).

This transitional grouping would run South Vietnam while an armistice was being administered under joint RVN/DRV supervision and with the assistance of international commissioners from a number of countries. The United States would at once withdraw all its remaining forces. (In fact, U.S. forces had already been thinned out to virtually insignificant numbers by late 1972.) In return, it would regain its prisoners of war and an accounting of its missing in action.

Thieu balked completely at all this. As the beneficiary of "Project Enhance," under which the United States had turned over to him in the fall of 1972 billions of dollars worth of arms and equipment, and still under the delusion that Vietnamization had really taken place and that he was in fact in command, Thieu demanded additional terms for letting the United States out from under. Nixon had already decided that he would quiet him by the unrestrained bombing of North Vietnam at the end of December 1972. By this bombing, Nixon seemed in effect to be telling the DRV: "OK now, I'm leaving, but before I finally do I want you to see how strong I still am and what dastardly deeds I can do. . . . Don't try anything funny; you can never tell, I'm unreliable, I'm mean, and I might return." At any rate, this was the effect Nixon most likely intended to have on the DRV.

By the same token he was also trying to project a somewhat similar effect on Thieu. With the Christmas bombing he was in effect telling Thieu: "Look, I'm leaving, but I leave you in charge and I've made it possible for you to handle the situation. I'm signing these accords which you say you can't abide, but I've also given you the stuff and shown you, by the bombing, the way to handle this; beat them hard over the head."

Accordingly, by signing the Paris Accords, but only in January 1973 after the bombing of December 1972, Nixon obtained: (1) victory in the U.S. elections; (2) U.S. forces out of Vietnam for good, and the return of U.S. prisoners; (3) DRV concern as to his later or ultimate intentions; (4) the Thieu regime's willingness to accept, not the terms of Paris, but the U.S. departure from Vietnam, with the firm afterthought that it might not be permanent or that if Thieu provoked the DRV enough, the United States might return to help him counter their counter-provocations. (It almost happened; and might have, except for Watergate.)

One can say that this clever policy worked. On the other hand, one can also conclude that a less cynical and immoral alternative policy would have extricated us from Vietnam much sooner under the same terms. It also might have had us participate honestly in the implementation of these terms. Had we done this in 1961, or 1963, or 1965, or even as late as 1970, we might have gained a viable coalition government which might have kept the Communists from obtaining full control of South Vietnam for at least some years. We would certainly have avoided hundreds of thousands of Vietnamese and U.S. casualties in-

curred between 1969 and 1972, and shortened one of the greatest tragedies of modern times. As it was, Nixon's cynical decisions of 1969-72
inexorably laid the groundwork for the ultimate collapse of the anti-
Communist Vietnamese regime in 1975.

10. Decision to Abandon RVN to DRV (SRV), 1975

A little over two years later, the tragedy of South Vietnam came to a
final close. Truculent from the outset, Thieu immediately challenged
the terms of the 1973 armistice by engaging in a series of military
actions designed to push NLF/DRV forces out of areas they had occupied before the armistice. At the same time, he firmly refused to
implement the critical political provisions of the Paris accords, by refusing to constitute the National Committee of Reconciliation and Con-
cord which was to nominate the transitional tripartite regime.[50] His
military sallies began to bring significant Communist responses by the
summer of 1973, and his political obdurateness led to failure to establish the tripartite government. By early 1975 the picture looked bleak
for Thieu, though neither he nor U.S. Ambassador Graham Martin
seemed to have fully realized how bleak.

A relatively minor Communist sortie against ARVN positions at
Banmethuot in Central Vietnam brought about the hurried and disor-
derly withdrawal of ARVN from the whole of Central Vietnam in
March 1975. In a matter of a few weeks, the entire ARVN military
position in South Vietnam collapsed. The DRV did not have to invade
massively again, as some commentators as well as Gen. Westmoreland,
showing a surprising lack of information and analysis, have averred.[51]
In the first place, the accords worked fully in the DRV's favor and it
was Thieu, not the DRV, who had interest in upsetting them. Secondly,
after the fall of Banmethuot and Central Vietnam, Vietnamese Communist forces had no need to engage in military actions, except to mop
up remnants and seek to keep orderly a situation which was rapidly
going totally out of control. Amidst scenes of indescribable panic and
confusion, ARVN-associated and related Vietnamese sought to flee the
country. In a short time, PAVN/PRG forces arrived in Saigon and took
the city. By mid-1975, the reunified "Socialist Republic of Vietnam"
was an established fact.

Our decision not to reintervene was logical and expected, however
fateful. After the 1972 election, and except for their last expression of
support for Thieu through the Christmas bombing of 1972, Nixon and
Kissinger had in effect washed their hands of Vietnam. It could go
down any drain for all they cared, whatever their pretenses or Ambas-

sador Martin's beliefs conveyed to Congress and the press during the last two years (1973-74) of the Thieu regime. And it did—oddly enough under the only U.S. president between 1945 and 1975 who had never made a single decision on Vietnam, Gerald Ford.

Notes

1. Based on personal recollection of contents of Dulles's cables after his conversations with Nehru in early 1956 regarding the TERM. This material should become available when the State Department releases *Foreign Relations of the U.S.* for 1956.
2. *See* Chapter III, Section 2.
3. Maxwell B. Taylor, *The Uncertain Trumpet* (NY: Harper, 1960).
4. *See* Tanham, *Communist Revolutionary Warfare*, Greene, *The Guerrilla;* F.M. Osanka, ed., *Modern Guerrilla Warfare;* (New York: Free Press, 1962).
5. Sir Robert G.K. Thompson, *Defeating Communist Insurgency: The Lessons of Malaya and Vietnam* (New York: Praeger, 1967); and by the same author, *No Exit from Vietnam* (New York: D. McKay, 1969); and *Revolutionary War in World Strategy, 1945-69* (New York: Taplinger, 1970).
6. *Pentagon Papers*, 2: pp. 84-102.
7. *Ibid.*, pp. 102-120.
8. Full text of this address is in Greene, *The Guerrilla*, pp. 54-61.
9. John Mecklin, *Mission in Torment* (New York: Doubleday, 1965), pp. 91-94.
10. One of Ngo Dinh Diem's prime opponents, the Harvard-educated nationalist leader Dr. Pham Quang Dan, was imprisoned in the cages beginning in 1960 or 1961 and released after the November 1, 1963 coup.
11. The Strategic Hamlet Program is covered in detail in *Pentagon Papers*, 2: pp. 128-59.
12. Kenneth P. O'Donnell and David J. Powers, *Johnny, We Hardly Knew Ye: Memories of John Fitzgerald Kennedy* (Boston: Little Brown, 1970, 1972), pp. 16-18.
13. Coup planning by the junta of generals, of which the United States was cognizant, had reached advanced stages as early as August 1963. *See Pentagon Papers*, 2: pp. 236-40. For a variety of reasons, the coup did not materialize until November 1. *See* Halberstam, *Best and Brightest*, pp. 326-58.
14. Theodore Sorenson, *Kennedy* (New York: Harper & Row, 1965), p. 660; Arthur M. Schlesinger, *A Thousand Days* (Boston: Houghton Mifflin, 1965); O'Donnell and Powers, *Johnny*, p. 17.
15. *Pentagon Papers*, 2: pp. 304-05.
16. Halberstam, *Best and Brightest*, pp. 326-27.
17. A record of this meeting can be found in *Pentagon Papers*, 2: pp. 741-43 (Document 135).
18. Material on this point is elusive. The writer can attest, from personal recollection, that Lodge tended to attribute such machinations to Ngo Dinh Nhu, based presumably on accounts Lodge received from both the Papal Nuncio and the Italian ambassador in Saigon. For an account lend-

ing some credence to this thesis, see Geoffrey Warner, "The United States and the Fall of Diem, Part I," *Australian Outlook* vol. 28, No. 3 (December 1974): pp. 255-57.

19. Charles de Gaulle, *Memoirs of Hope: Renewal and Endeavor* (New York: Simon and Schuster, 1971), p. 256.

20. *Pentagon Papers,* 2: p. 275.

21. Aside from the *Pentagon Papers* and the exhaustive treatment in Halberstam, *Best and Brightest,* see G. McT. Kahin and J.W. Lewis, *The United States in Vietnam* rev. ed. (NY: Dell, 1969); Ralph Stavins, R.J. Barnet and M.G. Raskin, *Washington Plans An Aggressive War* (New York: Random House Vintage, 1971); Robert L. Gallucci, *Neither Peace Nor Honor: The Politics of American Military Policy in Vietnam* (Baltimore: Johns Hopkins University Press, 1975); Leslie H. Gelb with R. K. Betts, *The Irony of Vietnam: The System Worked* (Washington, D.C.: Brookings, 1979).

22. DOS Bulletin LII, No. 1343, March 22, 1965, p. 402; *Ibid.,* No. 1344, March 29, 1965, p. 444; *Ibid.,* No. 1346, April 12, 1965, p. 529. *Also, Pentagon Papers,* 3: p. 723.

23. *See* Secretary of Defense Robert McNamara's Ann Arbor commencement address of June 16, 1962, *The New York Times,* June 17, 1962; Stewart Alsop, "Our New Strategy: The Alternatives to Total War," *Saturday Evening Post,* December 1, 1962.

24. For a cursory though useful discussion of the extent of North Vietnamese presence in the South before the bombing began, see Chester L. Cooper, *The Lost Crusade: America in Vietnam* (New York: Dodd Mead, 1970), pp. 264-66.

25. Halberstam, *Best and Brightest,* p. 631.

26. The origins of the aviary vocabulary which began to be used with such regularity in regard to Vietnam, first inside the government, after early 1965 are obscure. Since "dove" was the presumed symbol of the "peaceniks" who were increasingly besieging the White House, the responding symbol "hawk" was a natural one to denote macho, toughness, and American-ness.

27. Joseph C. Goulden, *Truth Is the First Casualty: The Gulf of Tonkin Affair* (Chicago: Rand McNally, 1969); Anthony Austin, *The President's War: The Story of the Tonkin Gulf Resolution and How the Nation Was Trapped in Vietnam* (Philadelphia: Lippincott, 1971); Eugene G. Windchy, *Tonkin Gulf* (New York: Doubleday, 1971).

28. Personal recollection.

29. Text of the Joint (Tonkin Gulf) Resolution can be found in *Pentagon Papers,* 3: p. 722.

30. The consensus of domestic, including media, support for the war (see Chapter VI) was then still so strong that the resignations, even with blasts, of low-level insiders would probably not have caused national attention. This was certainly my own reasoning when I contemplated the step early in 1965. Although I had worked within the group of escalation opponents in 1964, I was on a six-weeks trip to the Philippines when sustained bombing started in late February 1965, and unable to consult with anyone. Nonetheless, I have always regretted that I did not take the step at that time, however little fuss my resignation would have made.

31. *Pentagon Papers,* 4: pp. 615-19 (Document 260).
32. Poole, *The United States and Indochina,* pp. 150-52.
33. Reconstructed from memory. See L. Gelb and R.K. Betts, *The Irony of Vietnam,* for what is probably another fragmentary account of this episode. We will have to await the release of the State Department's *Foreign Relations of the U.S.* for 1965 to have all the documents. The official DRV statement of the Four Points, issued by Prime Minister Pham Van Dong in Hanoi on April 8, 1965, noted that the Four Points were "the basis for the soundest political settlement of the Vietnam problem." Senate Foreign Relations Committee, *Background Information,* p. 398.
34. *Pentagon Papers,* 3: pp. 720-43, (Public Statements).
35. The DRV may have regarded the U.S. military intervention in the Dominican Republic as evidence of the Johnson administration's frustration with its ineffectual bombing policies in North Vietnam, as does at least one American writer: Jerome Slater, *Intervention and Negotiation: The United States and the Dominican Revolution* (New York: Harper & Row, 1970), p. 32.
36. L. Gelb and R. K. Betts, *The Irony of Vietnam,* pp. 140-41.
37. Frances Fitzgerald, *Fire In the Lake* (Boston: Little Brown, 1972), esp. Ch. 8.
38. *Pentagon Papers,* 3: pp. 433-485.
39. Halberstam, *Best and Brightest,* pp. 662 ff.
40. The "Tuesday Luncheons" with President Johnson, Secretary Rusk, and Secretary McNamara, also occasionally attended by National Security Advisor Walt Rostow and an extremely limited number of other key subordinates to the President, became the principal forum for the finalizing of major policy decisions regarding the Vietnam War between mid-1965 and early 1968.
41. Townsend Hoopes, *The Limits of Intervention* (New York: David McKay, 1969).
42. *Pentagon Papers,* 4: pp. 546 ff.
43. The full text of President Johnson's March 31, 1968, address is in Department of State Publication 8376, April 5, 1968; *see also,* in Senate Foreign Relations Committee, *Background Information,* p. 282.
44. For congressional testimony by Harriman critical of President Nixon's Vietnam policies, particularly in relation to the negotiations for a settlement, *see Congressional Record,* vol. 115, part 13, June 24, 1969, pp. 17113-14; *Ibid.,* vol. 117, part 15, June 15, 1971, pp. 19896-97; *Ibid.,* vol. 116, part 28, Nov. 23, 1970, pp. 38442-44. Testimony by Cyrus Vance is in *Congressional Record,* vol. 118, part 14, May 16, 1972, p. 17553. Both men testified that the escalation of military activity in Vietnam in the Nixon administration hindered the achievement of a negotiated settlement, which they felt they were close to achieving in late 1968.
45. Kissinger's views on this point are expressed in DOS Bulletin, Vol. 68, No. 1755, Feb. 12, 1973, pp. 155-69; *Ibid.,* Vol. 68, No. 1762, April 12, 1973, pp. 388-98; *Ibid.,* Vol. 75, No. 1935, July 26, 1976, "Interview for *Die Zeit* of Hamburg." *See also* Tad Szulc, *The Illusion of Peace: Foreign Policy in the Nixon Years* (New York: Viking Press, 1978), pp. 27, 38. President Nixon's views can be found in *RN: The Memoirs of Richard Nixon* (New York: Grosset and Dunlap, 1978).

46. Tad Szulc, *Illusion of Peace*, p. 256.
47. *Aftermath of War: Humanitarian Problems of Southeast Asia.* Staff Report for Subcommittee to Investigate Problems Connected with Refugees and Escapees, U.S. Senate Committee on the Judiciary, 94th Cong., 2d sess. (Washington, D.C.: U.S.G.P.O., May 17, 1976).
48. Pat M. Holt, *The War Powers Resolution: The Role of Congress in U.S. Armed Intervention* (Washington, D.C.: American Enterprise Institute for Public Policy Research, 1978), p. 33.
49. For a persuasive statement of the view that the Founding Fathers intended Congress, and not the president, to authorize the exercise of the war-waging power, see Testimony before the Subcommittee on National Security Policy of the House Committee on Foreign Affairs by Professor Raoul Berger, Harvard University Law School, *Hearings on War Powers*, 93d Cong., 1st sess., House Committee on Foreign Affairs, 1973, p. 209.
50. Gareth Porter, *A Peace Denied: The United States, Vietnam, and the Paris Agreements* (Bloomington: Indiana University Press, 1975), p. 243.
51. Gen. William C. Westmoreland, *A Soldier Reports* (New York: Doubleday, 1976).

Chapter V

Winning Without Winning, 1961-72

"The collapse of the South . . . continued unabated. The Americans had always had the illusion that something might turn it around . . . Magically . . . the right program would emerge, blending arms and pig-fatteners together to make the peasants want to choose our side. But nothing changed, the other side continued to get stronger, the ARVN side weaker . . . The truth of the war never entered the upper-level American calculations; that this was a revolutionary war, and that the other side held title to the revolution . . . This most simple fact, which was so important to the understanding of the political calculations (it explained why their soldiers would fight and die, and ours would not; why their leaders were skillful and brave, and ours were inept and corrupt) . . . never entered into the calculations of the principals, for a variety of reasons; among other things to see the other side in terms of nationalism or as revolutionaries might mean a re-evaluation of whether the United States was even fighting on the right side. In contrast, the question of Communism and anti-Communism as opposed to revolution and anti-revolution was far more convenient for American policy makers. . ."

(Halberstam, *The Best and the Brightest*, pp. 561-62, paper ed.)

1. The Role of Toughness and Force

The thing that Johnson feared most was that history would write that he had been weak when he should have been strong, that Lyndon Johnson had not stood up when it was time to be counted, that his manhood might be inadequate. . . Did Johnson have as much manhood as Jack Kennedy? (Halberstam, p. 606, paper ed.)

155

While the existence and availability of abundant U.S. military power was certainly a prime determinant in the making of our policies toward Indochina in 1961-72, it is much more difficult to argue that our key military leaders played an equally determinant role. In fact, our military leadership was on the whole submissive and responsive as it allowed top civilian leaders to make virtually all the major decisions. The one great exception to this was Gen. Maxwell Taylor who, however, exercised his full impact on U.S. policy only during 1961-65, thereafter relapsing into the same type of submissiveness which the rest of our top military leadership tended to show.

Submissiveness of U.S. Military Leaders

Some writers have created the impression of a juggernaut-like U.S. military machine, run by impassioned and wild-eyed warmongers, somehow leading the country into an ever-expanding war in Indochina, which it then could not win.[1] The impression is incorrect. With the highly significant exception, already stated, of Gen. Maxwell Taylor, neither the chairman or members of the Joint Chiefs of Staff, nor theater commanders in the field like Admirals Sharp and McCain at CINCPAC, nor our military commanders in Vietnam proper—Generals Paul Harkins, Westmoreland and Abrams—had decisive input in the top policy decisions which affected the U.S. role in Indochina during the key years. It is true that these military leaders sometimes expressed themselves, occasionally in public,[2] and consistently in long and generally highly reflective classified messages to the president, the secretary of defense, or the JCS through their chains of command.[3] But their views were often simply noted and dismissed when their communications strayed in the slightest from their direct areas of tactical and technical competence; in other words, when these views strayed into higher strategy or policy.

Gen. Curtis LeMay, pleading to lay the North waste with bombs, was of course ignored and regarded as a rather comical figure by the top policy-makers. Gen. Westmoreland, going "political" in elaborating on his "search-and-destroy" strategy, supporting the bombing of the North, or asking for large increments of additional manpower, was often simply disregarded. (According to Halberstam, William Bundy called him "a blunt instrument." [4]) He was always, sometimes in nasty ways—such as by denying him command over certain elements within his jurisdiction—wholly controlled by President Johnson. Gen. Earle Wheeler, chairman of JCS in 1965-68, was held on a very short leash by his civilian superiors and so was Army Chief of Staff Gen. Harold K. Johnson. The CINCPAC commanders were frequently informed of key decisions, particularly those relating to negotiatory explorations with the enemy side, only late if at all; key commanders were often kept ignorant of the reasons for bombing pauses, presumably so they could not comment on them adversely; and sometimes their ignorance of ongoing political machinations explained untoward military actions that would take place—as in the bombing of Hanoi-Haiphong during Fanfani's mediation efforts in late 1965.[5]

As already pointed out, the bombing of North Vietnam was probably more tightly controlled from a civilian center than any other military operation in history. Major main-force military ground engagements were similarly controlled by Washington and the civilian element in Saigon, which did not prevent occasional lapses. Moreover, tight "rules of engagement" prevailed during the entire Vietnam War, binding the U.S. military on the ground to very closely enforced restrictions; again, this did not prevent rather frequent lapses as in the case of the massacre at My Lai.[6] As to most of the key political decisions affecting the war, the military commanders were either informed piecemeal and with few reasons given, or perfunctorily and with little hearing of their viewpoints, or not at all. Despite all of "McNamara's band concerts" [7] at Honolulu, Guam, Manila, Saigon or elsewhere, he and the president rarely got into detailed discussions with their military commanders on matters which primarily concerned the political and civilian aspects of the war—even key political relationships with top Vietnamese personalities.[8]

McNamara did seek the commanders' views, but only as inputs into his own decision-making process. And to make matters worse from the viewpoint of fighting men, McNamara would invariably filter the military views, even those bearing directly only on technical military matters, through his civilian whizz-kids, often M.A.'s in their twenties from the nation's business schools, who would subject them to merciless cost-benefit analyses in which considerations of great battlefield import were frequently disregarded. President Johnson used his secretary of defense to control and bargain with his military commanders;[9] basically to keep them doing the job that he and McNamara wanted them to do without many questions asked. Johnson's view of the bargain was about as follows: "I'm giving you a war to fight, and within reason all the means you need to fight it with; now, it's the only war you've got, so don't fight the problem, i.e., the war, because that is high policy and I decide it; and fight the war my way if you want to keep your job and have a war to fight."

The U.S. military took the brunt of U.S. policies in Vietnam, suffered the casualties, and made the sacrifices not only in men and resources but also in prestige. In doing so, the U.S. military took an extraordinary bum rap throughout the whole Vietnam engagement. It did not make the key decisions and policies; it failed in many instances even to be consulted on these, or to understand them fully. As a group, the U.S. military disliked and continued to dislike notions of limited war and refined deterrence; it tended to go for fighting all-out and for winning. Yet it was made to fight, but not with all it had; to win, but to spare the enemy; to maim, but not to kill; to hurt, but not too painfully. Why did our military leadership submit to all this? Why did it not come out loud and clear to protest and repudiate it, and to demand that we really go to war?

The U.S. military leadership found itself impaled on two propositions regarding its own relationship to the political forces at work in the U.S. which eventually became dilemmas from which it could not escape. Both propositions were tenaciously held by the military throughout the Vietnam War, less through careful analysis than through the long-range bearing of ancient lore.

The first was that the U.S. military leadership had no fundamental role in essentially political decision-making. Such compunctions did not keep our civilian leaders, politicians, diplomats and bureaucrats from turning into refined strategists, as we shall see! Of course U.S. military leaders have a role in political decision-making, especially in wartime, which they are in many respects as well or better qualified through training and experience to exercise than the civilian leadership. But to exercise it adequately, our military leaders would have had to eschew parochial advocacies of specific service or other causes, and rely more than was their custom on the intelligence, knowledge, experience and perspicacity of their key individuals. This is precisely what Gen. Marshall had done in World War II, Gen. Ridgway had done for Eisenhower, and also what Gen. Taylor did, first in resigning from the Army and writing his *Uncertain Trumpet,* then in assuming charge of both the military command and much of the civilian decision-making during the New Frontier years in Vietnam.

But who among the military leaders rose to counter Taylor's—and the prevailing—views, on counterinsurgency, for example? Who rose to say, as Ridgway had in 1954, that the United States should not conduct warfare on the mainland of Asia, not conduct limited warfare at all, and above all not involve itself in imperfectly constructed doctrines like counterinsurgency? Only General James Gavin, well nurtured by his European war experiences and his brief acquaintance with Indochina in the fifties, as well as by his conversations while ambassador to France with key French personalities, rose early from the ranks of the active or ex-military leaders to suggest lucidly alternative strategies for Vietnam. He backed the so-called enclave approach, which would have kept U.S. ground forces located only in static urban, largely coastal positions. Later, Gavin turned into an opponent of the whole U.S. war effort in Vietnam.[10]

Its fears of intruding into alien turf, bred from the traditional lore of its purely military role in a civilian-dominated environment, compelled U.S. military leadership into silence and acquiescence—as if no one in the military had ever read in Clausewitz that war is the continuation of policy by other means, which of course works the other way as well, and is a valid proposition.

Second, the U.S. military labored under the tremendous delusion that U.S. military power was equal to any challenge. Confident of its extraordinary successes in so many enterprises over so many decades, our military repeated this lore during the postwar period until it really came to believe it. Heroic pronouncements of this type, reminiscent of the World War II Seabee motto—"The possible we do today; the impossible we do tomorrow"—are primitive, boy scout-like morale builders which should not and cannot be taken seriously by senior leaders. Even today, there is in the U.S. military a tendency to believe it; how much more understandable that U.S. military leaders should have believed it when the country plunged into Vietnam at the crest of its world power.

But U.S. military power simply has not been equal to the challenge of nationalist revolutionary movements fighting on their home grounds at low, popular levels of warfare, either in 1959, 1961, 1965, or at any other time including the present. U.S. forces might today be able to help the Israelis repulse a new invasion by a combination of Arab states if this were to become necessary; but it is highly improbable that they could successfully assist them in putting down a major rebellion by hundreds of thousands of armed Palestinians if such a revolt should break out. U.S. forces might be able to help Iran repulse a Soviet invasion, but it is certainly improbable that they could have militarily assisted the Shah in putting down the kind of internal revolution which cost him his rule; and it is next to certain that they would fail totally if they were sent to help South Africa put down a black revolution on the scale of that in Indochina in 1959-75.

In fact, there are lots of challenges to which U.S. military power is not equal, and there will continue to be. Nor need U.S. military power be up to any challenge; it need be equal only to those challenges which directly and palpably threaten U.S. security interests in a way understandable to the American people, who support, make up and ultimately direct U.S. military power and leadership. In Indochina, U.S. military power was not equal to the challenge of infinitely resourceful, highly skilled and experienced, splendidly led guerrilla fighters who took their sustenance and support from the very population itself. U.S. military power would not have been equal to that challenge even if it had not been hamstrung, contained, controlled and restrained by a domineering and self-righteous civilian leadership basically unwilling to give the military a proper hearing.

But even if U.S. military leaders had recognized this, as basically General Gavin did, and even if they had demanded their rightful hearing, it is doubtful that they could have changed the course of events. Nonetheless, because they did not recognize it, and did not forcefully speak out, they share the blame with the civilian leadership for the misconduct of an impossible war which they could not have won.

Militarization and Machismo of U.S. Civilian Leaders: "Crisis Management"

We shall review in later parts of this book the degradation of diplomacy by strategy in the U.S. policies of the high cold war. Here, we wish to examine briefly the whys and wherefores of the enormous attraction which existing, available military power and its mechanisms and procedures relentlessly exercised over U.S. civilian leadership. It is a phenomenon thus far too little taken into account in studies of U.S. cold war foreign policies.

The United States had long prided itself on civilian virtues and the supremacy of the civilian over the military, going so far in fact as to have maintained only a minuscule military establishment, by world standards at least, before World War II. It did not even permit an integrated command structure to be established over the armed forces until well into World War II. Such a structure, the Joint Chiefs of Staff (JCS), highly and deliberately cumbersome compared to the integrated commands of other countries, was not given a statutory basis until passage of the National Security Act of 1947. Even then, JCS was hemmed in by civilian supremacy in the form of the new office of secretary of defense and, over that, by the creation of the all-civilian National Security Council.[11] What factors then explain the militaristic tendencies which developed in our politicians and civilian officials after World War II? The following deserve consideration:

1. Personal fascination with military gadgetry, introduced as a result of the World War II military or combat experience of many civilian principals and complemented on their part by deep respect for military effectiveness and efficiency, as compared to the inefficiency, diffusion, and red tape of

the civilian bureaucracy. President Truman was in awe of Gens. George C. Marshall and Omar Bradley as administrators and leaders of men. President Eisenhower had of course himself been a great military commander; President Kennedy had been a P.T. boat commander and minor war hero; President Johnson seemed all the more fascinated with military gadgetry, tactics and command, perhaps precisely because he had been deprived of military experience during World War II.

2. Fear of being perceived as weak, which led to overstating and overdoing the benefits of resort to force in discussions of policy and decisions of state. This macho or machismo factor seems to have become closely associated with political success in postwar America; and it transferred easily from domestic politics to foreign policy.[12]

3. Sincere belief in the capacity of U.S. military forces to accomplish virtually any mission; but the civilian leaders did not really believe postwar U.S. military leaders capable of thinking through problems of policy or even of high strategy.

4. Fear of losing policy control to military leaders unless civilian leaders and bureaucrats themselves gained the capacity of outdoing them at their game. In the State Department, this attitude was exemplified by the behavior and actions of Ambassador U. Alexis Johnson, who attained the post of undersecretary of state for political affairs and therefore of top-ranking U.S. Foreign Service officer in the late sixties and early seventies. This caused the State Department to open its doors to Pentagon exchange officers, who were rarely given anything to do, so that State Department officers might be given jobs in the Defense Department.

5. Associated with the macho mentioned above, sincere belief that the game of states was a game of men—somewhat like major sports—in which toughness in approach, the type of behavior associated with military deportment, and careful implementation of planned sequential moves would eventually gain the day. This was a natural concomitant of proceeding in world politics on the basis of the deterrence doctrines we have discussed in Chapter III and which themselves stemmed from the premises of Soviet containment, which turned our postwar foreign policy into an arena of confrontation rather than negotiation.

6. Most important, the abundant availability and pervasiveness of all forms of military power itself. (See "Role of Power" in Chapter III.)

But there were other reasons as well why the New Frontier, and after it the key leadership under President Johnson, approached the problem of Indochina in a specially tough, macho or militaristic spirit. A principal reason was the tendency, again part of the globalism covered earlier, to transpose method without much thought from one area of the world to another. We reviewed in Chapter IV how the New Frontier transposed refined deterrence as developed in Berlin and Cuba into what became graduated escalation as applied to Vietnam. These civilian-bred and civilian-led semi-applications of military power were an ideal way out for civilian leaders who somewhere along the way had lost the art of diplomacy—in which the Foreign Service itself was becoming highly inexpert—and yet wished to refrain from exclusive reliance on raw military power.

These leaders wanted—and sometimes, as in the case of Kennedy in late 1961, needed—to look and act tough, while keeping control of "crises" at all stages lest these degenerate into cataclysmic or irreversible manifestations of violence, such as nuclear war. The U.S. military leaders could not really be trusted with the key to this part-opened barn, which still contained most, and the most dangerous part, of their arsenal. The technique had been beautifully demonstrated by Bobby Kennedy during the Cuban Missile Crisis. All the while the military was deploying and partially mobilizing and dusting off its contingency plans, he was secretly negotiating with Soviet emissaries, and President Kennedy had remained in communications with Khrushchev. One can even wonder in retrospect whether force and its threatened or actual application had actually been of any real importance in the crisis. We know today that the Soviet offensive missiles in Cuba were removed at least partly because of our willingness to remove our own obsolescent missiles from Turkey, as well as because of our pledge not to invade Cuba. It is at least possible to argue that such a deal might have been obtained through normal diplomatic channels, without the quarantine and other military threats, since U.S. conventional military supremacy in the Caribbean was in any case never in doubt. But whether this was so or not, the end result of the crisis was that Kennedy had looked appropriately tough.

"Crisis management" became a favorite pastime of top U.S. civilian leaders in the high cold war because it provided the ideal outlet for machismo tendencies, for playing at soldier while harnessing the military leadership, for looking tough to the public, and for making decisions in an environment as nearly ideal as one could get in Washington. During crises, maximum secrecy was not only imposed but kept by the players in the decision-making game because of the gravity of the situations, permitting later public announcements to be made with appropriate drama. The number of players was sharply limited by the need for secrecy. And decisions were made in a mode approaching the rational as closely as one ever could in foreign policy, since the question was always to determine the national interest.[13] This compelled obliteration or at least dilution by decision-makers of any parochial advocacies or of bureaucratic or political tendencies which might prove obstacles to the determination of the national interest. Accordingly, after about 1959, we had crises in the Congo, in Berlin, in Laos, in Cuba, in Vietnam, in Berlin, in Cuba again, and again—this time almost uninterruptedly—in Vietnam.

In order fully to apprehend the importance of machismo and of the appearance of toughness, and accordingly of crisis management as the best vehicle devised by our top leaders to exhibit these qualities, we must return to some of the considerations we discussed earlier in our analysis of the United States in its role as superpower. The importance of toughness was largely dictated by the climate of anti-Communist opinion which continued to prevail in the United States throughout the entire high cold war, and by the need to placate Congress's almost blind resolution that we should never retreat before the Communist onslaught. In those times, diplomatic negotiation or accommodation was actually regarded as synonymous with retreat, and virtually any moves which Communists or suspected Communists made anywhere was an onslaught. By promoting the feverish anti-Communist climate of the earlier fifties our leaders had themselves created in Congress and in the mind of the public a sort of monster which now, in the sixties, was turning on them. The best control they had of their own glide into the unrestrained use of power and force was to devise crisis management, by which means they could use both the U.S. military and its arsenal and yet carefully tailor and control that use.

We indicated in Chapter IV (Decision 1) how the policy of breaking through the 1954 Geneva ceilings on U.S. military presence in Vietnam and implementing the Taylor-Rostow recommendations of 1961 to embark on counterinsurgency programs stemmed in large part from President Kennedy's imperative need to look tough after the Bay of Pigs, after Vienna, after Berlin, and after the decision to go soft in Laos. Similarly, driven to the wall by South Vietnam's incapacity to pull itself together in 1964 as well as by the siren calls claiming that bombing could do it, Johnson finally embarked on Rolling Thunder—but always provided he himself control it entirely. When bombing of the North in turn seemed to fail, Johnson turned to the direct entry of U.S. ground combat forces in the war; this too, he tried as hard as possible to manage and control. Even though it brought little success in 1965-67, a climate of opinion was deliberately created in which U.S. forces, together with ARVN, which they basically distrusted, seemed to be winning the day throughout Vietnam. There was, therefore, all the more a fall from grace at the top when the Tet offensive of early 1968 proved that, in fact, the crisis had not been solved. As Westmoreland and Wheeler acutely perceived, this would have been the moment to go for all-out war; but that was precisely what the civilian militarists emphatically did *not* want. The only way left was for Johnson to give up on the war and to abdicate his high post.

Nixon was in turn subject to the same tugs and pulls from the internal monster that America, with Nixon's considerable personal help, had created and which still existed. To have allowed Harriman and Vance in late 1969 or early 1970, to conclude the kind of peace to which Kissinger finally assented three years later would have appeared weak. As Nixon perhaps over-acutely sensed, the hawks were still howling in the corridors, though they had lost much of their force. But they had elected him—to make peace to be sure, but peace with honor as well. Nixon's entire personality was constructed on macho and toughness. Honor to him did not necessarily mean to do the honorable thing as some would conceive of the task; it meant that, if the bully forced you out of his alley, you went, but not without a last-ditch fight and a powerful final blow.

Nixon and Kissinger, as Johnson before them, allowed a false climate of opinion to be created in which Vietnamization seemed to succeed when it was in fact failing. When Nixon thought that our military as well as Thieu could be made to accept peace terms by one more thrust of military action, he authorized the ill-fated Cambodian invasion of 1970. This brought unexpected domestic results, for by then the domestic monster had finally been tamed—by the upheaval of the poor, the black, the students, and the flower children. All of a sudden, the United States was buzzing with love, and the code word had become, "Make love, not war." Nixon pulled back into peace with China and, at last, peace in Vietnam. Yet his perception of the political need to demonstrate toughness and force was such that he launched one last spasm of violence in the Christmas bombings of December 1972. Even President Gerald Ford succumbed to the temptation of macho in ordering the bombing that followed the incident of the *S.S. Mayaguez* in April 1975. If the United States was going to accept the inevitable in Indochina, it would first show that it was still a macho power to be reckoned with.

2. The Premium on Action, Determination, and Persistence

Action, determination, and persistence rate high in the American scale of personal values. U.S. leaders placed the same high premium on these traits as applied to policy virtually from the beginning of U.S. full-fledged involvement in Indochina in 1962. As we shall see, action was of the greatest import; but U.S. policy-makers were also determined that their course of action should continue and succeed, and persistent to the extreme in pursuing it. How can we explain determination in the face of mounting contrary evidence, and persistence in the face of repeated failure? Although rational analysis can to a certain extent account for these phenomena, an important element of irrationality is also involved.

Determination and Persistence

Rationally, several factors help explain our continued determination to pursue an erroneous course of action in Indochina, and our persistence despite failure to meet even minimally set objectives:

1. The lack of or failure to use appropriate knowledge and expertise—simply put, ignorance—part of a complex of analytic failure which we review in detail in the next section of this chapter.
2. Closed-system thinking, or insufficient appraisal and appreciation of viewpoints divergent from the set norm of the decision-making group, which we also review in some detail in Chapter VI.
3. Simple failure to accept the judgment that the course of action being pursued was erroneous, based on unshakeable conviction in its rectitude and therefore its necessity and on the incapacity of policy-makers to distinguish or to perceive acceptable alternatives.

More irrationally, it is very likely that our vaunted determination and persistence were simply a cover for an unwillingness to accept reality because of fear of its objective consequences, "Taylor was," writes Halberstam, "a desperate man in a desperate situation, unable to turn back, having come this far . . . and this was symbolic of all of them." [14]

This lack of courage among key policy-makers is what Hans Morgenthau, in a masterly essay written at the height of the Indochina war, has called their "sin of pride." [15] Not all our top policy-makers lacked courage in this sense; some—Secretary Rusk and Professor Rostow, for example—consistently remained blind to the policy's failure, which did not necessarily indicate a lack of courage, since it takes more courage for a blind man to persist in hitting a wall than for one who has regained his sight. Those who, at least some years after our engagement had started, had realized the error and the horror of it, are more to blame. Few among them dared jeopardize their positions or prospects by admitting error; for most of them, so much had been invested in the policy that not to persist even after the moment of truth had come— and this could be at any time between 1962 and 1968, and even later— would simply be too costly, too embarrassing, and too painful. In opting for persistence under these circumstances, those U.S. policy-makers were in fact serving only themselves and not their country, as they had sworn to do. But as Vietnam continued into the sixties, self came increasingly to rate above the national interest among these men.

They rationalized this, often subconsciously, by the simple expedient of identifying the national interest with the self.

Among the lower-echelon practitioners and military men, particularly in the field where Army, Marines, and Air Force men were fighting and dying daily, and where an enormously swollen civilian contingent was also making a daily investment of blood, sweat, and tears, persistence and determination could best be understood in terms of the credibility of U.S. power and leadership. "If we don't hack it here, no one will believe or trust us anywhere," would be the simplest way to put this rather crude but overwhelming field sentiment. Such expressions of faith then communicated themselves back to Washington to reinforce the sometimes flagging feelings of those at the top that U.S. credibility was really on the line. By just repeating that statement in public, however, top policy-makers could draw satisfaction from responsive chords in the public. "Yes," the public would in effect intone, "our word is on the line, we must be true to the test." Top policy-makers would then be presented with a new challenge: could they meet the public's expectations, which they had themselves engendered, that U.S. leadership would in fact be true to the test? Would their determination and persistence to see it through survive to the end? And to what "end"? Such were the circular dilemmas faced by Johnson and most of his top assistants as day after day between 1962 and 1968 the war went down the drain in Vietnam.

One more comment on determination and persistence, before turning to action. Although we shall analyze it in greater detail in the next chapter, it should be signaled here that in the real world of 1962-68, though not in the never-never world of U.S. policy in Vietnam, American power and leadership was in fact suffering a serious credibility crisis: not from lack of determination or persistence, but precisely from a surfeit of these traits in Vietnam. "When will the Americans cease this insane entanglement?" was the plaintive cry of thousands of Europeans, including some of the top European leaders, Japanese, and others during this period. After 1965 in particular, as U.S. combat forces bogged down in Vietnam, this cry became less plaintive and louder, though perhaps not less obscured from the top U.S. leadership itself.

Action

The premium placed on action by U.S. policy-makers during their Vietnam engagement is of great importance in understanding the U.S. predicament. The whole approach of the New Frontier when it took office was one of action. This was done at least in part by design, in order to distinguish the new administration clearly from what had been

depicted during the campaign as the do-nothing and la
Eisenhower administration. Thus in the U.S. State Departmen
ample, the demand for action was such that even low-echelon o.
mulling over a problem would at times find themselves engaged in t.
unprecedented process of responding to a telephone query from the
president himself. The White House, and accordingly its minions in the
executive-staff offices of the principal agencies—such as the executive
secretariat of the State Department or the office of the secretary of
defense—incessantly demanded a flood of instantaneous briefings and
"action memoranda."

Yet one of the best reasons for having a State Department, and a
fairly massive expert foreign-affairs bureaucracy, is precisely for a
country to possess a kind of "jelly bowl," as John Kennedy sarcastically
used to call this exasperatingly slow department—a sort of inert mass
handling foreign affairs. Foreign Service officers who largely staff foreign affairs ministries around the world, are aware of three things from
long professional experience in foreign affairs. First, having often
served long and repeated periods of duty in a particular region of the
world, and having frequently become experts in such regions, they tend
to realize that the problems or issues they encounter there are generally
more difficult and intractable than they appear in the press or even in
diplomatic reports to world capitals. There are always many more factors and nuances involved than appear in such reports. For a recent
example of this, recall the Angolan raid into Shaba Province of Zaire
in 1978.

Second, professional foreign affairs officers realize, also from long
foreign exposure, that world capitals (and particularly Washington,
D.C., as a superpower capital) are totally self-centered in their belief
that they can help solve problems by waving their own brand of some
magic wand; that is, these capitals see themselves much more seriously
and as playing a much larger role than they really do in problem areas.
To Washington, Washington looks powerful, big, and ever-present in
almost every place; but in these places, whether remote like Chile and
Indonesia or nearby like Quebec, Washington does not look all that
present or all that important. Accordingly, the tendency of perspi-
cacious U.S. Foreign Service officers is to rate Washington's capacity to
act in many situations as considerably lower than it is rated in Washington itself.

Finally, professionals in the foreign affairs business also know
through long experience that what appears as a great problem today
will often more likely than not simply go away if left appropriately
alone. In 1978, for example, the press and Washington made a great

deal of the events in the horn of Africa. However, whether or not by design, little if any U.S. action was taken. So much the better, since by 1979 the problem of the horn of Africa, which is in any case a very long-standing and long-range problem, has again receded into the relatively unobserved. *"Surtout, pas trop de zèle,"* [16] was Talleyrand's wise advice to diplomats, which the latter ignored to the country's peril in the grand action days of the New Frontier and Johnson administrations.

To the New Frontier, and to the Johnson White House later, the State Department and for that matter the entire foreign affairs and national security bureaucracies, were inert masses that had to be galvanized into performance, into action and running things. Eventually, as we shall see in the last section of this chapter, the premium for these bureaucracies was placed on their producing managers and on their demonstrating their adeptness at management. State, Defense, CIA, and other units of the national security bureucracy were turned into *action-producing* factories: counterinsurgency action; development or nation-building action; coordinated reconstruction (i.e., pacification) action; body-count action.

With the installation in about 1961 of the National Military Command Center at the Pentagon, the Operations Center at State, the Intelligence Watch Center at the CIA, and the White House "Situation Room," the entire foreign affairs-national security complex of the government was turned into a kind of Hospital Emergency Center from which the good doctors of the New Frontier and Great Society would administer first aid and, if possible at all, would operate on maimed and dying patients thousands of miles away—whether in Berlin, the Caribbean, or Vietnam. Such operations would symbolize *action,* whether or not the effective direction of such action was even known, and whether or not the operations were even required.

Moreover, what would the United States do if it didn't act? Would it just sit there, while Indochina was going down the Communist drain? This question, when posed by foreign affairs principals, was always difficult for subordinates to answer. The questioners had a ready-made course of action which might, to the subordinate, look erroneous. Did the latter then have a better alternative to suggest? If not, and the subordinate felt that the best action was to take no action at all and said so, the principal's tendency would be ruefully to point out that the subordinate would not be sharing the blame for the potentially disastrous consequences of non-action. These would fall squarely on the principal's lone shoulders. But the principal tended to feel differently about the consequences of wrong actions. He would feel that, at least, he had done or tried to do something. Why and with what result seemed to principals to matter much less than the fact of the action itself. Accordingly, the other side of the coin of regarding action as the essence of policy, was to regard non-action as the fearful peril of the policy-maker. The debate here was not really between action and alternative action, which is still action, but between action and non-action, in which the former was always judged preferable to the latter.

The consequences of the premium placed on action in Indochina by principal policy-makers of the New Frontier and the Great Society were obvious. The United States acted through counterinsurgency and nation-building to keep national liberation wars from spreading infectiously and damagingly; it acted through the deployment of U.S. military advisers and later ground combat forces to demonstrate that it was there when it counted and to uphold the credibility of its commitments; it acted through graduated escalation and bombing of the North to prove that it was strong and tough, and that the enemy would come around; it acted through AID, CORDS,[17] and CIA programs to show its determination and persistence in building a viable policy in South Vietnam; it acted through Vietnamization to leave something real behind while negotiating itself out; and to show its action capabilities it even bombed the enemy's main cities when it was on the verge of getting out.

The more the United States acted, the less it seemed to gain, and the more it seemed to need to act more in order to keep the enemy from gaining. As we shall attempt to demonstrate in the following sections, this was largely because it acted in a vacuum, in which the act of acting itself counted for more than the reasons for action.

3. The Failure of Analysis

The Saigon regime—cut off more and more from the rest of the country by its reactionary social policy, and from the politically alert youth and intellectuals by its denials of democracy—*never acquired any kind of valid social base*. Even before the fall of Diem its supporters consisted almost entirely of corrupt high bureaucrats, the systematically corrupted military and secret service leadership, the small body of landowners and the even smaller American-created group of native war profiteers.
(J. Buttinger, *Vietnam: The Unforgettable Tragedy*, pp. 44-45;
italics mine)

Despite the extraordinary refinements brought to it in the sixties with the introduction of systems analysis and other advanced statistical procedures, the analytical failure of the United States in Vietnam remained unmitigated. In this section we shall endeavor to show that this had little to do with analytic methods, and that even had these methods been yet more refined, and even if *political* analysis had been more objective, that still would have mattered little to the U.S. involvement and conduct of the war in Vietnam. We attribute the analytical failure of the United States in Vietnam to two major factors: the irrelevance of objectivity, and the relevance of subjectivity. We conclude, however, that the question of analysis was basically insignificant to what happened. Before touching the major aspects of the discussion, let us examine first the question of expert knowledge with respect to Vietnam and Indochina.

The Issue of Expert Knowledge

At the end of World War II, only a handful of U.S. officials with any field experience in Indochina were available to the State Department and the intelligence community. Not more than half a dozen U.S. officials at most could speak some Vietnamese. Although the fund of expert knowledge in the government was therefore low, the situation got progressively better in the late forties and early fifties as research and analysis on the Indochina scene in Washington was complemented by some work in U.S. academic institutions and especially by expert reports from U.S. consulates in Saigon, Hanoi and somewhat later Phnom Penh and Vientiane. These were written mainly by French-speaking personnel, of whom a number had significant expertise on Asia. By the early fifties, such nonofficial area experts as Ellen J. Hammer and Milton Sacks were publishing respectable books and periodical articles on Vietnam.[18] This was complemented about the time of Geneva by the works of Donald Lancaster;[19] a host of important correspondents' dispatches, particularly those of Robert Shaplen;[20] and especially by exhaustive official field analyses of every conceivable facet of the Indochina situation.

From the mid-fifties on, Bernard Fall's important work on Indochina began to appear with regularity;[21] and by the late fifties a handful of officials with Vietnamese language competence had been trained and were working in the field. This was to lead by the mid-sixties at the latest to a veritable outpouring of language- and area-trained officials and military officers from numerous civilian and military agencies. By the mid-sixties, the insufficiency of area expertise, if it had ever been as bad as sometimes depicted, had more than been made up. But it has always been incorrect to say that the United States was ever without experts; even for the late forties and early fifties, the writer could name at least a dozen officials and outsiders who had considerable knowledge of Indochina and the situation there.[22]

We shall try to give below what we hope is a fair summary of the overall appraisal that the area experts held of the situation in Indochina until about 1961. After 1961, their outlook began to change, not because there were now more or better area experts, but largely as a function of growing American involvement in Indochina; and because by turning Vietnamese contacts which U.S. experts maintained into cautious proponents of the war, U.S. involvement had the echo effect of reinforcing U.S. expert perceptions along optimistic, as against previously pessimistic, lines.

Before 1961, the experts generally tended to regard Vietnam as basically lacking in cultural and social cohesion. Pronounced regional differences could be observed, with the resources for potential industrialization strongly favoring the North, and the population of the North and Center prevailing over that of the South in almost every important qualitative trait—such as industry and hard work, aspirations for material betterment, nationalism, cohesion, martial quotient. Cambodia was viewed as culturally far more homogeneous and administratively as a less artificial construct than Vietnam under Bao Dai; and Laos as an undecipherable and isolated congeries of primitive tribes, also with pronounced differences between North and South.

Overall, the experts viewed Vietnamese nationalism as having found its major expression in the Viet Minh movement of Ho Chi Minh and his associates, who had led the 1945 revolution and established the DRV. Non-Communist nationalism, understood to have been extraordinarily weakened by French repression in the pre-World War II period, was generally regarded as not having significantly recovered after the war. Its small, artificial and incohesive political groupings (VNQDD, Dai Viet, religious sects, Catholics, etc.) had been caught and torn to shreds in the pincers of French control on the one side, Communist control on the other.[23]

The experts generally concurred that the great exception to the nonexistence of significant anti-Communist nationalism was Ngo Dinh Diem, who tried against great odds after 1954 to give his Vietnam Republic a coherent social and political base; but the experts generally recognized that some of Diem's instruments, such as the Catholic-run *Can Lao* Party, the growing influence of Diem's brothers Nhu (and his wife) in Saigon and Canh in Hue, and the repressiveness of the special forces and security services under the Ngo family, were potentially dangerous to the survival of the Diem regime.[24]

The experts on the whole perceived the Communist-run DRV as militant, tough, spartan, and extremely well-led. No major fissures had appeared within the top leadership—Ho, Dong, Giap and Truong

Chinh—until the purge of the party which resulted from the implementation of land-reform schemes in North Central Vietnam in 1956-58, and which led to the temporary demotion of Truong Chinh and the rise in importance of the southern leader Le Duan. The party under Ho seemed to have popular support not only in the North but throughout Vietnam, reinforced by its victory over the French; and it appeared capable of successfully running the North despite the enormous losses it had suffered in the First Indochina War.

Although Diem had survived in a truncated country following the 1954 Geneva Accords, the general view of the area experts before 1961 was that only a relatively short time-card had been gained in Vietnam; that sooner or later the revolution would start again; and that the South, with a basically unpopular government, ineffectual administration and a doubtfully trained and officered Army, would be highly vulnerable to internal guerrilla war supported by North Vietnam.

Most basically, the earlier (pre-1961) U.S. area experts, both inside and outside government, and whether in Vietnam or the United States, tended with some exceptions to sense clearly that if the revolution broke out again, we would be dealing with a civil war situation. In such a war, the differences between North and South or in the geographic origin of the combatants would be less significant than and overshadowed by the differences between those, northern and southern, who had previously opposed and those who continued to side with the Nationalist-Communist revolution, whatever its current functional name—Viet Minh, Viet Cong, DRV, National Liberation Front, or Provisional Revolutionary Government. Among the anti-revolutionaries, the experts recognized few sincere ideological-political opponents, but many who feared the Communists' potential repression against them for their previous role during the First Indochina War. They counted even more who had simply chosen the material comforts in the U.S.-supported anti-Communist region over the Spartan rigors, sacrifice-imposing, non-self-rewarding Communist-run region and cause.

Nature of the War

The issue of expertise and its role in U.S. policy revolves precisely over the question of the character and nature of the war. What kind of war was this? Was it, as many of the new nation-builders who were coming into Washington under the New Frontier claimed, a Communist bloc-directed aggression, an export of revolution from a clearly distinct entity called North Vietnam to an equally real and distinct entity called South Vietnam, which wanted none of it? Or was it, as many of the older area experts felt even if they did not always force-fully express it, the renewal of a by now ancient civil conflict, one started in both North and South Vietnam by Nationalist-Communists in 1945 as an anticolonialist revolution, not opposed initially by any significant force other than the French, and never abandoned despite the signing of a truce accord which the revolutionary leaders felt had been violated? However, by 1961 the revolution was opposed by those whom the French had eventually attracted and whom the United States, in substituting itself for the French in Indochina, had further cultivated and assisted until they possessed a respectable leader, a type of army and government, and a semblance of administrative structure, however weak and fragile the regime in the South might have appeared in the watershed year of 1961.

The older area experts never vigorously argued their case that this was a renewed revolution or civil war within the new United States administration which took office in 1961. Memories of Geneva had receded. Besides, as we have repeatedly pointed out, the Soviets had given the U.S. government justification for thinking of the partition as quasi-permanent. However, and leaving aside complex legal arguments about the sovereignty of the Republic of Vietnam—many of which in any case amount to rationales and are built on sophistries [25]—it is diffi-cult to understand why area experts did not argue more forcefully the case against the notion that revolution—particularly of the magnitude of that already existing in 1961 in South Vietnam—could be exported. Clearly, the revolution which resumed in the South in 1959 had enor-mous popular support there, or it would not have achieved the success that it had by 1961 or later. At the same time, there is also no gainsay-ing that though in no sense exported, the revolution was wholly and whole-heartedly supported by the Communist power center in North Vietnam.

At any rate, the experts who perceived that the war in Vietnam was civil war and revolution rather than outright aggression, felt rather than expounded their views. While it was of course neither easy nor popular to expound non-faddish, somewhat old-fashioned views at any time during the high cold war, and it was especially difficult to do this during early New Frontier days because of the intellectualism and cre-dentials which the new policy-makers brought to government, it is pos-sible that by their failure to do so, the area experts left the door open for the globalists. But even had they argued their case more forcefully and less equivocally, and presented in every possible decision-making forum of the sixties all the knowledge they possessed, it is still very doubtful that the area experts either from within or outside government would have been heard, by which we mean taken into account. We next turn to the major reason for this.

The Irrelevance of Objectivity

Those who came to power in Washington after January 1961 and dealt with Indochina were, for reasons already discussed, much less interested in learning facts which they believed they already possessed than in expounding and proffering their own ready-made explanations. As we have seen, these dealt largely with global considerations: the necessity to arrest Communist wars of national liberation lest these spread infectiously and contaminate the Third World against our own models of nation-building; the necessity to uphold U.S. commitments, no matter how informally made; the imperative of demonstrating toughness, and the availability if not the use of military power; as well as the necessity to show determination, persistence and action in the task of proving and reproving to the world, including the U.S. Congress and public, the credibility of American leadership and power. Accordingly, the leaders of the sixties had very little interest in the uniqueness or special circumstances of areas such as Indochina, of which area experts might have made them cognizant.

By ruling out particularisms and area knowledge, policy-makers of the sixties were ruling out of their consciousness and ken some of the most fundamental factors involved in understanding Indochina and Vietnam. We shall briefly treat three of these factors.

The French Experience. It was considered by New Frontier Washington, and later as well, basically irrelevant. There were always exceptions, of course; Max Taylor thought he understood the French experience, but that the non-colonialist United States would be immune from some of the problems that had plagued the French. The French had been fighting a colonial war; Americans would be fighting one of popular opposition to communism. The French had not been particularly sophisticated, unable to shake the opprobrium of their defeat in World War II and traditions like those of the unpopular African soldiery of the French colonial units and of the German-filled Foreign Legion, devious and narrow of vision; in other words, the French had been French. On the other hand, the United States would be militarily much stronger and more sophisticated, both in its arsenal and in its employment; unencumbered by colonial traditions; honest, straightforward, and broad of vision; in other words, inherently superior to the French.

Bernard Fall's wise experience of the French war, while frequently listened to by the lower-echelon U.S. military, was largely dismissed in upper-level Washington; studies of the 1950 China frontier battles or of the 1952 Tonkin Delta battles, or of the *Street Without Joy* in the Tuy Hoa area of Central Vietnam,[26] even if read, were ignored. We would not repeat such failures. (We repeated almost precisely the French Tuy Hoa experience at Khe Sanh later.) Even the battle at Dien Bien Phu was regarded as a sort of curiosity, in which weak and weary French forces, lacking a determined commander, had been rather easily shattered by the enemy's overpowering Chinese-supplied firepower. This type of account was very far from the truth—the French had fought with enormous determination and tenacity at Dien Bien Phu, and it was the enemy's manpower and even greater determination which decided the outcome.[27]

On the political side, French experience with the successive Bao Dai governments was dismissed. By the mid-sixties, hardly a single American in Vietnam even knew the names of the previous Bao Dai ministers who reappeared in the new South Vietnamese regimes, or their records in office or personal political histories. For example, few Americans realized that the South Vietnamese labor leader, Tran Quoc Buu, for years the darling of the AFL/CIO in Vietnam, had started out as a political informer for the French *deuxième bureau* in the mid-forties.[28]

On the human side, French experience with the cupidity, cowardice, and meanness of many of their Vietnamese collaborators was also ignored. Washington must have thought that corruption had ended with Diem and failed to realize that he had only contained it and was battling it continously with only slight success.

The Vietnamese Army. Warnings by experts against the unreliability of the Vietnamese soldiery and the lack of appropriate training and motivation of the officer corps, both direct descendants of the Vietnamese *supplétif* forces of the French army,[29] tended also to be disregarded. Even under Diem, and despite efforts to remedy it, soldiers were paid irregularly if at all; their tradition remained one of stealing what they could in the villages. As to the majority of officers, including those who might have received reasonably adequate technical and tactical training under U.S. MAAG auspices during the Diem regime, their general educational and moral background left much to be desired. With the exception of perhaps two dozen or so field and general grade officers, the top command was at best timorous and mediocre, at worst venal and corrupt.[30]

Apparently because of the presence of a large U.S. MAAG, later called MACV (Military Advisory Command, Vietnam), containing substantial numbers of U.S. special forces and counterinsurgency advisers, and later the presence of an overwhelming U.S. combat force, policy-makers in Washington seemed to imagine they could literally *wish* the ARVN to become infused with the leadership, command, morale and tactical capabilities of the U.S. forces. Perhaps simple propinquity would do the job. Except that most U.S. Army elements at all echelons quickly acquired enormous distrust for the Vietnamese, whom they too often saw lacking in even elemental courage, whatever reports went into MACV. Numerous exceptions to this have been and will no doubt continue to be noted by the type of U.S. commanders who can and will express themselves in publications. But it was the overwhelming impression left among GI's and U.S. officers, which one can easily glean from such firsthand accounts of the battlefield situation as those, for example, in Michael Herr's brilliant work, *Dispatches*.[31]

Moreover, despite the pretenses, language communications between the U.S. military and their Vietnamese counterparts remained a problem all through the war. Too few Americans spoke understandable Vietnamese; too few Vietnamese understood or spoke even passable English, although they would always nod affirmatively to their U.S. advisers; and too few Americans realized that most of the Vietnamese officer corps spoke acceptable French until at least the late sixties.

There were of course exceptions to all this. There can be no doubt that some Vietnamese, civilian as well as military, communicated well with Americans and showed guts, determination, courage, and even occasionally, though usually only in extremis, a willingness to fight.

Vietnamese Politics. U.S. policy-makers of the sixties regarded Vietnamese politics as difficult though manageable. At first, high hopes rested on Diem; but when his fall appeared imminent, it was assumed there would be others to take his place and the places of his small team of loyalists.

Appraisals of Minh's brief regime as being both incompetent and neutralist-trending were accepted without real analysis. Yet if a junta regime of the highest and best generals—those who ultimately dared take matters in their own hands to rid the country of a leader who after nine years of rule had become an unpopular dictator—was incompetent, then perhaps no one else could be more competent. Conversely, if a regime of such generals had concluded that some arrangement could be worked out with the southern Communists through Buddhist mediation, perhaps they had good reasons to believe that was the best that could be done in Vietnam in 1963-64, and the United States should at least have explored the possibility with them.

No one subsequently arose who proved much superior to Minh. Gen. Nguyen Khanh and the several civilian leaders who served under him were sheer opportunists; any U.S. expert with appropriate knowledge of politicians like Hung, Oanh, or Quat could have foretold their inevitable fall. Marshall Nguyen Cao Ky, who picked up the government after Khanh, was not much more than a show-off parading in silk uniforms with one of his many Franco-Vietnamese mistresses on his arm, making ridiculous remarks about his hero Hitler, and remaining full of empty braggadocio to the bitter end. It is almost incomprehensible that a U.S. statesman of Lodge's stature could have taken a clown like Ky seriously and sold him to Lyndon Johnson as a great war leader.

We have already (in Chapter IV, Decision 7) discussed Gen. Nguyen Van Thieu, who after 1967 and through Tet and Vietnamization finally emerged as the real leader of the existing Vietnamese polity, such as it was. He had long been the leader, behind the scenes, of the Vietnamese Armed Forces Council and had thrust Ky forward, biding his time until he knew for sure that the Americans were really serious about their involvement. Rigid, obdurate and repressive (as we indicated earlier), Thieu was a Diem without the knowledge of Vietnamese and European history, philosophy, and political theory that Diem had. Like Diem a sincere anti-Communist, he was also a rearguard conniver who shunned the frontal leadership of men. Like Diem he was an ardent Catholic, a fact virtually never reported by the U.S. press but which always remained of importance in a country where Catholics formed but a minuscule minority. Thieu struck no responsive chords in the hearts of the Vietnamese peasants or urban masses, even less among the urban bourgeoisie who despised him as a *parvenu,* as they did almost all other ARVN leaders, and who brought mean obstacles in his way. "Die for Thieu?" became the derisive expression of Vietnamese student youth which, in the late sixties, was avoiding military service by the hundreds of thousands.[32]

Apparently, U.S. policy-makers in the field or in Washington did not want to know, or fully to apprehend, that the nature of the regime, the character and composition of the ruling government of the South in Vietnam, was what the war was all about. Blinded by counter-insurgency and nation-building zeal, search-and-destroy mania, or clear-and-hold passion, U.S. decision-makers somehow seem to have persuaded themselves that was all that mattered; that you could build a viable polity, as they stated they wished, without politicians, through a military-administrative structure *devoid of real social and political base.* In the later stages of the war, virtually any Vietnamese whom U.S. officials did not know personally through his U.S.-connected work in ARVN, intelligence, psychological warfare, AID or in the CORDS-supervised provincial and village pacification efforts, came derisively to be called a *Saigon café politician*. Yet the Vietnamese were presumably fighting to establish a responsive, humane, understanding, capable and independent government! Whence was it to come?

Why did government and politics get excluded to such an extent from American analysis of Vietnam? Why was the analysis of Vietnamese politics so consistently and deeply erroneous after 1963? We shall review in the next section of this chapter some of the nefarious effects of the managerial-operational disease on the U.S. Foreign Service and on the intelligence community. In any event, the problem of politics and leadership in Vietnam seemed to elude the United States. It was either ignored or misrepresented. U.S. officials seemed to wish throughout to hide its true significance. As late as 1974, Ambassador Graham Martin was still claiming that there was no significant internal opposition to the Thieu regime, and what is more damaging, he may have really believed it.

The Relevance of Subjectivity

In Vietnam and in Washington, during 1962-72 and even, for some, during 1973-75, the U.S. government heard what it wished to hear. Reports were distorted at the base of the pyramid of command, often to the unmitigated disgust of the lower-echelon military and civilians who felt compelled to perform the distorting and knew perfectly well that in many instances the enemy body-count was lower than reported; U.S. and South Vietnamese casualties were higher than immediately reported; the enemy's military-political hold over regions was greater than reported; the South Vietnamese and U.S. control over regions was lower than reported.

These frequently doctored and sometimes even invented reports would then be sent up higher, there to be distorted or amplified some more; top staff officers would become exhilarated by the optimism exuding from the distortions made at the base to satisfy presumed desires at the top of the pyramid; and finally, at the very top in Washington, the distorted accounting and reporting, fortified by comments by the blinded staffs, would gain acceptance—sometimes against better judgment. Once solidly anchored in the form of key staff memoranda or estimates to principals in JCS, DOD, CIA, State and the NSC and White House, the optimistic reports would then acquire an aura of biblical veracity and god-given truth that only traitors, like some in the press, would dare question or deny. Hence, the stage was set for the battle royal between U.S. government and press on Vietnam, to which we shall return in later chapters of this book.

The only significant exception to all this, at any responsible level of government, was the cool and detached attitude of two of the principal offices in Washington producing intelligence estimates: the offices of current intelligence and national estimates under the deputy director of intelligence (DDI) at the CIA; and the bureau of intelligence and research (INR) at State. (The analytical offices in the Defense Intelligence Agency were not exceptions, nor were the systems analyses offices of the Secretary of Defense.) But at CIA/DDI and at State/INR there remained a few real area experts who examined reports with cold logic, a hard look unbiased by expectations or desired results, and the skepticism incumbent on those who knew Vietnam and its complexities: the drawing power and resilience of the Communists, the weaknesses and rifts of the anti-Communists, the potential frailties and errors of official American observers operating in a region so alien and remote from their knowledge and experience. These offices produced the less optimistic, sometimes pessimistic national intelligence estimates recorded in the *Pentagon Papers;* they also produced much of the staffing background which found its way into George Ball's memoranda of dissent. But these estimates too were dismissed or ignored as unwarranted conclusions by professional pessimists or particularistic analysts.

Why? Why were reports doctored at the base? Why were they distorted up the line? Why were top staffs blinded and unwilling to investigate or search further? Why were optimistic analyses accepted and pessimistic ones dismissed? Why were "we can; they can't" estimates pushed forward to the president and "doubtful that we can; doubtful that they can't" estimates locked out of sight? The answers lie for the most part in certain apsects of what we know of cognitive processes and the nature of action. They are not inherent in the specifics of the Vietnam situation *per se.* In other words, the relevance of subjectivity and the irrelevance of objectivity in Vietnam was not a unique phenomenon that had never occurred before and would not occur again; rather, it was typical of human behavior in the area of political analysis and appraisal.

Observation and Analysis. The predecisional phases of policy-making generally begin with (a) an observational phase; (b) an analytical phase. An event occurs somewhere that affects some people significantly enough to come to official attention. Data is then gathered through observation and contact-work to answer the relatively simple questions: What? Where? In the case of Vietnam, a struggle between Communist Nationalists and avowed non-Communist Nationalists for control of the government of South Vietnam. Once officials know, or think they perceive, what is happening where, they then move to analysis, that is to answering the questions: Why? How? In the issue at hand, why and how are these forces in contention? Who is likely to prevail and why? It is clear that the reliability of analysis is entirely dependent on the evidence and data gathered in the observational phase; and that the two phases are closely interconnected. They can also be regarded as potentially objective; that is, there is no inherent reason why subjective premises and value judgments, biases and assumptions, should enter into either the data-gathering on an event or in the analysis of that event.

If, to resort to a familiar and even trivial level, A leaves overwhelming evidence and in fact admits that he murdered B (his girlfriend), anyone at all involved, even A's father, can objectively agree that B was murdered and that A committed the crime. The investigative detective, analyzing the crime, can objectively discern motives for it; although if A's father analyzed it, he would probably, though not certainly, lay more stress on mitigating factors—such as possible provocations by B of A, or the ingestion of alcohol or drugs by A. That is why analysis is always only "potentially" objective. If the analyst is closely connected with the matter under scrutiny, his objectivity may become questionable, even if he tries as hard as possible to remain unbiased. (Thus for a recent example from diplomacy, it is possible that a degree of objectivity was lost by U.S. Embassy observers investigating allegations against the People's Temple in Guyana in 1978 because of the close relation the leaders of the temple maintained with the Guyana government and indirectly therefore with the U.S. Ambassador supporting that government.)

Appraisal and Recommendation. In the third predecisional phase of policy-making, officials move into the most significant area, that of appraisal, which tries to answer the question: What do the events observed and analyzed mean to their government? Thus, in the issue we are studying, "what do events in Indochina mean to the U.S.?" At this juncture, objectivity tends to give way to subjectivity even more than it does in analysis when a self-interested party participates. In foreign policy, no government can ever be totally disinterested in any foreign event. In the case of a superpower such as the United States, there are very few events in the world which if they gather any attention at all will not in however slight a measure affect it. If, moreover, a superpower like the United States is deeply involved in an area like Indochina or Vietnam, virtually any attention-gathering event there will most surely affect it deeply.

From appraisal, that is from subjectively judging how a given set of analyzed foreign events will affect a country, officials obtain the basic kernel of a foreign policy decisional output. If the response is that these events will affect a state a great deal, then governments will often obtain a more active or engaged recommendation for decision, and consequently a more involved set of policy actions than if the answer is that the events affect a state very little. Once officials move from the appraisal to the recommendational phase of the predecisional process in foreign policy-making, they are set for a decision. Based on appraisal, advisers and decision-makers recommend actions which are then taken, modified, or not taken. The policy actions decided upon are then implemented, after which the process repeats itself through feedback, that is through the gathering of new data and observation. See Figure 1.

FIGURE 1
Static Phases of the Foreign Policy-Making Process

Input	Process	Output
Observational Phase	Analytical Phase	Decisional Phase
Feedback	Appraisal Phase	Implementational Phase
	Recommendational Phase	Feedback

Of course, reality is never as neat as such a scheme. In the real world of policy-making, while the process tends to follow these basic outlines, it is in fact very messy, and all the phases tend to overlap.

Let us return to appraisal. A judgment is made here as to the importance of a given set of events to a state or government. If these events are likely to affect it highly, then it will in turn endeavor to affect them. Affectiveness means direction, that is, the wish to affect events in a desired direction. The all-important question now becomes: What is desirable?

The So-Called National Interest. In foreign policy, what is desirable is usually discerned in the standard way—what is desirable is what is regarded to be in the national interest. But regarded by whom to be in the national interest? The answer to this can only be, by the policy-makers of the moment themselves. The only way, then, to discern the national interest is to let the leaders of any country at any given moment of history interpret it in their own best, but always and inevitably biased, lights. This reasoning rejects contentions of the existence of a permanent, fixed national interest for any given country that can be discerned impersonally. The national interest exists, all right, but at any given time it is what the authoritative, i.e. legitimate, leaders of a nation-state declare it to be.[33] Viewed along a time-dimension, therefore, the national interest is a variable, not a permanent factor.

Subconscious Appraisal. How does appraisal, which as we have seen is a subjective cognitive exercise, come to get out of phase and to affect analysis, presumably an objective exercise of cognition? The answer lies in a phenomenon of cognition which we may term subconscious appraisal. This occurs during the analytical phase of a predecisional foreign policy-making process when the subsequent appraisal phase is of sufficient significance and importance to the lives and careers of those engaged in the analytical process. In simpler words, analysts are subconsciously appraising while analyzing.

This brings us back to the analogy of the crime committed by A against B. If all the persons involved in the investigation of this crime possess inherent sympathies for A similar to those of A's father, then it is likely that in the investigation of A's crime, mitigating motives or factors pertaining to A will be perceived and found which will tend to cast A in a more favorable light than if all the investigators had not been sympathetic to him. Accordingly, a cardinal principle of what was called "intelligence" in U.S. foreign policy-making, but was really analysis, used to be to keep the intelligence analysts completely separated and divorced from policy considerations and policy-makers.[34] This principle was never fully applied in practice; but in the analysis of the Vietnam War it was totally disregarded, other than in the exceptions in offices of the government mentioned earlier.

Actor Analysts. Official analysis in Vietnam was performed at all levels largely by persons who were also participants in the policy process and therefore sympathized with and had interests in the policies and programs being implemented. On the outside, however, the U.S. effort in Vietnam was being analyzed by the U.S. press which, whether or not it had other self-interests to pursue, was largely unencumbered by participation in pacification or in fighting programs in Vietnam, and therefore capable of reporting more objectively. Similarly with outside academic observers, some of whom quite early in the U.S. engagement provided analyses diametrically at variance with those of the government.[35]

Largely because of subconscious appraisal, official analysts often quite unintentionally and without specific instructions to do so colored their analyses in such a way that the programs and activities in which they were themselves engaged emerged as more successful than they really were, or than they seemed to disengaged observers. The phenomenon is really quite well-known. Forty years ago, in his book on the interwar crisis, E.H. Carr wrote on what he called "The Wish is Father to the Thought." [36]

One naturally perceives the results of one's own labor in terms more rose-colored than warranted and is naturally if not instinctively at odds with the critic or doomsayer. The Roman Consul Sulla had the messengers killed who brought him bad news in 87 B.C., and Cassandras before and since have been highly unpopular in ruling palaces and foreign offices. On the contrary, soothsayers have always been employed by rulers, and in Vietnam the soothsayers were the lower echelons of the military and civilian bureaucracies in the field and in Washington. Cassandras, dissenters, and other prophets of gloom could either be removed from the policy-making process altogether; or better, as in the case of George Ball, tamed with some comic amusement as dissenters-in-residence. Their presence ultimately legitimized the whole delusory process.

We stated earlier that not all analysts-participants approved this process and that many felt rancor, outrage and disgust at the deception in which they felt compelled by subtle psychological pressures, not by coercion, to participate. But with few exceptions like the well-known John Paul Vann, the dissenters in the field rarely aired their disgust publicly, resigned their jobs or commissions, or stopped doing what it was disgusting them to do. More often, they would anonymously communicate their feelings to U.S. reporters, whose own tendencies to skepticism at official analyses were thereby reinforced. Under the circumstances, this may have been the best that low-echelon personnel and officials could do. When an individual's life-goals and career are involved, it is asking a lot to make him place them on the line.

The Insignificance of Analysis

We noted in Decision 6 of the previous chapter what it took in the way of maneuver and persuasion to make President Johnson change course. We wish to conclude here with the proposition that analysis of the war and pacification efforts in Vietnam played only a very small part in the U.S. Vietnam enterprise altogether, although we have given the role of analysis much space and will return to it again in the final chapter. Appropriate analysis of where the United States stood in Vietnam would not have been significantly different in 1968 from 1963, 1965, or 1967. It always stood at the losing end, and hopes of surmounting and overcoming the obstacles were always extremely slender when analyzed in the cold light of objective premises and the real facts of Vietnam. The United States most probably would have gone on, even with appropriate analysis and even if subconscious appraisal had not invaded the objective analytic preserve.

Whatever Nixon and Kissinger themselves truly believed about the possibilities of Vietnamization—we conjectured in the last chapter, Decision 7, that they did not believe in them much if at all—many top U.S. policy-makers made themselves accept the notion even after 1969 that the Vietnamese could pull off alone what they had failed to accomplish with our massive engagement at their side in 1961-68. Cold, logical, and objective analysis still had little to do with U.S. officials' beliefs on the war, even after they had admitted to themselves the failure of analysis earlier.

It is in fact perfectly possible that President Johnson did not even believe, or at least fully believe, the faulty analyses with which he was presented in 1964-68; that he accepted them because he wanted to believe them so much. The point to make then, in the end, is that the whole question of analysis is basically insignificant to the question of why the United States went into, stayed in, or got out of Vietnam. It went in for a combination of the reasons treated in the previous chapters; and out for the reasons we shall consider later. Neither the issue of expert knowledge, nor that of the irrelevance of objectivity or the importance of subjectivity, were central to the case. Had thousands of knowledgeable experts been available in the forties, fifties and sixties; and had Washington really analyzed dispassionately and objectively rather than subjectively, not listening only to what it wanted to hear, the United States would still have gone in; and it would still have stayed in until new domestic and foreign pressures and perspectives finally forced it out.

The United States did not go in because of faulty analysis of the Vietnam situation proper; but because of containment, its superpower ethos, including its anti-Communist component, its appraisal of the danger of national liberation wars, and its firm belief that U.S. commitments everywhere would be jeopardized if it did not show firmness, determination, and persistence in Vietnam. The United States did not stay in because of defective analysis, but owing to its leaders' fears of the domestic consequences of losing to communism. It was for these reasons that the ten fateful decisions were made; and in order to demonstrate the credibility of U.S. leadership and power that the United States employed toughness and macho, applied controlled military power, and put the premium on action. Cognitive analysis had little if anything to do with all that.

The failure of analysis was in the final account an excusable failure of policy-making style; possibly, an incorrigible one. This failure was reinforced by the aspect to which we turn next: the managerial, operational, programmatic and technocratic fever which seized hold of U.S. policy in the sixties.

4. The Triumph of Management

We advance here the proposition that policy-makers at responsible levels of the U.S. government are motivated principally by three interdependent sets of factors: (1) what we may term an affective motivational set—those factors involving their will to modify the environment with which they are concerned in directions which they desire; (2) what we may term an effective motivational set—those factors involving their will to make the machinery or the institutions of government over which they preside run effectively, smoothly, and well; and (3) what we may term a recreative or gaming set—factors involving their will to remain engaged and to compete successfully in the play for political power and position. We shall not in this section be concerned with the last of these sets.

The Decline of Affective Motivation

Although affective motivation can be distinguished from effective, and from the recreative set, it must be conceded at the outset that affectiveness in a statesman or policy-maker need not necessarily or always be genuine, i.e., what it purports to be. President Franklin D. Roosevelt, for example, may in fact have been a lot less interested in improving the lot of poor people during the Depression of the thirties than he was in using such programs as the Works Project Administration, Social Security, the Fair Labor Standards Act and the Minimum Wage Act in order simply to obtain re-election in 1936 and then again in 1940. Whatever his ultimate motivation in political terms, however, President Roosevelt revealed from the very start of his administration a strong desire and determination to change the environment in which the Great Depression had occurred and, in order to accomplish this, to change the direction of policy. His programs were intended to serve that end. We can therefore say that, in President Roosevelt, the affective motivational set was highly developed. As he secured the assent of Congress, sometimes against considerable odds, and embarked on his programs, so many and sometimes overlapping new units of federal government were created that the U.S. federal bureaucracy and administration grew confusing to many people. Accordingly, we can probably say that President Roosevelt's effective motivational set was not highly developed as contrasted to his affective set.

Similarly, to take an example from foreign policy, President Truman and Secretaries of State James Byrnes and Dean Acheson were determined to halt Soviet and Communist power in Europe and to that effect conceived and implemented the Truman Doctrine, the Marshall Plan and the North Atlantic Alliance upon which President Eisenhower and Secretary of State Dulles later erected complex structures of consultations between governments in the North Atlantic area. These were meant to establish an ever firmer network of political, military, and economic interrelationships among the Western Allies. Much of this structuring during 1945-55 resulted in turn in an ever-denser network of relationships within Western Europe itself, which led eventually to the signing of the Treaty of Rome (1958), establishing the European Economic Community (Common Market) with the declared goal of creating the political union of Western Europe at a later stage. All these were affective moves on the stage of history, prompted and motivated by the will of statesmen and policy-makers to change the environment and in their judgment to improve it in directions they desired and expressly declared.

As the environment, both domestic and international, proceeded to change in the late forties and early fifties, and eventually froze into what we have been calling the high cold war, huge bureaucracies began to develop and grow—both in the United States proper and in and around all the regional and international organs created by the affective motivation of foreign policy-makers. As a superpower, the United States was drawn and felt compelled to engage itself heavily in world politics. As its search for security grew, along with its tendency to equate national security with the spread of its own values in various regions of the globe, so did U.S. military and civilian bureaucracies engaged in the making of foreign policy and national security. The machinery to effect, that is to implement and sustain, the strong affective motivational drive of U.S. statesmen and policy-makers thus became very large.

At the crest of U.S. power in 1959, the foreign policy-related bureaucracies, which had consisted of only a few thousand officials at the end of World War II, had grown into literally hundreds of thousands of civilians spread over some forty agencies of the federal government, to which could be added the several million men in the military forces. By 1959, the United States had become a very large national security state. The following were only some of the principal, i.e. most engaged, agencies and staffs that had emerged since the war:

White House

National Security Council and staffs
Variety of special advisers to presidents

State Department

Regional bureaus (EUR, EA, ARA, AF, NEA)
Functional bureaus, including Intelligence/Research
Over 100 field missions, including mission to the United Nations

Defense Department

Office of Secretary of Defense
Office of International Security Affairs
Joint Chiefs of Staff
Services top staffs
Defense Intelligence Agency
National Security Agency

Central Intelligence Agency

Intelligence production (overt, including technical)
Intelligence collection (clandestine)
Intelligence operations (clandestine)

United States Information Agency (Now called International Communications Agency)

Washington planning and program staffs
Several hundred field posts abroad
Voice of America

U.S. Agency for International Development

Washington program planning and administration
About 100 large field missions

Commerce Department

Bureau of International Trade
Field representation

Agriculture Department

Foreign Agricultural Service

Treasury Department

Field representation
Monitoring International Monetary Fund and Bank

Labor Department

Divison of International Labor
Field representation

From this brief sampling we can see why it became perilously diffi-cult for policy-makers in the late fifties or sixties to allow their affective motivational sets full heads of steam. Every indication of change, in whatever direction, would literally give rise immediately to huge obsta-cles. The lethargy and on-going momentum of the bureaucracy might absorb and overcome proposals for new directions; the bureaucracy might oppose change outright, as contrary to its growing vested interest in the status quo; the bureaucracy might misinterpret new policies and, not necessarily deliberately, give them precisely the opposite effect from that intended by the affective policy-makers.

The phenomenon of the imprisonment of potential policy change in the grip of an immovable bureaucracy has been well described and analyzed in Henry Kissinger's essay, "Domestic Structure and Foreign Policy," published originally in 1966.[37] By the early sixties, when U.S. involvement in Vietnam started in earnest, the United States was the archetypal *bureaucratic-pragmatic state* in the sense meant by Kissinger, and the affective motivational drive of its statesmen and policy-makers had become frozen in the concrete of bureaucratic policy-making.

This background makes it easier to understand why U.S. options in Vietnam and Indochina were not reviewed, in 1959-64, for example, in the light of ongoing new international developments such as the ap-proaching nuclear parity of the superpowers; the Soviet Union's greater capacity to extend its influence through conventional arms sales and deployments; Gen. de Gaulle's demand for an independent third-force Europe; and most significantly the developing conflict between the So-viet Union and the Chinese People's Republic over ideological, na-tionality, border, economic, and other issues. U.S. options were not reviewed because in so many ways it was simply easier to go on as before. The premium was placed not on reviewing why the United States was doing what, but on doing it better. This point is very impor-tant; for "doing it better" allows full rein to the effective motivational set of policy-makers while the affective set is kept in check.

The New Frontier on coming into office stated its desire to induce change, particularly in the Third World and in the firmly established direction discussed in Chapter III, namely nation-building and development. As we indicated, however, the nation-builders of the New Frontier were chiefly concerned with preserving and enhancing *their* models of development, less so with real change in the Third World. On balance, and although some leading policy-makers in the New Frontier and Great Society undoubtedly felt they were positively affecting history, the facts speak against this notion. The United States ended up by the late sixties and early seventies in a situation in which it was widely perceived all over the world, and by many people at home as well, to be supporting only the status quo, or unpopular dictators, as many critics put it. At the same time, the United States seemed everywhere to be opposing popular revolutions.[38] Let us examine these allegations briefly.

It is fundamental to the concept of affectiveness as a motivational drive of foreign policy-makers that the latter will examine and appraise politics, or the play for power and influence among leaders who hold or strive to hold power in a variety of extremely different and often highly perplexing situations, with a view to uncovering the political orientations and directions motivating such leaders. Logic would lead one to suppose that a group of strongly affectively motivated U.S. leaders would seek out and support men abroad who shared their own presumed devotion to such basic U.S. values as national independence, democracy, freedom and human rights, economic and social betterment of the masses, human change, and progress in the broadest sense.

A look, however, at an admittedly selective but not unrepresentative list of whom the leaderships of the Great Frontier and Great Society supported and opposed abroad, particularly in the Third World, reveals that what the American leadership of the sixties sought above all were stable regimes, i.e., regimes that would continue and maintain ongoing systems and processes of government and economy, and neither induce destabilizing reforms nor allow uncertain forces to reach power. Such regimes were generally regarded as most consonant with U.S. values. Thus in Brazil, Quadros and Goulart were regarded as too radical in seeking reforms and were replaced (with covert U.S. help) by a military oligarchy; in Iran, the Shah's autocratic regime continued to receive enormous U.S. support; in Korea, the United States placed itself squarely behind the dictatorship of Park Chung Hee; in Africa, there was hesitancy in supporting socialist leaders of uncertain tendencies; in Indonesia, the military dictator Suharto obtained U.S. military assistance.

In opting for stability as the highest political value in the international environment, the American policy-makers of the sixties and early seventies opted against "affect" in history, against political-ideological dynamics, and in favor of effectiveness, as we shall shortly see. This choice was conceptually confirmed for U.S. policy-makers by the "end of ideology" school of theory in politics,[39] which well complemented the "system theory" approach of nation-builders and economic comparativists discussed in Chapter III. The way was thus open for political affectiveness to be muted, while economic and technocratic effectiveness took over the central role in our policy-making.

The Rise of Effective Motivation

The passion for effectiveness stemmed, like all complicated phenomena, from a number of different sources and factors. We will discuss some of these here; they are all complementary.

"Can-Do" Ethic. The mentality that nothing was really beyond American achieving was a fundamental part of our superpower ethos and pervaded the whole American elite. No task was too hard, no challenge too great; in fact, almost any challenge that came along tended to be welcomed. Part of this ethic stemmed from American military success in World War II; part of it from our virtually unchallenged postwar supremacy in the world; part from the success of the U.S. economy at home and of U.S. business both at home and abroad. The "do what?" in "can do" became quite secondary.

Development of Macro Theories. Whether these theories referred to the world or to domestic economic systems (Keynesianism), economic development (Rostow's and associated and successor schools), political systems (Almond's and derived comparativist approaches), or world ideologies, they had in common a *system* approach derived in the social sciences straight from dubious analogies with the natural sciences, an approach with a built-in bias in favor of the status quo. As we indicated in Chapter III, system approaches wished to discern recurrent patterns and if possible quantify social and political data, giving to political leaders "roles" to play or perform, to masses "demands" to aggregate, and to institutions "outputs" to produce. The purpose of politics—that is, power in order to allocate values—thereby gradually slid out of the sight of the conceptualizers, as "system maintenance" became the dominant value attributed to "players in the system" (i.e., political leaders).

The tendency to espouse macro theories of political behavior built on system approaches had two disastrous effects on the conceptual baggage underlying the premises of U.S. policy-makers in the sixties, many of whom, with the arrival of the New Frontier intellectuals, were themselves theorists. First, it injected rigidity into policy evaluations, seeking to make these conform to the prevailing macro-theoretical concepts. By placing system maintenance at varying levels of analysis—international systems, regional systems, internal governmental systems—at the center of value considerations, it led to making global stability the prime value of U.S. policy and to closing the door to real change. Second, it induced the type of global approach which we treated in Chapter III and which regarded resistance to national liberation wars and the upholding of all U.S. commitments regardless of their nature as the only basis on which a world order congenial with U.S. values could be achieved.

Apotheosis of Technocracy. It stands to reason that if "we are up to any challenge," and the challenge discerned through macro-theoretical lenses is the maintenance of world stability, then what is needed are not experts in what moves men in what directions (affective), but experts in what keeps men going in their present directions, and makes them get there more smoothly and efficiently. Accordingly, U.S. policy in the sixties resorted principally to technocrats who were experts in how to produce at lower unit cost more of what had always been produced, and not in how best to organize economic or social activity toward the most desirable ends under the particular circumstances involved.

The technocrat is in essence an efficiency expert who optimizes what is; he is just the opposite of what political leaders have always been, that is, experts in optimizing what could be. The technocrat addresses what is, not what ought to be. It was rampant technocracy which performed Hitler's genocidal crimes, never raising the question of their propriety or value. It was rampant technocracy which would give the United States nation-building in the conceptual mode of the macro-theorists, counterinsurgency in the conceptual mode of the new warriors, and pacification of the countryside in Vietnam in the conceptual mode of the systems analysts.

Pervasiveness of Technocracy. The efficiency experts turned government technocrats came mainly from specialized graduate schools of business administration, but also from schools of engineering, public administration, agriculture, and other specialized fields such as defense studies. In such institutions, numbers, quantification, and statistics reigned supreme; they had invented refined cost accounting and had ultimately managed to bring sophisticated micro-organizational practices into congruence with new and still emerging macro-organizational theories.

This was the land of incremental decision-making and administration; of super-sophisticated deterrence doctrine; of political development by model-building. In the practice of American industry, it was the land of the quality car or shoe at lowest unit cost, the advertisement-driven consumer society in which what is bought and whether it is needed counts for less than buying it and making the best deal.

The U.S. of the late forties and the fifties produced a surplus of technocrats from every conceivable variety of civil and military institution of higher learning, and from industry and the private sector. They literally invaded and overwhelmed the U.S. government in the later fifties and sixties. Seeking the attractive benefits with which government would reward them, and above all the adventure which it would provide by sending them abroad, thousands of these technocrats ended up in defense, the services, the State Department, AID, U.S. Information, U.S. intelligence, and programs such as CORDS in Vietnam. There they would presumably produce not shoes or cars, but polity and administration, pacification and body-counts.

The Manager As Supreme Technocrat. The leaders of technocracy were quite extraordinary men called managers. Their intellects were ferocious; their bearing cool, unemotional, correct. Their moral sense was flexible on matters of broad public interest, such as corporate pricing policies, but tended to be rigid on matters of narrow private behavior. Their conduct was dispassionate, as it had been in the corporate chambers, foundation suites, high offices of institutions of higher learning, or large law firms whence they hailed. Their task was not to set tasks, but to perform them well.

Secretary McNamara and McGeorge Bundy exemplified this type of man. In them, on the surface at least, affective motivation had been suppressed by the effective set. Why else would a top manager (president) at Ford, and an administrator (dean) at Harvard, respectively midwestern and eastern WASPs, of undefined political or party hue, suddenly take such exalted offices under a liberally inclined Catholic Democratic president? And stay under a Texan ex-New Dealer who in his willful emotional character and impassioned conduct seemed the precise opposite of their cool and efficient temperaments? There were important managerial things to "do." [40]

Yet the things to do, and which the technocrats and managers proceeded in the sixties to do in Vietnam, seemed as we shall see in the next chapter to be only artificially and remotely related to the highly charged circumstances of men fighting and dying in distant jungles and paddies over causes which bore no resemblance to the production of cars or shoes at lowest unit cost—causes which were as profound and alien to the mind-sets of these technocrats as nationalism, imperialism, and social justice.

Notes

1. *See,* for example, Chapter 1 of Noam Chomsky's *For Reasons of State* (New York: Pantheon, 1973), pp. 3-171.
2. Public statements by Gen. Curtis LeMay, including his famous ". . . or we're going to bomb them back into the Stone Age" (May 6, 1964) and others of like ilk, are cited in Clyde Pettit, *The Experts* (Secaucus, N.J.: Lyle Stuart, 1975), p. 177. *See also The New York Times* (Oct. 4, 1968), p. 1.
3. The Pentagon Papers abound in such communications. *See,* for example, *Pentagon Papers,* 3 and 4, Documents.
4. Halberstam, *Best and Brightest,* p. 666.
5. Poole, *The United States and Indochina,* p. 151.
6. Seymour M. Hersh, *Mylai 4: A Report on the Massacre and its Aftermath.* (New York: Random House, 1970); Richard Hammer, *One Morning in the War: The Tragedy of Son My.* (New York: Coward-McCann), 1970.
7. Secretary McNamara's frequent conferences with his chief military commanders and civilian advisers during this period, often numbering several dozen persons, became known to insiders as "McNamara's band concerts."
8. Maxwell D. Taylor. *Swords and Plowshares,* (New York: W.W. Norton, 1972), *See* pp. 307 ff.
9. Halberstam, *Best and Brightest.*
10. James M. Gavin, *Crisis Now.* (New York: Random House, 1968). *See* especially chapter III, pp. 39-67.
11. A discussion of the National Security Act of 1947 and the institutions it created can be found in Lawrence J. Korb, *The Joint Chiefs of Staff: The First Twenty-Five Years* (Bloomington, Ind.: Indiana University Press, 1976), pp. 15 ff.
12. William P. Kreml, *The Anti-Authoritarian Personality* (Oxford: Pergammon Press, 1977). *See also* R.J. Barnet, *Roots of War.*
13. See Chapter VI, Section 3.
14. Halberstam, *Best and Brightest,* p. 588.
15. Hans J. Morgenthau, *A New Foreign Policy for the United States* (New York: Praeger, 1969), p. 155.
16. "Above all, not too much zeal . . ."
17. CORDS, acronym for Coordinator for Rural Development and Social Reconstruction. Heart of the Pacification Program headed during its key period by Ambassador Robert Komer.
18. Ellen J. Hammer, *Struggle for Indochina;* Milton Sacks, "Marxism in Vietnam" in Frank N. Traeger, ed., *Marxism in Southeast Asia* (Stanford: Stanford University Press, 1959).
19. Donald Lancaster. *The Emancipation of French Indochina* (New York: Oxford University Press, 1961).
20. The *New Yorker* correspondent in Indochina in the fifties and sixties. See Robert Shaplen, *The Lost Revolution* (New York: Harper and Row, 1955; rev. 1965).

21. Works by Bernard B. Fall: *The Viet Minh Regime: Government and Administration in the Democratic Republic of Vietnam* (Ithaca, New York: Cornell University, 1954); *Street Without Joy: Indochina At War, 1946-54* (Harrisburg, Pa.: Stackpole, 1961, 1963); *The Two Viet Nams; Viet-Nam Witness;* with Marcus G. Raskin, eds., *The Vietnam Reader* (New York: Vintage, 1965); *Hell in a Very Small Place: The Siege of Dien Bien Phu* (Philadelphia: Lippincott, 1966); *Last Reflections on a War* (Garden City, N.Y.: Doubleday, 1967).

22. Among outsiders, for example, the anthropologists John Embree at Yale; Lauriston Sharp at Cornell; Cora Du Bois at Sarah Lawrence; Richard Coughlin at Virginia; the historian John Cady at Ohio University. Among officials, Albert Seligmann at State; John Getz and Edmund Gullion at State; Chester Cooper, Paul Springer, and Luigi Conein among many others at the CIA.

23. P.M. Kattenburg, "Obstacles to Political Community: Southeast Asia in Comparative Perspective," *Southeast Asia Quarterly,* Vol. 2, No. 2 (Spring, 1973), pp. 193-209.

24. Shaplen, *Lost Revolution,* esp. Ch. IV.

25. Eugene V. Rostow, *Peace in the Balance: The Future of American Foreign Policy* (New York: Simon and Schuster, 1972), pp. 145-79, esp. pp. 162-63.

26. See Note 21.

27. Fall, *Hell.*

28. From personal recollection of documents of the early fifties. If this recollection is defective, I sincerely apologize.

29. See Chapter II.

30. *Ibid.*

31. Michael Herr, *Dispatches* (New York: Knopf, 1977).

32. While I have been unable to obtain accurate statistics as to the percentage of eligible Vietnamese evading military service in the Vietnam armed forces at given periods, this percentage can be stated with assurance to have been very high at all periods.

33. Edgar S. Furniss and Richard C. Snyder, *An Introduction to American Foreign Policy* (New York: Rinehart, 1955), p. 17; James N. Rosenau, *The Scientific Study of Foreign Policy* (New York: Free Press, 1971), pp. 239-49.

34. *See* Harry Howe Ransom, *The Intelligence Establishment* (Cambridge: Harvard University Press), 1970, p. 215.

35. An excellent example is Hans J. Morgenthau, "We Are Deluding Ourselves in Vietnam," *The New York Times Magazine* (April 18, 1965), pp. 25, 85 ff.

36. E.H. Carr, *Twenty Years Crisis,* pp. 67-71, 71-74.

37. *Daedalus,* Vol. 95, No. 2 (Spring 1966); the essay is also reprinted in *American Foreign Policy: Three Essays.* (New York: Norton, 1969, 1972).

38. Barnet, *Roots of War* and *Intervention and Revolution.*

39. Daniel Bell, *The End of Ideology: On the Exhaustion of Political Ideas in the Fifties* (New York: Free Press, 1962).

40. James M. Roherty, *Decisions of Robert S. McNamara: A Study of the Role of the Secretary of Defense* (Coral Gables, Fla.: University of Miami Press, 1970).

Chapter VI

Losing Without Losing, 1961-72

Thus did the Americans ignore the most basic factor of the war, and when they did stumble across it (as Taylor did in the report he brought back to the country at Thanksgiving time in 1964: "the ability of the Viet Cong continuously to rebuild their units and to make good their losses is one of the mysteries of this guerrilla war . . .") it continued to puzzle them. McNamara's statistics and calculations were of no value at all, because they never contained the fact that if the ratio was ten to one in favor of the government, it still meant nothing, because the one man was willing to fight and die and the ten were not.

(Halberstam, *The Best and the Brightest,* paper ed., pp. 562-63.)

1. The Heyday of the Managerial Approach

America's Indochina effort in 1961-72 was at all times conceived and controlled from Washington by an extremely small group of top policy-makers who planned and orchestrated it.[1] We shall term these top leaders the "principals," or the "inner circle," and further review their way of making decisions in the last section of this chapter. These men held enormous power and authority, not only within the executive but within the whole federal apparatus, as well as in the country at large, since at least until about 1968 the Congress remained generally passive and acquiescent.

We have already mentioned and discussed some of the principals in Washington. At various times during 1961-72 they included Presidents Kennedy, Johnson, and Nixon; National Security Advisers McGeorge Bundy, Walt W. Rostow, and Henry Kissinger; Secretaries of State

195

Dean Rusk and William Rogers; Secretaries of Defense Robert McNamara, Clark Clifford, and Melvin Laird; CIA Directors John McCone, Adm. William Raborn and Richard Helms. Other key, although slightly subordinate figures included Deputies and Assistant Secretaries of Defense John McNaughton, William Warncke, Paul Nitze, Cyrus Vance, and Allen Enthoven, and Undersecretaries and Assistant and Deputy Assistant Secretaries of State Averell Harriman, Roger Hilsman, William Bundy, Nicholas Katzenbach, U. Alexis Johnson, William Sullivan, Leonard Unger, and Philip Habib. Subordinate officials at the White House included Chester Cooper, William Jorden, and Richard Sneider. To this small inner group can be added U.S. Ambassadors to Vietnam Frederick Nolting, Henry Cabot Lodge, Maxwell Taylor, Ellsworth Bunker, and Graham Martin; and Saigon "Pacification" Directors Robert Komer and William Colby (the latter previously had also been the main subordinate figure at the CIA).

The forty-some individuals cited above, which include only one military personality, Gen. Maxwell Taylor, rotated in the principal policy-making positions during our Vietnam engagement from 1961-72. Many of these men have been exhaustively scrutinized, analyzed, and dissected in Halberstam's masterful *The Best and The Brightest.*

The inner circle shared the conviction that the United States could not afford to lose in Indochina and Vietnam. There has been confusion on this point, with the U.S. military during 1961-72 understandably taking the lead in conveying to the U.S. public the notion that the United States must have been out to win. On the contrary, the country was never out to win in Vietnam. It was out not to lose and, if possible, to win. Insofar as the U.S. objective in the war can be distinguished at all, and we shall return to this important point in a later chapter, it was to try to help the South Vietnamese forces defeat the Communists in the South and, failing that, to help them perpetuate a stalemate. Reduced to its essentials, the U.S. objective in Indochina was to avoid the painful circumstances which members of the U.S. inner circle perceived would befall them personally as well as the country at large in the event of a loss of Indochina to the Communists.

Much of the confusion that arose on the question of U.S. objectives in Indochina came from the fact that none of the three presidents involved, or any other in the listed group of principals, would ever declare candidly and unambiguously that perpetuation of a stalemate was their minimum objective. Nor would they commit themselves clearly to win; nor, at least until 1968, to withdraw, which was regarded as synonymous with losing. As we shall note again later, the objectives of our Indochina involvement were left open-ended.

The Policy of Stalemate

Given U.S. unwillingness to lose owing to the fear of the domestic political consequences, what were some of the principal reasons for preferring to perpetuate stalemate by keeping the war limited and controlled in the South, instead of going all-out against North Vietnam?

First, there always remained uncertainty as to the nature of the war. Throughout, there remained nagging doubts among the principals, whatever the certainties among the military or the bureaucrats below them and whatever the differences on this point between the principals themselves, as to whether the war was really one of aggression (before 1965), of provoked aggression (after 1965), or of revolution and counterrevolution.

Second, there was never any desire to eliminate North Vietnam. At no time during the entire period of U.S. massive engagement (1961-72) did top policy-makers ever seriously consider damaging the DRV to the point that it would cease to exist as a polity. The only objective was to compel it to desist from intervening in South Vietnam, so that the war in the South could be contained or possibly won. The reasons for this overall limitation, which in turn led to the bitterly resented specific limitations imposed on offensive military activities, lay in part in the never-abandoned conviction that China—and conceivably the Soviet Union—would intervene massively in Vietnam if it appeared that the DRV was going down to defeat. The reasons also lay in part in the nature of the effective, or managerial approach; the United States was simply engaged in maintaining or restoring the status quo, not in changing it.

Third, throughout the period of massive engagement, there was recognition among the top and revolving principals, that even when the going was roughest and the situation perceived as worst, as in 1964-66 and again after the 1968 Tet offensive, it was the South Vietnamese who would have to win the war. In final account, it was always felt the United States could only assist them not to lose. They had to do the ultimate winning, if such there was to be.

However, U.S. assistance went so far and so deep that the ruling Vietnamese elite never perceived it that way. After all, why had the United States supported Diem in preventing, in 1954-56, the logical conclusion of events that had begun as early as August-September 1945? Had not the United States come in with counterinsurgency and massive aid when the Viet Cong rebellion had seriously endangered Diem in 1961; and had it not encouraged Diem's fall in 1963 on grounds that the war could not be won under him? Had it not abided the overthrow of Minh in 1964 on grounds he was a neutralist, and assisted Khanh in the repression of Buddhist dissent which was interfering with the war effort? During the years of the massive U.S. engagement, the Vietnamese elite tended less and less to believe that it was their war to win and more and more that it was America's at least as much. This point explains some of Thieu's obdurateness in refusing to live by the Paris accords of January 1973. The South Vietnamese could never believe that the United States, some day, would simply walk away, pretending a stalemate had been achieved.

 • Finally, throughout the period of its massive engagement, the United States continued to operate on the basis of a genuine desire, however falteringly conveyed in its diplomacy, to settle the situation through negotiations. This desire was reinforced after 1966 by a gnawing and growing perception that world conditions were changing and that the United States might be weakening its superpower role in the world by its apparently endless engagement in Vietnam. Nonetheless, even on this point, considerable divergences continued to exist among the principals, some of whom (like Walt Rostow) never abandoned their conviction that the outcome of this conflict held enormous significance in the world power and political balance.

Out of the basic policy of stalemate, there emerged one of the most complex and, in hindsight, baffling concoctions of action programs that has ever been produced by presumably responsible and rational national leaders.

The Programmatic Mix

The highly complex, fluid and fluctuating mix of programs which the U.S. followed in Vietnam throughout the period of our massive engagement is illustrated in the simplified diagram found in Figure 2.

When reviewed today, the whole sweep of the U.S. approach, the various mixes obtained at various times, the fluctuating emphases, all look almost incomprehensible. They must certainly have so appeared to the military commanders in the corps headquarters and at MACV in Saigon, those at the theater headquarters at CINCPAC/Honolulu, and the Pentagon staffs of the services and JCS. As was indicated in Chapter V, Section 1, the principal military commanders involved (Gens. Earle Wheeler and Adm. Thomas Moorer at JCS; Admirals Harry Felt, Sharp, and McCain at CINCPAC; Gens. Harkins, Westmoreland, and Abrams at MACV) were denied both a clear mission to fulfill by all means at their disposal and authority to devise and follow a clear line of strategy to win the war. In a post-retirement speech which he delivered at the Naval War College in June 1972, Adm. Sharp inveighed

FIGURE 2
U.S. Programmatic Mix in Vietnam, 1961-72

Period	Civilian Program Mix	Military Program Mix
1961-63	Strategic Hamlets Budgetary Support Economic Development Assist.	Counterinsurgency ARVN Advisory "Covert" Bombing in South ("Farmgate")
1963-64	Political/Psychol. Pressures Review of Programs Econ. & Budgetary Assist.	Counterinsurgency ARVN Advisory Covert & Overt Bombing in South Coastal Patrols in South Tonkin Gulf Patrols Amphibious Operations Support Tit-for-Tat Retaliatory Strikes
1965-68	Pacification Exploration of Negotiations Budgetary Support Econ. Dev. Assistance	Search and Destroy Main Forces Overt Bombing, North & South Coastal Operations, North & South ARVN Advisory
1968-72	Vietnamization Negotiations Budgetary Support Econ. Dev. Assistance	Clear & Hold Secure Areas Overt Bombing, North & South Coastal Operations, North & South Bombing & Ground Ops., Cambodia & Laos ARVN Advisory & Enhancement

against the absence of clear strategy in Vietnam, as he had numerous times earlier in congressional testimony.[2]

But these policy/action "mixes" must have appeared equally confusing and frustrating to many if not all of the key civilian subordinates, either in Washington or in Saigon and its regional dependencies. They were also trying to make sense out of the effort in Indochina and for the most part equally in the dark about their real mission and the objectives of the president and his inner circle. They too were denied authority to devise and follow a clear line of policy to resolve the Indochina problem. While we need not, nor have we the space here to review all U.S. programs in detail (this has already been done in much literature [3]), a few summary points are nonetheless in order regarding the highlights of the U.S. engagement in 1961-72. We will look first at some of the negative or limiting elements in this strategy mix, and then turn to the various positive or sanctioned aspects of our programs.

Limitations in the Mix

While counterinsurgency was instituted in the early sixties, it at first entailed only few of the basic elements one would normally associate with hard-headed and repressive counter-terrorist warfare. The United States failed to establish full or even adequate control of Vietnamese police operations; "dirty tricks" were employed only with circumspection. Later, however, particularly under the so-called "Phoenix" program to eradicate enemy infrastructure, techniques such as torture and assassination became much more widely practiced.

Bombing of the North was instituted on a sustained basis early in 1965, but it proceeded on a relatively limited basis and its main impact was felt south of the 20th parallel, where targets were few and least significant, and where irreparable damage could not in fact be inflicted on the North. All sorties against the China border area, or in the Hanoi-Haiphong area, had to be specifically approved by the White House and each target cleared. Even after-strikes and reconnaissance patrols in those areas were cleared and approved at the presidential level. Moreover, throughout 1965-68, when it finally ceased—only to be resumed again under the euphemistic term "protective reaction strikes" during the Nixon administration—U.S. bombing policy against North Vietnam was frequently interrupted by pauses, which were sometimes prolonged, for the purpose of allowing negotiatory explorations to proceed, or in order to study the effects that particularly punitive bombing sorties might have had on the enemy's will, capabilities, morale, or action.

On balance, from 1965 to the initialling by Kissinger of the draft accord of October 1972, the bombing of the North was in no sense maximal or saturation bombing. The only saturation bombing engaged in was the bombing of Cambodia and Laos after 1969 and the Christmas bombing of North Vietnam in 1972. Nonetheless, if one totals up the amount of explosives dropped by air over Indochina between February 1965 and January 1973, it appears to amount to more than three times the total tonnage of explosives dropped over all enemy powers by the United States in World War II.[4] The conclusion is inescapable that much of this bombing was wasted. The damage to North Vietnam, while very severe when one considers the total of all military and civilian casualties and of all targets destroyed, was not irreparable. (The writer must add his own personal conviction that even so-called irreparable damage through bombing would not have brought the Vietnamese Communists to their knees.)

The United States remained, on balance, extremely careful about the so-called external "sanctuaries." Laos was not seriously touched by U.S. or South Vietnamese air or ground forces, except for border portions along the north-south trails, until 1969. Similarly for Cambodia.

While the United States dumped enormous bombing and artillery on the base sanctuaries or redoubts within South Vietnam proper, it never really succeeded, despite repeated raids and penetrations, in controlling such areas as the U-Minh Forest in the Camao Peninsula (IV Corps), the Cambodian mountain border area or the Iron Triangle area (III Corps), the Plateaux region (II Corps), or the DMZ (I Corps). Sufficient U.S. or ARVN forces were never stationed long enough in any of these redoubts to actually overcome or eliminate them. There is certainly a question as to whether this was due to policy limitations or to lack of capacity; but in any event the sanctuaries survived and many U.S. military blamed this fact on policy limitations.

On the other hand, there can be no question about the main sanctuary of North Vietnam itself: while the United States bombed it, it never invaded North Vietnam at any time on the ground—except for minor amphibious operations of short duration conducted by the South Vietnamese along the coasts south of the 20th parallel. Nor did the United States at the responsible policy level ever seriously contemplate a ground invasion of the North, for reasons already discussed and involving the risk of Sino-Soviet response.

Neither during counterinsurgency, nor during pacification, nor during Vietnamization, did the United States go all out with all means. First of all, use of either strategic or theater (tactical) nuclear weapons was ruled out. Second, certain types of covert operations were never approved, though they may have been practiced on occasion without sanction. Third, there were always strict limitations or "rules of engagement" on the employment of heavy weapons such as B-52s, and these limitations until the last year of the war (1972) included key infrastructural targets in North Vietnam such as the dike system. They seem to have permanently placed off-limits for bombing those targets in both North and South Vietnam where using the heaviest weapons would have caused more civilian casualties, and thus presumptively more bitterness and anguish among the masses of the Vietnamese people, than the targets appeared to be worth.

Fourth, while electronic counter-measures as well as fighter aircraft were used against North Vietnam's air defenses, the United States did not set out to destroy the DRV Air Force either on the ground or in the air. There seems to have been a tacit agreement with the North Vietnamese that as long as they did not employ offensive air power over South Vietnam, the United States would protect its raids against

North Vietnam but not destroy DRV air protection capabilities. At least, it seems to have worked that way.

Fifth, severe restrictions were placed in the "rules of engagement" of U.S. ground combat forces in South Vietnam. This is not to suggest that serious infractions—of which the horror at My Lai was but one example—did not occur, and probably quite frequently; but U.S. troops were not, at least officially, at liberty to kill and maim at will. Their actions were officially supposed to be limited to counterforce type operations; they were not sent out, despite so-called "free fire zones," to devastate regions at will or destroy targets of a predominantly civil character. A policy such as this is extremely difficult for troops in combat to follow, particularly where all Vietnamese, regardless of their side, appear indistinguishable to U.S. forces and where they all wear black pajamas. Nonetheless, it was a fundamental limitation under which all U.S. military commanders labored.

Finally, U.S. assets for the effort in Vietnam were not unlimited. Despite Congress's largesse and the clever funding methods employed, there were always clear-cut and severe financial constraints, even when the United States was spending in the neighborhood of $100 million per day (30 billion per year!) on its effort in Indochina.

In sum, then, there can be little doubt that the United States was conducting a limited and circumscribed war effort, one in which the military component was at least in theory never to predominate over, or control, the civilian mix of programs it was supposed to complement. The clearest indication of this lies in the fact that despite strong urgings by the military leadership, U.S. reserves were never called up nor was the full reservoir of U.S. manpower mobilized. Neither was the Vietnamese, for that matter. Throughout the war, Lyndon Johnson's Great Society programs were kept afloat; and the United States never really went to or admitted that it was at war.

We turn now to the mix of positive and presumably complementary programs the United States undertook to fulfill its engagement in Vietnam in the sixties and early seventies.

Positive Components in the Program Mix

It is probably fair to summarize the stated objective of top U.S. policy-makers, as presumably understood by U.S. military and civilian officials in Washington and Vietnam over the period 1961-72, as Admiral Sharp did in his speech to the Naval War College on March 27, 1972: "Extend the secure areas of South Vietnam by coordinated civil and military operations designed to assist the government of South Vietnam in building an independent, viable, non-Communist society."

This statement begs some fundamental questions. How can a foreign government assist another in building a society; and specifically, how could the United States help the fragile and rootless Vietnamese government in doing so? What could be meant by words like "secure areas" and "coordinated civil and military operations"? Nonetheless, it quite accurately represented the thinking at the top in Washington and what the inner circle hoped to bring about. As to method, the managerial approach was the key, as denoted by the word "coordination." The United States would deftly orchestrate, through the methods of the Harvard or Stanford Business Schools, a mix of programs that would turn the political, and accordingly the military, situation around.

In this approach, the failure of analysis combined with the vacuity of political thought and understanding in the apotheosis of management and managerial techniques. The effective motivational set was in full control; the affective had been overlooked. The United States did not really want to change the status quo; it just did not want to lose its already paid-up investment. It did not think politics, or diplomacy, or even war; it thought programs, and the U.S. approach was a programmatic one, bereft of real content. "Do, do, do; coordinate, coordinate, coordinate" became the order of the day repeated a thousand times at each echelon of activity. What was to be done and coordinated we shall briefly examine here; but it really matters little because all the activity and churning about brought virtually no results. Alas, the top policymakers never asked: "Why do? Why coordinate?"

The key issue in coordinating U.S. programs in Vietnam during 1961-72 was, of course, that of coordinating military with civilian efforts. This in itself became such an all-consuming task that it literally devoured the top of the U.S. government, leaving little time for the review and coordination of military programs proper on the one hand, civilian programs proper on the other. We shall focus briefly on each of these categories.

Military Programs. Counterinsurgency, the first major approach, failed in the absence of a strong political structure in South Vietnam; it addressed itself to impeding an ongoing revolutionary movement rather than to the building of a dynamic political counterforce—but the latter was essentially a Vietnamese task which no amount of U.S. programming could accomplish.

Search and Destroy, the strategy employed by Gen. Westmoreland against enemy main force units after his U.S. combat forces had been built up to approximately requisite numbers, succeeded within the limitations imposed in impeding to a degree the enemy's capabilities, in obtaining rising body counts, and in greatly prolonging the war. It did not succeed in destroying the enemy's will or ultimately, as shown during Tet, his capacity to win, even when accompanied by increasingly severe bombing of North Vietnam. This was because, essentially, the enemy matched U.S. actions step by step. As the United States incrementally increased ground combat forces in the South, so did the enemy; as the United States amplified firepower and stepped-up action, so did the enemy; as the United States took increasingly larger casualties, the enemy did not shrink from the increasingly growing cost in lives and treasure. From the first, Washington (as Paris before it in the fifties) failed to accept analyses which predicted this result; or to perceive that an opposing force, even if Vietnamese, could show the same or a greater amount of determination, motivation, persistence, leadership, skill, or appropriate technology than an American expeditionary force operating in the alien environment of Vietnam.

After 1968, the "clear and hold" strategy under Gen. Abrams also succeeded in further impeding the enemy's capabilities and further prolonging the war; it too failed to destroy the enemy's will or, more seriously, because this is what under Vietnamization it was presumably designed to do, to infuse the ARVN with a will to fight and to win even remotely equal to the enemy's. When the bombing went to its most sustained level, and was accompanied by excursions into the Laotian and Cambodian sanctuaries by U.S. as well as South Vietnamese ground forces, the South Vietnamese ally remained demonstrably unwilling to shoulder the full meaning and burden of the war.

As already indicated in Chapter IV, one of the cruelest deceptions of the entire Indochina war was to allow the impression to be created that ARVN had at least been turned into a serious fighting force with our help. Despite occasional brief and courageous stands by isolated units or commanders, ARVN never amounted to a real fighting force, even with the tons of rich equipment made available to it. The real weaknesses of ARVN were never better demonstrated than during its retreat from Laos at the first sign of serious enemy resistance after it had invaded the country in February 1971. This, not the truculent strutting of ARVN officers in Saigon in 1969-72, was the true harbinger of things to come.

Civilian Programs. Once undertaken, these programs seemed to acquire and run on an apparently relentless momentum of their own. U.S. officials down to the smallest villages were busy with charts and statistics; appropriations and budgetary assistance were flowing to the Vietnamese steadily; thousands of eager and busy pacification technicians and specialists were assisting in well-drilling, pig-raising, rice-planting and harvesting, harbor building, airfield construction, road improvements, war prisoner conversions, education, etc.

Yet on balance the verdict regarding the success or failure of all these programs must be negative. None of them, at any given time, produced what was hoped for. The strategic hamlet program of the counterinsurgency period succeeded only in angering villagers who did not want to be removed from their ancestral lands and graves, and actually diminished the already feeble allegiance to the Saigon government in the Mekong Delta. The pressures against Diem in 1963, and those against the Buddhists in 1964 and 1965, were not accompanied by the rise of a strong non-Communist Nationalist political force in South Vietnam. In fact, as already suggested earlier, U.S. assistance to ARVN in repressing Buddhism in Central Vietnam in the mid-sixties may have dealt the *coup de grace* to hopes of ever establishing such a political force in the South. The Buddhist movement, led in the mid-sixties by such vigorous, militant, and well-educated monks as Tri Quang, Ngoc Lien, and others, might have formed the kernel of a Third Force, incipiently allied with Big Minh's officers in ARVN, which might have survived a negotiated settlement, even if the Communist-led National Liberation Front had a role in what would have become a non-aligned government of South Vietnam.

In the absence of a strong political force, a "viable political-military-administrative structure" did not emerge. Pacification, also euphemistically called social reconstruction, ran into the problem that frequently the military need for a high enemy body count clashed head-on with the civilian need for access into allegedly insecure, enemy-penetrated areas. The wall maps in U.S. command stations and at MACV throughout this period tended to show a gradual accretion of secure and "mixed" areas, as well as a decline in the number of enemy-held villages and districts. But the facts were otherwise: throughout the long period 1965-68, the enemy penetrated all provinces and districts pretty much at will, securing everywhere what he needed most: (1) information; (2) access and passage; (3) places for weapons caches and weapons prepositioning; (4) food and water; (5) labor, mainly from the very young, for supply, communications, and logistical tasks.

As was frequently stated during this period and earlier, the United States and the ARVN held these areas in daylight, but night belonged to the enemy. Alas, too few were aware that exactly the same words had characterized the French effort throughout all of Vietnam in 1946-54. There can of course be little doubt that the general conditions of ineptness, corruption, and often high arrogance which tended to characterize the Vietnamese local administrators from province chief down contributed greatly to this situation. AID in Saigon and CORDS officers in the regions continued valiantly to preside over pacification and

to try as best as possible to coordinate their multiple social reconstruction activities with the military commanders at MACV and in the
corps areas. The latter always chafed at the bit and continuously requested intensification of the air war over South Vietnam, which frequently caused as much havoc with the pacification program as with
the enemy targets.

At the same time, the top of the government in Washington was also
negotiating, as part of the overall programmatic mix. The long and
abortive history of these efforts in 1965-68 has been told by Chester
Cooper in his *Lost Crusade,* as well as in other works.[5] They were
responsible for the frequent bombing pauses which occurred; but military commanders, as indicated earlier, were frequently left in the dark
as to the intent and nature of these negotiations. Actually, the negotiations did not amount to very much until 1968. The United States was
never willing to entertain the key point, the heart, of the Vietnamese
Communist demands: a voice for the southern Communists in the
Saigon regime. The Vietnamese Communists were never able to understand, much less to entertain, our key demand: that they leave South
Vietnam alone.

Why should they leave their own country alone? Besides, how could
the North Vietnamese do so since we were accusing them not just of
helping but of waging the war in the South? If they were doing the
fighting in the South, then surely "to leave the South alone" could
mean only to leave it, that is, to abandon the war and surrender. How
could the United States ask for surrender when intermediaries such as
the British, French, Swiss, Italians, Poles, Indians, and a host of others
stated we wished to "negotiate"? They might have settled for some
degree of withdrawal during 1965-68 in exchange for a permanent halt
in the bombing and a neutralist-leaning coalition government in Saigon, allowing the United States to phase its own withdrawal over time.
But the United States did not seriously test this until after 1968.

After the Tet offensive of early 1968, the United States gradually and
slowly prepared to withdraw. After Nixon entered the White House, it
moved to the Vietnamization program in which U.S. military operations, without losing all their sting, reverted to "clear and hold" during
a period of gradually increased U.S. troop withdrawals (1969-72). The
Vietnamization program too, failed dismally, though this was not fully
apparent to U.S. government and other American observers when the
United States finally completed its withdrawal with the signing of the
Paris accords (January 1973) and the return of U.S. prisoners of war
(March 1973).

Conclusions

The entire complicated mix of military and civilian programs which the United States undertook in Vietnam during the period of its massive engagement (1961-72) ultimately failed. This effort failed for a host of reasons, many of which have already been mentioned. A few additional points need to be made in conclusion.

1. Policy-making is not program management. The confusion between these two distinct types of activity during the period of major American involvement in Vietnam can be attributed in part to the infusion into government at high levels and below of system theorists, technocrats, and managers; and in part to the unspoken desire of the top leadership to stave off basic political decisions while allowing the stalemate to continue. They did just enough hopefully to maintain the status quo, but not enough either to upset it in the direction of major war or in the direction of real peace. The very fact that the top leadership shied away from the hard political decisions that had to be made about Vietnam in itself explains why technocrats and managers, whose job it is to be specialists and maintainers of the status quo, got such a large share of the action. But the managers failed because South Vietnam was not up to its share of the task and because the task itself was beyond achieving as well as beyond comprehension, particularly by the American people.

2. The approach attempted in Vietnam in 1961-72, and particularly after 1965, was far too refined and sophisticated either to be correctly implemented or even to be understood. It seemed as impossible to get military commanders to understand the reasons for the restrictions imposed on bombing as it did to persuade combat soldiers to accept those on killing. On the civilian side, a series of major programmatic efforts along U.S.-conceived lines, involving enormous financial inputs, seemed to the American overseers to be wasted when left to inadequately trained, poorly motivated and led, and often corrupt Vietnamese officials or lower-echelon military officers to implement.

   As a consequence, a constant tug was exerted by both U.S. military and civilian leaders in the field on the top commands in Saigon and Washington to take matters entirely in their own hands. Yet it was politically unfeasible and unacceptable that we just simply colonize South Vietnam. It remained their country; although in fact Americans were trying to run it all. U.S. political efforts failed, first to discern and then to assist any forces in the Vietnamese polity which might have infused the local scene with genuine political dynamism. The Vietnamese governmental, administrative, and even military structures remained to the end empty institutional shells with no real political content. Accordingly, this polity was no match for its strongly motivated, militantly and capably led, highly self-reliant and genuinely popular opponent.

3. The sublimation of the affective motivations of U.S. leaders into a purely effective and operational syndrome led to disaster. Even had the U.S. analysis of events and developments in Indochina been more objective, this would not by itself have changed our policies or approaches. But "doing and coordinating" while ignoring the political and social bases for action

ensured the paralysis of politics and the apotheosis of contentless activity. As we have suggested, management, operations, and programs deal with production at lowest unit cost and not with the nature of the product. Making policy is not like making shoes. Politics deals with values and with power. It has basically as little to do with management as the managerial leadership of the Ford Motor Co. has to do with national legislation. The task of politicians is not that of managers, and vice versa, no matter what the attractions of the latter may be to the former when the tasks of policy-making grow in complexity and risk.

2. The Domestic and Foreign Consensus of Support

John Kennedy in his inaugural address, pledged our nation "to bear any burden, meet any hardship, support any friend, and oppose any foe to assure the survival and success of liberty." Did he realize the purport and bearing of these words? Did he mull over his overarching rhetoric before he so eloquently expressed himself? Whether he did this or not, there can be little question that the American people as a whole believed his words and were deeply moved by them. "Ask not what your country can do for you," Kennedy said, "ask what you can do for your country." After the long, rather pedestrian, and to many young Americans, dreary days of the Eisenhower administration, the American public in 1961 was ready for Kennedy's brave and challenging words. Emerging from a rather severe recession and unconsciously undergoing significant generational, ethno-structural and denominational change, it was ready to increase but also to extend the bounty of the United States; ready to proffer sacrifice of effort, toil, and even blood to support causes in which it could believe.

Public Mood in the Early Sixties

The public's general sense of U.S. prestige was that it had somehow suffered considerably during the last years of Eisenhower's presidency. No doubt, the Kennedy electoral campaign in 1960 did much to propagate this belief. In the doldrums of the later Eisenhower years, U.S. progress toward strength, peace, and stability—the fact, which was stressed earlier, that the United States had reached the crest of its power in about 1959—was noted less than the suggested deficiencies of the U.S. superpower role and status, which Kennedy exploited to the fullest. Indeed, 1960 had been a difficult year. It had been the year of a still continuing though diminishing recession, of the U-2 incident and aborted summit, of Khrushchev's shoe-thumping display at the United Nations, of the problems in the Congo and in Cuba.

All this was exaggerated and proclaimed by a media complex growing daily in sophistication and influence, insatiable for more and preferably sensational negative events. Kennedy had won the campaign of 1960 at least partly on such blown-up non-issues as the fate of the islands of Quemoy and Matsu in the Taiwan Straits and the alleged missile gap in America's defensive posture. Now the United States had a young, vigorous, fresh president, who would "get the country moving again" and who, in foreign affairs, would show the world what stuff we were really made of.

The desire to support Kennedy, to endorse and encourage him, to push him into leading the United States and the world in great new works was as genuine and enthusiastic as it was largely irrational. Little of what Kennedy actually did in the difficult year of 1961 was calcuated to inspire much confidence in his foreign policy leadership— whether it was the appointment of the bland and colorless Dean Rusk as secretary of state, of the technocrat-manager Robert McNamara as secretary of defense; or policy moves such as the Bay of Pigs, the Vienna meetings with Khrushchev, the hesitant reinforcement of Europe after the building of the Berlin Wall, the failure to discern and analyze the growing Sino-Soviet rift, or the growing involvement in Southeast Asia. We have discussed 1961 at length throughout the previous chapters, and particularly in Chapter IV; as far as the then prevailing thrust of American foreign policy was concerned, it was a disastrous year and the watershed year which brought the United States down from the crest of its power to a new and less exalted world status.

Nonetheless, the American people wanted to believe, and believe they did. When the number of U.S. military men increased from under 1,000 to about 15,000 in Vietnam in a little over six months, few people realized that the New Frontier had in effect started the process of extending U.S. borders to those of Indochina with Thailand. And Indochina was still only faintly perceived as a problem area in U.S. opinion throughout 1962. It was not until Buddhist monks started burning themselves in the streets of Hue and Saigon in protest against the war and the repressions of the Diem regime, and until Mme. Ngo Dinh Nhu sneeringly referred to them in the late spring of 1963 as those "barbecued monks," that U.S. public attention was at least partly alerted.

But by 1963, when the issue of the war in Vietnam really began to hit home on the front pages and on television, something had happened which had infinitely reinforced the hoped-for belief in Kennedy as the prince of peace, charging forth to meet all comers at the head of our legions of goodwill. In the Cuban Missile Crisis of October 1962, as the accounts of the time had conveyed it, he had acted as a world leader should: with courage, immense poise, cold-bloodedly unblinking in the eyeball to eyeball confrontation (as Dean Rusk called it), holding Khrushchev at bay and then forcing him back, as in the best movie duels. He had been just like the lonesome sheriff in "High Noon," a film which had made Gary Cooper for years the subconscious model of what the American people really wanted to be in the world: standing alone for justice and righteousness. JFK was now clearly seen as acting in this mold. The American public was ready to follow him and his advisors and chieftains wherever they might wish to take them down the tortuous paths of confronting communism in Southeast Asia.

The positive response of the American citizenry in the early sixties to the "no burden is too great, etc." cast of New Frontier rhetoric was conditioned by years of automatic reflexes in an anti-Communist climate and buoyed now by the enthusiasm of demonstrated invincibility in the Soviet-Cuban backdown. America was economically refloated by 1964-65, at least in terms of gross national indicators, and once again, having overcome the mythical missile gap, it was militarily supreme and undeviatingly certain and serene in its assessment of communism as evil and of the Soviets and Chinese as both allied and aggressive—a line continuously promoted by the great bulk of our large-circulation media and press despite the conclusion of a nuclear test-ban treaty with the Soviets in 1963. America was ready for new crusades.

Tonkin Gulf and After

The leaders of the Johnson administration were perfectly aware of this general American sentiment when they began to prepare, early in 1964, various drafts of what would become the Tonkin Gulf resolution and would constitute, from their point of view, semi-permanent congressional authority for them to move ahead with their war plans in Indochina. After the incidents in the Tonkin Gulf in the summer of 1964, Congress rapidly enacted the joint resolution which legitimated the executive perception of a domestic consensus of support for its Indochina policy. Despite doubts about the binding nature of any such joint resolution on either the executive or the Congress, the signal had been clearly conveyed. Congress, representing the American people, was telling the president that it stood behind his efforts in Indochina, and that he should not hesitate to expand them if necessary in order to ensure the credibility of our power and leadership and the earnestness of our goals and efforts in Southeast Asia. That was really all the executive needed, or ever obtained or asked from Congress, to provide the war effort from mid-1964 on with the sanction of consensual domestic support.

We shall subsequently treat Congress's later adverse reactions to the war and its almost panicky and eventually extraordinary efforts from 1968 through 1972 to retreat from its earlier course, and to bring itself back into policy-making on Indochina instead of simply supporting the policy. For the present, it suffices to reiterate that Congress confirmed domestic support, in the view of the executive at least, by its 1964 joint resolution.

After 1964, however, and as we have seen earlier, the Johnson administration was hardly in a crusading mood with respect to Indochina. It was, almost desperately, trying to stave off defeat and to perpetuate stalemate until it could, presumably by sufficient infusion of U.S. force, ensure the survival of a non-Communist regime in the South. What the Johnson administration demanded from the American people after 1964 was not a crusade in the Kennedy spirit; but rather a long, costly, bloody, and persistent partial engagement in a constrained and limited mix of civil and military programs designed to extend secure areas and create viable government in South Vietnam.

Not at once, but in the longer run, this proved fatal to domestic support. If we could not get in there and win, the American people would increasingly ask, then what were we doing there in the first place? This would shortly lead many Americans to ask: "Why not get out?" The administration did not want to contend with getting out, which meant losing both in Indochina and obviously at home as well because, presumably, people do not vote for losers. But the administration was certainly never in there to win, in the knowledge that really winning would most likely have meant a much larger war with China or Russia or both. This, it did emphatically not want, even though the people in their relative shortsightedness might have been willing to contemplate or even tolerate it. Left with no clear alternatives it could accept, the American people, as we shall note further in the next chapter, drifted increasingly into grumbling about the rising losses and costs of the war as the war dragged on. This inevitably raised the question of the value of the stakes in Indochina, particularly as it became increasingly apparent that the objective was simply stalemate.

By 1968, the domestic consensus of full support under which the United States had so grandiosely started under Kennedy in 1961, had been permanently lost. But the consensus had not simply been lost with respect to Indochina alone. After 1968, it became clear that the specific anti-communist and anti-Soviet domestic popular consensus which had for so long undergirded and supported the U.S. policies of containment and had sustained them throughout the high cold war, had been fundamentally shaken in the whole of American foreign policy. It might, in fact, never be retrieved, at least in the form in which it had existed from 1950 to 1968. (See Figure 3.)

FIGURE 3
Domestic Support for American Foreign Policy

Time Period	U.S. Foreign Policy	Domestic Public Support
1945-50	Postwar Hesitation (Preservative Mode)*	Divided to gradually supportive
1950-61	High Cold War Confrontation (Promotive Mode)	Strong consensus of support
1961-65	Lowering Cold War Confrontation (Reduced Promotive Mode)	Strong consensus of support
1965-68	Defensive Stalemate in Indochina (Reduced Promotive Mode)	Perplexity; break in consensus
1969-75	Détente and Negotiations (Preservative Mode)	Gradual recovery of consensus based on new values

*Terminology derived from J. Rosenau, *Adaptation Theory*.[6]

Serious opposition to the war effort in Indochina began in the elites in about 1964-65; grew crescendo and extended to the "occasionally attentive public"[7] in 1965-68; and culminated in 1968-71, leading to Johnson's abdication, Nixon's election, and the post-Cambodian invasion youth revolts and riots of 1970-72. But we are not here concerned with the breakdown phase of the consensus, which we shall treat later in detail, rather with its phase of solid support for U.S. policy, which as we note in Figure 3 continued until about 1965.

It is at least interesting to observe that despite what we stated earlier regarding the readiness of the people in the early sixties for new crusades, very few people were willing to follow Senator Barry Goldwater in that direction when he advocated expansion of the war in the 1964 election campaign. This was not necessarily because people feared an expansion of the war at that time; they might in fact still have opted for such a policy in late 1964 had no better alternative been presented. But Lyndon Johnson presented a much better alternative indeed: that of victory at much lower cost.

The beauty of Johnson's clever and deceptive electoral rhetoric in

1964 was that it promised a strong stand against communism in Asia, no let-up in our military guard anywhere or in our unswerving willingness to help all who resisted Communist aggression, and at the same time that: "We don't want our American boys to do the fighting for Asian boys. We don't want to get . . . tied down to a land war in Asia." [8] This package was presented as in effect constituting victory to a populace still reeling under the misunderstood sacrifices of what it perceived as a half-lost (not half-won) war in Korea a decade earlier. Goldwater had been honest and blunt. We must win, he had conveyed, and to do it we must have the guts to extend the war if necessary and bear the risks and the costs. With this, he was sure to be defeated by Johnson's dishonest line: we will win, by sticking to our guns and keeping the war limited, never allowing Americans to fight in Asia again.

History has thus far omitted calling Johnson to full account for the cruel deception he pulled in the 1964 election campaign. For he knew much better than he let on what the future really harbored. If he could not necessarily have known that he could and would not win by sticking to his guns, he surely must have sensed in the fall of 1964 that by the early spring of 1965 he would be engaged in the program of graduated escalation and of bombing North Vietnam, a program which would without fail, if it was not successful, force him to consider the entry of U.S. ground combat forces. Far from ensuring victory, Johnson's post-elections program for Vietnam, which had been discussed with him for many months prior to the campaign, would actually ensure stalemate by bringing about the massive entry of North Vietnamese forces into the fighting. Stalemate eventually engendered defeat by causing the gradual loss of Johnson's domestic base of support.

The American Interest Complex in Vietnam

After 1965, and especially after 1966, the administration's support for its war effort in Indochina came far more from what we can call the American interest complex in Vietnam than it did from the increasingly perplexed and concerned American people as a whole. This interest complex was part of the "focussed" segment of American public opinion [9]—that segment which has a foreign affairs interest in only certain selected, specific issues. It is from the focussed segment of opinion that interest groups or lobbies traditionally draw their supporters. The American interest complex in Vietnam, which lobbied for continued involvement and vocally supported the Johnson administration in its war effort after 1965, was composed mainly of a rather large group of Americans who were, either directly or indirectly, personally affected by the war effort in Vietnam.

Principal components in the American interest complex were U.S. government employees or employees of government contractors who were themselves directly involved in the Indochina effort in Washington, elsewhere within the United States, or in Indochina proper. In Washington itself, a conservative estimate would be that probably about 10,000 government employees were in one way or another directly or indirectly engaged in supporting the war effort in 1965-68. To this number we can add the vast majority of the remaining federal employees who, though themselves not so engaged, nonetheless overwhelmingly and loyally shared the government's expressed viewpoint and stated policy. If dependents of these people are added we find a sizeable opinion group of several hundred thousand people. In the country as a whole, a conservative estimate would be that probably about 1 million people were, in one way or another, dependent for their livelihood on the war effort in Indochina; and to this million we may add several million more, including dependents, who belonged to the military-industrial complex as a whole and who, while not themselves directly engaged in producing, transporting, or selling for the 500,000 Americans in Vietnam, were nonetheless indirectly dependent on the continued strength and well-being of the U.S. military establishment there.

In Indochina proper, or in immediately surrounding zones—Japan, Korea, the Philippines, Guam, Hawaii, Okinawa, Thailand, and ships at sea—probably at least 100,000 civilians and close to a million military men, including dependents for those outside Indochina, were directly or indirectly involved in supporting the war effort. To these it is permissible to add, as a lobby group for U.S. policy in Vietnam, the remainder of the U.S. armed forces as a whole, who like the federal employees as a whole, loyally supported their government. All told, we approach a total of probably 10 to 20 million people whom we can include in a Vietnam interest complex which basically supported, sometimes very vocally, a war effort it regarded as necessary even if sometimes detestable.

Other Support Groups

The military, the technocrats in the military-industrial complex, the contractors and subcontractors,[10] the swollen group of Foreign Service and AID officers serving in or on Vietnam, and even the smaller group of sheer adventurers who found their way to the last frontier in Indochina, were vocal and outspoken advocates. At the crest of its superpowerdom, the United States was exporting surplus trained brains and energy abroad at an unprecedented rate; these were the mentors and emancipators the United States had naturally produced as a concomitant of its postwar superpower role. But they were not alone in advocating strongly the continuation of the Indochina effort and in lending welcome support to the administration's increasingly threatened effort to perpetuate the consensus of support.

The large mass circulation press of the United States and its editorial leadership also stood squarely behind the war effort at least until 1968. While dissent, as we shall see later, was in part led by smaller circulation, more elite-directed news organs such as *The New York Times* and *Washington Post,* the virtues of patriotism turned into nationalism and sometimes into strident chauvinism seemed to matter most to the publishers and editors of mass circulation organs and of smaller-town publications, those read by most Americans. Here the slogan "my country, right or wrong" seems to have prevailed until well into the later sixties and beyond.

Moreover, patrician and traditionalist members of the American legal, business, and political establishments, whose extraordinary influence in Washington made up for their lack of numbers, continued until very late to support the administration's policies. It was from this group, finally, that the principals were chosen who were to turn Lyndon Johnson around when, after the Tet Offensive and Westmoreland's subsequent major troop request, the effort in Indochina at last appeared to them to be more costly than it was worth.

There was also strong support for the war effort from among leaders of the major religious denominations in the United States, particularly the Catholic Church, although religious leaders were also at the forefront of the dissenting forces which began to group themselves into an anti-war lobby after about 1966. Among Catholic leaders in particular, the anti-communist factor played a major role; and there can be no doubting the sincerity of this group in supporting the war.

Finally, parts of the academic and general intelligentsia, many of whom were themselves dependent in some personal or institutional way on government interests or on governmental financial largesse, contributed strong support to the war effort and Johnson's policies. At the same time, it was from within this group more than from any other that opposition to the war rose after 1965-66 and that the anti-war lobby was eventually constituted and led.

Thus, the domestic base of support for the war, though losing in numbers, strength, and influence after 1965—largely because of the growing defection of the largest of all publics, the mass or amorphous public, which could not make sense of the war—still remained substantial until at least 1968. It was complemented by one critical element, which was at least as significant as domestic support in keeping Lyndon Johnson in the Vietnam business for so long: the foreign interest complex at work on the United States.

Foreign Forces at Work on the United States (*very weak section*)

We can basically distinguish two main groupings among the foreign elements who played a role in influencing or seeking to influence the Johnson administration's policies in Indochina: (1) major Western allies of the United States; (2) what we may term U.S. client states in the immediate vicinity of Indochina or elsewhere.

Western Allies. Relevant major Western allies during the period of our massive engagement in Indochina included Britain, France, West Germany, Canada, and Japan. The posture of all of these states is interesting. Virtually from the outset, France was a clear skeptic and no-sayer. While she imposed no real obstacles on the United States effort, she provided no real help to it either—whether in Indochina proper, where France possessed some remaining influence, or in fortifying U.S. domestic support. At various stages, de Gaulle, as indicated earlier, tried to talk us out of our course of action and to bring about a negotiated settlement. He proposed an international conference in 1964, transmitted the DRV Four Points in 1965, and France in 1968 allowed Paris to be selected as the site for the negotiations which eventually ended the war.

Japan, by contrast, was neither a yes-sayer nor a no-sayer, though there is ample reason to believe that the Japanese government and people had major reservations as to the conduct, if not necessarily the reasons, of U.S. operations.[11] Japan had not yet, in the sixties, assumed the conduct of a really independent foreign policy; she could not, accordingly, have been expected to present serious opposition to the U.S. use of bases in Okinawa, for example, for B-52 operations against North Vietnam. But if Johnson and the U.S. government thought they had Japan on board, it was more because they assumed her support in the absence of vocal opposition than because of any specific Japanese statements or actions. It is clear that because Japan presented no obstacles to the use of Okinawa, and also profited from the war through the very substantial purchases of the U.S. military in Japan, the Johnson administration was basically justified in assuming Japanese support.

West Germany probably also harbored reservations, but in the face of an imperfectly understood U.S. effort in an area remote from direct German concerns, these were understandably sublimated, with Germany preferring to play the role of faithful U.S. ally, demonstrating sympathy and concern for the U.S. plight as the war effort bogged down. Germany's posture tended to become more critical after 1969.

As early as 1964, the United States had maneuvered Canada under Prime Minister Pearson into believing that, as a member of the 1954 Geneva International Control Commission—then still represented in Vietnam although wholly ignored by both the U.S. and the South Vietnamese—it had a continuing useful role to play in bringing about negotiations for a settlement, presumably on terms favorable to the United States. While the Canadian government and people harbored reservations about the reasons, nature, and character of the U.S. effort in Indochina,[12] the Canadians offered no serious objections to the U.S. course during most of the war and even swallowed rather crude U.S. moves to exploit Canada's goodwill as a potential mediator with Hanoi, as in the abortive Seaborn mission to Hanoi (1964).[13]

Similarly, Britain harbored serious reservations about the U.S. course and conduct throughout the war.[14] After he took office, Prime Minister Harold Wilson almost uninterruptedly tried to bring about serious negotiations.[15] But the British, our oldest friends and chief allies, no more than the Canadians found the strength or the will to tell President Johnson and the American public squarely and forthrightly that they were engaged in the wrong course, one which would eventually seriously endanger the defenses of the West and America's capabilities to continue to lead it as before. (By contrast, when U.S. interest groups and the media overly agitated the U.S. government on the question of possible Soviet intervention in Africa in 1978, Prime Minister Callahan almost ended U.S. debate on the matter by sharply questioning America's competence and tendency to reach instantaneous conclusions about events in that complicated continent.)

These remarks bring up our chief point. By failing to object vigorously and strongly to a misguided and costly U.S. involvement in a region intrinsically remote from the chief interests of the U.S. and its Western allies, the latter—with the major exception of France—reinforced the administration's domestic consensus of support for the war. In the minds of Johnson and his key policy-makers, major Western allies and U.S. public opinion tended to be linked as a natural constituency. Moreover, the views of close and trusted allies are generally of enormous importance to an American administration deeply bogged down in a difficult problem. It is not at all impossible to conjecture that if the allies, the British in particular, had been willing to shoulder the burden of Johnson's displeasure by telling him outright that his objectives were ill-conceived and unattainable and his conduct detrimental to the welfare and security of the West, U.S. policy might have been more quickly modified.

But none of the Western allies, save the French in a detached and aloof manner, said so to Lyndon Johnson, and French influence in

Washington was at its lowest point in the sixties during de Gaulle's stewardship. One possible reason for allied reticence, in addition to the sheer difficulty of risking Lyndon Johnson's strong temper and displeasure, was the fact that while no one was saying "no," many of the smaller client states of the U.S. and of other Western allies, including predominantly of the British, were saying "yes." We turn next to this aspect.

Client States. The importance of sycophantism among the smaller U.S. client states in regard to the Vietnam War cannot be exaggerated. This was particularly the case owing to President Johnson's susceptibility to cajolery and flattery, especially at moments when his tasks appeared heaviest and most difficult. Client states managed to exploit this susceptibility to the fullest, and in so doing they played a significant role in bolstering the domestic consensus of support for the war. The client states, among whom Singapore is particularly to be singled out, consistently fueled the allegations by President Johnson and some of his chief advisors that U.S. credibility was continuously in question and that any weakening of our resolve in Indochina would lead to immediate disaster.

One of the chief actors in this role was Prime Minister Lee Kwang Yu of Singapore. The Republic of Singapore has not only not gone under with the defeat of South Vietnam and its absorption into the new Socialist Republic of Vietnam, with which Singapore is now entering into relationships, but it has prospered incredibly since then and seems today to be indeed quite secure. Lee could have been just simply wrong in continuously encouraging President Johnson's belief that he was saving Southeast Asia. But it was worse than that, for Lee knew perfectly well what he was doing, which was not at all giving honest counsel or advice on international politics to a distant, somewhat forlorn, but enormously important protective superpower. Lee was a sycophant, buying U.S. favors in Singapore through his unstinting declarations of support for the U.S. effort in Indochina. Those favors he received, in ample measure; and from the standpoint of Singapore, Lee served his country well. From the standpoint of the United States, he was unhelpful, because he made it so easy and so telling for President Johnson and others to point to Lee as a potential victim we were saving in Southeast Asia—a line which the Congress, the press and the U.S. public accepted unthinkingly.

President Marcos of the Republic of the Philippines followed much the same course, but in a more subdued vein. Besides, every U.S. administration was on guard against Filipinos seeking favors. Nonetheless, Marcos was handsomely rewarded for joining the "many flags in

Vietnam" program which Johnson instituted with almost fanatical fervor in 1965-66.[16] Marcos sent two non-combat engineer battalions to Vietnam; and Thailand and the Anzus powers (Australia, New Zealand) each sent one combat battalion. Nonetheless, the "many flags" program basically floundered, despite a large expenditure of U.S. diplomatic and financial effort on its behalf.

The Republic of South Korea was another matter; for Korea, although handsomely paid to do it, actually sent two fighting infantry divisions to Vietnam and suffered heavy casualties there. Thus Korea was genuinely supportive; not basically a sycophant state like Singapore, or a semi-sycophant like the Filipinos or the Thais. The latter, against the expenditure of billions of U.S. dollars, allowed the construction between 1965 and 1969 of five major airbases and the stationing of some 100,000 U.S. forces on their soil. These bases permitted the stationing of B-52s and of other advanced sophisticated aircraft and intelligence equipment in the vicinity of Vietnam, thereby constituting an essential contribution to the war effort. Their presence on Thai soil also amounted to a virtual act of war against the Indochinese Communists and to a final departure from the traditional Thai posture of neutrality in Southeast Asian conflicts—a posture which, in the previous century and in this, had saved Thailand from Western colonization.

While the Thais never received more of a formal assurance of U.S. protection than the Rusk-Thanat Executive Agreement of 1962, mentioned earlier, it was clear that the United States had purchased in Thailand an ally which it would, if necessary, protect. The United States paid for its purchase through military construction expenditures and through budgetary and economic assistance to Thailand. In defense of Thailand's choice, it must be indicated that U.S. pressures to permit the construction of the bases was tremendous, to say the least. But the Thais might have had another way out. They might have remained or become neutralist like Cambodia before 1970, and made deals with both sides. On the other hand Thailand like the Philippines, was a SEATO ally of the United States. At least, the United States could feel that it got something out of Thailand's risky course of support for its Indochina involvement. In the long run, however, Thai-U.S. relations were basically weakened by the whole episode.

Another state in Southeast Asia, Indonesia, played a much more muted role. While never breaking its long established relations with the DRV, it nonetheless managed to convey to the United States, after Sukarno's demise and replacement by Suharto in 1965-66, a much stronger impression of support than it had previously. The belief that the United States was saving Indonesia in the long run by saving Viet-

nam in the short run took firm hold in Washington, where it contributed further to the creation of a general impression in the country that
the administration's actions in Indochina were essential to the safety
and security of the Free World. This was precisely the impression the
administration wanted to convey, and which it hoped would sustain its
domestic consensus of support.

The Israelis, whose continuing interest was to keep the United States
mobilized against communism (read, the Soviet Union), also had a
share in the process of building the consensus of support for the Indochina war. Despite the deepening U.S. embroilment, and the emergence in the mid-sixties of a precarious stalemate which might come
later to signify a decline in the image of worldwide U.S. power and
military supremacy, the Israelis apparently calculated that on balance it
was better to keep the U.S. military-industrial complex strong by its
involvement in the Indochina war effort than having it possibly wither
on the vine for want of a U.S. war to be fought somewhere in the
world.

The only country really hurt, in the long run, by the U.S. withdrawal
from Indochina—besides South Vietnam and the United States itself—
turned out to be Israel, which in the later sixties and seventies had to
contend with the rise of the pro-Arab extreme left in U.S. politics, with
congressional and general domestic fears of another foreign engagement, and with the weakening of U.S. forces morale and of U.S. anti-
Soviet and anti-Communist political resolve. In retrospect, it might
have been more farsighted from their point of view, if the Israelis had
early capitalized on their enormous influence on domestic U.S. opinion
in order to join the French as no-sayers to an involvement which, given
their knowledge and experience, they might have judged would turn
into a disaster.

Several other client states gave the U.S. administration moral support
in Indochina—among them Iran, Belgium, Holland, Greece, Turkey
(before the Cyprus crisis), and Latin American countries. These states
all contributed to building the consensus of support for the war which
kept the United States involved in Indochina for so many long years.

3. Closed-System Decision-Making

We close this chapter with a review of the decision-making process at
the top of the U.S. government in 1961-72, and of its chief and most
alarming characteristic: its imperviousness to those inputs from outside
the charmed circle of "The Best and The Brightest" which argued contrary to the prevailing views within this circle.

Decision-Making Models

The pathbreaking work of academic thinkers like Graham Allison, Morton Halperin, Alexander George, and others [17] has widely increased discussions among both practitioners and observers of international affairs and of the making of U.S. foreign policy of what is termed "bureaucratic politics." By this is meant the tugs and pulls of organizational and political advocacy among the leaders of agencies and units involved in the making of key foreign policy decisions. Similarly, "organizational output" has through this literature become an important term to signify the manner in which decisions which are largely sequential rather than basic in character [18] are routinely made according to the standard operational procedures, organizational repertoires, and the on-rolling momentum of large bureaucratic organizations.

Allison and others usefully distinguished the bureaucratic-political and the organizational modes of decision-making from what they called the "rational" mode, previously virtually the only implicit or explicit model used in the study of the processes by which foreign policy decisions are reached. Both the bureaucratic-political and the organizational models get us away from the enduring notion of diplomatic historians, commentators, and others that foreign policy decisions are reached in a generally sane and rational atmosphere, in which the costs of various alternative courses of action are carefully laid side by side with their potential benefits for the policy-maker to make judicious and wise choices and calculations of optimal conduct. The reality of decision-making is indeed far removed from such a model.

At the same time, the rational mode, or something approximating it, is forever present in the background and always conditioning the real decision-making process. Accordingly, we can never ignore it—if for no other reason than that it is the model by which decision-makers *think* they are reaching decisions. For example, as we have seen in previous chapters, the general atmosphere of containment played an overwhelming role in conditioning U.S. policy decisions on Indochina throughout 1950-68. The question was always asked by key decision-makers: "What course of action at this time is most conducive and least risky in advancing our objectives of containing or halting the spread of communism or weakening Sino-Soviet incentives for aggression?" It was always within the framework of such an overall "rational" perspective that initial calculations of U.S. moves were made.

It would therefore be incorrect to focus purely on the bureaucratic-political and organizational models in examining the processes of our decision-making with respect to Indochina in 1961-72. These models are in any case too tidy and neat, as their authors would be the first to admit, and they are not designed to be mutually exclusive one from the other in determining the actual decision-making process in any given issue. Allison himself interweaves all of them carefully in his study of the Cuban Missile Crisis.[19]

In respect to Vietnam and Indochina in 1961-72, three particular aspects of the decision-making process distinguished it throughout the entire period. First, the dominance of the president in the process; second, the limitations presidents imposed on the number of advisors they chose to include in the process and the reinforcing, rather than actual policy-making role these advisors performed; and third, the imperviousness of the process in operation to inputs from outside the presidential circle itself—that is, the "closed-system" nature of the thinking in the decision-making process.

Dominance of the President in Decision-Making

At all times during the entire period, on all key issues, the president of the United States was the dominant and controling figure in U.S. policy-making on Indochina. It was Truman in early 1950 who, in the wake of the Chinese Communist victory on the mainland, the conclusion of the NATO Treaty, and the primacy of European considerations in the face of the perceived Sino-Soviet challenge, decided on the recognition of the Associated States and the material support to France in its colonial war in Indochina. In this, he was certainly pushed ahead and fully supported by his secretary of state, Dean Acheson, and the latter's assistant secretary for Far Eastern affairs, the same Dean Rusk who later became secretary of state.

But had Truman not chosen to see a direct connection between Communist China's victory on the mainland and its participation in the Korean War on the one hand and the Soviet threat to Europe on the other; and had Truman chosen to regard the Viet Minh as a Nationalist though Communist-led force fighting in its own right to liberate Indochina from France, the decision might have been entirely different. This is not to say that a rational mode prevailed in decision-making; for, on the contrary, a rational calculation of interests might well have favored a different course of action. Moreover, it is clear that both domestic political considerations and the greater bureaucratic power of those decision-making units favoring France over those arguing the case of the Indochinese Nationalists within the U.S. government played a major role in the decision outcome. The point is that the president was the dominant actor in the decision-making process.

Again, in 1954, it was President Eisenhower, opposed initially by Secretary of State Dulles, who decided against direct U.S. intervention in Indochina during and after the battle at Dien Bien Phu; and it was President Eisenhower who authorized U.S. Undersecretary of State Gen. Walter Bedell Smith's approval, with reservations, of the Geneva Accords of 1954. Again, this point does not argue for a rational decision-making mode against another model; for in this case in particular, an enormous bureaucratic-political battle took place, which was mentioned in Chapter II.[20] We are simply arguing the predominance of the president, whatever cognitive model the latter chose to employ in making the final decision.

The point repeats in 1954-56 when, despite considerable in-fighting within the U.S. government, also described in Chapter II,[21] President Eisenhower authorized the support of Diem, the engagement of the United States in SEATO, and the perpetuation of the partition in Vietnam. These decisions might certainly have been entirely different, whether or not they were made largely on rational or on bureaucratic-political grounds, if the president at the time had decided that non-alignment by the Southeast Asian states was preferable from the U.S. point of view to a lineup of states in the area alongside the United States in confrontation with communism. But it was the latter course which the president favored, and that was the course adopted.

In 1961, it was President Kennedy, supported by Secretaries Rusk and McNamara, who made the watershed decision of our entire post-war policy in Indochina by accepting the recommendations of the Taylor-Rostow mission to vastly increase the U.S. military advisory component in Vietnam and to engage in counterinsurgency programs. As we have seen, this decision was in our view in large part dictated by considerations affecting the president's domestic image of strength or weakness, both in the Congress and the country at large. Suppose the decision had had to be made in the early spring of 1961, before either the Bay of Pigs, the Vienna meeting with Khrushchev, the Berlin Wall, and the decision to tread softly in Laos. This is of course purely conjectural, but it is not impossible to speculate that Kennedy might have adopted an entirely different route on Vietnam—let us say, to reconvene the Geneva Conference and to seek a settlement allowing the formation of a coalition regime including the Communists. This is admittedly unlikely, but it is not impossible. Accordingly, the question whether rational considerations were predominantly involved, or considerations of domestic or bureaucratic politics, or the resultants of organizational outputs and momentum by major units of the government, is less important than the fact that the decision was made by the president, at the time and in the manner that he felt he had to make it.

In 1963, Kennedy changed ambassadors to Vietnam and acquiesced in the climatization of atmosphere which resulted in the ARVN coup against Diem. Had Kennedy firmly resisted such a course, there is no question that the coup would not have taken place, whatever tugs of war were going on among his advisors. But in mid-1963 Kennedy felt that a change of regimes in Vietnam would be more likely to strengthen the Vietnamese war effort (or to open the way to possibilities for a negotiated settlement; we shall never be sure, since Kennedy died shortly after the coup). Again, it was the president who was the decisive element, and not the particular model of decision-making adopted.

Similarly, despite the enormous bureaucratic-political battles of 1964, as well as the growing pressures of organizational outputs by the many large governmental units engaged in Vietnam decision-making, it was President Johnson who early in 1965 decided to adopt the policy of graduated escalation and the bombing of North Vietnam. As we have seen in Chapter IV (Decision 3), this was in no sense a decision made in a rational decision-making mode either. In that particular decision, organizational outputs and bureaucratic politics clearly dominated the process, since many rational-mode-type studies made before the decision clearly pointed to the probable failure of the policy on rational grounds. Again, the decision-making mode *per se* was irrelevant. What was relevant was the position of, and the considerations inspiring, the president himself. This is best demonstrated by the fact that he delayed the decision for the better part of a year, until after the elections of November 1964. Even then, it was not certain until the very last moment whether he would make it at all. And once he had made it, his next major Indochina decision, the entry of U.S. ground combat forces, following inexorably from it, was not even the product of anything we could call a systematic decision-making process at all.

It was also President Johnson himself who decided the manner, and the timing, of the U.S. decision to end our Vietnam engagement—by his decision not to run for another term, to end the bombing of North Vietnam, and to seriously seek negotiations. None of this was the result of any particular process, following any given model or mix of models. Another president might have acted in an entirely different way.

President Nixon acted in an entirely different way when together with Henry Kissinger and without any other formal or informal process of consultations within the government, he decided to withdraw "with honor," which in effect prolonged our engagement for another four years—until after the November 1972 elections. The Johnson decision to get out of Vietnam had now in effect been reversed by the Nixon decision to stay in Vietnam as long as necessary in his judgment, while publicly saying that we were getting out. Had this decision been made in a rational, bureaucratic-political, or organizational mode, it would probably have turned out entirely differently. We might well have disengaged from Indochina by 1970 at the latest, following upon the lines of the potential settlement that Vance and Harriman felt they had been able to reach with the North Vietnamese toward the end of 1968. But Nixon wished it otherwise. Again, the president was supreme in the process, if there was a process at all. He was also supreme, and virtually alone with Kissinger when he decided to invade Cambodia in 1970, to authorize the initialing of the draft Paris accord in October 1972, and to proceed with the massive Christmas bombing of North Vietnam at the end of that year.

Finally, it was President Ford who decided not to re-intervene when the final collapse of Vietnam occurred in 1975. If he, as a non-elected president, wished to do otherwise, could he have? It might have caused an enormous domestic crisis in the United States, particularly after Watergate, but if the president had decided in April 1975 to confront the Congress with the fait accompli of a re-intervention, say in the nature of resumed bombing of North Vietnam, the armed forces would probably have loyally followed him. Moreover, some of his advisers certainly were pressing him to take this course, even though after enactment of the War Powers Act of 1973 his authority to do so would have been very constrained. In this ultimate decision, perhaps more than in any other in the long course of our Vietnam engagement, the president's hand was forced by the country's sentiment; yet even then, the president remained supreme. It was his decision and his action or lack of action that counted most.

Of the presidents we have mentioned Johnson and Nixon were by far the most dominant and singly determinative in the decision-making process; but all of them were the chief determiners of their country's course of action in Indochina, even if the underlying architecture of the decisions was often supplied by advisers. Accordingly, the factors which principally motivate and impel a president in the making of policy are those that must be focussed on if one wishes to understand and explain the reasons, if not necessarily the processes, of U.S. decision-making in Indochina during the period of our massive engagement. We suggest that these factors group themselves into the following three clusters: (1) those relating to the presidents' personal perceptions and calculations, conditioned by those of their advisers, of our status in world politics and the requirements of our security at the time they are acting; (2)

those relating to the presidents' perceptions of the domestic political situation at the time of their actions; and (3) those relating to the personalities and styles of the presidents themselves. We shall examine each of these briefly in turn.

Status and Security Perceptions. All five presidents involved in decision-making on Indochina shared the same basic perception of Indochina's importance to the U.S. role in the world: that it was a fundamental arena of confrontation in the Third World between forces of an inimical ideology supported by major hostile powers, and forces friendly to the United States and its objectives; and that U.S. status and accordingly security would suffer if the friendly forces did not obtain our full support. Whereas Truman, Eisenhower, and Kennedy drew the line short of the entry of U.S. forces in a full combat support role, Johnson and Nixon—the former, however, being the only one of the five to be fully tested by the question—did not. This basic perception continued to be shared by all our presidents from 1950 to 1970; after 1970, however, with the initiation of a worldwide policy of détente with the Soviet Union and President Nixon's trip to and rapprochement with Communist China, it slowly began to erode.

Domestic Political Perceptions. Within this major premise of the importance of Indochina to the security of the United States, considerations dealing with the presidents' reading of the domestic political situation played a principal role. All five presidents read the situation in a basically similar vein. A loss of Indochina, or a substantial victory of communism in Southeast Asia, would lose them the office of president and would lose their party its majority in the country and its position in Congress. They read the domestic political situation this way because of their unmitigated conviction that the American people saw the world simplistically, as basically divided between white hats (anti-Communists) and black hats (Communists) and because to a surprising extent they personally shared this outlook. The only possible exception to this shared perception of our presidents was Nixon after the 1972 elections, when he probably sensed that a combination of his policies of worldwide détente and rapprochement with China had resulted in considerably defusing the earlier black versus white U.S. public view of the world. When Nixon had come into office in 1969, this process of defusion had already been set in motion by Johnson's abdication, the initiation of the Paris Peace Conference and—most significantly—by the youth rebellion and the anti-system demonstrations of the late sixties and early seventies within the United States.

Presidential Personalities and Styles. Finally, the personalities and styles of the presidents significantly affected their decision-making.

Generalizing broadly, it is possible to say that Truman was obdurate, tough, and determined to demonstrate these traits in his policies. Perhaps more like Johnson than any other of the Indochina-period presidents, he felt personally challenged by the rise of communism in Southeast Asia and became determined to arrest it. Eisenhower, far more at ease in the office, accustomed to high command, and not in need of establishing his credentials as a tough leader with the Congress, was relatively relaxed and more aloof. He alone among the five presidents involved was able to absorb a defeat to communism in Indochina and to provide such a defeat with a domestic appearance of success by way of gradually increasing U.S. responsibility in Southeast Asia. He rebounded resiliently to lead the United States to the crest of its status as a superpower. Kennedy was sophisticated, eager, and daring to the point of adventurousness. He accordingly did not shy away from undertaking new commitments which he did not, however, necessarily believe would permanently involve the United States.

Johnson suffered from the combination of an enormous inferiority complex in regard to handling affairs of state, and an enormous feeling of superiority, experience, and self-confidence in handling and manipulating the movers, shakers, and sleepers in American politics. His inferiority complex in regard to foreign affairs put him in wholly unwarranted awe of the national security and foreign affairs expert advisers he inherited from Kennedy, the intellectuals who surrounded him, and certain foreign leaders and heads of state. On the other hand, his superiority complex led him to disregard or treat cavalierly the very arena in which he should have been the master: Congress. Accordingly, Johnson accepted the ill-conceived scenarios of the graduated escalation school of thought in regard to Vietnam, and misled the Congress in the Tonkin Gulf resolution and the entry of U.S. ground forces into the war.

Finally, Nixon combined the negative manipulative traits of a highly insecure (proto-paranoid) but extraordinarily ambitious power-seeker with the constructive manipulative traits of a highly developed affective motivational set. Nixon's style and personality led him to deceive the public into believing that he was withdrawing from Vietnam, when in fact he was not only continuing but intensifying the war while managing to reduce our forces component in Vietnam at the same time—a remarkable feat. But he managed also to convince the public that he was turning defeat in Vietnam into standoff. He did so by changing the most fundamental premise of American foreign policy, namely the co-equation in the U.S. public's mind of American security with the defeat of communism everywhere. This was the result of his and of Kissinger's genius in conducting worldwide détente and obtaining rapprochement with Communist China.

We attempt in Figure 4 to represent in simplified tabular form what has been stated in the previous paragraphs.

Narrowness of the Advisory Circle

Three excellent authors have subjected the small advisory coteries surrounding Presidents Kennedy and Johnson, particularly the latter, to close scrutiny from three distinct perspectives.[22] From a largely sociological perspective, Richard Barnet examined the narrow socio-economic base of origin and background of these advisers, and how their societal conditioning as members of the U.S. upper elite was in turn reflected in their cognitive processes as policy-makers.[23] From a largely personal and human perspective, David Halberstam subjected the key dozen or so persons most involved in Indochina policy-making in 1961-68 to a relentless examination of their backgrounds, traits, frailties, foibles, and relative strengths.[24] Finally, Irving Janis, using a socio-psychological perspective, scrutinized how an in-group of peers reinforce each other's perceptions of the world and of events and, almost subconsciously, come in their group cognitive patterns to exclude intrusive inputs and viewpoints that do not correspond to those of the in-group.[25] There is little we can add here to the telling points these authors have made.

We may observe, however, that the same patterns and processes generally prevailed also in the Truman, Eisenhower, and Nixon periods. The last is particularly easy to study because Nixon acted with only one real adviser, Kissinger, and by design those two admitted no one else to their closed circle and communicated none of their most significant views and plans to other top associates, either in the executive or in Congress. As to Truman, his main advisory element was also very small: Acheson and the latter's closest associates at the State Department, particularly Undersecretary Robert Lovett and, on this issue, Assistant Secretary Dean Rusk. Eisenhower's top Indochina advisory group was not much larger, consisting in the main of Secretary of State John Foster Dulles, the latter's brother Allen Dulles at CIA, J.F. Dulles's deputies at the State Department, Robert Murphy (a career Foreign Service officer) and Walter Robertson (a Richmond banker) and, to a more limited degree, Gens. Walter Bedell Smith (at the 1954 Geneva Conference) and J. Lawton Collins (in 1954-55 only). _At all times we are thus dealing with a very small group of top advisers surrounding a dominant president._

FIGURE 4
Presidential Roles in Indochina Policy-Making

President	Perception of Indochina in U.S. Security	Domestic Political Calculus	Personal Style	Indochina Policy Output
Truman	Important to demonstrate U.S. power and credibility	Avoid second loss to communism in Asia	Truculent	Assistance to French
Eisenhower	Important as U.S. strongpoint in worldwide containment	Settle for half loss; avoid further loss	Aloof and detached	Assistance to Republic of Vietnam
Kennedy	Important in worldwide struggle for Third World	Restore confidence in U.S. prestige and power	Sophisticated and adventurous	Counterinsurgency role for United States
Johnson	Vital bastion of U.S. security position	Maintain foreign policy consensus to move on with New Society at home	Deferential until election; high-handed after election	Perpetuate stalemate through U.S. combat interventionary role
Nixon	Dispensable if appearance of honor maintained	Reduce anti-Communist hostility by design	Secretive; manipulative; affective	Disengage over prolonged period; retain unpredictable posture; finally abandon

Role of Executive Branch Advisers

In the case of Indochina, the presidential advisory circle consisted mainly of reinforcers of the president. These men acted as presidential echoes, and as presidential supporters and interest-servers. If this was the case for chief advisers, it was all the more true for middle- and lower-echelon counselors of the presidents.

It is relevant here to digress on some fundamental structural aspects of the American political system. In the executive branch of the U.S. system, the president is the only elected official, and therefore the only official who is directly accountable to the people. This sometimes ne-glected if simple truism forces us to realize the trump card the presi-dent holds in arguments with advisers. "I must live with the decision," says the president, "you can come and go at will; and since I alone stay or fall on it, the decision matters a good deal more to me than to you. Therefore, I must ultimately be guided by my own sense of what is the correct decision rather than by yours, and by my own sense of what the public will accept or tolerate, about which you need not be so directly concerned." This is indeed a hard argument for advisers to contradict, and it lies at the heart of the advisers' passivity and their tendency to become reinforcers and supporters rather than molders of the presi-dent's mind.

We should note here the sharp distinction between the American and European governmental systems. In European and other parliamen-tary-type governments, the responsibility for key foreign as well as do-mestic decision is much more diffuse, since a collective of individuals and not a single one responds to the electorate, and since in final account it is a political party in European-type systems rather than a single individual who stands or falls in elections.

Furthermore, American advisers serve purely at the pleasure of the president and not because of their existing or potential role in the collective leadership of a political party. If President Giscard d'Estaing, even in the strongly executive-dominated Fifth French Republic, wishes to replace his foreign minister, he still has his party to reckon with; but the president of the United States can easily dismiss or re-place anyone in the executive branch who does not give him pleasure, including a secretary of state like William Rogers or secretaries of de-fense like Robert McNamara or Melvin Laird. This places advisers in the American system—even members of the Cabinet—in a role much inferior to that of Cabinet ministers *vis-à-vis* a prime minister or presi-dent in European-type systems. U.S. advisers feel a strong compulsion to assent, lest they find themselves seeking their pleasure outside the government.

Executive branch advisers in the American system hold no relative monopoly on advice, similar in any sense to that held by cabinet ministers in European systems, who belong and are ultimately responsible to a political party—a party which also controls the fate of their leader. American political parties are almost pure fiction; but the existence of potential non-executive branch rival advisers is an intense reality. What keeps President Carter, or any American president, from asking the head of the AFL/CIO, the president of Yale, the head of General Motors, or the chairman of any Senate committee (to use only four from a potential multitude of examples) for key advice on an issue in foreign policy? Nothing, really, but the resistance of executive branch-appointed advisers, who therefore seek to fill every nook and cranny in the advisory basin and to leave no void unfilled. For reasons best explored fully by social psychologists, the nature of their advice is likely to be pleasurable to the president; and they are conversely unlikely to turn into Cassandras or bearers of bad tidings. Thus, the advice presidents in the U.S. system receive from their top appointed subordinates in the executive branch is likely to reinforce their own inclinations, dispositions, and outlooks—and frequently tends less to be advice in the generic sense of the word than expressions of willingness to perform and to achieve tasks which the president, with their concurrence, wants done.

The Problem of Confronting Presidents

U.S. policy-making toward Indochina during 1950-72 operated within the parameters set by U.S. presidents. They made all the fundamental decisions; their outlooks cast the framework and tone within which all decisions were made. This is not the place to treat the phenomenon of awe for the presidency in the American polity, a subject which has been covered thoroughly in much first-class literature.[26] It is appropriate for us briefly to treat here, however, the problem that arises when individuals either within or outside the U.S. government attempt to confront presidents with views diverging from theirs, or outlooks that do not correspond to their particular perceptions.

When the president starts from a given set of assumptions, and furthermore assumes or credibly appears to assume that others with whom he consults are starting from the same set of assumptions, it is indeed difficult to move against or thwart the strong current set by the president's cognitive givens. For example, Senator Wayne Morse of Oregon, who argued for years, beginning as early as the late fifties, against U.S. involvement in Indochina in any form, was simply not heard—ignored— by a number of the presidents involved, even though he held a respectable and fairly senior position in the Senate and had served on both the Republican and the Democratic sides of the aisle.

Similarly, though to a lesser degree, Senator Mike Mansfield who had the most experience with Indochina (Cambodia as well as Vietnam) of any Senator, and whose political career was so distinguished that he followed Senator Johnson as Senate majority leader when the latter was elevated to the vice presidency and presidency, was unable, though listened to on frequent occasions, to make himself heard. If it is that difficult for a respected, high-ranking political partner of the president to be heard, what are we to make of the chances that a second or even first-echelon bureaucrat, or a less exalted political figure in the White House or from outside the government will manage to do so?

The first obstacle to overcome in approaching a president, even if someone is of high general repute, is that presented by the door guardians of high office holders like the president. Such men hold their positions in part because of their uncanny ability to distinguish doomsayers from soothsayers, even from afar. Even without specific presidential instructions, their natural sycophantic instinct is to protect the president from prophets of gloom. Just getting an appointment can become an inordinately difficult task if a door guardian suspects that some of a president's most cherished assumptions are about to be assaulted. But supposing that this obstacle is overcome, how would a president respond to an input directed strongly against a course of action in which he has for some time been engaged, when the underlying premises of his action appear to him to be entirely correct, and upon which he assumes there is widespread agreement? Stated another way, how would Truman or Eisenhower react if a visitor, though highly respected and important in his or her own right, argued with them that support to the French or to Diem in Vietnam should be discontinued? Or how would Kennedy, Johnson, or Nixon react if a visitor told them that they were supporting the wrong side or a lost cause in South Vietnam?

Most likely, and there is some slight evidence to support the conjecture,[27] presidents would first threat the visitor with studied disbelief, offering regret that, on this issue, the visitor had gone astray, but consolation in the fact that the president would proceed to show him the error of his ways. The president would then probably follow this with a strong entreaty to the errant confidant or adviser to come on board all the way, "so I can show you that my policies will really work." If the adviser demurred and stuck to his or her guns, the president would most likely lose confidence in him or her, at least on this particular issue, and sadly dismiss the visitor without much further comment—then turning to his sycophants and having the visitor discreetly watched or blatantly blacklisted.

Of course, each president has his own particular style with dissenters. Kennedy tended to grill potential or real dissenters on Indochina with questions and would then suggest that Robert Kennedy keep an eye on them.[28] Johnson often showed direct irritation but managed to salve his conscience by literally training himself to listen to, and occasionally even to hear, George Ball; from this, he would operate on the illusion that he had heard all sides of the question. Note that while George Ball was given frequent access to the president, particularly in 1964-65, he was carefully kept at all times from actually playing a real decision-making role in the daily sequence of events. His purpose was, in fact, to serve precisely as a domesticated in-house dissenter, not allowed to touch actual policy-making on Indochina. Nixon possibly found the easiest way out of the particular dilemma of confrontation. He simply isolated himself, along with Kissinger, behind a veil of total secrecy. Since he let no one in, including supporters, he did not have to let dissenters in either.

These remarks on presidential dominance of our policy-making in Indochina over twenty-five years lead us to the conclusion that its product was rigidity of assumptions, and constraints on the decision-making latitude of the subordinates serving the presidents. Its chief characteristic was narrowness of the circle of intimate advisers. These increasingly came to contain only those who loosely shared the viewpoints, biases, and outlooks of our presidents.

Role of Congress

We next ask: Why was the charmed circle of executive branch policy-making on Indochina not broken before 1968 by loud and raucous political voices from outside the executive branch? Why was the Congress so passive and why did congressional support for executive policy-making on Indochina persist for so long?

This question is particularly relevant if we think of Congress as a more-or-less natural political adversary of the president in the American political system, as in a sense a substitute for the opposition that would exist for the government to contend with in a parliamentary system. In this perspective, the two real political parties competing for public allegiance in the United States are the executive and the Congress, not the Democratic and Republican. If we think about it, this is about the situation that has prevailed in the U.S. system with respect to foreign policy-making since the beginning of the second Nixon administration (January 1973). On virtually every major foreign policy issue, there has been vigorous if not virtually irreconcilable debate between the executive and Congress—issues such as Angola (1975-76), Panama (1977-78), Horn of Africa (1978), Taiwan (1978), SALT (1973-79), and a host of others, including energy policy and other major economic issues.

On the other hand, when Congress does not fulfill the role of loyal opposition in foreign policy, this role does not seem to be fulfilled at all. The appearance of consensual support for ongoing policies dominates thinking in the executive, and the charmed circle of executive decision-making remains unbroken. Accordingly, the ultimate breakdown of the domestic foreign policy consensus over the issue of Vietnam and Indochina, forced on by the wave of public sentiment in 1968 which overwhelmed both Congress and the executive, was at bottom a highly salutary development in the American system. It brought the Congress back to the adversary role decreed for it by the Constitution, in foreign as in domestic matters. Before the congressional hearings on national commitments began in the late sixties, and before Congressional resolutions like Cooper-Church (1970) constrained the executive in Indochina and led finally to the enactment of the War Powers Act of 1973, the situation had been quite different. The leaders of Congress had, most simply put, in effect sold out the constitutional role of Congress in American foreign policy in order, variously, to buy the president's support for domestic legislation the Congress desired or in order to obtain his support in the re-election of members of Congress.

Virtually from the time of the enactment of the NATO Treaty in 1949 through the high cold war to 1968 at the earliest, the Congress had in effect copped-out and become the handmaiden of the president and his small coterie of advisers in national security and foreign policy matters. This passivity or acquiescence by Congress, rather than any genuine massive support in the country, is what was really meant by the term "foreign policy consensus" during the high cold war. The consensus in effect meant "no one says no" to whatever it was the executive desired done in foreign policy; and in practical terms the "no one" in this expression meant Congress.

We do not mean to suggest that sincere and able leaders of Congress—among whom, with respect to Indochina, we can single out in particular Senators Wayne Morse and Ernest Gruening (the earliest dissenters) and later among others Senators John Sherman Cooper, Albert Gore, Frank Church, George McGovern, J. William Fulbright and Mike Mansfield, whose role as Senate majority leader placed him in a particularly difficult position—did not do their best to persuade the president that he was embarked on the wrong course of action. Church found himself in almost violent altercations with Johnson as early as the winter of 1965-66 [29] and Mansfield tried repeatedly in a highly dignified but firm manner to change the president's mind. Fulbright, who held the important post of chairman of the Senate Foreign Relations Committee, went courageously public, beginning in about early 1966, with his dissent earning the lasting enmity of Johnson. But as an institution, and whatever the intentions of some of its leaders, Congress failed to perform its proper constitutional role.

The bluntest way to explain Congress's failure to play its constitutional role of ensuring that the appraisal of the national interest prevailing in the executive be healthfully complemented by that of the Congress is simply to say that the American public was asleep under the soporific effects of simplistic anti-communism and the black versus white convictions of the high cold war. Why then should Congress disturb the sleeping dogs which regularly re-elected it? But these sleeping dogs finally awoke, and when they did the Congress too awoke with a vengence to reassume its proper role under the Constitution, a role which it should always have played.

Conclusions: Thinking in the Closed System

We have examined the two chief characteristics which we contend dominated our Vietnam policy-making process throughout the period of our involvement with that tragic country, 1950-72, and most specifically during the period under major consideration in this chapter, 1961-72. First, the decisive role of the president himself as policy-maker; second, the limited number of advisers admitted or heard in the charmed inner circle, and the constraints implicit in the roles such men played, which led them to be reinforcers and supporters rather than true co-makers of national policy with the president. We have seen that these constraints applied even to very major figures of leadership in the Congress; and that, as an institution, Congress failed during this period to perform its properly assigned role under our system as a political adversary to the president, supplying the missing element of a true opposition political party.

In regard to the substantive character of thinking in the presidential inner circle, we have in previous sections outlined and discussed many of its essential aspects. These consisted in the first place of the perceptions and effects born from the containment doctrine applied continuously—in the manner interpreted by a succession of presidents and secretaries of state—as the major premise of American foreign policy in

1950-68. Secondly, thinking in the inner circle consisted of the perceptions and effects born from the twin and parallel lines of appraisal we had made of our presumed commitments and their credibility on the one hand, and of the potential effects of victorious Communist-inspired national liberation wars on the other. In the third place, thinking in the inner circle consisted of the perceptions and effects born from our stress on machismo, toughness, and the role of force in the international politics of the second half of the twentieth century, as well as from the premium value we had placed on action, determination, and persistence. Finally, the thinking in the inner circle was affected by the misperceptions and effects stemming from our failure properly to analyze the chief political components of the Indochina issue, and from a technocratic-managerial approach which found its product in the application of a multitude of programs based on the ill-conceived premise that our military and technical superiority enabled us to surmount any and all challenges. All these aspects of our thinking must be set against the specific cultural-political ethos the U.S. brought to its role as superpower.

Thinking with the president in the small inner circle were men who believed in the sixties as they had in the fifties that the Sino-Soviet bloc must be contained at its minimal periphery (established about the end of the Korean War), and that its slightest gain over that line would redound to the immediate danger of the United States. They did not review the premises that after 1960 China was still allied to or the puppet of the Soviet Union, or that the regimes of other Communist states, for example the DRV, could not in any sense act independently of the Soviets. Nor did they question the outlook that wars of national liberation were externally inspired, propagated, and supported, or that their success in one place would automatically infect the world against the influence or presence of the United States.

These men judged the U.S. word as sacrosanct, and as being everywhere on the line; they judged the United States to be determined, persistent, tough, and strong; they saw the virtue of acting as much superior to that of reflection or contemplation; they perceived the non-Communist regimes of Indochina as weak but basically virtuous and deserving by resisting threats these men regarded as almost wholly external in inspiration; and they saw the Communists in Indochina as strong but basically evil and externally dependent. Finally, they thought the United States capable, with its means of technology and weaponry, of managing and operating a series of highly sophisticated, complementary, overlapping, and complex military and civilian pro-

grams which would result in preserving open options in Indochina—
that is, an indefinite stalemate.

Much of this thinking was, as we have seen at length, incorrect and
based on serious misconceptions. But that in itself is less important
than the fact that this thinking was impervious to contrary views and
inputs from outside the inner circle, and that it found an echo of support in the American population, to whom our leaders had initially
taught the same thought pattern. In other words, *the system was a
closed one.* Leadership, from its original postwar and early cold war
perceptions, had created a framework of thought from which public
opinion would not let it escape. Of course, so long as public opinion
held to it firmly, there was no real incentive on the leadership to wish
to escape. Its wish, after all, was fundamentaly the same as that of any
leadership anywhere, to remain in power.

In the longer run, however, and as the course of our involvement in
Indochina progressed, reality began gradually and amorphously but
inevitably to impose itself on the cognitive processes of our leaders and
policy-makers, forcing them in turn to recast the public mind and
mood. We have repeatedly observed that U.S. leadership did not really
wish to win in Indochina—that was the job of the South Vietnamese;
the leadership only wanted not to lose. The very conception of our
program mix was designed basically to perpetuate stalemate. We shall
see in subsequent chapters how, gradually but inevitably, new perceptions arose in the minds of top U.S. leaders as the Sino-Soviet rift
developed into major conflict, as nuclear parity and multipolarity
emerged in world politics, as the fissiparous and polycentric tendencies
became more apparent and inescapable in the communist world, and
as confrontation and hostility in the high cold war eventually gave way
to the more relaxed stance of détente and negotiations.

We now turn, therefore, to examination of the reasons why the long
course of U.S. involvement in Indochina was finally reversed.

Notes

1. *See* Chapter VIII, Section 1, for the description of orchestration given by
   J. Thomson.
2. Admiral Sharp's views on the strategy of the war are conveyed most fully
   in his *Strategy for Defeat: Vietnam in Retrospect* (San Rafael, Calif: Presidio Press, 1978).
3. *See* in particular W. Scott Thompson and Donaldson Frizzel, eds., *The
   Lessons of Vietnam* (New York: Crane, Russak and Co., 1977); Gloria
   Emmerson, *Winners and Losers* (New York: Random House, 1976);

Guenter Lewy, *America in Vietnam* (New York: Oxford University Press, 1978).

4. Statistics compiled by the Indochina Resources Center, Washington, D.C., based on Pentagon figures supplied by Senator Stuart Symington and Representative Les Aspin, and introduced into the *Congressional Record* on May 14, 1975, by Senator Abourezk, show that a total of 6,723,644 tons of bombs was dropped in 1,899,668 total sorties over all of Indochina (South Vietnam, North Vietnam, North Laos, South Laos, Cambodia) between 1965 and 1973 (inclusive). *See Congressional Record—Senate*, 94th Cong., 1st sess., vol. 121, no. 77, p. S 8155 (May 14, 1975). If this total, which has been reflected in subsequent literature and which has not been denied by Department of Defense, is accurate as it appears to be, it represents more than three times the total tonnage dropped by the United States over all enemy powers in World War II. George C. Wilson, "Hard-Learned Lessons in a Military Laboratory," in *A Short History of the Vietnam War*, ed. Allan R. Millet (Bloomington: Indiana University Press, 1978), pp. 57-66, makes the point that the total tonnage dropped works out to "289 pounds of explosive for every man, woman, and child living in the four nations of Indochina" (p. 63).

5. *See also* David Kraslow and Stuart Loory, *The Secret Search for Peace in Vietnam* (New York: Random House Vintage, 1968); *Pentagon Papers* volume on negotiations (not part of the *The New York Times*, Gravel, or Government Printing Office editions) recently declassified in part under the Freedom of Information Act, and made available to L. Gelb and R. Betts, *Irony of Vietnam.*

6. James N. Rosenau, *The Adaptation of National Societies* (New York: Mc-Caleb-Seiler, 1970).

7. In the sense used here, the occasionally attentive public is that portion of the public which is neither always attuned to foreign policy and events (attentive or elite public), nor simply attuned to given issues (lobby groups or focussed public), nor generally inattentive (mass or amorphous public). The occasionally attentive public in the case of Vietnam in the sixties predominantly and preeminently included the student bodies on U.S. campuses.

8. President Lyndon B. Johnson on September 25, 1964, as quoted in Pettit, *Experts*, p. 190.

9. Other writers often call this portion of public opinion "lobbies and interest groups."

10. Among major contractors for the U.S. government in Vietnam, the construction firm of Morrison-Knutsen, headquartered in Texas, particularly stands out as it employed tens of thousands of American civilians in Vietnam throughout the sixties.

11. R.P. Deere, "Japan's Place in the World," in *Japan in Current World Affairs*, ed. Marinosuke Kajima (Tokyo: Institute of International Peace, Japan Times Ltd, 1971), pp. 293-306; Douglas H. Mendel, Jr. "Japanese Opinion on Key Foreign Policy Issues," *Asian Survey* IX, No. 8 (August 1969): pp. 625-39; Seymour Broadbridge and Martin Collick, "Japan's International Policies: Political and Economic Motivations," *International Affairs* 44, 2 (April 1968): pp. 240-53; Teruo Kobayashi, "A Great Debate

in Japan: The Fate of the U.S.-Japan Security Treaty in 1970," *Journal of Politics* 30, (August 1968), pp. 749-79.

12. Peter C. Dobell, *Canada's Search for New Roles: Foreign Policy in the Trudeau Era* (London: Oxford University Press, 1972), pp. 24, 80; Richard H. Leach, ed., *Contemporary Canada* (Durham, N.C.: Duke University Press, 1967), pp. 288-89.

13. C. Cooper, *Lost Crusade.*, pp. 325-26.

14. F.S. Northedge, "Britain As A Second-Rank Power," *International Affairs* 46, 1 (January 1970): pp. 37-47.

15. C. Cooper, *Lost Crusade*, pp. 350-68.

16. At the time President Johnson decided to implement the policy of graduated escalation and sustained bombing against North Vietnam, he also decided that as many nations as possible should demonstrate concrete participation alongside the United States in the Indochina effort. He accordingly instructed U.S. diplomats abroad to spare no efforts to obtain gestures showing the presence of nations other than the United States in Vietnam. This unsuccessful enterprise became known as the "Many Flags in Vietnam" program.

17. Graham Allison, *Essence of Decision: Explaining the Cuban Missile Crisis* (Boston: Little, Brown, 1971); Morton H. Halperin, *Bureaucratic Politics and Foreign Policy* (Washington, D.C.: Brookings, 1974); Alexander George, "The Case for Multiple Advocacy in Making Foreign Policy," *American Political Science Review* 66, (September 1972): pp. 751-95; A. George et al. *The Limits of Coercive Diplomacy: Laos, Cuba, Vietnam* (Boston: Little, Brown, 1971); A. George and Richard Smoke, *Deterrence in American Foreign Policy: Theory and Practice* (New York: Columbia University Press, 1974); H. H. Lentner, *Foreign Policy Analysis* (Columbus, Ohio: Charles Merrill, 1974).

18. Lentner, *Foreign Policy Analysis*, usefully distinguishes sequential or routine type decisions from those he calls basic and which introduce fundamental change in a country's foreign policy.

19. Graham Allison, *Essence of Decision.*

20. *See* Chapter II, Section 2.

21. *Ibid.*

22. For a listing of members of the inner circle, see Chapter VI, Section 1.

23. Barnet, *Roots of War.*

24. Halberstam, *Best and Brightest.*

25. Irving L. Janis, *Victims of Groupthink* (Boston: Houghton Mifflin, 1972).

26. *See* essays by Thomas E. Cronin (pp. 168-83) and F.G. Hutchins (pp. 35-55) in *The Presidency Reappraised,* Rexford Tugwell and Thomas E. Cronin, eds. (New York: Praeger, 1974). *See also* James D. Barber, *The Presidential Character* (Englewood Cliffs, N.J.: Prentice-Hall, 1972); Erwin C. Hargrove, *The Power of the Modern Presidency* (Philadelphia: Temple University Press, 1974), pp. 1-32.

27. The only evidence I have for this conjecture is an informal conversation I had in 1966 with Hon. Francis R. Valeo, then secretary of the U.S. Senate and former chief of staff in Senator (then Senate Majority Leader) Mike Mansfield's office. We discussed some of Mansfield's efforts to impart dissenting views to President Johnson and the latter's responses. The literature

I consulted on the presidency, including Doris Kearns', *Lyndon Johnson and the American Dream* (New York: Harper & Row, 1976), offers no insights on the question.

28. Reconstructed by memory from oral accounts at the time by persons who had direct access to President Kennedy. O' Donnell and Powers, *Johnny*. corroborates only that Kennedy was angered by Mansfield's vigorous and persistent dissents on Indochina (pp. 13-18). Donald C. Lord, *John F. Kennedy: The Politics of Confrontation and Conciliation* (New York: Barron's Educational Series, 1977), pp. 228-29, says basically the same thing.

29. Halberstam, *Best and Brightest,* pp. 742-43.

Chapter VII

Disengagement from Indochina, 1968-73

1. Changing Perceptions of the War

Changing perceptions of the war at home led the American public, including its elites, gradually to reverse the U.S. slide into the never-never land of Vietnam and to force a return to reality. Among these perceptions, the growing and gnawing feeling that the very reason for fighting the war was itself in question, even among our top policy-makers, played an important role. The longer-range effects of fighting a war for apparently open-ended and ambiguous objectives, along with the loss of international prestige and goodwill attendant on such a long war fought under such apparent discrepancies of power, similarly contributed to reversing the U.S. slide. Moreover, the ongoing changes in the international system which imperceptibly but gradually over a period of twelve years modified the apparent stakes in Indochina contributed to changing the U.S. perspective. We shall cover each of these factors at some length, paying special attention to two dominant critical explanations of the prolonged involvement in Indochina: the quagmire theory; and the explanation that the United States deliberately sought to prolong the stalemate as long as possible.

Nature of the Casus Belli

We have discussed earlier [1] the failure of top American leadership to resolve the key question whether the war was a revolutionary civil or internal war, an aggression by one state against another as claimed, though not necessarily fully believed, by U.S. leadership in the heyday of escalation and even in 1969-72, or some other type of undefined war. The view expressed in this book was that the Vietnam War was an internal revolutionary or civil war. It should have been viewed in that

241

light from its inception in the August 1945 Viet Minh revolution, through the first eight years of the French Indochina war, the period of reduced violence or remission in 1954-59, the period of so-called insurgency before the massive entry of U.S. ground forces in 1959-65, through the eight years of full-fledged U.S. combat involvement in 1965-73 and the last two years of internecine struggle in 1973-75.

The substantive merits of the controversy over the nature of the war are less important than the fact of the controversy itself. Whatever the U.S. leadership contrived to say or do, it never succeeded in persuading the public that the war had been an unambiguous aggression, similar say to an attack by an independent Thailand on an independent Malaysia in Southeast Asia. It was also unwilling to admit to itself or to the public at large that the war was indeed an internal revolution; it could not do this because it had presumably committed itself to the support of one of the two state entities which had emerged in Vietnam after 1954 and which were both contending for the control of South Vietnam. The result was growing public confusion in the United States which would sooner or later lead to large domestic political consequences. It is clear that rising public doubts about the nature of the war and the validity of the *casus belli* during 1964-65 to 1968-70 contributed in major measure to the growing opposition to the war and ultimately to U.S. abandonment of the enterprise.[2]

The problem of the *casus belli,* of fighting for poorly understood reasons in a remote area alien from American experience, comprised essentially three elements: First, when and how and why did North Vietnam commit aggression, and against whom? Second, who precisely among the Vietnamese was the enemy? Third, what if any was the broader significance of the enemy, i.e., did the enemy pose a serious menace to the United States or to interests palpably connected with the security of the United States? This in turn raised the question whether the presumably assailed and aggrieved party in Vietnam, i.e., South Vietnam, was important enough for the United States to defend directly with its own forces, and whether it was doing enough in its own self-defense.

On the first point, a vocal though at first tiny minority of opinion in the United States began arguing from about 1961 on, and increasingly after 1964, that no aggression had in fact been committed by Vietnamese in Vietnam. This group, which became a substantial minority of U.S. opinion in about 1965-66, adopted generally two parallel and complementary, though distinct, lines of reasoning.

1. There was a revolution in progress against the established regime in South Vietnam, this revolution being southern in inspiration though clearly led by

Communists called Viet Cong who were supported though by no means necessarily controlled by Communist North Vietnam (the DRV). This revolution counted in its ranks many nationalist and repressed elements in addition to the Communists themselves.[3]

2. The revolution in progress in the South in the sixties was a direct and linear continuation of the popular Viet Minh or DRV-led revolution against imperialism and its puppets in all Vietnam. Although the DRV was leading and perhaps controlling this revolution, it could not be regarded as aggression since the Vietnamese Communists had been deprived by the great powers of their legitimate right to contend for the leadership of all Vietnam. This right had been accorded them in the unimplemented provisions of the 1954 Geneva accords. Accordingly, the DRV was in no way committing aggression but instead acting under permissible standards of international behavior in setting forth on its temporarily interrupted revolt against what it viewed as externally imposed authority in South Vietnam.[4]

In either view, whether the rebellion against repressive southern authority was primarily southern aided by the North, or primarily northern-inspired against imperialism in Vietnam, the only aggression being committed in Indochina was that of the United States. The latter had acted unilaterally, without any form of international sanction, intervening directly in the internal affairs of Vietnam to keep in power a regime which, in this U.S. opinion perspective, had lost all semblance of popular mandate or support. In doing so, moreover, the United States had itself violated its 1954 Geneva pledge not to block implementation of the accords by force.[5]

As to our second point: the minority view that there was no real *casus belli* compelling the United States to fight in Vietnam grew over the sixties and early seventies into a majority of opinion along with the realization among the general U.S. public that the Communists in Vietnam were really Vietnamese, not essentially distinct or clearly distinguishable from other Vietnamese. The single most important contributing element to this changing viewpoint were the stories and reports from returning U.S. military men who disseminated widely within the country their own incapacity to distinguish among the "gooks," "dinks," and "slopes," [6] their bafflement at the infinitely superior performance of "their" Viets over that of "our" Viets, and their disappointment and bitterness at the South Vietnamese's corruption, inefficiency, and lack of popular support.

The changing perception of the nature of the enemy, as seen from the perspective of the mass public in the United States, forms a particularly interesting psychological aspect of the Vietnam War. There is little doubt that the public in 1961-65 had no clear idea of the enemy. Who was Charlie? Certainly not Chinese, for the administration was repeatedly stressing that it was not at war with China, or with any other state in Asia either, including the DRV for that matter. For the amazingly long period of some five years it seems to have sufficed that the enemy was Red, or Charlie. After that, with the multiplying effect of soldiers' letters and oral accounts, the enemy suddenly seemed to manifest itself in the surprised American mass mind as Vietnamese who were better led, more willing to fight and sacrifice and die, and above all more self-reliant and independent than the South Vietnamese. The South Vietnamese were armed, fed, and led by the United States; the Communists seemed to be on their own. Moreover they kept on coming, and there seemed to be no end of them.

The U.S. public perception changed slowly after 1965 from an initial and fairly general understanding that external aggression was being resisted by the South Vietnamese (1961 to 1965-66), to a largely unexpressed image of Vietnamese, both southern and northern, resisting the imposition by U.S. means of a type of U.S.-made order upon Vietnam (1966 onwards). This new image was being in part created and fortified by direct television displays of battle scenes, such as the fight for Hue during Tet; or even earlier the urban battles against the virtually unarmed Buddhists; or by media pictures such as the brutal point-blank killing of a suspect by a high-ranking South Vietnamese police officer. The imagery of a different type of war from the one initially assumed and expected solidified itself in the public mind well before the later depiction in the mass media of atrocities committed by exasperated U.S. forces against Vietnamese civilians at such a place as My Lai. By the time My Lai was revealed (September 1969), the U.S. public was well conditioned to sympathize with the GI's against a U.S. war leadership which had seemed to place them in an untenable position toward all Vietnamese.

The change in the U.S. domestic optic on the war was a matter of cardinal importance, for with it the stage was set for a turn-about in the U.S. involvement. The reversal of policy which came in 1968, however, was further touched off by the growing conviction that the enemy was not a really significant threat to the security of the United States or to interests palpably related to those of the American people as a whole.

When the issue of saving South Vietnam from communism had hung in the balance in 1964-65, Joseph Alsop and other like-minded and equally influential commentators had over and over challenged the president and the administration to respond with guts, courage, and the necessary escalation and involvement to what they depicted as a major threat to U.S. security.[7] The suggestion was quite literally made by Alsop and others that if this threat was not contained or defeated in

Vietnam proper it would sooner rather than later have to be met in Hawaii or the West Coast of the United States. While the administration did little to foster this point of view, it did even less to discourage it, despite Johnson's false rhetoric in the 1964 electoral campaign that fighting a land war in Asia was the job of Asian boys.[8]

Though the administration was essentially getting itself into war through the gradually incremented escalation of 1965, it never asked Congress to declare war or made clear to the American people what it was in fact trying to do, as we have repeatedly seen throughout this book. On the contrary, it took pains in both 1965 and 1966 to establish for public consumption that it was *not* going to war. It explicitly rejected thoughts of direct hostile engagement with China; it refused to say that it was at war with North Vietnam; it refused to mobilize the reserves or the national guard; it refused to moderate or sacrifice its Great Society domestic programs for the sake of the war. In the strategic sense, it refused even to consider unleashing anything like its full conventional force capabilities against the enemy's rear base in the North, that is, to raise publically or even internally the issue of a possible ground invasion of the enemy's territory.

Under those circumstances, how could anyone logically have expected the American people to perceive a serious security threat coming from this enemy? If the administration was fighting without really admitting it was at war, if it was keeping the character of the fighting strictly limited, if it spoke only of holding South Vietnam but never of winning the war or beating the enemy, then was this enemy really worth the effort, the blood, and the cost?

Such doubts pervaded U.S. opinion as escalation reached its peak in 1966-68 and as the military situation in Vietnam turned into long stalemate. Then, after two and a half years of U.S. combat, the Tet offensive of early 1968, at least as pictured to the U.S. public, suddenly revealed the enemy as barely dented and our own Vietnamese as weaker than ever. U.S. opinion inchoately but unmistakably began to sense that if the administration was unwilling to win, the public itself should not continue to support a fight which might be disagreeable and inconvenient but in no way fatal for the United States to lose.

The Effects of Open-Ended Objectives

We have had repeated occasion to point to the ambiguous and open-ended character of U.S. objectives in the Indochina intervention, at least as perceived by the U.S. public during the succession of administrations between Kennedy and Nixon.

Kennedy's decisions of 1961 were, as we have seen, the most significant taken during the course of our intervention from 1950 to 1973. Yet, the objectives of the decisions were never adequately specified. Had he wanted to defeat the Viet Cong, he would probably have had to intervene with ground forces and, at a minimum, order the same type of escalation against North Vietnam that Johnson ordered later. Had he wanted to settle the war in the South on more or less even terms, he would have had to induce the Vietnamese Communists into some form of reformulation of the Geneva 1954 provisions in which they would have obtained some type of guaranteed participation in the governance of the South. But both these courses of action were clearly discarded by the Kennedy administration, which merely indicated that it would support the presumed U.S. commitment to South Vietnam's defense against allegedly externally directed and supported aggression. As we just pointed out, this statement of objective lost force with the passage of time.

Johnson offered more of the same. By the time he came on the scene, the enemy had so gained in strength and the political-military situation in the South had so deteriorated that more U.S. action was required just to stay even. Thus, Johnson ordered escalation, but graduated escalation, and the intervention of U.S. combat units, but only incrementally. His objective still remained to help the South Vietnamese defend themselves against presumed external attack, even after North Vietnam had introduced major regular units of its army into the South in response to the air war being waged against it. In other words, Johnson's actions had the general effect of a self-fulfilling prophecy, this not being at all lost on perceptive U.S. observers. Like Kennedy, he remained adamantly unwilling to wage real war, war to defeat the enemy; while at the same time he also, despite all pretenses, remained unwilling until 1968 to offer the only possible types of concessions which might have induced the enemy to end the war. Accordingly, like Kennedy, Johnson was pursuing the objective of stalemate, but without clearly so indicating to the American public and Congress.

Both presidents were apparently caught in a trap—a trap essentially of their own making since they had both personally contributed to the creation of the adamant, or presumed adamant, domestic atmosphere in the United States regarding losing to communism or losing a war, even an undeclared one.[9] The trap was essentially this: if they went to full-fledged war, their estimates were that they would inevitably have to confront China, or the Soviet Union, or both. Neither president at any time wished for a host of good and sufficient reasons to engage the United States in major hostile confrontation with these world powers. On the other hand, if they chose negotiations, the conjuncture of events in South Vietnam was such that a coalition government including the Communists would have to emerge. Yet the emergence of such a coalition would take, within the United States, precisely the appearance of defeat to communism, which both presidents feared most. They feared genuinely and profoundly that it would, at a minimum, cost them and their party the next elections; moreover, they feared that it was virtually certain to provoke a wave of reaction and vigilantism against alleged traitors such as had followed the loss of China in 1949.

As a result, both presidents chose to "tough it out," that is, to continue what they were doing, doing more of it as become occasionally necessary in the course of the war between 1961 and 1968. Both hoped that the American people would follow them and bear the necessary sacrifices while they waited for an indefinite something to turn up that would permit them somehow to escape the trap. The result was the policy of stalemate and of unspecified, open-ended objectives in which it was always suggested that there would, someday, be light at the end of the tunnel.[10] The tunnel analogy was a particularly poorly chosen one, as we shall see; for as the exercise became prolonged in years, the American people felt themselves more and more buried and crawling in an endless cave.

Nixon's objectives, by contrast, were clearly and firmly declared. Announcing himself as the peacemaker during the 1968 electoral campaign, he would get the United States out of Vietnam and he would do so honorably. The latter provision left Nixon the loophole he needed to once more perpetuate the policy of stalemate. Moreover, while Nixon clearly stated his goals, he left his means completely and deliberately in the dark. Nixon was, as Jonathan Schell has suggested, continuously playing with illusions and treating the country to an enormous shadow play.[11] An ill-defined policy of Vietnamization was to be Nixon's essential means to his end; but, paradoxically, as the war was in fact being Vietnamized between 1969 and 1972 and as more and more Americans were in fact being withdrawn from Vietnam, the war itself was somehow and inexplicably expanding. Beginning in 1969, Cambodia was being secretly bombed (though the American people didn't know it); in 1970 and 1971 both Cambodia and then Laos were invaded with massive air support to the U.S. and Vietnamese units involved; and in 1971-72, South Vietnam's ARVN was being provided with virtually the entire available U.S. arsenal in the South, while bombing resumed over North Vietnam, ending with an enormous and devastating crescendo at Christmas, 1972.

Tunnel Image. Successive administrations helped perpetuate the confusion in the U.S. public mind by the unfortunate image, created by

President Kennedy and carried further by his successors, of comparing Vietnam with a tunnel. A tunnel, through which one must necessarily pass before reaching the other side of the mountain where there is light again, can also become a cave if one never reaches its end, and a cave subconsciously tends to evoke the image of a grave. In the case of Vietnam, there was still no light at the end of the tunnel when Kennedy was killed in November 1963; still no light in November 1965, after the United States had committed itself to sustained bombing of the North and to the massive introduction of U.S. ground combat units; and still no light in November 1966 when there were almost 500,000 U.S. troops fighting savagely there. By November 1967, the tunnel had begun to look like a cave; and by November 1968, at the time of Nixon's election, like a grave.

In 1969, Nixon promised to bring the United States out, again suggesting that there was light at the end of the tunnel, light this time to be seen by the Vietnamese themselves after they finished the crossing on their own while the United States slowly evicted the tunnel. For four more long years the tunnel effect remained, however, as thousands of U.S. casualties were incurred, fighting and dying took place throughout Indochina, and our prisoners, unliberated, remained at the bottom of the cave. By the beginning of 1973, Americans were free, at last breathing fresh air again; but after two more years, it was the Vietnamese Communists who emerged from the tunnel into the sunshine, leaving the U.S.-backed Vietnamese buried in the grotto.

Quagmire Myth vs. *Stalemate Machine.* Two contending theories about the character of U.S. intervention in Vietnam have been held by American critics and opponents of the war. Argued originally by Halberstam in his first work on Vietnam,[12] the quagmire theory, also initially supported by Arthur Schlesinger [13] and in part by Roger Hilsman [14] and others, held that the U.S. sank itself step by step deeper and deeper into quicksand. Each step being insufficient to accomplish even the limited aims stated for it, a series of endless successive steps were needed, but with each successive step we sank deeper into the quagmire.

In arguing the theory of the stalemate machine, Daniel Ellsberg suggested that the United States, primarily through the decisions of its presidents, deliberately chose not to work itself out of the quagmire.[15] It chose instead to perpetuate it as long as possible, and through as many presidential elections as possible, ultimately walking out of the quagmire only when it had become apparent that it was truly sinking—and then walking out quite easily, and without major moral compunctions.

Ellsberg argued in his work that each U.S. president, from Truman to Nixon, knowingly did the least he needed to do in order not to be thrown out of Vietnam by the Communists, and thereby to perpetuate the stalemate until the next U.S. election. Every president *knew* that what he did would be insufficient, not only to win in Vietnam but even to get out of the quagmire. The purpose of the perpetual stalemate was of course not to have to face the domestic political consequences which every one of the five presidents involved similarly judged would be fatal to him and his party if they had to bear the onus of losing to communism. Ellsberg consequently traces the source of the stalemate policy to the effects of the loss of China to communism in 1949 and to the creation within the United States by the American leadership itself of the anti-Communist monster mentioned earlier, whipped into fury and a wild search for treasonous scapegoats by such politicians as Senator Joseph McCarthy of Wisconsin, Pat MacCarran of Nebraska, and others.[16]

Ellsberg's theory of the stalemate machine does not dismiss or vitiate many of the objective reasons for involvement in Indochina which we have discussed earlier—such factors as containment; resistance to the spread of national liberation wars; preserving the sanctity and credibility of U.S. commitments; the role of macho and force; the New Frontier and successor administrations' premium on action and persistence; the programmatic and managerial (i.e., "effective") motivations of a generation of American leadership; the domestic consensus of support; the homogeneity of peer thinking in closed system decision-making. All these factors were no doubt present in varying degrees at various times. However, according to Ellsberg, rather than being central concerns or objectives of the presidents involved, they served rather as rationales for each president's determinant and central goal: not to be pushed out of Indochina during the term of his administration for fear of the ensuing domestic political consequences.

Ellsberg's thesis rests on the foundation that no president ever did more than was absolutely necessary to preserve the stalemate; and that in taking all of the successive incremental steps which bogged us deeper into the quagmire, each president knew perfectly well that each step was in itself insufficient to preserve the stalemate for very long, but hopefully just long enough to maintain it until the next step would be required.

The thesis of the stalemate machine can be supported by a great deal of empirical evidence, as demonstrated in the *Pentagon Papers* and in the recent book by the chief compiler of the *Pentagon Papers,* Leslie Gelb.[17] Clearly, a quagmire is something from which one can never escape; yet ultimately, when it wanted to break the stalemate, the United States simply did so, and fled from Indochina. We have repeatedly stated throughout this work that the U.S. might have obtained the same if not better terms in 1963, 1965, and most likely even as late as 1969 than it obtained in 1972-73. Then, why did it not do so? The answer simply cannot be that the terms at those times were unacceptable in the light of specific objectives set for the war; for in terms of these vague objectives, they were certainly still unacceptable in 1972-73.

The only reasonable answer is that indeed the objectives of the United States in Indochina were neither to win at a cost which presidents knew would be exorbitant, nor to lose in the sense of a negotiated settlement incorporating the Communists in the government of South Vietnam. The objectives were open-ended. At any time one considers them during our long involvement—whether in 1950, 1954, 1955, 1956-61, 1961-64, or 1964-68—they were simply to keep the stalemate going, always hoping that something would turn up, but if not, then as long as possible or necessary in terms of a domestic political judgment.

Abandoning the Stalemate. The United States abandoned the stalemate machine in Indochina only after Nixon and Kissinger had carefully worked out the U.S. rapprochement with Communist China. The disastrous effects of our presumed loss of China had hung over U.S. politics like an evil-smelling but inescapable cloud for some twenty-three years as of 1972 when Nixon signed the Shanghai Communique. Its last vestiges now dissipated as the rapprochement turned into a domestic political gain for the president who had done so much to create the cloud of suspicion in the first place. Having regained China, which the Democrats had lost in 1949, Nixon could now afford to lose Vietnam, particularly if he hid the loss in the glorious-sounding public relations techniques of successful Vietnamization. Moreover, Nixon was being inexorably pushed in this direction by domestic public opinion. The miserable stalemate which had so long seemed necessary in Indochina could now be broken. After the corner of the 1972 elections had been safely turned, the trap was sprung. The stalemate machine was abandoned, and so was Indochina.

The effects of waging a war of open-ended and ambiguous objectives, a war of stalemate and attrition, of perpetuating involvement merely for the sake of involvement, were devastating upon the U.S. public in the longer-run. Continuing such a war after 1968, when the public had compelled the president to promise withdrawal as his objective, was particularly devastating. After 1968, we had a closed-ended objective for the war, which was to get out of it, and the public clamored vociferously for results. While at first it trusted the new Republican leadership to quickly accomplish its stated goal, it simmered and occasionally exploded in rage when the goal did not soon materialize and the war expanded instead of contracting.

Instead of denouncing the dissidents, student riots, and activists of the late sixties and early seventies as the administration (then carefully preparing its rapprochement with China) had hoped, the public at large basically condoned and even sympathized with "the kids" leading the anti-war movement and even with the growing refusal of young men to respond to the draft or continue military service. Authority in the United States started very seriously to erode toward the end of the first Nixon administration (1970-72).

Nixon and Kissinger judged that they too needed the customary four years until the next elections before they could risk the abandonment of a policy followed by all their post-World War II predecessors. This does not necessarily indicate that they judged the public mood differently than did the majority of their fellow Americans, including the leading members of the Congress, although Nixon was certainly particularly sensitive to the hawkish feelings of hard-core right-wing Republicans and of populist-nationalist Democrats like George Wallace. Yet it is difficult to accept the notion that he really believed in the so-called "Silent Majority," presumably a majority favorable to continuing the war as long as necessary to obtain what Nixon termed "peace with honor." He induced Vice President Spiro Agnew to conjure up the silent majority and then to inspire it through a series of carefully calculated addresses. At the same time, Agnew was also instructed to tackle the anti-war media head-on and to make anti-administration reporting on the war as difficult and nasty a business as possible. In doing all this, Nixon was systematically using the best public relations techniques that he and his advisors could think up to keep the policy of stalemate in the war going as long as possible.[18]

As we have indicated, the real purpose was to gain the necessary time to set in motion and achieve the rapprochement with China, as well as to permit the new policy of détente with the Soviet Union to show some results in Europe and elsewhere. By 1971, significant results emerged in the Berlin Quadripartite Agreements. By 1972, the SALT I accord was signed with the Soviets. By 1973, Brezhnev and Nixon were reaching accords on the future of Europe and of East-West trade and exchange, premised on recognition of the existing status quo. The Soviets could claim that the United States had at last accepted the postwar division of Europe; and the United States could point to significant gains in opening up the Soviet Union to trade and exchange, and even to the emigration of Soviet Jews. The groundwork was laid for the Helsinki accords signed by President Ford in August 1975.

The rapprochement with China having been crowned by the Shanghai Communique, and détente in Europe having made significant gains, Nixon and Kissinger could at last bring their policy of disengagement from Indochina to its ultimate conclusion with the least possible fears of adverse domestic consequences. For insurance, they waited until after the November 1972 elections in any case. And to show their ill-temper to the victorious Vietnamese Communists, and their qualities of macho to what may have remained of recalcitrant Americans, they engaged in the Christmas bombing of 1972. Watergate overtook them soon thereafter and engulfed Indochina in domestic forgetfulness. It re-emerged only briefly with the final collapse of Vietnam in 1975 and President Ford's impetuous and costly action in the Mayaguez incident.[19] After January 1973, American relief to be rid of Indochina was immense. So was the world's relief at the ending of American immersion in a war which had, over the intervening period, come to be seen abroad as increasingly costly, wasteful, and wrong.

The War Seen From Abroad

"There is not a single independent state in Europe or Asia," writes Mr. Lippmann, "which follows our lead. . . No European government could survive today if it joined us on the battlefield. . . As for the Asian peoples we are supposed to be saving, no independent Asian state—not Japan, India, Pakistan, Burma, Malaysia, Indonesia—is giving us even token support." (Cited in A.M. Schlesinger, *The Bitter Heritage*, Greenwich, Conn: Fawcett Books, 1968 rev. ed., p. 69.)

The foreign forces working to reinforce the domestic consensus of support for the war were discussed in Chapter VI. We grouped these forces into (1) Western allies, including Japan; (2) U.S. client states, particularly those bordering or close to Indochina in Southeast Asia. As the twelve long years of our involvement progressed, however, different perspectives of the war as seen from outside the United States came more and more to reinforce elements in the U.S. proper opposing our continued engagement in Indochina. By the late sixties and early seventies, only a few sycophantic governments remained favorable to the U.S. war policy. Most others were more and more openly voicing their doubts and misgivings. This fact played a role at least as important in our disengagement as the earlier foreign support had played in keeping us engaged.

Indifferent World. A large part of the world remote from Indochina remained indifferent to the U.S. ordeal in Vietnam. There may occasionally have been raised eyebrows or even secret smiles of satisfaction at U.S. discomfiture among leaders of certain countries in Latin America, Africa, or the Middle East. By and large, however, these governments showed little interest in the Indochina question and little if any sympathy for the U.S. entreaties of support occasionally made of them. It apparently continued to elude President Johnson why so many countries seemed so unconcerned. When he or his emissaries would raise the issue, they tended to be met with polite demurral at the provision of any, even purely rhetorical, support. No doubt some of the indifferent governments, like that of India, were privately scandalized at the spectacle of the U.S. giant daily exerting a substantial portion of its enormous power on a relatively minor and backward Asian peasant state. If so, they did little if anything to express their concern publicly, where it might have helped the mounting anti-war forces in the U.S.

Adverse World. At the opposite extreme were the Communist regimes and a small number of governments, like that of Sweden, who earned President Johnson's lasting enmity for strongly and openly berating the U.S. role in Indochina, sparing no words or even actions to depict the U.S. as guilty of crimes against humanity, and as engaged in a senseless war pursued by wholly disproportionate means for no discernibly valid objectives. Untrammeled by NATO affiliation, the Swedes could afford to utter with impunity what were probably the sentiments of most Scandinavians, if not most Europeans, about the war. There is certainly much evidence that alert opinion in Northern, Central, Western and Southern Europe generally shared the view of the war as an abomination. It began to be freely expressed by student movements in such countries as France, Netherlands, West Germany, the United Kingdom, and Italy as early as the mid-sixties and reached crescendo point during the student rebellions in some of these countries in 1968.

Vocally adverse opinion of the war was of course held also in the communist countries, as well as in most of the officially non-aligned or neutralist world. In such countries as Algeria, DRV propaganda proved itself very effective in mobilizing anti-Vietnam War sentiment.

Shocked World. Such governments as the French, British, Japanese, and Canadian grew increasingly disenchanted with America's adventure in Indochina as the war went into its violent and prolonged stalemate in the years after 1965. These governments were restrained from expressing themselves directly or forcefully because of their traditional ties and alliances with the United States, their continued dependence on U.S. leadership, and their fear that decisive policy changes in the United States might be jeopardized if they interceded too directly. For the most part, therefore, they confined themselves to assisting the various mediation and peace efforts which the Johnson administration seemed to wish to see promoted. But both governments and peoples in Europe and Asia watched with growing stupefaction and concern as the United States bogged down in an apparently endless Asian land war fought for dubious causes in a region which they tended to regard as of little if any intrinsic significance to the security of the West or the developed world. By the early seventies several Western governments were almost desperately hoping that the United States would soon liberate itself from the Vietnam yoke in order to resume the leadership of the non-Communist world in coping with a variety of new and serious problems then arising in relations between the developed and less developed countries, in functional areas such as international resource and financial problems, and in such regions as Africa and Latin America.

Sycophants. Finally, a few sycophantic governments continued to praise and encourage the U.S. effort in Vietnam to the last. Among these, the Thais deserve special mention because they perhaps stood to lose the most if the U.S. effort in Vietnam failed. Korea, the Philippines, Taiwan, Australia, and of course Singapore also played this role. Yet, except for Thailand's contribution of the bases mentioned earlier and of some troops, and Korea's significant contribution in manpower and lives lost, the sycophantic governments on the whole contributed very little concrete support. They were in many cases themselves dealing with student and other segments in their populations turning increasingly hostile to the war. This was particularly true in Australia, where a vocal and militant labor opposition eventually succeeded in gaining control of the government largely on the issue of Australian support for what was viewed as an unpopular, unjust, and imperialistic war in Southeast Asia.

Net Effects of World Public Opinion. There is little doubt that the clear shift in world public opinion outside the United States against the war after about 1966-67 played an important if indirect role in bringing about the similar shift within the United States itself. This would be true even without considering such extreme manifestations of anti-war and anti-American feeling as the mock trials of American war criminals organized by Lord Bertrand Russell in Stockholm in the late sixties and early seventies. Increasingly, as manifestations of anti-war and anti-U.S. sentiment abroad percolated through to the American public, the public perceived that American prestige was slipping badly abroad, and that instead of being able to count on the moral and political leadership of the United States, the world was now turning fearful, distrustful, and unfriendly. If there was a single factor which, more than any other, had sustained the domestic consensus of support for U.S. leadership in the high cold war, it had been the American public's feeling that U.S. presence and leadership in so many areas and issues abroad were required, desired, and gratefully received. Disillusion on this score set in among older Americans in the mid and late sixties, just as new generations, less concerned with an American leadership role in the world, were ascending on the American firmament.

By the late sixties and early seventies, and not without a part attributable to very effective DRV-inspired propaganda throughout the West and the Third World, the same perceptions were affecting U.S. opinion at home as were affecting world public opinion. These included apparently endless U.S. involvement in a seemingly unwinnable war, taking the United States away from urgent tasks elsewhere, both at home and abroad; disproportionality of means to the perceived and ambiguous ends of the U.S. enterprise in Indochina; rising costs for uncertain and shifting stakes; disappointment at the lies and deceptions about the war in which Washington seemed to get continuously caught; and finally, and also probably most important, the pangs of conscience arising among millions of individuals about the morality of the continuing war, given the apparent power discrepancy on both sides of the Vietnam equation.

Changes in the International System

The changing character of world politics during the lengthy period of the massive U.S. engagement in Indochina, 1961-72, also played a decisive role in changing American perceptions of the war, and particularly the appraisal by American leadership of the importance of the stakes in Indochina to the interests of the United States. This factor proved particularly telling on the group of "wise men" assembled by Secretary of Defense Clark Clifford on President Johnson's behalf to advise him in early 1968 as to the future course of our engagement, and which recommended U.S. withdrawal from the war. Four interrelated developments on the world stage had had a dramatic effect in changing world power and political relations during 1961-72.

1. Emerging parity between the superpowers. By the mid to late sixties, nuclear parity had been substantially achieved by the Soviets, with the result that a type of checkmate had developed permitting both superpowers to begin considering reciprocal arms control measures. At the same time, the new balance provided the medium-sized powers, especially France, which under de Gaulle had obtained its own small nuclear strike force, the opportunity to assert a much greater say in world politics. France under de Gaulle took the lead in trying to edge Europe toward a third force or

independent position between the superpowers; while in the Eastern sphere Rumania embarked on a similar course of maneuver and independent conduct. In the Third World, both China and much later India obtained nuclear weapons capability.

2. Polycentrism and multipolarity. A loosening of the frozen lines of the high cold war tended to emerge everywhere. The U.S. involvement in Southeast Asia, combined with the emergence of parity, had placed in question in the minds of some European leaders the capacity and reliability of the United States to fulfill its guarantees to Western Europe. This sent the NATO structure into the beginnings of a sort of limbo, from which it has yet to recover fully. At the same time, organs of the European Economic Community, in which the United States had far less influence, tended to assume growing importance in European affairs. The mounting Soviet concern on the other side of the globe with the rise and political assertion on the world stage of the People's Republic of China provided Eastern Europe as a whole with a somewhat similar opportunity to evolve in self-chosen directions. When this evolution proceeded too fast or far, as it did in Czechoslovakia in 1968, the Soviet Union intervened directly, thereby severely damaging its worldwide prestige and position.

In a somewhat similar development in the Western Hemisphere, the United States intervened directly in the Dominican Republic in 1965 when a regime not to its liking seemed about to take power. Independent centers of power and influence have been emerging in the non-Communist world steadily since the U.S. hold relaxed simultaneously with our deep engagement in Southeast Asia. The Soviet hold in the Communist world has been similarly weakened by an ever wider spread of polycentrism—many paths to socialism, and many power centers—within the former bloc.

3. Weakening U.S. economic position. During the sixties and due in large part to its Indochina embroilment, the United States started incurring increasing deficits in its balance of payments. These were to assume gigantic proportions in the seventies, thereby leading to a major world financial and monetary crisis. The deficits were due to unwillingness or incapacity to reduce U.S. expenditures and private investment flows abroad. At home, the United States was incurring growing deficit spending, contributing to a mounting inflation which in turn reduced U.S. export capabilities. The situation was only briefly arrested by a series of measures, including a surcharge tax on imports, taken in 1971 by Secretary of the Treasury John Connally on President Nixon's behalf. The United States rather high-handedly decided not to inform its principal trading partners ahead of time of its actions. The deteriorating economic situation, caused initially by U.S. unwillingness to retract at home in order to finance its increasingly costly involvement in Vietnam, suffered a further serious blow from the 1974 embargo of the oil-producing countries organized by the Organization of Petroleum Exporting Countries (OPEC) in the wake of the Middle Eastern war of 1973 in order to influence Western policy toward the Arab-Israeli conflict.

With the cost of the Indochina war rising to almost $100 million per day in the peak final years of 1967-69,[20] and the absence of economy measures designed to restrain federal expenditures in the United States or otherwise to finance the war by special measures, domestic inflation rose rapidly. Its effects were first felt abroad, in regions of basic U.S. economic hegemony such as Western Europe, Canada, and Japan. After 1971-72, the dollar fell from its dominant and freely convertible position of being the world's de facto monetary standard and reserve currency. It had to be devalued on repeated occasions while a complex and difficult to manage system of floating exchange rates and reserve currencies was adopted by the International Monetary Fund. From the mid-seventies on, inflationary effects aggravated by the world oil shortage were severely felt at home.

4. Sino-Soviet conflict. Competition and hostility between the Soviet Union and the People's Republic of China grew unabated during the sixties and reached a climax when military clashes occurred on the Issuri River in 1969. These led to refusal by the People's Republic of China for a period of some months to continue to allow the transshipment of Soviet war material destined for North Vietnam. (This action, strenuously objected to by the DRV, played an important role in causing the roots of the present-day conflict in Indochina and of continuing Sino-Vietnamese difficulties.) After 1969, it became impossible for the U.S. administration to continue to act as if it were blind to the Sino-Soviet conflict. Accordingly, Nixon and Kissinger seized the opportunity to explore and eventually to bring about Sino-U.S. rapprochement.

In the most fundamental sense, Sino-U.S. rapprochment relieved Soviet pressure on Europe by forcing the Soviet Union to pay constant attention to its Asian second front, where the possibility had now been opened of a Sino-U.S. alliance directed against it. This development signified a permanent change in the calculus of world security faced by the United States since the end of the World War II. It was consequently bound to engender major changes in U.S. foreign policy in the seventies. But such changes could not be initiated until the Indochina engagement had been permanently abandoned.

Further Effects. The United States was so fixed and concentrated on Indochina in the sixties that it was unable to give proper attention and leadership to the grouping of nations that expected and assumed its leadership, especially NATO Europe. U.S. schemes for arresting nuclear proliferation, such as the idea of a multilateral force to be created in Europe, floundered in futility. At the same time the European powers, within the context of mutual cooperation in EEC, developed large and rival arms exporting industries.

Straining to give due attention to the Arab-Israeli War of 1967, the United States permitted that conflict to end without any sort of permanent solution being found and with the seeds laid for renascent conflict a few years later. The United States also failed, owing to its preoccupation with the remote arena of Southeast Asia, to concern itself properly with the problems of energy source availability and consumption. It had no advance planning to cope with this problem when it arose dramatically after the OPEC boycott and oil price rises following the

Middle East war of 1973. Furthermore, Latin America was neglected and the problem of Panama repeatedly shelved for later, more onerous and difficult resolution.

In sum, almost all of U.S. foreign policy had become U.S. policy in Vietnam after 1965, and in the longer range, such a situation of single issue concentration was highly dangerous if not untenable.

2. Loss of the Domestic Consensus

As we have just seen, the perceptions of the war, of why the United States was present and fighting in Vietnam and Indochina, and of what it was trying to do there were gradually but unmistakably changing both at home and abroad from 1961-72. The cumulative effect of changing perceptions resulted, by late 1968 but certainly as indicated in all the major polls not later than 1970-71, in the loss of the domestic consensus favoring the war and supporting American foreign policy.[21] This consensus, as we saw in Chapter VI, had been very firm in the fifties and only slightly less so in the first half of the sixties.

The reversal of the American course of action occurred when the domestic consensus of support for the war had become irremediably and perceptibly shattered—precisely as had happened in the French case some fifteen years previously. Three domestic factors contributed in major fashion to the changing perspectives we have discussed and to the ensuing loss of consensus. These were: the rising economic costs of the war; the growing gap between the official and unofficial, including media, accounts of the war; and the impact of generational change in the United States. The anti-war movement brought public opinion to a head and provided the requisite means to deal a shattering jolt to the top leadership. Riding the crest of the domestic unrest provoked by swelling resistance to the war among the people, particularly among the young, the Congress began to reassert the role of leadership in the realm of foreign policy-making which it had virtually abdicated since the beginning of the high cold war in the late forties and early fifties.

Under these simultaneous onslaughts, the policy of perpetuating stalemate in Vietnam crumbled and the United States ultimately abandoned Indochina (1973-75). The single most telling blow dealt to the administration's policy of endeavoring to keep the policy of stalemate from collapsing until after the November 1972 elections was the release to the *The New York Times* by Daniel Ellsberg, a former Defense Department official turned anti-war activist, of an official history of U.S. policy-making on the war until 1968, which had been compiled in the Pentagon at Secretary McNamara's direction and was baptized *The*

Pentagon Papers.[22] These papers revealed enormous discrepancies between the administration's publicly avowed aims and means and what it had in fact been doing in Vietnam—and how. The scandalization of the elites and of a portion of the mass public which resulted from publication of the papers overshadowed the question of the legality or legitimacy of Ellsberg's action, on which the administration unsuccessfully tried to focus attention. The administration's actions became lost in the morass of the Watergate revelations which followed upon the November 1972 elections.

In the process, and without ever fully admitting to itself that it had lost a war, the United States nonetheless experienced the prime lesson that all nations learn from losing in war: that of the frailty and perishability of their domestic authority structures. The lesson was experienced in the painful and frightful events of Watergate, but it took its source in the tragic history of the American involvement in Vietnam.

The Effects of Rising Costs

The costs of the war in direct economic and financial terms were staggering, not to mention its longer-range costs in terms of national inflation, national insolvency, and the export of economic problems abroad through the depreciation of U.S. currency and the weakening position and role of the dollar. This resulted in the early seventies in enormous U.S. balance of payments deficits, which were shortly to be further aggravated by the rising world market price of oil.

Despite various "magic" funding formulas and devices conjured up by the Department of Defense and the Office of Management and Budget to hide U.S. war costs in a variety of ways during the sixties, and somehow to absorb them in the congressional appropriations to fund the U.S. military services, it became increasingly difficult during the later sixties to keep from Congress and the public the total of sums going directly to support the South Vietnamese government and military services and all U.S. military and civilian programs in Indochina. U.S. costs, over the years in question, rose as indicated in Figure 5.[23]

We may therefore conclude that over the key years of the fighting period, 1965-72, the United States spent an annual average of about $21.5 billion in support of its effort in Indochina. If these sums had been spent at home, they could have purchased, for example, the total urban renewal of most large U.S. cities.

The problem of rising economic costs in relation to Indochina emerged in acute form domestically because it coincided with a period during which socioeconomic deprivation was being sharply felt in the United States by groups whose political and social awareness had dra-

FIGURE 5
Financial Costs of Indochina War Effort to U.S., 1965-1972

Fiscal Years	Input attributable to War Fighting and Other DOD Support Programs ($B)*	Economic and Supporting Assistance ($M)**	Total U.S. Funded ($B)
1965	5	275	5.3
1966	20	737	20.7
1967	30	568	30.6
1968	35	537	35.5
1969	30	414	30.4
1970	23	477	23.5
1971	15	576	15.6
1972	10	455	10.6

Total U.S. Financial Input, FY 1965 through 1972   172.2

*Source: DOD outlays cited as "War Related Costs over FY's 1965-1973," extrapolated from complex graph on Chart I, opposite Appendix D, p. D-1, of Secretary of Defense James R. Schlesinger's *Annual Defense Department Report for FY 1976 and FY 197X*. (Figures are in constant FY 1975 dollars.)
**Source: *U.S. Economic Assistance to Vietnam, 1954-75*, "U.S. Overseas Loans and Grants: Vietnam Program Summaries," AID Statistics and Reports Division, Washington, D.C.: Agency for International Development, 1975. (Amounts apparently not adjusted for fluctuations in $ value.)

matically risen, largely as a result of the civil rights battles of the fifties and sixties. For the first time in decades the problems of rural poverty, urban blight, unequal employment opportunities, and sex and race discrimination were making themselves seriously felt on the home front. The surging demands of the blacks and the poor for a greater share of the economic pie seemed aggravated when seen in the light of the elusive and extremely costly policy being pursued in Indochina. Little by little, but very saliently after 1968, the war came to be seen as simply not important enough in view of the many problems at home to justify its cost.

The enormous discrepancy that had arisen by the late sixties between any possible and increasingly dubious security benefits the American population at large could perceive from the pursuit of the war and its staggering economic and financial costs was made the more dramatic and anguishing by the simultaneously occurring cost in lives and wounded of war. Between 1961 and 1972, the U.S. lost 46,163 killed in action and 10,081 who died of non-hostile causes in Vietnam; 270,000 were wounded.[24] In addition. 1,916 of our combat soldiers and civilians in Vietnam were listed as prisoners of war or missing in action by the Defense Department on December 31, 1972.[25] Of these, 133 were still officially listed as missing in action in April, 1979.[26] The number of blacks among these casualties was disproportionately high, an effect of the highly objectionable educational deferment provisions and other loopholes of the Selective Service Act, which resulted in a disproportionate number of blacks performing combat or other field service in Vietnam.

Amorphously, the U.S. public realized that the dead may have died well, though in vain, and that the problem of the wounded and incapacitated veterans would be with us for a long time. It accurately gauged what actually happened: to this day (1979), the problem of the wounded and other veterans of the Vietnam War continues to plague us without an adequate solution. For psychological reasons too deep to fathom here, the United States like France after its own Indochina war, is showing itself indifferent to the survivors of a grim, dirty, and unfortunately lost war.

The costs of the war in 1961-72 were not confined to money or lost and wounded lives. There were also great costs in diplomatic and psychological terms. We have alluded in the previous section to some of the diplomatic costs caused by U.S. neglect of relatively vital tasks in Europe, Latin America, the Middle East, international economic relations, and specifically the relations between rich and poor countries. Moreover, the Indochina war drained and strained America's reservoir of best-trained and most proficient national security and foreign affairs specialized personnel, as well as the best officers in the armed services. Those who either eschewed service in Indochina for reasons of conscience or disinterest, or who were regarded as inadequate for it, suffered reductions in rank and career opportunities. Some of the least adequate personnel ended up with roles in some of America's most vital foreign policy issues or areas. Some of the best personnel, who served in Indochina, were shunted aside after the end of the war.

The psychological costs of the Indochina War on the U.S. population as a whole were also very high. The refusal of thousands of young men to respond to the draft summons, and the desertion from the armed forces of thousands of others,[27] caused major social disruptions and a judicial-administrative problem which still exists.[28]

The nation was torn by uncertainties and hesitations during 1961-72. Was U.S. security really threatened? Was the enemy really as dangerous and ruthless as depicted? Were "our" Vietnamese really pulling their weight in defending themselves? Was the war a just and moral one? Was U.S. intervention with the means employed, particularly heavy bombing, justified? Was this massive foreign burden bearable when so many unsolved problems were crying for attention at home? Was the South Vietnamese government with its corruption, venality, and occasionally graphically reported brutality one worthy of the all-out support we were providing? Were the official reports telling the whole story? Was the war progressing as scheduled and claimed, or bogging down as the media were reporting? Most anguishing of all, were the American people perhaps being systematically denied the truth?

The Media and the Credibility Gap

In an essay entitled "Lying in Politics" [29] Hannah Arendt has explored the capacity for self-deception and delusion among the neat-looking, youngish public relations experts who have in the past two decades brought their image-making skills to the forefront in the formerly smoke-filled rooms of traditional American politics. She extends this capacity to the problem-solving systems analysts whose ascent in U.S. policy-making we discussed at some length in Chapter V. These are the rationalists whose effective motivational set overwhelms their affective set and who go about reducing the realities of the world to quantifiable variables neatly aligned in problem-solving equations. The sad fact is that, whether consciously or unconsciously so designed, the whole period of massive U.S. engagement in Indochina was an exercise in illusions which resulted in a tremendous loss of touch with reality on the part of U.S. policy-makers. This was bound sooner or later to catch up with them. It did, when the American public, well-nudged in that direction by the much more realistic media, ceased altogether to believe in the pronouncements of their leaders about the Indochina war.

Between 1961 and 1972, the gap between media and other unofficial accounts of events in the war and the official versions and rationales grew continuously. We can to some extent discern and follow the growth of this gap if we take five of the principal aspects of the Indochina war from 1961 to 1972 and attempt to examine their treatment by both sides over the entire period. In doing this, we are necessarily generalizing and abstracting greatly. Both space and the generally deductive method of this book preclude a systematic, accurate, and detailed work of survey research here. It is essential to point out, therefore, that thousands of different media covered the war and U.S. policy, frequently in vastly different reporting and editorial fashion. Official versions and rationales also came in many different forms, from presidential news conferences to daily handouts and releases by the State Department, Defense Department and other executive agencies, to formal speeches by the president and hundreds of other officials.

Nonetheless, much of the media coverage, including radio and television as well as the print media, was based on only one major source of information: wire service accounts provided by either Associated Press or United Press International. This ensured a large degree of uniformity, at least in the items selected for coverage. Moreover, it is quite evident to anyone who read the press and watched television between 1961 and 1972 that editorial slant and coverage assumed an increasingly uniform orientation over this whole period. Similarly, official versions ultimately all tracked back to a single major originating and orienting source—the White House. Accordingly, the exercise below may have some value despite its obvious limitations.[30]

Reasons for U.S. Presence and Actions. Official versions explaining the reasons for U.S. presence and actions in Indochina continued to emphasize security as the principal factor until sometime after Johnson's abdication speech of March 31, 1968. After Nixon's assumption of office, the search for an honorable peace was generally given as the principal explanation. Security was given slightly differing emphases in the period 1961-68. During the period of intervention and counterinsurgency, 1961-63, official versions generally claimed that security imperatives dictated limited U.S. intervention. In the aftermath of the Diem coup, 1963-64, official versions stressed that security considerations dictated increasing involvement. In the period of the air war against the North, of ground combat intervention in the South and of pacification, 1965-68, all these programs and actions were again justified on grounds of security, the official versions after 1966 stressing the security of all Southeast Asia against the menace of potential Chinese aggression.

Media reporting and editorial slant generally accepted the tenor of official versions in 1961-63. Some doubts as to the validity of explanations premised on U.S. security interests tended to appear in 1963-64. By 1965-68, media accounts tended to differ much more from official versions, with the lead media (such organs as the *The New York Times, Washington Post, Los Angeles Times,* and CBS News) appearing increasingly doubtful of the vital nature of U.S. security interests in Indochina and Southeast Asia. This is the period during which the media focussed a maximum of questioning and doubt on the validity of all official explanations. During the period of disengagement and Vietnamization, 1968-72, the media continued to treat official versions with skepticism and to view U.S. security interests in the region as secondary. It also continued to regard U.S. aims in Indochina as being ambiguous and shifting, despite the official line that the United States was seeking "peace with honor."

Nature of Enemy. Official versions first depicted the enemy in Indochina as externally supported communist insurgency, an explanation which was apparently too abstract ever to be really understood by the public. After 1963, the enemy was increasingly depicted officially as closely identified with China and as threatening most if not all of Southeast Asia. After 1968, the enemy was continuously projected as aggressive, obdurate and inflexible.

Media treatment of the enemy differed earlier from the official versions than it had in the case of explaining U.S. presence. Almost from 1961 on, the principal media treated Communist-led instability in Indochina as stemming from multiple causes, including internal repression by the Diem government. In 1963-64, the media generally saw the enemy as local Communists winning the guerrilla war in South Vietnam. After 1965, the lead media tended to regard enemy actions as basically reciprocating those taken by the United States. It tended also to de-emphasize the significance of Chinese and Soviet support of the enemy, in sharp contrast to the official versions. The rest of the media was slower in differing sharply from official accounts. After 1968, the lead media tended to treat the enemy in Vietnam as militarily invincible. The mass media was much slower in reaching an overall appraisal that the United States had neither the need nor the resources to defeat the enemy.

U.S. Power and Credibility. Official versions remained hortative on this point: the United States must fulfill its commitment to South Vietnam (1961-64); it must protect Southeast Asia against the threat of Chinese expansionism and Communist aggression in accordance with its SEATO obligations (1965-68); it had the power, the means, and the capacity to do so provided it demonstrated patience and determination (1961-68); and it must show staying power in order to obtain the best possible settlement (1968-72).

While general media treatment concurred initially with the official version that U.S. credibility was important, the growing realization by most of the reporters in the field and eventually by editorialists and commentators at home that U.S. engagement in Indochina was likely to be long term caused a sharp media reappraisal in 1965-68 of U.S. capacity to support this type of engagement almost indefinitely. The media put stress during this period on the limitations in the mix of means being employed and on the absence of light at the end of the tunnel. In 1968-72, the media as a whole clearly took a view at variance with the official versions: namely, that peace was being achieved too slowly and at too great a cost.

South Vietnam. The sharpest difference between official versions and general media accounts of the South Vietnamese was in the relative stress accorded to this factor. Official versions throughout 1961-72 tried to keep South Vietnam in play and repeatedly to assert the secondary and supporting role of the United States in contrast to the primary and cardinal role of the South Vietnamese. The official line remained that initiated by President Kennedy in 1963, that ultimately it was *their* war and *they* must win it. Media accounts, on the other hand, tended throughout to downplay the role of South Vietnam, particularly in the pictorial coverage of the war after 1965. Even during Vietnamization— after 1969—the war was covered as if it were almost entirely an American exercise.

Aside from stress, the qualitative difference of accounts from official versus media sources was also marked on this point. Official versions faithfully and expectedly depicted South Vietnam as a solid and worthwhile ally (1961-63), as restabilizing after internal turmoil (1963-65), as recovering in stability and capacity (1965-68), and as capable of holding out even after U.S. withdrawal (1968-72). Media accounts, on the other hand, revealed doubts as to the viability and determination of South Vietnam as early as 1961-63, depicted South Vietnam as unraveling in 1964-65, as weak, unstable, and unworthy in 1965-68, and as not really capable of holding out alone in 1968-72.

Estimate of Outcome. It was on this point that official versions and media accounts of the war diverged most. It was essentially over the promises of the government as to an eventual outcome in Indochina, and the ending of the U.S. engagement, that the media created the expression and subsequently demonstrated the existence of a credibility gap.

Official versions stressed time and patience from the outset. No exaggerated promises were made in 1961-64. Nonetheless, as we have seen Kennedy promised "light at the end of the tunnel" as early as 1962 and each subsequent administration found itself under increased pressure to put a definite term to its open-ended engagement. As we suggested earlier, the miscalculation of the top leadership was probably greatest on this point. The American public, though influenced as well as represented by the media, appeared unwilling to commit itself to an indefinite engagement for undefined ends. Repeatedly in 1965-68 the president and the top leadership felt themselves compelled to give progress reports which, whether always consciously or not, considerably exaggerated the positive elements in the situation. Thus, the theme of progress in official reports and accounts changed from "U.S. efforts are progressing as well as possible" in 1961-64 to "patience and determination are required, but U.S. efforts are progressing well and will undoubtedly succeed" in 1965-68. After 1968, the general official theme remained that "U.S. efforts are succeeding as planned."

The media was in sharp disagreement on this point. Lead media such as *The New York Times* reported serious doubts as to the progress of U.S. efforts as early as 1961-63. We suggested in an earlier chapter that reporters like Halberstam and Sheehan were closer to reality than the official reports from the field during that period.[31] Beginning in 1963-64, the mass media generally tended to support the lead media in treating progress as doubtful. A note of pessimism crept into wire service and other reporting that resulted gradually in a tone of almost perennial skepticism on the part of columnists, editorial writers, and editors generally. Television began to emphasize what war and government supporters started to call the dark side of the news.

By 1965-68, the media were in effect conveying almost daily that the United States was failing in Vietnam. (President Johnson and his cohorts, by contrast, were exhibiting continued though cautious optimism.) The media found justification for their earlier pessimism in the Tet offensive of early 1968. The government, on the other hand, found it almost impossible to justify its earlier estimates after Tet occurred. Even though Tet was perhaps not as severe a defeat as depicted in the media,[32] the credibility gap which resulted from it was surely one of its most serious consequences. After Tet, the media stuck to the general position that U.S. war efforts were doubtful, and U.S. peace efforts failing. The official line that the United States was slowly succeeding basically failed to persuade the American public.

Significance of the Gap. The American mass media played a central role both in creating the notion and the fact of a credibility gap between government and public. This gap would probably have come into existence even if the media had not played such a role, for sooner or later the reality of U.S. failure in Indochina would have caught up with the illusion of success. Nonetheless, it must be concluded that the media's role greatly accelerated the process. Why did things happen that way?

The side of the media and of the press is probably easier to explain than that of the government. In the first place, and as we indicated in an earlier chapter,[33] the press was an independent analyzer and not a participant-analyst. This fact alone placed it under much less constraint to distort, doctor, or otherwise present field reporting in such a manner as to show our policies, programs, and actions in the most favorable possible light. Next, it is probably fair to surmise that the media, over the whole period of U.S. engagement, probably saw itself as having a special role to play, an important and somewhat mystical function to fulfill. This was, after all, one of the most difficult periods of recent American history, in which U.S. forces were being pitted in ruthless war, in a remote and alien environment, against an ill-defined enemy, for ambiguous and debatable reasons. Was it not the duty of the media as a whole to provide them protection if not extrication from what appeared as a hopeless and worthless situation?

Was not Congress succumbing completely to the executive's decision-making, failing time and again to review the stakes in the exercise? In these circumstances, did not the media, the print media in particular, have a duty to become a real fourth branch of government which would compel both the executive and the Congress to pay attention, to learn, and if necessary to change policy? Only the public as a whole could bring about a reversal; but who other than the media could play the necessary brokerage role in bringing public opinion's critical pressure sharply to bear directly on both branches of the government?

In addition, there was glory, careers, and business to be made by the media in making of this war their own *casus belli* against the government. Numerous young reporters, belonging to the rising generation we will discuss in the next section of this chapter, felt themselves morally and politically outraged by the war. Not having grown up under the atmosphere of fear and blind anti-communism which was still conditioning if not dominating the beliefs and actions of government officials, they could take a much more independent view of the conflict in Indochina and appraise it in quite different terms. They could, for example, conceive the ideas that perhaps it was the United States which was the aggressor in Indochina, and the Communists who had the just cause, that perhaps the South Vietnamese were not angels of virtue nor the Communists agents of unmitigated evil, that possibly there was little if any relation between U.S. security and this local guerrilla war in a former French colonial territory in Southeast Asia. Not only would such views, if reported in articles and published in periodicals and books, make much noise at home and possibly start important journalistic and literary careers, but the media would sell, business would swell, and their own ranks would be augmented by new waves of young reporters and writers similarly inclined.

Finally, there can be little doubt that the media as a whole were also affected by a great sense of power. The more they played the game of the credibility gap, the more the gap widened and the more the game's challenge increased. We referred above to the media's own *casus belli* against the government. This particular war had its quite rough moments: efforts by the government to intimidate, silence, or otherwise to harass the media, during all three administrations of the 1961-72 period; counter-resistance and counter-threats by the media which, for its part, was determined that it was not going to lose its war.[34]

Taking the side of the government, we have to account briefly for at least three important factors which dominated its handling of media and public relations during the period under consideration: (1) bureaucratic uncertainty as to substance of events and policy, aggravated by lack of effective coordination; (2) the difficulty of selling the war to the public, even under the best of circumstances; (3) the "upbeat" and optimistic tone generally characteristic of the approach of American politicians of the sixties and early seventies.

Lower echelon bureaucrats charged with informing the media and the public were frequently themselves poorly informed as to what was really happening in the field and as to the specific policy tone desired by the White House at any given time. The lack of effective coordination between the various federal agencies, and between them and the White House, hampered the media information and public relations program of the government in 1961-72 as much as it hampered policy-making itself. At least four major units were involved: the Joint U.S. Public Affairs Office in Saigon (JUSPAO), itself a sometimes calamitous exercise in civil-military coordination; the assistant secretary for "P" (Press and Public) at the State Department; the assistant secretary for public relations at the Defense Department; and the White House press secretary's office. Frequently ludicrous results emerged from quite contrary briefings on various events by all these units on a virtually simultaneous basis. The press, of course, rarely missed an opportunity to point up discrepancies.

The Indochina case was indeed a difficult one to sell. Even major public information efforts by the government, such as the issuance of White Papers on the North Vietnamese role in South Vietnam during the period 1961-65 by the State Department [35] proved unconvincing because they were compiled with obvious bias and from scarce and doubtful evidence. Few of the later major documentary issues fared any better. Speeches by officials were generally lacking in powerful and comprehensible rationales. It was not until 1966 that Secretary of State Rusk first seriously invoked the SEATO commitments of the United States in a major statement.[36] Full use of the rationale of Chinese Communist ambitions, agressiveness, and potential intervention in Southeast Asia came at about the same time, after Marshall Lin Piao's famous address of September 1965 had been fully absorbed in Washington.[37] When these rationales were trundled out, the general reaction on the part of the attentive public was not to accept them at face value but to wonder instead why, if they had been valid all along, they had been surfaced so late in the long Vietnam night. Johnson's explanations of bombing pauses and of unsuccessful negotiations efforts turned out to be similarly unconvincing.[38] Nixon's opaque earlier explanations of his peace and Vietnamization plans were trusted for the brief period of about a year (late 1968 to 1969). However, they tended to lose conviction with the expansion rather than the contraction of the war in 1968-71 and with U.S. personnel withdrawals taking place so mysteriously and incrementally. This was all too reminiscent of the manner of their earlier dispatch to Vietnam under Johnson in 1965-66.

The apparent need of the top U.S. leadership in the sixties and early seventies to appear always upbeat and continuously to project an image of optimism and progress requires somewhat more commentary than that given other factors. The quasi-universal tendency on the part of the leadership to accentuate the positive was probably a direct result, as already suggested, of the entry into politics in a major way of image building and public relations techniques beginning with the Kennedy election of 1960. With and after Kennedy, the question of the image of the president seems to have become central in American politics. Transcending even the president's own personality, the constant preoccupation of the president's advisers was with the image he projected of being at all costs and all times on top of every problem, every detail and facet of government and foreign affairs. The president must never be caught without ready and presumably workable solutions. He must in fact appear virtually infallible.

Such an image-building focus tended to give the media and the press a focal point, a target on which to aim their harpoons; it virtually invited skeptical press attention instead of diffusing presidential responsibility and response amidst a large and ungraspable bureaucracy.

Furthermore, by making the president appear bigger than life, by personalizing government almost entirely through him, by constantly placing him front and center on television and the airwaves, the image-makers played into the hands of a media system only too eager to oversimplify complex issues and to personalize difficult situations. From being McNamara's war, the small war in Vietnam soon became Johnson's war, and later Nixon's war. In response, the image makers redoubled their efforts to make the president look, feel, and act upbeat, positive, successful, confident, and victorious. Here again they invited counter-response. The more the need to be upbeat on the president's side, the more the need on the part of the media to examine critically whether or not the president in fact measured up to all the standards set for him by the image-making illusionists.

Indochina was a terrible public relations trap, into which each president fell deeper and deeper. An enormous gap opened between the initial public expectations, the longer-range presidential performance, and the ultimate presidential results. The media communicated and widened the gap, resulting ultimately in virtual total public disbelief of anything at all said by the president and other official sources about Indochina.

Since the reality of events in Indochina never did conform to the wishes and expectations of the policy-makers, much less the image-makers, one cannot fault the media for signaling and emphasizing the credibility gap. Such newspapers as the *The New York Times, Washington Post, Christian Science Monitor, St. Louis Post Dispatch, Los Angeles Times,* and many others, who were among the first to call for halt of executive abuses and distortions of the truth, performed a praiseworthy task. Doubtless, distortions in press reports accompanied the emotion and limited vision of an immediate battle account. Nonetheless, it was the duty of the press to call it as it saw it, to stress the ferocity and savagery of the war, the excesses on the part of Americans and of allies as well as of enemies, to show Tet for what it had been—an unexpected and formidable assault by an enemy supposed to be on his last gasp.

A final word on the release to the public of the *Pentagon Papers*. This illicit act might not have occurred had the executive acted faithfully on its public promises to withdraw from and end the war. When Daniel Ellsberg released classified documents to the *The New York Times* in the spring of 1971, all of which were then at least four years old, he acted out of desperate though reasoned conviction that no reliable evidence existed within or outside the government, that President Nixon would *ever* get out of a war which seemed instead to be expanding day-by-day. Under these circumstances, to defy rules of classification which seemed to make little sense in the first place and to be breached daily in selective releases to favored sources by the government itself,[39] was a forthright gesture of attachment to the higher values of the American republic, even if it transgressed its technical rules and thereby subjected Ellsberg to an eventually abortive trial.

Once the publication of the *Papers* in mid-1971 demonstrated the depth of discrepancy between image and reality in Indochina, as well as the lies and distortions to which the public had been so constantly subjected over the previous decade, a permanent seal of public disapproval settled itself over U.S. intervention in Indochina and its elusive objectives.

The Impact of Generational Change

The coming of age of a new generation in the United States made its full impact felt on Indochina policy in the late sixties and early seventies. It is an interesting though conjectural question whether this impact would have been felt as severely and decisively in the absence of the other factors we have already treated, such as the shifting perceptions of the war arising at home and abroad owing to its apparent endlessness and aimlessness, the increasingly less tolerable economic and psychological costs of the war, and the growth of the credibility gap.

The generation gap would probably have arisen in any case. The "kids," as millions of people called the hirsute and uniformly jean-clad youngsters who showed up by the tens of thousands for marches and demonstrations against the war in Washington and virtually everywhere else in the country, interestingly defined themselves as limited to those under thirty. "Over thirty, you can't be trusted" went the saying of the times. To be under thirty after 1968 meant one had to be born after 1938, and thus one had to have escaped the formative effects of some of the most significant events of World War II and the immediate post-World War II period—such as the beginnings of the cold war, McCarthyism and ideological anti-communism, and the Korean War. The kids held different life styles and values and, accordingly, different perceptions. They were very different. A male who had just graduated from college in 1968, most likely under a student draft deferment, had been only fifteen years old when Kennedy took office and only seven years old at the end of the Korean War.

Generation Born Circa 1920. This generation, born during, just after, or in the half decade following World War I, had directly experienced the Depression of the late twenties and thirties; the great war of 1939-45 in which most of its males saw some form of active military service; the gradual rise of the cold war and the accompanying and paralyzing development of virulent ideological anti-communism in the U.S.; the Korean War, in which many of its males again served in the armed forces; and the advent and development of the high cold war in the fifties and early sixties. The median age of this group was about forty when Kennedy took office in 1961 and the Vietnam involvement began in earnest. Its members had been decisively marked and tempered by the apparently central role of force and war in the affairs of men. They readily exhibited some of the cognitive characteristics we have treated earlier in this volume: reflex anti-communism, a preference for force and diplomacy premised on force (deterrence) over the politics of compromise and diplomacy premised on accommodation, the tendency to reason by historical analogy and to see in present events consequences of the past which might have been avoided if matters had been handled properly (as they conceived it) in the past.

Generation Born Circa 1945. It might be difficult to find other examples in history of more divergent life experiences in two successive generations. The children of the post-World War II period were probably in incipient rebellion against their parents almost from the time they were born. Contrary to their elders, they had experienced neither World War II, nor the virulent anti-communism of the postwar period which had substituted for the anti-totalitarian passions of the war, nor the Korean War and the beginnings of the high cold war in any meaningful sense. Above all, they had not experienced the economic strains and deprivations of the prewar Depression.

On the contrary, the kids had been brought up in relative luxury, lacking for little in their early childhood and youth, fortified and nurtured by the passionate determination of their parents that their own children should not again be deprived. Rapid if not instant gratification has often been mentioned as a characteristic of this generation, which had been well-fed, well-housed, well-clad. It had, moreover, become accustomed to widespread travel and mobility and to the ready availability of electronic means of communications. This had tended to make the 1945 generation far more cosmopolitan and certainly far less parochial than the previous one. It had been brought up in a more open atmosphere of views and exchange where family antecedents or racial, religious, ethnic, or linguistic differences counted for less than they had at the time of their elders.

The post-World War II world had grown smaller by the day and year owing to the advances in communications and many of the youths of the late sixties and early seventies had lived and traveled as civilians where previously their fathers had trudged only as soldiers, if at all. In fact, a substantial number had been brought up abroad as dependents of U.S. military and civilian official personnel serving over the vast confines of the postwar "American Empire," in an Americanized atmosphere perhaps but a basically cosmopolitan one nonetheless. The post-World War II generation was as naturally rebellious as any previous one, but—for the first time in history—it was particularly affected by the existence in the world it inherited of huge arsenals of truly abhorrent weapons of absolute destruction.

When the older generation refers to living in a dangerous nuclear world, it seems rarely to be fully conscious of the portent of these words to their young, who have never known another type of world. In many respects, the connotation of the word "war" to the 1945 generation in the United States and other advanced industrial countries is only and totally that of nuclear war; another type of war involving them is quite inconceivable to many of them, although such wars have been replete throughout the world in localized areas since 1945. The general turn-off of the young to war in the sixties and seventies is therefore in essence a reflection of their fear of nuclear war and, in an elemental sense, a drive for survival. This has perhaps been insufficiently understood in connection with the youth rebellion against the Indochina war.

Generation Gap. It is perhaps instructive to recall that the youth turn-off and later its opposition to the Indochina war was preceded by a considerable cultural divergence between the two generations even before the U.S. involvement in Indochina reached its peak in the mid-sixties. The rock music of the late fifties and early sixties, the beginnings of pot smoking and the careless taking of drugs, the refusal to act in a "civilized" way according to previously set and accepted patterns of behavior, the failure to learn the classics, to take to better music or the fine arts, to study in a disciplined manner, the increased use of profanity and obscenities in everyday language—all these culture traits were well in progress before our war in Vietnam reached the stage where it involved large numbers of our youths directly.

Once called upon to fight in something as distant and apparently worthless as Vietnam most of this youth of the new mores and cultural spheres, of ease of living and instant and taken-for-granted gratification, never understood why its sacrifice was needed or demanded. Almost from the first, and with notable exceptions only in the South, the farm belt, and among certain ethnic groups (blacks and Eastern Europeans for the most part), youth tended generally to be against the "whole lousy business," as it saw the war.

Effects of Youth Rebellion. The effects of the generation gap and ensuing youth rebellion against the war were felt primarily in two areas: (1) in relation to military service obligations; (2) in relation to the politics of the war at home. With respect to military obligations, millions of U.S. youths avoided military service by taking advantage of loopholes in and uneven administration of a biased Selective Service Act which permitted student deferments and a large number of other type exemptions.[40] Many thousands either fled abroad (Sweden and Canada turning into preferred havens) before being drafted, or deserted from the service after being drafted. Best available data places the total number of U.S. military desertion incidents during 1965-72 as high as 550,000.[41] This does not include the millions who committed technical desertion by crowding the colleges and universities, or otherwise avoiding the draft.

The entire phenomenon was unprecedented in American history. Never before had so many thousands defaulted on the most elementary obligation of citizenship. The general population without doubt sensed the desertion of its young, whether real or technical, and this contributed as much as any other factor to the American public's turnabout on the war after the United States had entered it directly in 1965. While much opprobrium was cast upon real, and some upon technical, deserters during the high period of our engagement in 1965-72, such opprobrium tended to tone itself down when a member of one's own direct or extended family deserted, and this eventually happened to thousands of families touched directly by the Vietnam War. On the other hand, the country did not seriously prepare itself to take care of this problem in the period after the war. This resulted in much ill-feeling and in considerable though muted unhappiness throughout the country until after President Carter's general amnesty declaration upon assuming office in January 1977.

On the domestic political front, youth played a decisive role in leading the anti-war movement, as we shall note further below. Such important groups as the National Mobilization Committee to End the War (Mobe and later New Mobe), the Vietnam Moratorium Committee, the National Peace Action Coalition, and a host of other movements resisting the war in Indochina from 1965 to 1973 [42] found their leadership largely dominated if not in fact consisting almost solely of students and young people. The professional student or perennial campus hanger-on category of young people which was largely responsible for creating the "New Left" of the late sixties and early seventies finds its origins during this period. The first generation of these hangers-on was originally compelled to remain campus-oriented because of the requirements of anti-war activism. The political action of disaffected students and youths was thus a major factor in bringing about the breakdown of the original consensus of support for the war.

The Congressional Assertion

Responding to the new perceptions slowly emerging about the war in 1966-68 and later, as well as to the effects of rising costs, the growing credibility gap, and the youth rebellion, the Congress came ultimately to play a major role in reversing the U.S. policy of massive engagement in Indochina. We have earlier alluded to Congress' role on numerous occasions. As we indicated, certain individual congressmen and senators had long harbored great misgivings about the Indochina enterprise and some, like Senators Gruening of Alaska and Morse of Oregon, had opposed it from its earliest days.

It was not, however, until the chairman of the Senate Foreign Relations Committee, Senator Fulbright of Arkansas, began himself to sense strongly, in about late 1965 and early 1966, that the Executive had badly deceived Congress over the Tonkin Gulf incidents and that it was continuing to deceive it in its accounts of the progress of the war,[43] that Congress could be considered as a significant element in the gradual breakdown of the domestic consensus.

In the spring and summer of 1966, Congress began an assiduous effort, under Fulbright's leadership and with Senate Majority Leader Mike Mansfield's tacit blessing, first thoroughly to investigate and later to halt the headlong plunge of the executive into the Vietnam stalemate machine. During the period 1966-72, both houses of Congress held numerous, in some committees almost incessant, hearings on virtually every facet of the war, from its diplomatic, to its military, economic, moral, and political aspects. Among Senators, besides Fulbright and Mansfield, Eugene McCarthy of Minnesota, George McGovern of South Dakota, Robert and later Edward Kennedy of New York and Massachusetts, respectively, Frank Church of Idaho, and Mark Hatfield of Oregon were among the most prominent earlier leaders in the movement to halt the war. They received strong support from Sens. Harold Hughes of Iowa, John Sherman Cooper of Kentucky, George Aiken of Vermont and several others.

All the hearings, whatever their specific theme or the committee involved, had significant and cumulative effects in terms of their bearing on the domestic political scene. They all contributed to a general critique, which was both responsive and stimulating to the overall sentiment of opposition rising in the country; and they all tended to place the executive increasingly on the defensive and to force it to reveal its goals and ends, although the Congress would still not deny the executive the means it sought to conduct the war. The national commitment hearings in the Symington subcommittee of the Senate Foreign Relations Committee, which were mentioned previously,[44] proved among the most important of these hearings because of the legislative measures which eventually resulted. In a larger sense, these hearings constituted a review and critical evaluation of the whole of post-World War II American foreign policy. In a narrower sense, they provided opportunity for the exposure and wider public dissemination of anti-war and pro-withdrawal views. Parades of prominent citizens from the professions, the churches, the academic world, even the military and foreign and national security policy-making communities appeared before these and other hearings.

The Congress set in motion in the late sixties and early seventies the machinery which would eventually formulate and secure passage of the War Powers Act of 1973, which sharply limited the executive in the combat actions he could undertake abroad without the expressed sanction and review of Congress. However, until about mid-1970 the Congress remained unwilling or unable to halt the executive's basic control of Indochina policy. This began to change only after the enormous popular outcry which followed President Nixon's move into Cambodia in March 1970. The main reason for Congress's previous apparent paralysis was that while sentiment in both Houses after 1968 clearly reflected a slowly gaining preponderance of views in the country favoring withdrawal, Congress remained unwilling to cut or to clearly signify to the executive that it would cut the ongoing appropriations supporting American fighting men in the field. This is of course an extremely difficult action for any Congress to take at any time during a *de facto* war in which U.S. fighting men are engaged.

It took the culminating shock of the unexpected Cambodian invasion to push the so-called Cooper-Church amendment through both houses in mid-1970, by which Congress effectively denied the executive further authority to expand operations in Indochina. This and similar measures taken by Congress during 1970-72 forced the executive to speed up its timetable of withdrawal. After the U.S. withdrawal and the signing of the Paris Accords of January 1973, Congress ultimately denied further funds, even to continue support of the South Vietnamese regime.[45]

On balance, the significance of Congress' gradual intervention in the Executive's Indochina war policy probably lay more in what it signaled in terms of long-range relations between the executive and Congress in the formulation of U.S. foreign policy than in its immediate effects on the course of the Indochina war itself. By the War Powers Act of 1973, the Congress not only symbolically but in fact as well, reasserted its important constitutional role in America's foreign relations. By sharply dividing each of the key powers in foreign affairs between Congress and the executive, the framers of the Constitution had made clear they did not desire these powers to be exercised by only one of the two branches. Under the Constitution, Congress was given the power to declare war, the executive to wage it; Congress the power to advise and consent, that is to be involved, in the making of treaties, the executive to actually make and conclude them; Congress the power to constitute and maintain armed forces, the executive to employ and lead them. Ever since the Curtiss-Wright decision by the Supreme Court in 1936,[46] the executive had increasingly been arrogating the foreign policy-making power to its own single bosom. Congress, from that time on until the late sixties, had been playing a relatively insignificant albeit decorous role of assenting, and thereby signifying to the world the domestic consensus of support.[47] This has changed. Since 1973, Congress has not only been vocal but sometimes obstreperous in claiming and asserting its powers to engage or refuse to engage the United States abroad, and in asserting its right to be consulted fully before as well as after major foreign policy actions by the executive. In its actions of 1966-73, the Congress, slowly pulling together a majority for disengagement from Indochina in both houses, reflected and perhaps best symbolized the gradual but inescapable breakdown of the domestic political consensus of support for the foreign policies of the successive U.S. administrations which had conducted the high cold war.

The Anti-War Movement

The anti-war movement was an extremely loose, diffuse, and group- (rather than individual) led organization which emerged in the early sixties to catalyze and solidify in the public mind the breakdown of the domestic consensus of support for the war. It brought together and mobilized popular resistance to the war by harping constantly, first in small and subsequently in ever larger popular marches and demonstrations, on all of the many factors being discussed in this chapter. It helped awaken new perceptions of the war by questioning the nature of the *casus belli* and advertising the imprecise and ambiguous character of U.S. objectives and the rising opposition to the U.S. war effort abroad. It vented the deep resentment of growing segments of the American people about the costs in treasure and lives. It questioned the morality of fighting the wrong war at the wrong time in the wrong place. It relentlessly rejected the credibility of official versions of the war and disseminated instead the critical views presented by the media, returning soldiers, and an ever larger number of skeptical civilian observers. Above all, it furnished an effective and relatively practical vehicle for American youth to demonstrate its generational rebellion and its aversion for the war.

The movement, as it was called, started in about 1962-63 as a small collection of conscientious objectors and pacifists, local religious and women's groups (such as Women's Strike for Peace, which lobbied the State Department against the war as early as 1963 [48]), and some leftist-oriented student activists, particularly in the Berkeley area. Within a decade, it had grown to become a tremendously effective nationwide political force, capable of threatening the paralysis of the nation's capital in Washington and of provoking something akin to terror and a siege mentality in the White House itself. It had developed an extraordinarily effective system of national and worldwide communications. It penetrated the Armed Forces (particularly in Vietnam itself), and was capable of attracting hundreds of thousands of people to demonstrations, marches, and protests in many and varied forums.

It can be said that, as an organization, the movement never really existed in well defined form, that it lacked hierarchical structure or traditional lines of command and authority, that it was administratively weak, and at best multi-headed, at worst devoid of identifiable leadership altogether. But some of those characteristics were precisely what gave the movement its force as one of the strongest if not the strongest spontaneous, genuinely popular movements ever to emerge in the United States to serve a specified and limited political purpose. It was also surely one of the most successful ones. This was recognized in the 1969-1972 efforts of the Nixon administration to suppress or otherwise hamper and constrain the movement in a variety of ways.[49] For these reasons the anti-war movement deserves far greater study, in all its many dimensions, than it has yet received in the literature of American politics and history.[50]

There are several aspects of organization and style that should be noted in our extremely abbreviated account of this movement. (1) It had a large number of component organizations or groups, crisscrossing many aspects of social life in the United States and including predominantly church groups, student groups, and somewhat later than the others, professional and business groups. (2) The movement was widely dispersed geographically throughout the entire country; while its accent was on youth, it received vital logistical and other type support from a cross section of the American population much wider than youth alone. (3) Stylistically, the movement resorted largely to interesting and, for the United States, relatively new techniques of massive and nonviolent demonstrations and resistance, first developed on a large scale during the civil rights struggles of the sixties. Such techniques included consenting to or even inviting mass arrests by the authorities, thus flooding the jails and making later judicial proceedings virtually impossible. The one major exception to the generally nonviolent methods of the movement was the provocation of violent incidents at the Democratic Party convention in Chicago in mid-1968. The Chicago police fell too easily for this provocation, using repressive methods of such severity as to bring about precisely the results sought by the war opponents: great attention to their actions and public outrage at both sides. This can be contrasted to the methods employed two years later during demonstrations at Kent State University in Ohio, when public outrage ranged itself almost entirely on the side of the youthful victims of savage repression by a unit of the National Guard. (4) The movement was notable for the absence of conventionally prominent U.S. political leaders in and by the shifting and undefinable character of its top operational leadership. The latter included such disparate and separately motivated but effective individuals as left-wing student activists

Tom Hayden, Jerry Rubin and Abby Hoffman; lifelong left-wing activist lawyer David Dellinger; morally-outraged former Marine and
Indochina policy-maker Daniel Ellsberg; pediatrician Dr. Benjamin
Spock; actress Jane Fonda; former Yale University chaplain William
Sloan Coffin; singer Joan Baez; Harvard historian Staughton Lynd;
scientist Linus Pauling; Quaker pacifist Cora Weiss; feminist organizer
Bella Abzug; former civic action worker in Vietnam Don Luce; and
literally dozens of other well-known personalities, including some professional military.

One of the reasons for the movement's great success was its convergence in the mid to late sixties with the civil rights movement, stemming from a decision on the part of the Rev. Martin Luther King and
other prominent black civil rights leaders to join forces with it in endeavoring to resist and halt further U.S. involvement in Indochina. As
already suggested, the involvement was causing a disproportionately
high number of black casualties and was becoming increasingly unpopular in the U.S. black community because it tended to focus attention and resources away from domestic socioeconomic programs
considered as essential counterparts to the political rights being won by
blacks. We have neither the space nor the intention here to write the
history, including the stresses, of the convergence of the black power
and anti-war movements in the United States in the sixties, but this
history deserves to be written and assessed in all its complex dimensions, its failures as well as successes.

3. Concluding Thoughts on Losing from War

We close this analysis of the principal factors that led the U.S. ultimately to disengage from its twelve years' enterprise in Indochina
by advancing some basic conclusions concerning the Vietnam War.
Though never winnable in the field within the limitations set for it
from the outset and retained by every administration involved, the
Vietnam War was not lost in the field, but at home. It was not lost at
home only because the people perceived that under its constraints it
was a doomed military enterprise in the field. Under normal circumstances, and if the American people could have justified the war to
themselves as they had other wars, this would have led to crescendo
demands on the government by the public for the use of ever-stronger
means, possibly not even excepting the eventual use of nuclear weapons, to reverse the course of events and to win the war in the field.

The war was lost at home when the American people began overwhelmingly to perceive it as both doomed within the limited means

used to pursue it, and—this is the essential point—as *wrong* in its moral and political aspects. The people long sought to understand U.S. objectives and the methods the United States employed; ultimately, both failed to be understood and accepted because of an essential moral judgment on the part of the people that the United States was wrong. When it dawned on the American people that the country was wrong, having engaged in the wrong war against the wrong enemy at the wrong place and time and with the wrong means, the people themselves brought an end to the Indochina phase of the U.S. role as full-fledged superpower. They did so by letting Congress know their views, by demonstrating massively against the war, and by sanctioning massive anti-war demonstrations while refusing to join administration efforts to suppress the anti-war movement. They breached the long-standing consensus of support for the executive in foreign policy and forced the executive and Congress to extricate the United States from Vietnam. They opposed any further steps which the executive might take to prolong the agony for security reasons which they no longer felt to be compelling, or on behalf of an ally which most Americans felt had received more than its due share of consideration.

To fail to understand this, and to continue to argue today long after the end of our engagement, that the war could have been won if we had but used the right means and shown the necessary staying power,[51] reveals total ignorance of the profound moral dimensions of the war and of the chasm this opened in U.S. public opinion. In Vietnam, it was precisely the use of means disproportionate to the ends sought, as the people understood these limited ends, which led to the polarization and subsequent potential disintegration of the domestic value structure. This was particularly so after the decision had in fact been made and communicated to the people in 1968-69 to get out of the war with or without victory, and this decision had been sanctioned by elections. The means finally proved disporportionate to the ends sought in Vietnam, not because they were insufficient but because they were too large, too costly, and ultimately perceived as too inhumane for the ends advanced to justify them. The war in Vietnam was lost at home and not because of inadequate means in Vietnam. Twice the means used in Vietnam would have lost the war even faster at home, because of the aggravation of the existing perceptual disproportionality that would have ensued.

The most important effect, not of losing the war, but of losing from the war, was division of the deepest kind at home. The domestic division and disunity, and the effects it portended for the future of the American polity itself, were infinitely more significant than any temporary or even quasi-permanent effects that might result in American foreign policy. Accordingly, it is at home, and not in foreign policy, that one must look for the lessons of Vietnam.

The division at home was not really between that part of the population which sought a final and unequivocal end to the war, its horrors, and its illusions, and another part representing a presumably "silent majority" which did not. The myth of the silent majority exploded in the face of those who had created the expression. By 1971, Americans were basically united in opposition to the war. Only a small portion of the elite, that which happened to be in power, and of the military and civilian bureaucracy continued to support our Indochina war effort after 1970. It was here that the division at home lay: between an overwhelming majority determined to see the war finally end, and a very tiny minority in control of the government.

It is really not surprising, and probably less speculative than we suggested earlier,[52] that the basic conflict that split America in the early seventies came to a head in the Watergate affair, the most serious constitutional and domestic political crisis this country has faced since the civil war. Watergate was a linear and natural descendant of Vietnam and its excesses. It was the fear of the anti-war movement, and the fear of compromise of national security plans set in motion in secrecy, that caused the Nixon administration to concoct the horrors of the Cointelpro; the Huston plan; the Plumbers; the wiretapping of officials, newsmen, and others; and the rest of the illicit White House machine which was caught, exposed and dismantled as a result of Watergate.

Losing from war, therefore, led in 1974–76 to a purge of values and of structure, a cleansing of souls, and a final upheaval in leadership which the U.S. successfully survived. It emerged, after the Ford interregnum and the 1976 elections, as a stronger democracy than it had been before Vietnam. It was rid, hopefully forever, of the fears and suspicions, the abuses of ideology and of power, which had for so long dominated its behavior in the high cold war.

Notes

1. *See* Chapter V, Section 3.
2. *See* Arthur M. Schlesinger, Jr., *The Bitter Heritage,* rev. ed. (Greenwich, Conn: Fawcett, 1968) esp. Ch. IV.
3. "In sum, the insurrection is Southern rooted; it arose at Southern initiative in response to Southern demands." George Mc T. Kahin and John W. Lewis, *The United States in Vietnam,* p. 119.
4. *See,* for example, Chapter 1 in R. Stavins, R.J. Barnet, and M.G. Raskin, *Washington Plans an Aggressive War.*

5. See Chapter II, Section 2.
6. For a feel of GI lingo in Vietnam, particularly their characterizations of the Vietnamese, *see* Michael Herr, *Dispatches.*
7. For one of Alsop's early columns along this line, *see Washington Post,* Jan. 1, 1965, p. A 13, in which Alsop compares President Johnson's choice in Vietnam to President Kennedy's choice in Cuba in 1962.
8. *See* Note 8, Chapter VI. President Johnson made this statement in a speech at Muskogee, Okla., Sept. 25, 1964. *See The New York Times,* Sept. 26, 1964, p. 1, col. 5.
9. President Johnson repeatedly stated to intimates and to leading members of Congress that he would not be "the first president to lose a war." See Halberstam, *Best and Brightest.*
10. President Kennedy first used the tunnel analogy in a press conference held Dec. 12, 1962. See *The New York Times,* Dec. 13, 1962, p. 4, col. 5.
11. Jonathan Schell, *The Time of Illusion* (New York: Random House Vintage, 1975).
12. David Halberstam, *The Making of a Quagmire* (New York: Random House, 1965).
13. A. M. Schlesinger, Jr. *The Bitter Heritage.*
14. A. Hilsman, *To Move A Nation.*
15. D. Ellsberg, *Papers on the War.*
16. *Ibid.,* pp. 91 ff. *See also* Gelb and Betts, *Irony of Vietnam,* which further demonstrates Ellsberg's thesis.
17. Gelb and Betts, *Irony of Vietnam,* became available to this writer only after he had substantially completed this manuscript.
18. J. Schell, *Time of Illusion,* pp. 55 ff.
19. On the Mayaguez incident, *see* U.S. Congress, House Committee on International Relations: *Seizure of the Mayaguez,* Hearings Before Subcommittee on International Political and Military Affairs, 94th Cong., 1st sess., (Washington D.C.: U.S.G.P.O. 1975-76); *see also* Ray Rowan, *The Four Days of Mayaguez* (New York: Norton, 1975); Charles Bennet, "The Mayaguez Re-examined: Misperception in an Information Shortage," *Fletcher Forum* 1 (Fall 1976): pp. 15-31.
20. See Figure 5.
21. In answer to the question: "Do you approve or disapprove of the way (the president) is handling the situation in Vietnam?" the Gallup Poll showed the following percentages of approval in the representative years indicated: 1965–fifty-eight percent; 1968–thirty-nine percent; 1971–forty-one percent, George H. Gallup, *The Gallup Poll: Public Opinion 1935–1971* vol. 3, (New York: Random House, 1972), pp. 1967, 1982, 2074, 2099, 2190, 2244, 2291. To the better question: "Do you think the U.S. made a mistake getting involved in Vietnam?" the following percentages answered positively (that we made a mistake) in the representative years indicated: 1967–forty-one percent; 1968–forty-five percent; 1969–fifty-two percent; 1970–fifty-six percent; 1971–sixty-one percent; 1973–sixty percent, George Gallup, *Poll,* pp. 2189, 2254, 2309, 2074, 2099 and George Gallup, *The Gallup Poll: Public Opinion 1972–77* vol. I (Wilmington, Del: Scholarly Resources Inc., 1978), p. 87. The Harris Survey yields the following percentages who felt, in response to the same question, that it had been a mistake to get involved: 1971–seventy-one percent; 1973–seventy percent.

Only nineteen percent in 1971 and twenty-one percent in 1973 felt it had not been a mistake, with ten percent and nine percent unsure in 1971 and 1973 respectively, *The Harris Survey Yearbook of Public Opinion: A Compendium of Current American Attitudes–1971*, and *Ibid.*, 1973, (New York: Louis Harris and Associates, 1975 and 1976 resp.).

22. The study, officially entitled "History of U.S. Decision-Making Process on Vietnam Policy," was commissioned by Secretary of Defense Robert S. McNamara on June 17, 1967. It took a governmental team of thirty-six authors, of whom Ellsberg was one, a year and a half to complete. Only fifteen copies of the original report were produced and distributed to selected policy-making principals of the Johnson administration. See Neil Sheehan et. al. *The Pentagon Papers: The Secret History of the Vietnam War As Published by The New York Times* (NY: New York Times Co., 1971), pp. xviii-xxv.

23. It is extremely difficult to obtain accurate statistics on the total financial cost of the Indochina war to the United States. The writer determined to use the statistics in Figure 5 largely because they provide a compatible total in terms of constant 1975 U.S. dollars. Taking the fiscal years 1966–1974 (mid-1966 to mid-1974) instead of those used in Figure 5 (mid-1965 to mid-1972), and using a more conservative calculation of U.S. military operations expenditures based on Congressional Research Service, *February 1974 Update of Total War Cost Figures*, the Indochina Resources Center (IRC) arrived at a different grand total, namely $140.2845 billion, or $31.9 billion lower than the total in Figure 5. However, the fiscal year 1965 is not included in the IRC calculations, while the lower expenditure in fiscal year 1974 (left out of Figure 5) is included. Moreover, the IRC carefully points out that its figure "should not be taken as representing the full cost of the war. Senator Mansfield . . . cited the *Statistical Abstract of the U.S.* figure of $352 billion *(Congressional Record,* March 21, 1975, S4642)." *See* "Indochina War Statistics–Dollars and Deaths," *Congressional Record* Senate, 94th Cong., 1st sess., vol. 121, No. 77 (May 14, 1975): S 8152. The total figure of $172.2 billion in 1975 dollars arrived at in Figure 5 is probably as close to the actual sum of U.S. financial expenditures over the eight peak years of the war as one can hope to get.

24. Lawrence Baskir and William Strauss, *Chance and Circumstance: The Draft, The War, and the Vietnam Generation* (New York: Random House Vintage, 1978), Fig. 3, p. 53 and notes 7 and 8, p. 283. The original source for these figures, compiled for the Ford Clemency Board is *Selected Manpower Statistics*, DOD-OASD (Comptroller), May 1975, pp. 39, 46, 61, 108.

25. Department of Defense Comptroller, as listed in Douglas Clarke, *The Missing Man: Politics and the M.I.A.* (Washington, D.C.: National Defense University Research Directorate, U.S.G.P.O, January 1979), Table 2, p. 10.

26. Joint Casualty Resolution Center, Hawaii, *Monthly Statistical Summary for 1–30 April, 1979* (Unclassified).

27. See Notes 40 and 41.

28. The problem was eased by the Carter amnesty program, introduced in 1977.

29. Hannah Arendt, *Lying in Politics: Reflections on the Pentagon Papers*, Pa-

per prepared for a Conference of the Council on Religion and International Affairs, Wash. D.C., October 1971. (Available to the writer in unpublished form only.)

30. Basic information for what follows was drawn from the *Pentagon Papers*, 1, 2, 3, 4: "Public Statements" sections of each volume (for official accounts) and from a review of press and television coverage of the period (for lead and mass media accounts).

31. See Chapter V, Section 3.

32. This is argued by Peter Braestrup in his *Big Story: How the American Press and Television Reported and Interpreted the Crisis of Tet 1968 in Vietnam and Washington* (Boulder, Colo: Westview Press, 1977). On the other hand, *see also* Don Oberdorfer, *Tet!* (New York: Doubleday, 1971).

33. See Chapter V, Section 3.

34. The writer apologizes for having abstracted and generalized so widely about the media. He is confident that future historians will tell of particular episodes and analyze the specific organs and individuals involved.

35. *See,* for example, *A Threat to the Peace: North Vietnam's Effort to Conquer South Vietnam,* Department of State (DOS) Publication 7308, Far Eastern Series 110, July 1962; also in *DOS Bulletin* 47 (July 30, 1962): p. 202. This report carefully documented available statistics on North Vietnamese infiltration and the return of Southern cadres from North to South Vietnam, but failed to mention South Vietnamese breaches of the 1954 Geneva accords. Another White Paper, *Aggression From the North: The Record of North Vietnam's Campaign to Conquer South Vietnam,* was issued in February, 1965 (DOS publication 7839) and was similarly unconvincing.

36. Before the Senate Foreign Relations Committee in February 1966. *See Pentagon Papers,* 4: p. 640.

37. This was the address in which Lin Piao characterized China as leader of the Third World "countryside" which would inevitably invest and overwhelm the "cities" of the world (i.e., the advanced industrial countries). *See Pentagon Papers,* 4, p. 643. President Johnson had pointed to Peking's role in masterminding aggression in Vietnam as early as April 1965 in an address at Johns Hopkins University, *Ibid.,* 3, p. 730.

38. For example, President Johnson's offer made in a speech in San Antonio on September 29, 1967, to trade-off a bombing halt for "productive discussions" with the North Vietnamese. *See* C. Cooper, *Lost Crusade,* p. 381.

39. Henry Kissinger was a master of the selective release process both during his tenure as national security advisor (1969–72) and as secretary of state (1973–76). He did it both directly in private briefings and by arranging the dissemination of certain documents among favored press and electronic media sources. See Marvin and Bernard Kalb, *Kissinger* (New York: Dell, 1974), *passim.*

40. U.S. males of draft eligible age (19 to 26) during the Vietnam era are estimated at 26,915,000 of whom 10,935,000 served in the military and 15,980,000 did not. (Of the 8,615,000 who served in the military during the Vietnam War, 1965–72, only 2,850,000 served in Southeast Asia, of whom 2,150,000 served in Vietnam proper. Of these, 1,600,000 served in combat and 550,000 in non-combat capacities.) Of the 15,980,000 who never served during the Vietnam era, 6,641,000 were disqualified, 8,769,000 were

deferred or exempted, and 570,000 were listed as apparent draft offenders, of whom 209,517 were actually charged. L. Baskir and W. Strauss, *Chance and Circumstance,* Fig. 1, p. 5; Fig. 2, pp. 30–31; Fig. 3, p. 53.

41. *Ibid.,* Fig. 5 p. 115. The total number of less than honorable discharges during the Vietnam War is given as 563,000.
42. G. Louis Heath, *Mutiny Does Not Happen Lightly: The Literature of American Resistance to the Vietnam War* (Metuchen, N.J.: Scarecrow Press, 1976), pp. xxxi-xxxiv, lists a total of 329 U.S. war resistance organizations and groups.
43. J. William Fulbright (Sen.), *The Arrogance of Power* (New York: Random House Vintage, 1967).
44. See Chapter VI, Section 3.
45. The following is an abbreviated list of measures in Congress to limit Executive actions in Indochina during this period. *1970:* HR 19911 endorsing Cooper-Church and Hatfield-McGovern Senate Ammendments *(Congressional Quarterly Almanac* (CQA), 1971, pp. 120–24); *1971:* S2819 and HR 9910, attempts to limit numbers of troops in Indochina, defeated *(CQA,* 1972, pp. 409–14); *1972:* HR 15495 and 16029 endorsing Senate amendment to end the war in four months, defeated in House *(CQA,* 1973, pp. 19, 123); *1973:* attempts to limit aid programs in Indochina *(CQA,* 1974, pp. 792, 832); *1974:* S3394, placing ceiling on aid appropriations to Southeast Asia *(CQA,* 1975, pp. 536–47); *1975:* defeat of further requested aid package to Indochina *(CQA,* 1976, pp. 295–315).
46. Justice Sutherland in *U.S. v. Curtiss Wright Corp* 299 U.S. 304 (1936).
47. See Francis O. Wilcox, *Congress, The Executive, and Foreign Policy* (New York: Harper & Row, 1971).
48. I distinctly recall receiving a delegation of ladies from this group at the State Department in early July 1963. They creditably refused to be convinced by the official briefing I provided.
49. See J. Schell, *Time of Illusion, passim.*
50. Although scores of journal articles, pamphlets, and books were written in the passion of the hour (1968–73), there seem as yet to have been few if any systematic and scholarly studies of the anti-war movement. See G. L. Heath, *Mutiny.*
51. Gen. William Westmoreland has essentially argued this thesis in his *A Soldier Reports,* and in speeches and other writings.
52. See Chapter IV, Decision 9.

Chapter VIII

Vietnam as Lesson of History, 1973–

1. Vietnam as Moral Problem

Herbicides, defoliation, the burning of hooches and of whole villages, free fire zones, the massacres of civilians by artillery or by millions of tons of air-dropped ordinance, the forcible removal or other dislocation of hundreds of thousands of villagers, the widespread use of napalm, the massive problem of refugees, the shooting and torture of prisoners and political suspects, the other horrors that took place in Indochina during the period of our massive engagement: are all these to be shrugged off as the natural concomitants of war? It can be and has been argued that the constraints and limitations the United States placed on its mix [1] go a long way toward absolving it from immoral conduct.[2] But the problem is not easy to resolve, and absolution from the charge of immorality, not to speak of genocide, not easy to obtain.[3]

More than three decades have elapsed since the Nuremberg judgments of Nazi war criminals established the principle that state leaders are themselves accountable for state actions desecrating presumed norms of acceptable civilized human behavior. At about the same time, the trials of Japanese war leaders in World War II resulted in the execution of several top military leaders. Yet most of the American foreign policy elite has continued until quite recently to be basically comfortable with fundamental assumptions of *realpolitik* which include the belief that a state's morality in international affairs cannot be judged by the same standards applied to ordinary individuals in orderly society, and that special rules apply.

This outlook, almost always assumed and rarely examined, has seemed faulty in a host of recent cases. In respect to Chile, ITT, Lockheed, the FBI and CIA, and above all the abuses of Vietnam, the pretext of national security interest covering the actions of leaders has been mercilessly stripped off by popular scrutiny with ensuing public accounting on the part of individual leaders. Except in the case of Watergate, this has not led to public prosecutions, but the threat of these in future cases cannot be ruled out. It is remarkable in retrospect that as an outcome of Watergate, a former attorney general of the United States as well as several other high-ranking officials served sentences of federal imprisonment for authorizing actions which, in their own minds, had been designed at least as much to protect the national security as to advance the political interests of their cohorts.

The imaginary concretization or reification [4] by leaders and peoples of such conceptual symbols as "national security," "national interest," even "state," "nation," "government," or "law," tends to blind us to the real people and situations which are implicit within these symbols. If we do not start with human beings, the problem of morality in foreign policy remains obscure, and meaningful answers cannot be found. Concepts like the state, national security and interest, even law and government, are after all only abstractions shielding real people who, whatever their titles or elite roles, actually guide human affairs. In the last analysis, we are always dealing with leaders who speak for people so long as the latter consent, or in case of tyrannies or autocracies, so long as the leaders can maintain their control.

Only leaders, in the name of law, enforce commonly agreed-to standards that remain valid only so long as the values underlying them are shared and accepted. (For example, was it the leaking of secret government communications that was the illegal activity, or were the illicit means used to prevent such leaking what was illegal?) Only leaders tell other people on their behalf or as their targets what the national interest is supposed to be. Leaders are, in the end, only human beings with all their capacities and flaws, as we are so painfully reminded when we contemplate our presidents during the period of U.S. involvement in Vietnam.

Reification is what makes possible the phenomenon of bureaucratic detachment so elegantly described in the following quotation from James Thomson's all too brief but scintillating study of how the United States got into Vietnam:

> In quiet, air-conditioned, thick-carpeted rooms, such terms as "systematic pressure," "armed reconnaissance," "targets of opportunity," and even "body count" seemed to breed a sort of games-theory detachment. Most memorable to me was a moment in late 1964 target planning when the question under discussion was how heavy our bombing should be, and how extensive our strafing, at some midpoint in the projected pattern of

systematic pressure. An assistant secretary of state resolved the point in the following words: "It seems to me that our orchestration should be mainly violins, but with periodic touches of brass." [5]

Games-theory detachment enables decision-makers to engage in what Irving Horowitz once dubbed "the Howard Johnson-sanitized vision of conflict." [6] Abstract concepts and distant human relationships mesh into imaginary problem situations or "scenarios" wholly distinct in the minds of statesmen and decision-makers of lesser breed from the real world in which they themselves operate. Thus, the savage fighting in Vietnamese villages turns into pacification; the terrors of North Vietnamese civilians into graduated pressure or escalation; the bribing of foreign publishers into preservation of press freedom; the tapping of subordinates' phones into leak plumbing. In each instance, the effects on individuals are submerged by the necessities of programs which run on momentum, impervious to review, dictated by the alleged requirements of the higher abstractions. Owing to the reified presumption of national security interests, the question of morality, of the personal suffering of some and the possible personal responsibility of others, simply need not arise. Real people, whether the victims of such actions or the consciences of those who perpetrate them, simply cease to count—all in the name of a higher morality, that of the interests of the state.

This is what is changing. If we wish to come to grips with the problem of morality in foreign policy today, and specifically with that of Vietnam, we must return to human beings and realize that it was the inner circle and in the first instance the president in the Kennedy and Johnson administrations, and later Nixon and Kissinger, who were and are accountable for the actions of the United States in Vietnam. Nuremberg may have been early though not necessarily premature in convicting men whose defense it was that they acted in the name of the state. But toward the end of the twentieth century, it has become apparent that such defenses would no longer easily be accepted by publics. Publics the world over now increasingly demand that men be judged, with all the complexities such judgments imply, not the reified abstractions under which they have been acting in the past.

Despite the absence as yet of universally applied moral standards, the obligation of leaders and statesmen to act morally within their own temporal and cultural codes is fundamental. This is prudent and expedient in statecraft because necessary if the character of interstate interaction is to remain consonant with the hoped-for progress of humanity. And it is ethical because it is the best that can be achieved, up to this point. A rational foreign policy is therefore a moral one, and vice versa.

The question in international affairs can never be whether a state's behavior can be judged normatively, or expected to be normative, for all rational behavior including that of the state is logically normative in that it seeks to advance or delay certain ends and proceeds on the expectation of some value realization. Moreover, the state is a reified abstraction hiding the reality of human beings acting for the state. The real question is what kind of ethical standards and norms govern the behavior of a state's leaders. As a problem in practical statecraft and as a moral test of a state's policy, it might be asked as follows: "Does the behavior of a given state's leaders conform with the values and norms that prevail both among that state's people and in the world at the time they are acting? "

We can thus begin to equate moral foreign policy with behavior by state's leaders which conforms to the prevailing ethical and value standards of their time. Time provides a key to the understanding of values, which may help explain why the value of resisting aggression in Europe in the thirties and early forties could not automatically be transferred to the civil wars of Indochina in the sixties. The shift of values with time also helps explain why it is so unlikely that statesmen, contrary to their general conviction, can in fact learn from the lessons of history. History, regrettably, is a mighty poor teacher since values, or if not values then at least the identification of events as manifestations of particular values, are constantly in flux. It is almost impossible today to imagine that the Zulu War or the repression of East Indian rebellions could look righteous to men of rectitude in pre-World War I Britain; or the eradication of native Americans be applauded as heroism in frontier America. Similarly, it will most likely be very difficult to persuade the next generation, as it was the one rising in the sixties, that the United States engaged in a moral course of action by wreaking havoc and destruction upon Indochina to save it from itself.

The inseparability of morality and foreign policy is demonstrable in innumerable examples. When we analyze these, we perceive that choices of ends and means in foreign policy are invariably normative and that moral choices—choices conditioned by prevailing norms of a culture and a time—do not, in fact, should not, require consideration of absolute ethical standards. Morality in foreign policy, as in other domains, is not necessarily synonymous with perfection but minimalist in nature. It is to seek the best possible, that which is the most conducive to mitigation of tragedy in the human condition under the circumstances. In assessing the question of how the American people can test the morality of a foreign policy advanced by their government, we must assume the policy to have been constructed within the limitations of a non-perfectionist ethic, and within the bounds of its own culture and time. A judgment of morality can then perhaps be made in accordance with the following basic prescriptions.

First, a test of means to ends must be continuously applied in foreign policy. Are the means used commensurate and in harmony with the ends sought? Is this relationship of means to ends proportionate and humane, or disproportionate and thus inhumane? In U.S. culture, the ends do not and cannot justify the means. Were the United States to begin claims to the contrary, its own value structure would rapidly begin to disintegrate. This must be one of the principal lessons of Vietnam, and also of Watergate, where means like wholesale wiretapping and enemies lists proved quite disproportionate to the relatively low-threshold threat that may have existed in the perceptions of U.S. leaders. In Vietnam, as already indicated at the end of the last chapter, the use of means disproportionate to their ends led to the polarization and threatened disintegration of the domestic value structure of the United States, particularly after the decision had been made in 1968–69 to get out of the war with or without victory and this decision had been sanctioned by elections.

Second, foreign policy must constantly be tested as to its ends. The test of ends lies in finding out whether the policy objectives to which their affective motivations drive statesmen and leaders, and for which they seek to earn public acceptance, are in fact properly in harmony (a) with the essential norms of the domestic value structure; and (b) with prevailing international standards of opinion and conduct. When the affective behavior of leaders is allowed to serve abstract ends of reason of state, devised in the remote scenarios they tend to conjure up in their role of powerful and self-confident elites, the chances are strong that the ends of policy will fail to justify the means used. The latter will then cease to be forthcoming in democracies like the United States and policies will fail. On the contrary, when U.S. leaders develop and explain policy objectives tangibly and palpably related to prevailing world standards and to sentiments and currents pulsating among the American people, the chances are strong that the means forthcoming will be commensurate with the ends sought, and that policies will succeed.

American values and norms, though changing over time, continue to be first and foremost related to fortifying the domestic structure and homogeneity of the United States itself. As we stated earlier,[7] unlike the older states of Europe and Asia, the United States does not begin to approximate even that limited measure of ethnic homogeneity and cultural impermeability existing in such states as France, Italy, Germany, the United Kingdom, or China. It must accordingly rely far more on centrally accepted principles of government and on "rules of rule" around which people of extremely diverse origins, who have lived in the same territory together for only a very brief historical period, can rally. As a result, American foreign policy can never really be divorced from the necessarily continued striving for harmony, cooperation, and preservation of understood principles of governance by Americans at home.

The Morality of U.S. Involvement in Indochina

By the tests we suggested, it would be difficult to characterize initial U.S. involvement in Indochina in the fifties and its far more serious engagement after 1961 as immoral, though as we have seen there is certainly ample reason to judge it as unwise. It was unwise because of the whole range of factors we have tried to analyze in this book. But unwise and unsound as it may have been, it was not intrinsically immoral in terms of a test of commensurateness of means to ends, and an appropriate test of announced ends to the values prevalent in the fifties and early sixties in the U.S. domestic structure.

In such a test, the United States as a superpower with a huge presence in the general area of Asia, an emancipator mentality, and a perception of being guarantor of the integrity of states in the area, did not act immorally in making a value choice favoring an allegedly independent and anti-Communist leadership over a Communist albeit Nationalist one in Vietnam. Nor did it act immorally in assisting the non-Communist leadership by appropriate political, economic, and military means to preserve its status and power against the assault of the militant revolutionary leadership which was determined to destroy it.

To argue otherwise is essentially to argue that all interventionism by one state in the affairs of another is intrinsically immoral. This argument is not only highly unrealistic, particularly in the age of nuclear power and the superpowers after World War II, but largely self-defeating, since it presumes a type of valueless behavior on the part of states' leaders which is not very different in kind from that argued by the proponents of pure *realpolitik*. If it was immoral to intervene in Vietnam in support of a leadership of choice—so long as this leadership at a minimum declared itself bound to norms of behavior acceptable to the American people and to world public opinion as a whole—then it would be equally immoral to intervene in Uganda against the butcher Amin or in South African affairs to ease the burdens of *apartheid*. A human rights policy of any kind would certainly become impossible.

Nor was it basically immoral in terms of these tests for the United

States to engage itself directly with military forces on the side of what U.S. leaders perceived as the defending and aggrieved party against what they viewed as its attacking aggressor opponent. Again, this is not to suggest that these judgments, premised as we have seen on seriously faulty analysis, were necessarily sound; only that they were not intrinsically evil. It would be difficult to argue that by the reservation it stated at Geneva in 1954 that it would not use force or the threat of force to overthrow the Geneva Accords, the United States had in effect pledged itself to permanent non-intervention in Indochina.[8] This is particularly so in the light of seven years of subsequent internationally recognized existence of a U.S.-supported South Vietnamese regime under Ngo Dinh Diem. Moreover, as we have noted, the Soviet Union, the other superpower in the high cold war, in effect sanctioned the *de facto* partition of Vietnam by failing to act significantly to repudiate Diem's violation of the political provisions of the 1954 accords and by proposing both Vietnamese states for membership in the United Nations as early as 1957.[9]

The United States may certainly correctly be accused of having acted unwisely in breaking through the Geneva Armistice ceilings on military advisers in 1961; and of having unwisely misread what was in reality an internal civil war, resuming again after 1959, as being an external war of aggression. But it is quite another matter to judge it as having acted immorally because of its violation after seven years of a pledge not to upset through use of force the existence of an international agreement of which the principal (political) provision had remained unimplemented. There is no doubt that the United States directly and crassly intervened in the internal affairs of another country (Vietnam) in 1961. But direct intervention of this type, whether or not politically wise or legalistically justified, is not ground for moral judgment *per se,* as we have just suggested—provided, again, that the U.S. value structure justified active interventionism of this type in this instance, which it is fair to judge that it did; and provided the general norms of international behavior prevailing at the time tolerated such behavior by superpower guarantor states, which again it is fair to state they substantially did. U.S. interventionism in Vietnam in 1961 was not politically, legally, or morally different in kind from U.S. or Soviet interventionism in Cuba in 1959-62, or in the Congo over about the same years. Undoubtedly politically unwise and misjudged; but not intrinsically immoral.

The morality of the U.S. involvement, however, must further be judged in terms of its ultimate results. Did the United States by intervening mitigate more pain and suffering than it caused by intervening, or than would have resulted if it had not intervened? By this test, the morality of U.S. intervention is extremely difficult to justify. Even if one judges that U.S. engagement was not intrinsically immoral, it would be hard to assess it as not having resulted ultimately in more pain and suffering than if it had not intervened at all.

Even accounting for the good the United States may have brought to Indochina, at least in Vietnam and to a lesser degree in Laos, in terms of its economic and developmental programs—the United States input of economic and social assistance into the area was enormous during the crucial years 1961–72—the judgment still appears inevitable that more suffering was caused through war and destruction than was mitigated by assistance. This judgment must persist even if one accounts for the harm done by the enemy side in its own intervention. The overwhelming reason for this judgment is that had the United States not intervened in the first place, Communist control of all Vietnam would probably have been secured relatively quickly and certainly much less painfully than was ultimately the case. A relatively painless Communist victory would have reflected the preponderantly Nationalist-Communist sentiment which we have argued throughout this book existed in Vietnam virtually from the beginning of the August 1945 revolution. Accordingly, early acceptance on the part of the United States of a probably inevitable outcome would not have been immoral; it would in fact have been more moral by America's own standards of values, i.e., self-determination, than intervention to prevent it.

Finally, it should be pointed out in regard to its own calculus of morality in intervening in Vietnam that the United States could not have known the outcome with certainty beforehand. Its political analysis certainly failed; and it was certainly deluded in its various estimates of the situation and of the forces at play in 1959–62, and even more so in 1965. But state leaders cannot be judged immoral simply for reasons of political miscalculation.

The Morality of U.S. Means and Ends

Were the means used in Vietnam and Indochina proportionate with and commensurate to the ends sought? We have noted at length in previous sections the constraints and limitations imposed upon the U.S. engagement in Indochina, as well as the fact that stalemate, in the sense of avoidance of the appearance of defeat both for the United States and for the South Vietnamese, remained throughout the major real goal being pursued. In his recent work,[10] Guenter Lewy has made much of the limitations and constraints, imposed and generally observed, concluding that in essence the horrors and the wreckage wrought were considerably more limited than those who have continued to accuse the United States of having committed war crimes and genocide represent them to have been.[11]

There can be no question, however, that the United States used savage means of war. Its forces defoliated and possibly put permanently out of commission thousands of acres of forests and of formerly and potentially productive lands. They burned and otherwise destroyed thousands of villages; forced the departure of hundreds of thousands of peasants from their cherished ancestral lands; literally dotted all of Eastern Cambodia with deep craters; [12] maimed, burned, and killed civilians as well as enemy soldiers on a massive basis with napalm on both sides of the DMZ; occasionally engaged in vicious interrogation techniques and in what cannot be otherwise described than as torture of defectors and prisoners; whether intentionally or not, destroyed at least some dike systems in North Vietnam, thereby contributing to the aggravated problems of the Vietnamese economy after 1975; bombed and virtually destroyed all major infrastructural and industrial targets in North Vietnam as well as many in the South; conducted occasional mistaken or accidental raids against civilian hospitals; profoundly dislocated the system of economic, social, and political relations among the more primitive Montagnard tribesmen of Vietnam and Laos; and on and on. This litany of horrors is not a minor one. The tragedies and sufferings the United States caused will remain forever embedded in the hearts and minds of millions of Vietnamese, Laotians, Cambodians, and Montagnard tribesmen whose hearts and minds it tried to win.

At the same time, at least until 1969, the United States fought a limited and constricted war of stalemate, in which most of the suffering its forces and the South Vietnamese forces and authorities inflicted was matched if not exceeded by the Vietnamese Communists. For them, the war was certainly *not* limited or circumscribed and the ends justified *all* means. Occasionally, and to their credit, U.S. forces restrained, purged and punished excesses, as those of My Lai. They canceled bombing and ground warfare missions if it appeared that the results in civilian suffering might exceed the military stakes of operations. While the enemy used terror tactics and assassination at will, at least in rural areas, the United States protected urban centers from wanton terrorism; there were probably fewer incidents of urban terrorism in the Second than in the First Indochina War. On some occasions, U.S. elements were actually able to help villagers build roads, sanctuaries, sanitary facilities and wells, to raise pigs or cattle, to cultivate or harvest crops. The United States brought the dubious benefits of urban material welfare to towns like Danang and Saigon in which Hondas, cars, other facilities and conveyances, artificial prosperity and employment, burgeoned along with prostitution and corruption.

What then is the verdict to be drawn? With regards to means and ends, we are drawn to a split verdict. Until the United States, in and after 1968, clearly and unequivocally changed its objective in Vietnam, U.S. means may be considered to have been on the whole, and despite their more horrifying aspects, at least basically in harmony and commensurate with the relatively limited ends sought. These were the ends of stalemate and the avoidance of the appearance of defeat, under the guise of resistance to externally inspired aggression. The morality of U.S. ends must be judged essentially in terms of values held by Americans, not Vietnamese, and condoned if not necessarily shared by the international community. In that context, it seems difficult to establish that the U.S. failed the test of means to ends before 1968.

A special point must be made here about the air war against North Vietnam before 1968. The act itself of engaging in strictly limited and militarily targeted air operations against an enemy using his territory as sanctuary and as logistical base for continuing and reinforcing his assault on territory defended by the United States cannot *per se* be viewed as immoral, so long as the enemy matched U.S. actions by his own massive ground presence in U.S. protected territory. The key point is that U.S. ends before 1969 were what they purported to be: a limited military exercise of defending what was perceived as a protected state against an externally induced and conducted assault or aggression.

In and after 1968, however, United States ends avowedly changed to disengagement and withdrawal, whether or not the Communists gained their repeatedly stated and permanent objective of obtaining a role in the government of the South. This objective on their side never changed from 1945 to 1973 and even to 1975, when circumstances rather than their own volition gave them total control almost certainly sooner than they had expected. The problem with post-1968 U.S. ends involves the caveat "with honor" attached in 1969 to the declared aim of withdrawal. Withdrawal was the promise that had been made to the American people by the presidental candidates in 1968. It becomes extremely difficult, however, to justify the means used by the United States in Indochina after 1968 in relation to the elastic concept of honor.

In what sense could it have been honorable to withdraw from a war over four long years of intensive fighting, which caused a large additional number of casualties and wreaked more widespread havoc and destruction than the six years of previous fighting? How can honor be invoked to justify the sneak and secret bombing of Cambodia and

Laos, the invasion of Cambodia, the raids in and invasions of Laos, the much less discriminate bombing north of the 20th parallel after 1970, the sustained bombing of Hanoi, the mining of Haiphong harbor, the vicious Christmas bombing of 1972?

In light of the Johnson decision to end bombing and to negotiate, the Nixon promises to end the war and withdraw, and the American people's demonstrated concurrence in these redefined objectives, vague in their details as they may have been, the results of a test of means to ends change dramatically. What could morally justify incurring some 75,000 additional total U.S. casualties (including wounded) in 1969–72 (as against some 135,000 in the previous seven years of direct engagement) when withdrawal was the objective understood and accepted by the American people? What could morally justify dropping twice the amount of ordinance by air on Indochina in 1969–72 that was dropped by the United States on all enemies in World War II while the United States was at the same time negotiating with the North Vietnamese in Paris? [13] How could honor justify the employment of means of repression at home in order to veil the plans and actions of the top leadership in complete secrecy? Above all, how could honor justify lying to the American people in 1969–72 about U.S. involvement in operations like the bombing of Cambodia and Laos, or lying to the Vietnamese or the American people about Vietnamization or about U.S. post-withdrawal intentions? [14]

Accordingly, while we have concluded that the tag of immorality cannot validly attach to the U.S. effort in Vietnam before 1968, unwise politically as that effort may have been, the war waged by the United States in Indochina after 1968 was immoral, failing both the test of means to ends and the test of ends.

This discussion has been about morality, not about politics. We have shown earlier [15] the political reasons why some of the methods used, including the delay of the final withdrawal until after the achievement of détente results in Europe and the rapprochement with China, were conceived and even employed with telling effect in the Nixon-Kissinger period. We have even conceded that the policy may have been very clever. But throughout, its declared end remained U.S. withdrawal and its undeclared end a peace settlement which gave the Communists essentially what they wanted and which could, as we suggested, have been obtained in 1969 or 1970. Vietnamization was no excuse; as we have seen, it was a temporizing expedient to gain time while results were being achieved in Europe and China. At heart, as far as the top leadership was concerned, it remained a sham. In moral terms, this makes the Nixon-Kissinger policy in Vietnam all the more reprehensible. On every count, it fails morally to meet a test of means to ends, and a test of ends to the domestic value structure. This was *realpolitik* in its very essence; and it is a classic example of action that fails because of its lack of concern for the moral content of policy.

Instead of obtaining "peace with honor" at minimum cost, Nixon ultimately obtained peace with dishonor to him, at very great cost.

The Morality of U.S. Abandonment of Vietnam

The U.S. aim to disengage and withdraw, announced in 1968, had been actively supported in demonstrations by the anti-war movement and passively supported by the remainder of the public in its toleration of the anti-war movement's actions and its refusal to support the administration's efforts at suppression and at silencing the media. It had moreover been sanctioned in the 1968 elections and demonstrated as the people's will in repeated public opinion polls after 1968.[16] In taking four long years to implement this goal, the Nixon administration caused enormous damage to Vietnam and Indochina, to the domestic fiber of the United States, and to the U.S. image in the world. The United States has been paying for this sin many times over since it occurred, particularly in the despair of American youth. It is still paying in such delayed manifestations of the anguish it caused as the existence and tragic demise of the People's Temple cult in Guyana, many if not most of whose members were originally recruited because of their despair at the continuing war.

It can be argued that the United States deprived the non-Communist Nationalists in Vietnam of whatever slender chance they might still have had to survive in a coalition government if one had been created in 1969-70. Because of a new rising generation, there were more capable and clean individuals on the anti-Communist side in the late sixties in Vietnam than there had been earlier or than would remain later, after Thieu's political repression of the early seventies. It was therefore profoundly wicked to carry on for another four years, at extremely high cost in lives, treasure and human welfare, in order to come out, in January 1973, only with what could have been obtained in terms of a settlement in 1969-70, or in 1965 for that matter.[17]

Through clever public relations, the announced goal of Vietnamization was made to appear successful. But within two short years (1973-75) the South Vietnamese military position at Banmethuot in II Corps crumbled under a slight Communist assault in March 1975, and with that the entire South Vietnamese military and political structure collapsed at one blow. The naked reality of South Vietnamese weakness, even after six years of Vietnamization (1969-75) stood fully revealed in April 1975. The final U.S. evacuation of Vietnam took place in shameful disorder and indignity.[18] In numerous instances, the proper Vietnamese were not evacuated while thousands of panicked individuals of little consequence, many of them hardly knowing what they were doing, overcrowded the badly strained evacuation facilities and forced departing U.S. military and officials to carry them along, sometimes at gunpoint. The shamefulness of the episode overshadowed even that of the grim baby trade in which many Vietnamese families had been engaged shortly beforehand, literally selling babies for adoption in the States to commercial agencies only too willing to oblige.

Ultimately, of course, and irrespective of any promises that may have been made or intents allegedly conveyed by Nixon, Kissinger or U.S. Ambassador Graham Martin to the Thieu government in Vietnam, the United States did not return to save Thieu from the results of his own follies and excesses in terms of the implementation of the 1973 Paris Accords.[19] The United States never again returned to Indochina, and probably never will. Its last gesture, a final wicked episode closing the whole tragedy as far as the United States was concerned, was the bombing on President Ford's ill-conceived order of a Cambodian naval base from which Khmer ships acting without responsible authority had temporarily detained U.S. seamen of the *S.S. Mayaguez*. Again, American as well as Indochinese lives were unnecessarily lost. Yet America did seem to breathe a little easier after this final display of presidential macho.

Did the United States act immorally in ultimately abandoning South Vietnam? Should it have returned in 1975 to try once more to stave off the collapse and save what was left to be saved? The arguments invoked for this view remain the same as earlier ones: the United States should have reintervened to preserve the sanctity and credibility of its alleged commitments; to avoid a humiliating defeat; to rescue those who staked their future on U.S. presence; to save its honor.

These arguments are as vacuous and fallacious when invoked for 1975 as they were at any time during the long period of U.S. engagement. As we observed much earlier in this book,[20] most of the Vietnamese the United States would have gone gack to save always knew that their days were numbered and that there would have to be a reckoning sometime for the lies and deceptions that their own colonial traditions, cowardice, and preference for material comfort had for so long induced them to employ in persuading Americans of their worthiness. A caveat stated earlier again applies: by no means can all "our" Vietnamese be included in such a blanket statement of disapproval. There were always, and there remain today, some very tragic exceptions.[21]

The final abandonment of Vietnam in 1973-75 may have been cynical because of what Nixon, Kissinger, or Ambassador Martin may have led Thieu and his colleagues to believe, but it was certainly not immoral. It met the test of means to ends, and of ends in terms of the wishes, desires, and values of the American people and of the international community. What was cynical, if not immoral, was the make-believe, the illusory success of Project Enhance and of Vietnamization presumably proceeding apace under the paternalistic and watchful eyes of Ambassador Martin. The latter meanwhile remained blind to Thieu's political repressions and South Vietnam's violation of the political provisions of the Paris Accords. This violation could not be excused by mutually provoked breaches by both sides of the military truce provisions in 1973-74.

It was high time for the United States to leave Vietnam for good in 1975. After eight years of combat with U.S. forces and two more of South Vietnamese military truculence with an incredible arsenal provided by the U.S., after a total of nearly $200 billion spent from the American treasury, after 55,000 American lives lost and nearly 300,000 wounded, it seems impossible to argue that the United States had not done enough in what had from the start been a limited engagement in a very poor cause. Its final abandonment of Vietnam in 1975 was at worst only cynical behavior. But so in fact had been the whole of its policy since 1954. For as we have repeatedly pointed out, the truth is that the successive U.S. presidents, if not all the top policy-makers in their respective administrations, never thought they could do more than merely avert the appearance of defeat in Indochina.

It is then not too surprising that even when the war was lost, the United States never squarely and openly admitted losing it. This truth was better left unspoken, to simmer in semi-consciousness, relegated as far as possible to the rear of newly arising concerns. Ultimately, by being able to abandon Vietnam after the "decent interval" of two years following its military withdrawal, [22] the United States had managed to place the final onus for losing on the Vietnamese themselves. As cynically as U.S. leaders had fought throughout to avert the appearance of defeat, they could now claim to have escaped defeat itself.

Individual and Collective Responsibility for the War

The issue of individual responsibility for the tragedy of Indochina in U.S. foreign policy has repeatedly been raised by some American opponents of the war,[23] more so during its later stages (1968-73) but recurrently also since the U.S. withdrawal in early 1973. This issue should now be closed.

The reasons for this are not solely related to the need for unity or domestic equilibrium within the United States, the necessity, as President Nixon of all people put it in his 1969 inaugural address, "to bring us together again." The same need was also strongly felt by President Ford when he assumed office after Nixon's resignation in mid-1974. Interestingly enough, Watergate coming immediately on the heels of Vietnam in a way took care of the problem of individual responsibility for the war and its attendant "crimes against humanity" insofar as President Nixon personally was concerned. Moreover, the political bloodletting which followed Watergate seemed to have calmed spirits and diminished the search for retribution among those in the anti-war movement who had clamored to bring policy-making perpetrators of the Indochina outrage to accountability at the bar of justice.

As suggested, however, the urge to unity and the priority need to reestablish domestic equilibrium are not the sole reasons for arguing against the notion of individual responsibility and accountability for the war. Another reason is the absence of authoritative consensus as to the nature of the norms or laws under which any responsible policy-maker could be made to account. The case of Indochina is hardly comparable to those of the World War II genocidal or war crimes. The Nazi war criminals embarked systematically and deliberately on a policy of genocide, of extermination of human beings (notably Jews, but also gypsies, Communists, Eastern Europeans, and others including even useless old people) whom they defined as not belonging to the privileged and superior caste of which they considered themselves a part.

Nothing comparable at all occurred in Vietnam, whatever tragedies might have been committed against the Indochinese people in the course of U.S. intervention in a misapprehended revolutionary civil war.[24] The acts of U.S. agents in Indochina were committed as part of an unwise and unsuccessful interventionary action erroneously designed to protect these people from external aggression. Even prolonging the war in 1969–72 and extending it in full to Laos and Cambodia, can only with difficulty become grounds for charging that the Nixon administration concertedly and by design entered into a genocidal policy of extermination.[25] Contrary to arguments attempted in that direction, it is difficult to show anything designed at any time in U.S. policy in Indochina to serve other than military-political purposes in guerrilla-type war, or deliberately to exterminate selected human ethnic, religious, economic, or social groups. This goes even for the Phoenix program of eliminating enemy infrastructure in South Vietnam through selective terror and assassination techniques.[26]

If there was controversion by agents of the United States of the laws of war, the terms of the U.S. military Code of Justice, or of other accepted international or municipal laws or established norms of wartime behavior—a matter certainly subject to debate, in which one side by no means has all the monopoly of knowledge or wisdom—then individuals so accused should not find themselves any more immune from accountability at the bar of justice than were the top Japanese military commanders after World War II. A clear-cut agent transgression, such as that at My Lai, was brought to trial despite popular sympathy for the responsible Lt. William Calley and opposition to the Army's way of handling him.

If, as we argued, U.S. policy does not fail the tests of morality until its declared ends changed with Nixon in 1969 without the means to the ends changing commensurately, then how could the inner circles of the Kennedy and Johnson administrations, including a general like William Westmoreland, be made individually responsible for war crimes? If, on the other hand, there was far greater justification for bringing such charges against the inner circle of the Nixon administration, because of the basically immoral nature of its policies, then we have seen that that circle consisted essentially of only two individuals— the president himself and Henry Kissinger. Neither Secretary of Defense Melvin Laird, who favored speedier withdrawal, nor Secretary of State William Rogers, who was not privy to top planning, can be included. President Nixon has been made to atone for his sins through the ordeal of Watergate, and presumably continues in publically imposed exile to pay his debt to society. This would leave only Secretary Kissinger subject to punishment, and would lead to the ludicrous conclusion that he alone should pay for the sins of a U.S. policy which started under Truman, continued with Eisenhower, and took its most decisive turns under administrations of which he was not a part. Kissinger, moreover, turned out to be the individual who more than any other with the exception of Nixon was responsible for finally, however late, managing U.S. exit from the war, and thus for turning U.S. policy away from the crimes for which he would be charged.

The judgment of U.S. leadership and of the United States as a whole for collective responsibility for the tragedy of the Indochina War lies properly before the bar of history. To say so is not a trite cop-out or a disingenuous effort at absolution. For the United States as a nation will be judged harshly by future generations, here and abroad, for its role in Indochina during the third quarter of the twentieth century.

The American people will pay a price, both at home and abroad, for the errors of analysis, the faulty judgments, the misplaced exertions, the immorality and cynicism of leadership, which brought such calamitous

results in Indochina. In many ways, they are already collectively paying, as is apparent in lowered U.S. international posture and prestige,
the deplorable international financial and resource position of the
United States and above all in America's continued failure to rebuild a
strong consensus at home as to the proper role it should play in the
world.

2. Vietnam As Policy Problem

The trauma of Vietnam reveals lessons with respect to five fundamentals of foreign policy: the relativity of security and of power; the
purpose and significance of diplomacy; the importance of analysis; the
role of affect and values; and finally, the inseparability of domestic
politics and foreign policy.

Relativity of Security and Power

Security, presumably, was the main goal of post-World War II
American foreign policy; yet security seemed for several decades into
the postwar period to remain unattainable by the United States. The
more the United States did to achieve security, the more it seemed to
have to do. Containment and the Marshall Plan in Europe were devised to achieve it; shortly the United States found it had to spread
containment and Marshall Plan equivalents throughout the globe. Deterrence and interlinked chains of U.S. commitments were conceived
and proffered in the name of security; yet war ensued in Korea, the
tensions of the high cold war developed in Europe, conflict and wars
broke out in the Congo, Cuba, and the Middle East. Finally, the
United States went to war in Vietnam. Why was it that the more effort
it devoted to security, the more security seemed to elude it?

A major reason was a serious misconception of the meaning of security. Security in foreign policy cannot, any more than in interpersonal
relations, be attained by the sheer threat of force. The shopkeeper or
home-owner who lives in fortress-like conditions, surrounded by warning devices and guns, may thereby prevent or at least delay the chances
for assault on his possessions. But it is doubtful that he will feel more
secure than his counterpart who works or lives unarmed. Security, in
such a case, is not obtained as a result of anything the shopkeeper or
owner does or does not do for protection; it is a function rather of the
state of health of the society within which he is living. If that society
has a high incidence of crime, whatever the causes, the person involved
will continue to feel insecure, whether or not he is armed or
forewarned.

In foreign policy similarly, inhabitants of a nation-state which is not ready to go to all-out war as the allies did against the Axis in 1939-45, will not feel more or less secure in accordance with the amount of weapons they hold. They will feel so in function of the health and peacefulness of the international environment. A state, even a super-power, cannot disseminate or construct security in the international system only by providing weapons, warning systems, or guarantees of the use of force. It can do so even less by spreading a chain of bases containing its own response-ready weapons across a line of contain-ment of a presumed enemy power. All such means invite response and riposte by the presumed enemy. The result, barring all-out war, is an armaments race and a mutual, eventually multilateral, rise in the sense not of security but of insecurity.

Security, then, is above all a psychological sense or state of mind. Less than twenty years before our first intervention under President Truman to help the French in Indochina, President Franklin D. Roose-velt had reminded Americans that the only thing they needed to fear was fear itself. These were wise words, whether used in relation to the massive economic problems faced at home in Roosevelt's time, or to the problems of foreign policy faced in the post-World War II period. For the sense of security lies in the absence of fear.

The absence of fear in turn means the absence of a perception of threat. Secure people are fearless people because they do not feel threatened; they do not feel threatened because they do not perceive, or have no reason to perceive, that there is hostility toward them. Like people, secure states are those which do not perceive a threat because they have no reason to believe that the external environment is hostile. In order to render itself secure, a state which is unwilling or unready to go to war must consequently realize that it cannot negate the threats it may perceive by interposing its own threats. It must seek instead to assuage the hostility which caused others to threaten it in the first place.

In relation to Vietnam, the United States failed singularly to com-prehend the nature of the threat it feared, and it failed totally to seek to assuage it. It perceived the Vietnamese threat as an extension of a larger threat, that of the entire Sino-Soviet or Communist camp, and sought to meet it, as it was seeking to meet the larger threat, largely with means of force. Counterposing power to what it perceived as hos-tile power, the United States reached a dead end in Vietnam after 1961. Politics and diplomacy were essentially absent from its arsenal; the use of power alone led it to war. Although it wished to circumscribe and restrain its use of power lest it be led into an even wider war, the

United States was unable to transcend its use of power by the use of diplomacy at least until Nixon and Kissinger reached the scene.

What we may call the dilemma or paradox of security [27] was not, for the United States, confined to Vietnam. The entire postwar foreign policy of the United States, from the inception of the high cold war in 1948 until Nixon and Kissinger set in motion the machinery of détente and the U.S. rapprochment with China after 1969, was premised on the ever-growing extension of U.S. objective power without a concomitant growth in the role of U.S. diplomacy. Deterrence, the parrying of a threat by the interposition of a counter-threat, could not by itself resolve U.S. threat perceptions and accordingly diminish fears and bring about a sense of security. Yet with such significant exceptions as the Austrian Peace Treaty of 1954 and some international agreements reached with the Soviets in the early sixties, diplomacy was almost entirely absent during the high cold war.

Power overwhelmed U.S. diplomacy during the high cold war (1948–69). In falling into the trap of power, the United States in the Indochina phase of its superpowerdom failed to appreciate or ignored the relativity of power with respect to issue, to time, and to place. The effectiveness of power, even very great power, depends entirely on what it is applied to, where and when. Indochina in 1945–75 was one of the most difficult, if not impossible, areas in which to apply power. The issue was intractable; the place conducive to forms of war with which the United States had become unfamiliar; and the time one in which the population, galvanized by the Japanese occupation, motivated by the desire to be rid of colonial masters, and mobilized by extremely able and adaptable leaders, was ready to proffer almost unlimited sacrifices. It is important to remember that not all issues everywhere in the world are tractable, even by superpowers such as the United States rising to its crest in 1945–59 and declining only slightly in 1959–75.

Security for the United States, as pointed out much earlier in this book,[28] does not have to be equated with the creation of a world order in which U.S. values or the U.S. system prevail everywhere. A congenial world order in terms of U.S. values, which include preeminently the maintenance of world peace and of U.S. security, can be created provided the United States makes proper use of diplomacy.

To repeat, security is in essence a subjective commodity connoting the absence of fear and threat perception; the best means to achieve it, given the relativity of power to issue, time, and place, and therefore the inherent limitations on the effectivness of power, is the proper use of diplomacy.

Purposes, Death, and Revival of Diplomacy

One of the great weaknesses of diplomacy and of the diplomatic profession in the second half of the twentieth century has been its incapacity to communicate clearly and intelligibly to governments and to peoples what it practices and what it seeks to achieve. Diplomacy in the sense intended here is not simply synonymous with the conduct of foreign relations, in which case its craft would become merely administrative, bereft of soul and substantive content. Nor is diplomacy simply synonymous with foreign policy, as when diplomatic historians employ the term to speak, for example, of "American diplomacy." The misuse of the term by historians, politicians and statesmen on the one hand, combined with its bastardization by public administrators and with the failure of diplomatists clearly to convey their functions on the other, has debased the term "diplomacy" almost to the point of meaninglessness. Little wonder that its practice fell into disuse, if not disrepute, when compared with the rise of strategy and of strategic thinking during the nuclear age.

What we intend here to convey by "diplomacy" is the intensive process of cross-cultural communication between two or more governments or authoritative decision-making centers. The purpose of such communications, whether they are written, oral or tacit, is twofold. On the one hand, a decision-making center reciprocally communicates with others as to the nature of its structure, that is of its processes for making policies and decisions. On the other, it communicates reciprocally with others as to the nature of its soul, that is of its history, traditions, values, its fears, concerns, wishes, and intents.

The process of diplomacy, of communications between decision-making centers, goes on permanently though sometimes only tacitly. It is occasionally deliberately interrupted in its explicit phase, as it was between the United States and the People's Republic of China between 1949 and 1971, or between the United States and Cuba between 1959 and the mid-seventies. The tacit phase of diplomacy, which predominantly involves bargaining, nonetheless continues permanently, as bargaining is an unstructured form of communications between decision-making centers. When bargaining structures itself explicitly to resolve certain defined issues at a specified place and time, it transforms itself into negotiations. In the structured process of negotiations, decision-making centers continue to bargain with each other explicitly over an indefinite period until they resolve conflicting issues or agree to leave them unresolved but hopefully undisturbed.

In the sense just described, diplomacy is the best means yet devised and available to governments in a still very conflict-filled world of multiple sovereign states, to achieve reciprocal understanding of their operational structures, recognition of their aims, resolution of at least some of the issues that divide them, and ultimately peace and a sense of security.

Given the general ethos and outlook of the United States as a superpower at the onset of the high cold war in the late forties and early fifties, there arose in the United States, as suggested in Chapter III, an enormous emphasis on geostrategic thinking and on the use or threatened use of force in the form of deterrence appropriate to the nuclear age and later of refined deterrence. The temptation to apply policy models derived from the use of refined deterrence techniques from one to another area of the globe grew irresistibly.

Superficially, there appeared no good reason not to apply models derived from confrontation with the Soviets in Berlin or Cuba to areas such as Vietnam. As we noted earlier, however, Vietnam was an Asian peasant state of entirely different character; and the Vietnamese, whatever their relations with them, were not the Soviets operating in the sophisticated environment of strategic scenarios adapted to nuclear confrontation. Whereas refined deterrence did not apply and could not work in the issue of Indochina, diplomacy in a far more traditional sense might have succeeded, as it succeeded for a period of some years (1962–69) in Laos. Having become a lost art, however, diplomacy was not employed. In that sense, we can speak of the death of diplomacy during the high cold war.

Diplomacy as a method in the conduct of American foreign policy similarly died during the high cold war in regard to a large number of other issues. For example, it was certainly insufficiently employed or not employed at all in relation to France's effort under the leadership of General de Gaulle to rise as an independent power center between the two world blocs. De Gaulle indicated to the United States and United Kingdom as early as 1958 [29] his desire to form a concert of leadership and power to guide the destinies of the North Atlantic alliance. This approach, which might have averted the later problems of nuclear proliferation and the fiasco of the multilateral force proposal in NATO, and brought about a quicker end to the high cold war in Europe, was rebuffed by the United States. Similarly, the United States rebuffed de Gaulle's efforts to bring diplomacy back into the Indochina question by organizing a multilateral forum, such as a reconvened 1954 Geneva Conference, to discuss and hopefully resolve the issue.

The U.S. emphasis on geostrategic thinking and on the use of force and of deterrence, combined with the frozen ideological posture of anti-communism of the United States during the high cold war, also led to the rise in U.S. policy-making circles of the civilian militarists we discussed in section I of Chapter V. Crisis management satisfied both the effective and the recreative motivational drives of such men, and provided them the means to control U.S. military leadership at one end of the spectrum, and the affectively motivated politicians or diplomatists who might have changed the rules of the game at the other. Among the results were the maintenance of the status quo in Europe and the Third World and the complex mixes of highly sophisticated but publicly incomprehensible programs developed to maintain stalemate in Indochina. In its death period, diplomacy could not overcome or break the log-jam of programmatic approaches and managerialism in which our foreign policy had become mired.

One of Henry Kissinger's signal contributions to American foreign policy was that he produced a true revival of diplomacy after the Nixon administration took office in 1969. Kissinger's intellectual knowledge of diplomatic method, along with his extraordinary personal gifts for communicating lucidly and profoundly with high-level personalities across cultural boundaries, resulted almost overnight in an enormous thaw of the long-frozen ice of U.S. relations with its major partners in Europe as well as with the Soviet Union, and later China. Détente and the Sino-U.S. rapprochement ensued. Kissinger's understanding of the purposes of diplomacy, his willingness to reach across the abyss to reach and comprehend the enemy while similarly having the enemy comprehend us, and President Nixon's willingness to authorize Kissinger to speak and act for him, produced the long-sought peace in Vietnam.

The terms of that peace were no more or less onerous than they would have been earlier in our long Indochina involvement if diplomacy had been employed in the manner Kissinger used it. The peace, as settlements of war always do, reflected the fundamental military and political situation on the ground. The fact that the peace settlement in Vietnam did not last was in no sense an indication that diplomacy had, after all, failed. On the contrary, considering the hopelessly incurable weaknesses of the South Vietnamese political-social and military edifice, it was rather a marvel of diplomacy to have been able to achieve it at all.

The revival of diplomacy, however, brought its own costs. Kissinger wrapped his moves in Europe, the Middle East, Asia, and elsewhere in the inordinate secrecy that has traditionally been the companion of diplomatic method. Diplomacy's achievements are in fact largely made possible by assuring its agents, acting on behalf of states, that their statements will remain strictly confidential, so that they can communicate as frankly as possible with each other. In such frank communications, positions and intents can be unveiled which might greatly imperil if not devastate statesmen and leaders in their respective domestic political settings if prematurely revealed. It was one of Kissinger's remarkable talents that he was able to keep the U.S. media reasonably well informed, or at least thinking they were well informed, while in fact revealing little of major import until the precise moment that it would serve his purposes and those of diplomacy or politics. The secrecy of Kissinger's diplomacy nonetheless contributed to a further sapping of the U.S. domestic underpinnings of the war. The repressive tactics used by the Nixon administration to protect it added, as we suggested earlier, to the growing erosion of the American people's confidence in the basic authority structures of American society.

The Importance of Analysis

We devoted a long previous section of this book to the failure of analysis.[30] Our purpose was to explain and stress the insignificant role that analysis played in the specific context of Vietnam and Indochina, in the light of the predetermined or, as we called it, closed system of decision-making which prevailed for so long in U.S. policy toward that issue. It must nevertheless be clear from previous comments made throughout this book that analysis, done as objectively as possible under the specific circumstances of an issue, is of the highest importance in foreign policy. As we noted earlier, foreign policy generally undergoes four pre-decisional phases: observation, analysis, appraisal and recommendation. At least the first three of these phases deeply involve and engage the diplomatist; the third and fourth also involve and are sometimes made the exclusive preserve of policy-makers at the center of the decision-making process. Analysis, then, is among the diplomatists' most important tools; and on its appropriate performance depends much of the success of diplomacy and, ultimately, of foreign policy.

Analysis in foreign policy is the objective explanation of the how and why of politics in foreign areas. It should play a fundamental role in determining the results of the subsequent phases of appraisal, recommendation and decision. In the feedback cycle of foreign policy,[31] analysis evaluates implementation and can thus recondition and redetermine appraisal and policy. All this, provided analysis is at least reasonably objective and performed in thorough and competent fashion. But proper analysis of events, their sources and causes, seems to have eluded the United States in Indochina during its deep involvement in the issue. More recently, appropriate analysis of social and political events abroad still seemed to be eluding U.S. foreign policy, as in the case of Iran in 1978–79.

We reviewed the reasons for the failure of analysis in Indochina at length in Chapter V and need not repeat them here. In brief, analysis failed because of the subjectivity involved in its process and the predetermination of those portions of analysis which would enter the decision-making process and those which would not. Adequate and objective analysis in Vietnam and Indochina throughout the period of the high cold war, but especially after 1961, might have allowed healthier appraisals of both South Vietnamese and Vietnamese Communist capabilities, of the chances of U.S. efforts to affect the issue, and of the true state of Sino-Soviet and Vietnamese-Sino-Soviet relations during the years of U.S. involvement.

Rigorously objective analysis is vital to the development of a foreign policy which properly serves the security interests of the American people. It is also achievable, as demonstrated by those in the media, the attentive public, and the academic world who forecast accurately the probable outcome of our Indochina involvement.[32] But decision-makers must be willing to accept its results. In the issue of Indochina, they were not and the danger of closed-system decision-making is consequently one of the great lessons of Vietnam.

Affect and Values

If security in the sense of absence of fear and threat perception remains the essential goal of American foreign policy, then we must ask: "Security of what?" The answer cannot be the traditional one involving reified concepts of the state or the nation. The security of the "United States" means above all the security of values which the inhabitants of the United States wish to protect and enhance. The "United States" is a term which cannot be separated from its people. Americans might not, for example, wish to protect the security of the United States if it were a fascist dictatorship instead of a democratic republic. On the other hand, Americans might wish to protect their democratic principles and institutions even if they decided to merge their present state into, say, a larger federation, for example, the British Commonwealth or a world government. In that unlikely case, however, they would no longer be protecting the security of the United States *per se,* but of a larger agglomeration of peoples.

The values for which security is sought in foreign policy are those which the American people, who have lived together for only a brief period of time on the same territory in the Western hemisphere,[33] share, cherish, and desire to uphold at home. These values are invariably related in the first instance to the social, political, and moral cohesion of the American people at home. They form the bases of the "rules of rule" which are so central to the American experience.[34] It follows that foreign policies which tend to weaken rather than enhance such values are counterproductive and conducive to insecurity. The deep American engagement in Indochina was a case in point.

Foreign policy should seek the extension or protection of our interests in territories or issues abroad which the American people understand and with which they can palpably and readily identify. Identification with peoples, territories or issues abroad will shift with time and will vary as circumstances may dictate. Black Africa and portions of the Middle East (such as Israel and the oil-producing Arab nations) are of much greater interest to many Americans today than they were in even the recent past. While American identification with Japan, democratic Western Europe, and portions of the Western Hemisphere remains great, there is little understanding for or identification with most of Asia, except China and Australia/New Zealand. In the nature of politics, specific interests apply pressures on the leadership of the United States, or of any country for that matter, in order to obtain the desired identification of their interests with those of the nation. When specific interests are themselves a virtual part of the government, as in the case of the U.S. military-industrial complex for example, it is difficult for the government under the best of circumstances to curb the identification of specific with truly national interests.

Specific interests, such as those seeking new advanced nuclear delivery systems, or military basing rights for the United States in the Indian Ocean for example, often manage to relate their needs to presumed higher needs of the national security. It is then the task of wise leadership and *ipso facto* its moral duty, to sort out such claims on national attention and carefully to distinguish spurious claims on the national interest on the part of specific interests from the genuinely national interest itself.

The latter is best viewed as that which will be congruent and in harmony with the values preponderantly held at home. Currently, it is doubtful that the American people would support a military engagement in the Indian Ocean or in Southern Africa, or in Korea or Southeast Asia if wars were to break out there again. Wise and correct statesmanship will recognize these limitations from the very outset of the political effort by various specific interests to determine the general or national interest. This difficult task imposing itself on leadership cannot be performed in the absence of a strong affective motivational

set within leadership itself. If leaders are purely effective, that is operators and do-ers, rather than oriented to the values held and prized by
Americans in their time, the danger of slippage in the determination of
the national interest is great. This is one of the great lessons of Vietnam, as we saw in Chapter V.

At the same time, affectively oriented leaders, in the first instance,
the president and secretary of state, have the opportunity which they
have presumably been seeking throughout their political careers to condition as well as to express the values held by the people. Their capacity to do so is a function of their political skill, and of the degree of
identification that people can muster for the changing or new values
the leaders are prescribing. Thus, Nixon and Kissinger were able to
reduce the fear of losing to communism and replace it instead by a
desire to promote the relaxation of world tensions and to reach accommodation with the other super or great powers through diplomacy.

Inseparability of Politics and Policy

Indochina and Vietnam demonstrate more clearly than any other
recent episode in the history of American foreign policy the inevitable
and necessary connection between foreign policy and domestic politics.
The evolution of the United States has been somewhat unusual in this
respect, as compared with other major states, including the Soviet
Union. The role of domestic politics in nineteenth century U.S. diplomacy was probably more pronounced and surely more apparent than
in the foreign policies of Britain or France during that period. The first
decades of the twentieth century saw a continuation of the same trend.
The evident primacy of U.S. domestic politics caused European powers
to despair that the United States would understand or accept the imperatives of power politics as demonstrated in the post-World War I
settlements, or even those of idealism and internationalism expressed in
the doctrine of collective security and in the League of Nations that the
United States failed to join. Could this age of what was sometimes
called innocence on the part of the United States have in fact been an
age of greater realism in terms of what it was and could be in the
world?

There was an extremely sharp break during and after World War II.
From little power, the United States went to superpower; from waning
parochialism it moved to extreme internationalism; from regional imperialism to the worldwide extension of American bases and economic
interests; from destiny in the continent to eagerly grasped global destiny, marked by a desire to achieve universal emancipation through the
spread of American values. Foreign policy suddenly became a category

of state activity apart from domestic policy; just as the study of international relations in American universities split off from political science or history and asserted its separate existence as a scholarly discipline.

The U.S. foreign affairs and national security establishment grew by leaps and bounds until, as we have noted, it became almost unmanageable in size and capable of conditioning and influencing presidents as much if not more than their natural political constituency, the people. It also grew very separate from the people as a whole, carrying the Congress along with it in the absence of perceptible popular opposition to the assumption of a dominant world role by the United States. As we indicated, there was a strong consensus supporting not only the Indochina policy but the entire foreign policy of the United States during the high cold war.

At the heart of the problem was the fact that the consensus of support had not been inspired by the people themselves but rather by the leadership of the post-World War II United States. Foreign policies stemmed full-blown from the minds of a leadership convinced almost from the onset of the post-war period that the Soviet Union, and later, the Sino-Soviet bloc presented dangers of immense potential consequence to the security of the United States. We detailed how containment was conceived and why. The policy of worldwide containment, leading to that of worldwide expansion, had to be explained to the American people by overarching rhetoric. Virulent anti-communism, in radical ideological form suited to the people's mood though not necessarily comprehended in the same way by the elites governing our conduct in the world, came to propel and drive the policies of the United States. As we suggested much earlier, a sort of Frankenstein monster developed which held the leadership itself in its grasp.

Vietnam and Indochina represented at the beginning of massive U.S. engagement the culmination of elite-inspired foreign policies, incomprehensible to the people and followed by them largely out of blind ideological fear and misapprehension. They represented at their catastrophic end the revulsion of the people and their recovery of control over the direction of foreign policy. America's experience in far-flung exercises in the manipulation of power had resulted by 1968 in what all policy must above all seek to avoid: the revolt, disunity, and repudiation of the people at home.

Since 1973 and more so since 1975, the U.S. tendency to look at national security and foreign policy as a political and cognitive category separate from domestic and other policy has considerably receded. Once more Americans seem to understand better that foreign policy, no more than civil rights policy, energy policy, or agricultural policy, is a separate category of state activity that can be divorced at any stage from the people's involvement and concern. When this happens, as it did in the U.S. engagement in Indochina, the people will tend to turn on the policy and its elitist authors. They will bring both back from the abstractions of international relations models to the realities of their everyday concerns, and to the principles and values which they understand and uphold.

3. Vietnam as Problem of History

Mr. Speaker, over this weekend we have learned the extent of the disaster that has befallen China and the United States. The responsibility for the failure of our foreign policy in the Far East rests squarely with the White House and the Department of State. The continued insistence that aid would not be forthcoming unless a coalition government with the Communists was formed was a crippling blow to the national government. So concerned were our diplomats and their advisers, the Lattimores and the Fairbanks, with the imperfection of the democratic system in China after twenty years of war and the tales of corruption in high places that they lost sight of our tremendous stake in a non-Communist China.

Our policy, in the words of the premier of the National Government, Sun Fo, of vacillation, uncertainty, and confusion has reaped the whirlwind. This House must now assume the responsibility of preventing the onrushing tide of communism from engulfing all of Asia. (Rep. John F. Kennedy, D-Mass., addressing the House of Representatives for one minute on Jan. 25, 1949; Congressional Record-House, Jan. 25, 1949, pp. 532–33.)

To read in such a book as Tang Tsou's *America's Failure in China* (arresting title), the list of measures that were proposed for the United States in China but not tried—including large-scale use of advisers, logistic support, intelligence and communications assistance, the overthrow or replacement of Chiang, transport, combat air support, large-scale training, U.S. combat units—is to read the list of measures that *were* successively tried in Vietnam. ("Leverage" for reform and for broadening the government was urged in both cases, tried in neither.)

These measures had been rejected in China because, in the judgment of General Marshall and others—almost surely correct—they were unlikely to prove adequate. In Vietnam, the Pentagon Papers reveal that many of the corresponding judgments, at the decision-points of escalation, were scarcely more sanguine; but this time the measures were used anyway. Why the difference? Because Vietnam was more important? Hardly. Because of the difference in scale? But the measures urged for China were not very large, and the actual programs in Vietnam, in the end, were too small. Because the Marshall-Acheson policy in China was proved mistaken? One doubts that many officials in the 1960s believe that.

Almost surely, among the generation of officials who survived the purges of the Asian bureaus in the fifties, it was not the worries of foreigners
that they remembered, as the epitaph to the Marshall-Acheson course of
cutting losses in China, but the famous charges that this policy exposed
Marshall as "a living lie . . . a front man for traitors" and Acheson as
"the Red Dean." (Daniel Ellsberg, *Papers on the War*, New York: Simon
and Schuster, 1972, pp. 91–92.)

Summary

In summary, the United States got involved in Vietnam after a brief
hesitation following World War II because of domestic anti-communism, its dynamism as a superpower, and its nearby presence which
made the exercise of influence in Southeast Asia easy and cheap. Mis-
interpreted and misapplied concepts of containment, impelled by the
ideological distortions of anti-communism at home, caused the United
States to rally to the assistance of a colonialist European ally while
discounting the forces of nationalism in Asia and vastly overestimating
the Sino-Soviet threat and its possible consequences in the region.

As U.S. involvement persisted because of containment and the desire
to camouflage the setback of 1954, the United States gradually began
to gain momentum and to take over the fight against the revolution in
Indochina. To rationalize doing so, it conjured up theories of worldwide interlinkage of national liberation wars and the credibility of U.S.
commitments. The United States invented refined deterrence and the
limited-mix programmatic approach to war as an exercise in crisis management. Failing properly to review the stakes and to incorporate the
critical results of objective analysis at crucial moments in the enterprise,
it pursued stalemate in a closed system of decision-making in order to
continue to avoid the dreaded domestic consequences of defeat or the
appearance of defeat.

As the war continued in prolonged stalemate, new perceptions of its
stakes and of its costs gradually arose among the American people and
even in the leadership. A vast credibility gap developed between the
official versions and accounts of the war and the willingness of Americans to believe them. With the rise of a new generation, lacking the
memories and set outlooks of the past and no longer fearful of accusations of betrayal, an anti-war movement grew to large proportions in
the United States. Reinforced by the black civil rights movement, it
succeeded in swamping both Congress and domestic opinion. After an
engagement in Vietnam which lasted over six presidential elections, the
United States finally reversed course and abandoned Indochina. It is
doubtful that it will ever return there again.

It is difficult to judge U.S. intervention in Indochina as intrinsically immoral, since its ends accorded with deeply held convictions among the American people at the beginning of the high cold war, and since its means were generally limited, in consonance with the relatively limited objectives being pursued. After the declared ends of U.S. policy changed in 1968, however, it was immoral as well as cynical for the United States to continue waging war another four years, regardless of the time needed for clever political and diplomatic maneuvers of extrication to be worked out.

Ultimately, the American people and their leadership cannot escape collective responsibility for having inflicted gross injury on the peoples of Indochina, on themselves, and on their previous image as contributors and leaders in the development of a civilized world conscience. Individual responsibility cannot be attributed in practical terms; but the collective memory of guilt cannot be escaped. The United States learned history's lesson of disapproval by disregarding some of the most basic principles of sound and wise policy—among them, the relativity of security and power, the proper role and purposes of diplomacy, the significance of objective analysis of foreign political events, the importance of affect in leadership, and the inseparability of foreign from domestic policy.

Paradoxes of History

The one sharp lesson that Vietnam teaches almost savagely is that the most astute leaders, the finest minds, the smartest strategists, the most dedicated decision-makers, the most effective politicians, the best and the brightest, in short, could and can be all wrong. Not just wrong in terms of mistaken assessment of conditions, events, and consequences, though they were that too. But wrong in the more important, normative sense of the word. They could *be* wrong, and partly because they were, they could *do* wrong.

There are still people in the United States today who continue to contend that the United States won in Vietnam, though it lost at home. The notion that the United States could be defeated is as hard to accept as the elementary Clausewitzian dictum that war and peace are not two separate states, but two extremes in a continuum of politics and policy. Those who argue that the United States was winning in Vietnam still do not see that it was the growing perception at home that the war was wrong, and the leadership pursuing it all wrong, that caused it to fail in Vietnam. A million more men and machines, several billion more dollars, could neither have been forthcoming nor would they have made any difference. The simplest way to put it is also the best: the United States lost the war when Americans overwhelmingly ceased to accept it as right and came to regard it as wrong.

In Vietnam, neither the government's best hopes nor its worst fears were realistic. This is not really surprising since its best hopes were a function of and dependent on its worst fears, and it was the perception of these fears which came into question. The American people began to see, as in plain fact *most* of the Vietnamese people had seen long before, that there was in fact little to fear. Whatever that elusive something was—the hostility of the Vietnamese Communists, no doubt, and beyond that the hostility of other Communist and non-Communist powers and of the American people to losing to communism—was not worth assuaging at a cost which finally became intolerable because it induced other fears of far more serious consequence in terms of the domestic fabric of the United States itself.

The question we now pose and try to relate to the vast and mysterious realm of history is, "Why were the Best and the Brightest all wrong?" Why was it wrong to be fearful in the first place, and then to compound that wrongness by pigheadedly going ahead even after it had become almost universally apparent that both the original and the subsequent fears were essentially groundless? An attempt can be made to answer this puzzle by trying to penetrate and understand the thicket of the interrelationship between the historical perceptions of statesmen and their motivational sets. This interrelationship is dominated by normative considerations.

Historians and philosophers remain the major sources for most of the conceptual frameworks of statesmen, politicians, diplomats, policy- and decision-makers of lesser breed. It is still from the history they have learned that most of the images that national leaders carry in their heads are derived; and from the history of political thought that they derive most of the value structure which guides their operations. That is what they impart to colleagues, whether domestic or foreign, with whom they communicate in the processes of decision-making, negotiation, or efforts to resolve differences by accommodation or confrontation. Ultimately, and we have said it earlier in this book, hardly anything is more important in international affairs than the historical images and perceptions that men of action carry in their heads, and the values and norms they believe in upholding and promoting.[35]

(One might note in an aside that statesmen have always tended to be more sanguine than historians in asserting the value of history as guide in shaping their own and other leaders' mind-sets; the real doubters have been scholars and historians who, of course know far more about history and its endless paradoxes. Historians may not doubt the importance of history in shaping contemporary decisions: what they doubt is its prescriptive value when used by statesmen.[36])

Clearly, the mind-sets and cognitive processes of the American leaders of the Vietnam period were replete with historical images, analogies and conceptions. Clearly also, most of this conceptual baggage came from the history that had been taught and conveyed to them, as to most of us: a distorted, selective narration and judgment of portions of past reality. This left them, as all of us, filled with a vast variety of impressions and judgments about which there ultimately are no agreed standards of appraisal. This is in the nature of history. As the historian H. Stuart Hughes so correctly put it in a remark far more profound than the quip it purported to be: "History continues to be what the historians say it is." [37] (Similarly, the national interest is at heart what the president says it is.)

A paradox of history, inasmuch as it is conveyed, is that it may well be prescriptively powerful; to the same extent as experience in life, inasmuch as it is learned, prescribes elements of behavior. But in the same circumscribed sense: that is, both fail to prescribe the *value* which patterns of behavior undertaken in the past will have if once again undertaken in the future. They both leave us necessarily in the dark about present values since the value context is forever changing. History does not tell us whether what may have been right or wrong yesterday would be right or wrong, even if seemingly practical, today. Experience does not teach us whether repeating past behavior will gain us value (approval, success) in the context of today or tomorrow.

With respect to Vietnam, the decision-makers' images from history told them to be fearful of what they regarded, though erroneously, as aggression. The prescription was to deter and defeat it in Indochina, lest it lead them again to defeat at home, as it had after the fall of China, or confront them elsewhere in the world. But these images from history could not and did not tell them whether stopping presumed aggression, which would have been valuable in pre-war Europe and presumably had had value in Korea, would be equally valuable in Indochina. This value judgment had to be applied by the decision-maker himself, in the context of his own and contemporaneous value structures. Since what is of value in one period and circumstance is not necessarily so in another, roads taken largely on the premise of history's prescriptive power, even if correctly assessed, have no certainty of leading to valuable results.

In Indochina, the decision-makers piled misperceptions upon misperceptions: they were unable to distinguish Vietnamese communism from other communisms; nationalism from communism; Vietnam and Indochina from Europe and other Southeast Asian or Asian political settings; civil war and revolution from externally directed interstate war; they were above all unable to recognize that the aggression they feared represented in a changed context of values a liberating force, and that the alleged freedom they supported represented a sham. When these new perceptions dawned on the American people, the result was that the value context within which the decision-makers were operating changed toward the judgment that while perhaps stopping communism had been valuable in general, or in Europe or Korea, it was not valuable at the required cost in Indochina. Therefore, the prescriptive lessons of history ceased to have bearing of value in Indochina.

To make prudent and hopefully successful policy in terms of goals they set, statesmen must inevitably make value choices which accord as well as possible with the contemporaneous but always changing value structures that prevail when their decisions are made. History, though presumably prescriptive, has very little guidance to offer in that respect. The statesman's choice, however, should be guided by some relatively simple logic. Presumably, his affective motivational set has led him on his course in order that he may place his finger on the pulse of history and, to whatever small degree, affect its general direction. In using history prescriptively, he tends *ipso facto* to diminish the range of his affective motivation. The view that history is prescriptive and repeats itself condemns him to a sort of historical determinism. He becomes, in a sense, a prisoner of history. Acting on George Santayana's old dictum that those who ignore history are condemned to repeat it, he may in actual fact produce the opposite result, and by repeating history he may condemn his own future.

U.S. leadership in Vietnam overwhelmingly opted for the course proferred by Santayana. It took the simpler and more traveled road. It rejected, whether consciously or unconciously, the more arduous task of applying new value judgments to what it essentially, and erroneously, regarded as a sequence of old events repeating themselves from Europe to Southeast Asia during the high cold war. This rejection was best expressed in the American leadership's refusal to review the stakes in Indochina at crucial or watershed moments of the enterprise.

It did not do so in 1949, after the Chinese Communist victory and significant French defeats; nor in 1955, after Geneva; nor in 1961, at the inception of the Sino-Soviet conflict and near collapse of the Saigon regime; nor in 1965, prior to the introduction of U.S. combat forces and after settlement proposals had been received; nor in 1969, after Tet and Johnson's abdication and the initiation of the Paris Peace Talks. The creative act of value review and new value interposition finally could be avoided no longer. It was made slowly and deliberately, after 1969, in function of the rapprochment with China: once the Chinese Communist menace had been removed—a fundamental value judgment—opposition to communism in Indochina had also lost its value, as Nixon and Kissinger correctly calculated.

Acting predominantly on their *effective* motivational sets, U.S. decision-makers of the pre-1969 Vietnam period undermined their own thrust as potentially creative leaders. They came to view themselves primarily as managers and operators in an essentially engineering enterprise. Using perceived history's presumed prescriptions as guide, they undercut their own *affective* potential. Such are the paradoxes of history, and in the Vietnam case the choice of effectiveness over affectiveness ultimately guaranteed failure. They were wrong, and in the course of time came to be seen as doing wrong.

Perhaps these and other paradoxes of history can be resolved only by those who construct holistic explanations of history—total systems à la Toynbee, Darwin, Freud, Lenin and Marx. If a statesman accepts a construct of history such as Marxism-Leninism, his affective motivational set has been in effect pre-empted; he needs then only be effective, and he will inevitably do his necessary and predetermined part in affecting the processes of a history whose laws have been unambiguously discovered and prescribed. In that view, it is a culminating irony of history that the Vietnamese Communist leaders were those who triumphed in Indochina. By sticking with effectiveness, they triumphed; by chosing effect over affect U.S. leaders discarded the one great option that was denied the Communists. They acted, in sum, as determinists, and failed.

History will continue to provide presumed prescriptions; and most probably statesmen will continue to act on the basis of the distorted and selective images of history that they carry in their heads. It could well be that in the present post-Vietnam period of mounting American disillusionment with world affairs, for example, the United States will conclude from "the lessons of Vietnam" that it should never re-engage its military power at all. The lesson of history in Vietnam, as applied to conflicts elsewhere, is precisely *not* that U.S. security is never involved or that U.S. power should never be engaged; but rather that global approaches and global laws do not work, and that each case must be regarded on its own merits.

Turning this to present dilemmas in any of the numerous crises the United States faces almost daily in international affairs, the United States should not regard involvement here or there as bad because it was bad, or wrong, in Vietnam. That is what history now seems to prescribe; and if statesmen are allowed to take the easy course, they will. The right questions to ask are: "Who is engaged in this conflict and what strengths and forces do they represent?"—"What is the justice of this issue as seen by the people who are themselves most directly involved?"—"What are the actual situations in all their local perplexities?" Once answers to these questions are obtained, one can then ask: "What are our interests, if any, and why?"—"What are our capabilities and the limits to them in affecting this issue?"—"What is sufficiently clearly right to such an overwhelming number of Americans that there can be no question later on if much larger sacrifices are called for?"

Further, Americans should seek to ensure at every turn that their leaders and statesmen actually exercise the normative and qualitative functions, the affect, that motivated them in seeking responsibility in the first instance. The more they are exposed, in an open society like that of the United States, to the value judgments of the people at the time they act, the more affective they will be, and ultimately therefore the more effective. Allowing them to be motivated predominantly by "effect" for so long caused the engineering-operational approaches which set the stage not only for failure but for their doing wrong. The people too, then, were wrong in not measuring and asserting value earlier, no matter what the apparent misperceptions and alleged prescriptions of history may have been.

It is consequently essential that social science and historical research face up to rather than eschew philosophical and normative-value questions. They must not be allowed to seek refuge in the type of nominally value-free research which will tend increasingly to lead to safe, technocratic and non-creative findings, to mechanical policies and sterile politics, to effect rather than affect on the part of statesmen and policymakers. If the United States is to avoid another generation of the best and the brightest being all wrong, the American people must seek above all to help those charged with its destinies to discern the values by which they should be guided.

Toward the Future

At the beginning of its third century as a sovereign republic, the United States has now undergone the trials and tribulations caused by the effects of a lost war abroad in which it was deeply engaged. Founded in an anti-colonial revolution in which the aspirations of the people counted far more than the apparent power of the guns involved, the United States ironically faced a reverse situation in Indochina at a moment when its power appeared supreme in the world. The defeat of the forces which the United States supported in Indochina has led to

recalculation abroad, not so much of the power as of the character of
the United States. It is devoutedly to be hoped that the fissures and
divisions which the U.S. engagement in Indochina provoked in the
domestic fiber of the country will continue to lead to similar recalcula-
tions at home.

If the United States is a superpower, which cannot be denied, it can
demonstrate such status only as a result of the closest bond between its
leadership and its people, and only if the leadership faithfully responds
to aspirations and values genuinely held within the people. American
leadership, in possession of great power after World War II and intent
on building a world order co-equal with its perceptions of American
values, provoked frightening ideological hostility within the people in
order to mobilize them into continuing action and involvement in
world affairs. The blind hostility of ideological anti-communism among
the American people ended by controlling the reason and actions of
those who had inspired it. It eventually trapped them into sustaining a
stalemate in Indochina which nearly destroyed the country at home,
and which the people themselves were ultimately able to break only at
great risk and peril to the fundamental institutions of the republic.

The main lesson of Vietnam lies at home. Vietnam led directly to
Watergate and to the severest constitutional crisis in U.S. history since
the Civil War. The United States was and remains a relatively hetero-
geneous grouping of diverse peoples and interests who have not yet
forged a genuine bond of people to land. The "rules of rule" under
which the United States governs itself remain the paramount element,
the essential cement, by which the United States can survive. These
rules demand a sharing of power between the executive and the legislative in foreign affairs, the continued subordination of the military arm
to responsible civil authority, an emphasis on the moral values of the
Bill of Rights, and most important, the harnessing of all foreign policy
to the central purpose of reinforcing the domestic homogeneity and
social cohesion of the United States.

There have been many changes since the beginning of the high cold
war. Initially conservative and preservative despite U.S. misperceptions,
Soviet policy, which later showed itself aggressive and truculent, has
again reverted to a largely preservative mode. It appears today to be
most concerned with what should also most concern the United States:
the preservation of its threatened domestic structure from internal challenges. Nuclear parity has emerged and from this fact it can be reasonably safely inferred that nuclear weapons will not be used in a
confrontation of the superpowers, provided their respective leaders remain rational men—a premise which must be accepted if any projec-

tions are to be made at all. The world has also witnessed the breakup of monolithic world blocs, the rise of the People's Republic of China, and the continuing trend toward multipolarity and polycentrism. In the second phase of its superpowerdom, which began after Vietnam, the United States is neither unchallenged nor supreme, nor is it the focus of all attention, nor does it need to focus its own attention on every single issue arising anywhere in the world.

We can tentatively discern four emerging trends in world politics to which it will be the task of American foreign policy to adapt slowly and prudently over the next two decades. [38] The first of these is a worldwide process of fragmentation, demonstrated in the assertion of an ever-increasing number of smaller and smaller units seeking recognition of their identity and legitimation of their authority as new decision-making centers. While predominantly national-ethnic in character, such units also include other groups seeking identity recognition. Contrary to the dreams and hopes of federalists and integrationists, the world in its currently high phase of transnational business and functional activity is not drawing closer together but, in terms of politics, pulling further apart. The process of fragmentation involves virtually all states, in their domestic structures as well as in their international relations. It is a problem which will tax the imagination of future generations of policy-makers throughout the globe.

Second, global managerialism by leaders of multinationals whose strongly developed effective motivational and recreational sets determine their incessant quest for adventure, profit and action challenges the traditional authority structures of states in all world areas. It will not be easy over the next twenty years to accommodate the power and ruthlessness of multinational corporations to the requirements of traditional state units. This will demand new solutions and new forms of diplomacy on the part of the United States as of all other major powers.

Third, the world will face continued global irresolution by governments in the face of mounting transnational problems of the greatest difficulty. There are as yet no obvious solutions on the horizon for such complex issues as international monetary and financial relationships, the development of poor countries, technology and population transfers, competitive trade and investment policies by the advanced industrial states, energy-producing resources, availability and distribution of other scarce resources, environment, population control, and Law of the Seas.

Finally, the United States and other major powers will continue to face both at home and abroad the reassertion of the type of terrorism, symbolic violence, and low-level warfare which is symptomatic of pop-ular anomie and the rebellion of youth in all ages of transition from one historic period to another. It accompanied the ushering in of the age of industrialism as it now attends the dawn of the post-industrial age.

Prudent, wise, cautious, and restrained maneuver in foreign policy is the order of the day under these circumstances. The theory of inter-linked worldwide credibility of U.S. power and commitments will have even less meaning in such a world than it did earlier, when its quixotic pursuit led the United States into Vietnam. Ideological crusades will appear similarly meaningless. The pile-on of armaments, nuclear or otherwise, will mean very little to most people in the world—other than those whose livelihood depends directly on the continued production of such weapons.

As previous U.S. commitments sink slowly into the limbo for which they are probably destined, the U.S. executive in consultation with Congress should seek to cast U.S. foreign policy in a mold which will allow the option of selective engagement. Before any intervention on the part of the United States, the American people must be fully con-vinced of its judiciousness. The means in any such interventions should be almost solely diplomatic. U.S. arms, whose effectiveness will depend entirely on the uncertain will of the young to employ them, should be reserved only for last-resort instances of necessary and legitimate self-defense.

The U.S. should avoid precipitous involvements in deep-seated and localized conflicts abroad which are largely incomprehensible to the people, and eschew automatic responses of engagement premised on Manichean outlooks or false premises of international interlinkage. Whatever its errors of style, the Carter administration has succeeded in greatly diminishing fears abroad of an imperious, self-willed, misper-ceiving America, rushing headlong into fires it cannot then extinguish. Carter's policies have confirmed long-held beliefs among many Euro-peans for example, that the true character of America was not repre-sented by its leaders during the heydays of its superpowerdom. This has consequently enhanced a desirable intent on the part of other powers to do more to promote their own security and welfare, if the United States will only let them.

Inevitably, waiting in the wings, there will always be forces of reac-tion, imperialism, militarism, and ideological hatred, which will depict such policies as isolationist, weak, vacillating or incompatible with the responsibilities of power. The macho phenomenon is still very much present. Easy answers, never to be trusted, will always suggest themselves in the exciting and sometimes malevolent prose of columnists inspired by special-interest groups. Nonetheless, a president who avoids the snakepits and who permits himself to look indecisive while avoiding such potential errors as intervention in Africa, Latin America, or for that matter (except diplomatically) in the Persian Gulf, will rank higher in history, if he keeps the bond with the people's values and their trust, than those of his predecessors who showed their alleged decisiveness by taking the United States into and keeping it in the snakepit of Vietnam.

The national interest of the United States has little to do with arranging regions of the world in some frozen geopolitical pattern, founded on the armed means of the last great war that the United States or others fought. It has everything to do instead with domestic values and with accurate perceptions reflecting them; with a view of security as absence of fear; with the use of analysis and diplomacy as means of adaptation in a rapidly changing world of ever-fluctuating values; with the understanding of the inseparability of foreign policy from domestic policies.

If Americans correctly understand these fundamentals, they may hope that the future will spare them a repetition of the trauma that was Vietnam in the foreign policy of the United States.

Notes

1. *See* Chapter VI, Section 1.
2. This is substantially the argument made by Guenter Lewy in his *America in Vietnam.*
3. Portions of the immediately following passages are adapted from my "Moral Dilemmas in U.S. Human Rights Policy," Chapter 1 in Natalie Hevener, ed., *The Dynamics of Human Rights in United States Foreign Policy* (New Brunswick, N.J.: Transaction Books, 1980). I hereby gratefully acknowledge the publisher's and the editor's willingness to let me adapt *in extenso.*
4. The term reification signifies that one infuses an abstract concept with the characteristics of a concrete object or living organism. For example, though we speak of government as existing concretely, it cannot in reality be separated from the people who constitute the government.
5. James Thomson, "How Could Vietnam Happen? An Autopsy," *Atlantic Monthly* (April 1968): 47–53.
6. Irving L. Horowitz, *Ideology and Utopia in the United States 1956–1976* (New York: Oxford University Press, 1977), p. 279.
7. *See* Chapter III, Section 1.
8. The text of this reservation, which is mentioned in Chapter II, Section 2, can be found in *Pentagon Papers*, 1, p. 570 (Document 93). Note that the United States not only declared that it would refrain from the threat or

use of force to disturb the agreements, but also that "it would view any renewal of the aggression . . . with grave concern and as seriously threatening to international peace and security."

9. See Chapter II, Section 3.

10. Guenter Lewy, *America.*

11. For an example of views accusing the United States of genocide in Vietnam, see Noam Chomsky, "The Remaking of History," *Ramparts Magazine,* July 1975 (reprinted as *Lessons of Vietnam #1,* Phila, Pa.: Indochina Program, American Friends Service Committee).

12. As the writer observed first hand when he flew over Eastern Cambodia in small observation aircraft in June 1974. On the effects of the war on Cambodia, see William Shawcross, *Sideshow: Kissinger, Nixon and the Destruction of Cambodia* (New York: Simon and Schuster, 1979).

13. Casualty figures supplied by Pentagon Information Office, *see* source cited immediately below. Of the total of 6,727,084 tons of bombs dropped by the U.S. over Indochina (according to the Indochina Resources Center from statistics originally supplied by Department of Defense to members of Congress), nearly 4,000,000 tons were dropped from January 1969 to January 1973 (U.S. Congress, "Indochina War Statistics," *Congressional Record,* May 14, 1975, p. S8155), double the amount the United States dropped on all enemies in World War II. This takes no account of the some 6 million tons of artillery shells expended by the United States in Indochina in 1965–72, or of the even larger quantity of artillery exploded by the ARVN from 1961 on. See Daniel Ellsberg, *Papers on the War,* p. 241, fn. 3.

14. On the confused subject of statements of U.S. post-withdrawal intentions allegedly made by President Nixon and Secretary Kissinger to President Thieu in connection with his assent to the Paris Peace Accords of January 1973, see Tad Szulc, "Behind the Vietnam Cease-Fire Agreement," *Foreign Policy* 15 (Summer 1974): pp. 21–69; also Frank Snepp, *Decent Interval* (New York: Random House Vintage, 1978).

15. See in particular Chapters IV, Decisions 7, 9, 10 and Chapter VII, Section 1.

16. The 1968 Gallup Poll showed fifty-six percent of respondents approving a policy of gradual withdrawal from Vietnam (Gallup, *Poll,* 1972, p. 2115); in 1969, a total of eighty-one percent favored either immediate or gradual withdrawal *(ibid,* p. 2232); in 1970, the percentage favoring withdrawal had risen to eighty-four percent *(ibid.,* p. 2240); in 1971, seventy-eight percent of those 18–21 years of age and sixty-six percent of those over 21 years of age favored withdrawal by the end of that year *(ibid.,* p. 2301). The 1971 Harris Survey showed sixty-one percent of respondents in favor of U.S. withdrawal by the end of that year; and in 1972, seventy-six percent favored bringing home all U.S. troops immediately (Harris, *Survey,* 1975, pp. 120, 180).

17. The key provision of the Paris Accords of January 1973 gave the National Liberation Front (Viet Cong) a voice and role in the formation of a new South Vietnamese government; this provision, which the United States had been unwilling to accept in earlier years, had always remained the irreducible heart of Vietnamese Communist demands. *See* Porter, *Peace Denied.* Text of the so-called Paris Peace Accords can be found in DOS *Bulletin* 68 (February 12, 1973): pp. 169–88.

18. Snepp, *Decent Interval*.
19. Porter, *Peace Denied*.
20. *See* Chapter II, Section 2.
21. For example, the Saigon lawyer Tran van Tuyen, who courageously remained his own master and is today paying for his independence through a prolonged sojourn in Communist re-education camps.
22. The expression "decent interval" was recurrently used by Henry Kissinger during the period of his 1969-72 negotiations with the Vietnamese Communist representative Le Duc Tho and can be attributed to him. *See,* inter alia, Snepp, *Decent Interval;* Ellsberg, *Papers on the War*.
23. For example, Ellsberg, "The Responsibility of Officials in a Criminal War," in *Papers on the War,* pp. 275 ff.
24. However, *see* Telford Taylor, *Nuremberg and Vietnam: An American Tragedy* (New York: Bantam Books, 1971)..
25. As argued by Chomsky and others, *see* Note 11.
26. However, review the arguments in Taylor, *Nuremberg and Vietnam;* Richard Falk, Gabriel Kolko, and Robert Lifton, *Crimes of War: After Songmy* (New York: Random House Vintage, 1971); and Richard Falk, *The Six Legal Dimensions of the Vietnam War* (Princeton, N.J.: Center of International Studies, 1968).
27. *See* Wolfers, *Discord,* particularly Chapter 10, "National Security As An Ambiguous Symbol."
28. *See* Chapter II, Section 1.
29. Willis, *France, Germany,* p. 320.
30. *See* Chapter V, Section 3.
31. *See* Figure 1, Chapter V, Section 3.
32. For example, the prescient article by Hans Morgenthau, "We Are Deluding Ourselves in Vietnam," *The New York Times Magazine* (April 18, 1965). This article was appropriately subtitled: "The Only Way Out of Vietnam Is Out."
33. *See* Chapter III, Section 1.
34. As we stressed earlier in the present chapter.
35. Paul Kattenburg, "Détente, Security and the Social Sciences," *Social Science* 51 (Winter 1976): pp. 12-13.
36. For an illuminating discussion of the uses of history by statesmen, and an attempt to show how history could be used prescriptively, *see* Ernest May, *Lessons of the Past: The Use and Misuse of History in American Policy* (New York: Oxford University Press, 1973, 1975).
37. H. Stuart Hughes, "The Cold War and Detente," *New York Review of Books* (Feb. 19, 1976): pp. 3-6.
38. Paul Kattenburg, *Observations on Some Forces of Change in the Contemporary World*, Essay Series No. 8 (Columbia, S.C.: University of South Carolina, Institute of International Studies, Spring 1978).

Bibliography

Public Documents

The Pentagon Papers: The Defense Department History of U.S. Decision-Making on Vietnam, Senator Gravel Edition volumes 1–4. (Boston: Beacon Press, 1971).

U.S. Congress. *Congressional Quarterly Almanac.* (Washington, D.C.: U.S.G.P.O., 1970, 1971, 1972, 1973, 1974, 1975).

U.S. Congress, House. Committee on Foreign Affairs. Hearings on Termination of Hostilities in Indochina. 92d Cong., 2d SESS., May 16, 18, 23 and June 1, 1972 (Washington, D.C.: U.S.G.P.O., 1972).

U.S. Congress, House. Committee on International Relations. Seizure of the Mayaguez, Hearings Before Subcommittee on International Political and Military Affairs. 94th Cong., 1st sess. (Washington, D.C.: U.S.G.P.O., 1975–76).

U.S. Congress, House. Select Committee On Missing Persons in Southeast Asia. Final Report, HR 1764: Americans Missing in Southeast Asia. 94th Cong., 2d sess. (Washington, D.C;: U.S.G.P.O., December 13, 1976).

U.S. Congress, House. Subcommittee on National Security Policy of House Committee on Foreign Affairs. Hearings on War Powers. 93d Cong., 1st sess., (Washington, D.C.: U.S.G.P.O., 1973).

U.S. Congress, Senate. Committee on Foreign Relations. *Background Information Relating to Southeast Asia and Vietnam* 6th rev. ed. (Washington, D.C.: U.S.G.P.O., June 1970).

U.S. Congress, Senate. Committee on Foreign Relations. U.S. Involvement in the Overthrow of Diem, 1963. Staff Study Based on the Pentagon Papers. (Washington, D.C.: U.S.G.P.O., July 20, 1972).

U.S. Congress, Senate. Committee on Foreign Relations. Hearings on SR 151, U.S. Commitments to Foreign Powers. 90th Cong., 1st sess. (Washington, D.C.: U.S.G.P.O., 1967).

U.S. Congress, Senate. Committee on Foreign Relations. Hearings on Moral and Military Aspects of the War in Southeast Asia, May 7 and 12, 1970, (Washington, D.C.: U.S.G.P.O., 1970).

U.S. Congress, Senate. Committee on Foreign Relations. Hearings Before Subcommittee on U.S. Security Agreements and Commitments Abroad, Broader Aspects of U.S. Commitments, 91 Cong., 2nd sess., (Washington, D.C.: U.S.G.P.O., November 24, 1970).

U.S. Congress, Senate. Committee on the Judiciary. Aftermath of War: Humanitarian Problems of Southeast Asia. Staff Report for Subcommittee to Investigate Problems Connected with Refugees and Escapees, 94th Cong., 2d sess. (Washington, D.C.: U.S.G.P.O., May 17, 1976).

U.S. Congress, Senate. "Indochina War Statistics: Dollars and Deaths," *Congressional Record* 94th Cong., 1st sess., vol. 121, no. 77 (May 14, 1975): S8152–56.

U.S. Congress, Senate and House. *Congressional Record,* vols. 115, 116, 117, 118 (1969–72).

U.S. Department of State. U.S. Participation in the U.N.: Report by the President to Congress for 1957. Released June 19, 1958.

U.S. Department of State. *Department of State Bulletin,* Selected and referenced volumes for 1945–75.

U.S. Department of State. A Threat to the Peace: North Vietnam's Effort to Conquer South Vietnam. Publication 7308, Far Eastern Series 110, July 1962.

U.S. Department of State. Aggression From the North: The Record of North Vietnam's Campaign to Conquer South Vietnam. Publication 7339, February 1965.

Articles and Papers

Alsop, Stewart. "Our New Strategy: The Alternatives to Total War." *Saturday Evening Post,* December 1, 1962, pp. 13–19.

Arendt, Hannah. "Lying in Politics: Reflections on the Pentagon Papers." Paper prepared for a Conference of the Council on Religion and International Affairs, Washington, D.C., October 1971. (Not available to the writer in published form.)

Bennett, Charles. "The Mayaguez Re-examined: Misperception in an Information Shortage." *Fletcher Forum* 1 (Fall 1976): pp. 15–31.

Broadbridge, Seymour and Collick, Martin. "Japan's International Policies: Political and Economic Motivations." *International Affairs* 44 (April 1968): pp. 240–53.

Chomsky, Noam. "The Remaking of History." *Ramparts Magazine,* July 1975. (Reprinted as *Lessons of Vietnam #1,* Philadelphia: Indochina Program, American Friends Service Committee, 1975).

Chomsky, Noam. "Vietnam, The Cold War and Other Matters." *Commentary* 48 (1969): pp. 12–26.

Dulles, John. "Principles in Foreign Policy." *Department of State Bulletin* 826 (April 25, 1955): p. 671.

Dulles, John. "The Peace We Seek." *Department of State Bulletin* 813 (January 24, 1955): pp. 123–25.

Gelb, Leslie. "The Essential Domino: American Politics and Vietnam." *Foreign Affairs* 50 (April 1972): pp. 459–75.

George, Alexander. "The Case for Multiple Advocacy in Making Foreign Policy." *American Political Science Review* 66 (September 1972): pp. 751–95.

Hammer, Ellen. "Perspective on Vietnam." (Review Article) *Problems of Communism* 25 (January 1976) pp. 81–84.

Hughes, H. Stuart. "The Cold War and Detente." *New York Review of Books,* February 19, 1976: pp. 3–6.

Kahin, George. "The Pentagon Papers: A Critical Evaluation." *American Political Science Review* 69 (June 1975): pp. 675–84.

Kattenburg, Paul. "Vietnam and U.S. Diplomacy, 1940–1970." *Orbis* 15 (Fall 1971): pp. 818–841.

Kattenburg, Paul. "Obstacles to Political Community: Southeast Asia in Comparative Perspective." *Southeast Asia Quarterly* 2 (Spring 1973): pp. 193–209.

Kattenburg, Paul. "Detente, Security, and the Social Sciences." *Social Science* 51 (Winter 1976): pp. 10–15.

Kattenburg, Paul. "Observations on Some Forces of Change in the Contemporary World." Essay Series 8, Institute of International Studies, University of South Carolina, Columbia, S.C. (Spring 1978).

Kennan, George, et. al. "Mr. X Revisited." *Foreign Policy* 7 (Summer 1972): pp. 5–53.

Khanh, Huynh. "The Vietnamese August Revolution Reinterpreted." *Journal of Asian Studies* 30 (August 1971): pp. 761–82.

Kissinger, Henry. "Domestic Structure and Foreign Policy." *Daedalus* 95 (Spring 1966): pp. 503–29.

Kobayashi, Teruo. "A Great Debate in Japan: The Fate of the U.S.–Japan Security Treaty in 1970." *Journal of Politics* 30 (August 1968): pp. 749–79.

Mackinder, Harold. "The Round World and the Winning of the Peace." *Foreign Affairs* 21 (July 1943): pp. 595–605.

Mendel, Douglas. "Japanese Opinion on Key Foreign Policy Issues." *Asian Survey* 9 (August 1969): pp. 625–39.

Morgenthau, Hans. "We Are Deluding Ourselves in Vietnam." *The New York Times Magazine,* April 18, 1965: pp. 25, 85 ff.

Northedge, F.S. "Britain As A Second-Rank Power." *International Affairs* 46 (January 1970): pp. 37–47.

Ravenal, Earl. "Consequences of the End-Game in Vietnam." *Foreign Affairs* 53 (July 1975): pp. 651–67.

Szulc, Tad. "Behind the Vietnam Cease-Fire Agreement." *Foreign Policy* 15 (Summer 1974): pp. 21–69.

Thomson, James. "How Could Vietnam Happen: An Autopsy." *Atlantic Monthly,* April 1968: pp. 47–53.

Walker, Steven. "The Interface Between Beliefs and Behavior: Henry Kissinger's Operational Code and the Vietnam War." *Journal of Conflict Resolution* 21 (March 1977): pp. 129–68.

Warner, Geoffrey. "The United States and the Fall of Diem, Part I." *Australian Outlook* 28 (December 1974): pp. 245–58.

Westerfield, H. Bradford. "What Use Are Three Versions of the Pentagon Papers?" *American Political Science Review* 69 (June 1975): pp. 685–96.

Books

Allison, Graham. *Essence of Decision: Explaining the Cuban Missile Crisis.* Boston: Little, Brown, 1971.

Almond, Gabriel and Coleman, James. *The Politics of the Developing Areas.* Princeton, N.J.: Princeton University Press, 1960.

Alperovitz, Gar. *Atomic Diplomacy: Hiroshima and Potsdam.* New York: Random House, 1965.

Arendt, Hannah. *On Revolution.* New York: Viking Press, 1963.

Aron, Raymond. *The Imperial Republic: The United States and the World, 1945–73.* Cambridge, Mass.: Winthrop, 1974.

Austin, Anthony. *The President's War: The Story of the Tonkin Gulf Resolution and How the Nation Was Trapped in Vietnam.* Philadelphia: Lippincott, 1971.

Barber, James. *The Presidential Character.* Englewood Cliffs, N.J.: Prentice-Hall, 1972.

Barnet, Richard and Müller, Ronald. *Global Reach.* New York: Simon and Schuster, 1975.

Barnet, Richard. *Intervention and Revolution.* New York: New American Library Mentor, 1972.

Barnet, Richard. *Roots of War.* New York: Atheneum, 1972.

Baskir, Lawrence and Strauss, William. *Chance and Circumstance: The Draft, The War, and the Vietnam Generation.* New York: Random House Vintage, 1978.

Bator, Victor. *Vietnam, A Diplomatic Tragedy: The Origins of the United States Involvement.* Dobbs Ferry, N.Y.: Oceana, 1965.

Bell, Daniel. *The End of Ideology: On the Exhaustion of Political Ideas in the Fifties.* New York: Free Press, 1962.

Bell, David. *Resistance and Revolution.* Boston: Houghton Mifflin, 1973.

Bienen, Henry. *Violence and Social Change.* Chicago: University of Chicago Press, 1968.

Blachman, Morris. "The Stupidity of Intelligence." In *Readings in American Foreign Policy,* ed. Morton Halperin and Arnold Kanter. Boston: Little, Brown, 1973.

Black, Cyril. *Communism and Revolution: The Strategic Uses of Political Violence.* Princeton, N.J.: Princeton University Press, 1961.

Braestrup, Peter. *Big Story: How the American Press and Television Reported and Interpreted the Crisis of Tet 1968 in Vietnam and Washington.* Boulder, Colo: Westview Press, 1977.

Brandon, Henry. *Anatomy of Error: The Inside Story of the Asian War on the Potomac, 1954–69.* Boston: Gambit, 1969.

Bryan, C.D.B. *Friendly Fire.* New York: G.P. Putnam, 1976.

Buttinger, Joseph. *The Smaller Dragon: A Political History of Vietnam.* New York: Praeger, 1958.

Buttinger Joseph. *Vietnam: A Dragon Embattled.* 2 vols. New York: Praeger, 1967.

Buttinger, Joseph. *Vietnam: The Unforgettable Tragedy.* New York: Horizon Press, 1977.

Cady, John. *History of Postwar Southeast Asia.* Athens, Ohio: Ohio University Press, 1974.

Cantrill, Albert. *The American People, Vietnam, and the Presidency.* Princeton, N.J.: Princeton University Press, 1970.

Carr, E.H. *The Twenty Years Crisis.* London: Macmillan, 1946.

Chen, King. *Vietnam and China, 1938–54*. Princeton, N.J.: Princeton University Press, 1969.

Chomsky, Noam. *At War With Asia*. New York: Pantheon, 1970.

Chomsky, Noam. *For Reasons of State*. New York: Pantheon, 1973.

Clarke, Douglas. *The Missing Man: Politics and the M.I.A.* Washington, D.C.: National Defense University Research Directorate, U.S.G.P.O., January 1979.

Colbert, Evelyn. *Southeast Asia in International Politics, 1941–56*. Ithaca, N.Y.: Cornell University Press, 1977.

Cooper, Chester. *The Lost Crusade: America in Vietnam*. New York: Dodd Mead, 1970.

Cressey, George. *Asia's Lands and Peoples*. New York: McGraw Hill, 1951.

Dallin, Alexander. *German Rule in Russia, 1941–45: A Study of Occupation Politics*. London: Macmillan, 1957.

Dallin, David. *Soviet Foreign Policy After Stalin*. New York: J.P. Lippincott, 1961.

Deere, R.P. "Japan's Place in the World." In *Japan in Current World Affairs*, ed. Marinosuke Kajima, pp. 293–306. Tokyo: Institute of International Peace and Japan Times Ltd., 1971.

De Gaulle, Charles. *Memoires de Guerre*. 3 vols. Paris: Plon, 1959.

De Gaulle, Charles. *Memoirs of Hope: Renewal and Endeavor*. New York: Simon and Schuster, 1971.

Devillers, Philippe. *Histoire du Vietnam: de 1940 à 1952*. Paris: Editions du Seuil, 1952.

Dickson, Paul. *Think Tanks*. New York: Atheneum, 1971.

Dobell, Peter. *Canada's Search for New Roles: Foreign Policy in the Trudeau Era*. London: Oxford University Press, 1972.

Dommen, Arthur. *Conflict in Laos: The Politics of Neutralization*. New York: Praeger, 1964.

Draper, Theodore. *Abuse of Power*. New York: Viking Press, 1967.

Duncanson, Dennis. *Government and Revolution in Vietnam*. London: Oxford University Press, 1968.

Eckstein, Harry, ed. *Internal War: Problems and Approaches*. New York: Free Press, 1966.

Ellsberg, Daniel. *Papers On The War*. New York: Simon and Schuster, 1972.

Emerson, Gloria. *Winners and Losers: Battles, Retreats, Gains, Losses, and Ruins From A Long War*. New York: Random House, 1976.

Falk, Richard. *The Six Legal Dimensions of the Vietnam War*. Princeton, N.J.: Center of International Studies, Princeton University, 1968.

Falk, Richard; Kolko, Gabriel; and Lifton, Robert, eds. *Crimes of War: After Songmy*. New York: Random House Vintage, 1971.

Fall, Bernard. *Hell in a Very Small Place: The Siege of Dien Bien Phu*. Philadelphia: Lippincott, 1966.

Fall, Bernard. *Last Reflections on a War*. Garden City, N.Y.: Doubleday, 1967.

Fall, Bernard. *Street Without Joy: Indochina At War 1946–54*. Harrisburg, Pa.: Stackpole, 1961, 1963.

Fall, Bernard. *The Two Vietnams: A Political and Military Analysis*. New York: Praeger, 1967 (2d ed.).

Fall, Bernard. *The Viet Minh Regime: Government and Administration in the*

Democratic Republic of Vietnam. Ithaca, N.Y.: Cornell University Press, 1954.

Fall, Bernard. *Vietnam Witness 1953–66.* London: Pall Mall Press, 1966.

Fall, Bernard and Raskin, Marcus, eds. *The Vietnam Reader.* New York: Vintage, 1965.

Fishel, Wesley, ed. *Vietnam: Anatomy of a Conflict.* Itasca, Ill.: F.E. Peacock, 1968.

Fisher, George. *Soviet Opposition to Stalin.* Cambridge, Mass.: Harvard University Press, 1952.

Fitzgerald, Frances. *Fire In The Lake: The Vietnamese and the Americans in Vietnam.* Boston: Little, Brown, 1972.

Fulbright, J. William. *The Arrogance of Power.* New York: Random House Vintage, 1967.

Furniss, Edgar and Snyder, Richard. *An Introduction to American Foreign Policy.* New York: Rinehart, 1955.

Gaddis, John. *The U.S. and The Origins of the Cold War, 1941–47.* New York: Columbia University Press, 1972.

Gallucci, Robert. *Neither Peace Nor Honor: The Politics of American Military Policy in Vietnam.* Baltimore: Johns Hopkins University Press, 1975.

Gallup, George. *The Gallup Poll: Public Opinion 1935–71.* Vol. 3. New York: Random House, 1972.

Gallup, George. *The Gallup Poll: Public Opinion 1972–77.* Vol. 1. Wilmington, Del.: Scholarly Resources Inc., 1978.

Gati, Charles, ed. *Caging The Bear: Containment and the Cold War.* Indianapolis, Ind.: Bobbs-Merrill, 1974.

Gavin, James. *Crisis Now.* New York: Random House, 1968.

Gelb, Leslie and Betts, Richard. *The Irony of Vietnam: The System Worked.* Washington, D.C.: Brookings, 1979.

George, Alexander et al. *The Limits of Coercive Diplomacy: Laos, Cuba, Vietnam.* Boston: Little, Brown, 1971.

George, Alexander and Smoke, Richard. *Deterrence in American Foreign Policy: Theory and Practice.* New York: Columbia University Press, 1974.

Giap, Vo Nguyen. *People's War, People's Army: The Viet Cong Insurrection Manual for Underdeveloped Countries.* New York: Praeger, 1962.

Goulden, Joseph. *Truth Is The First Casualty: The Gulf of Tonkin Affair.* Chicago: Rand McNally, 1969.

Gurtov, Melvin. *The First Vietnam Crisis.* New York: Columbia University Press, 1967.

Gurtov, Melvin. *The U.S. Against The Third World: Antinationalism and Intervention.* New York: Praeger, 1974.

Halberstam, David. *The Best and the Brightest.* Greenwich, Conn.: Fawcett Crest, 1972; New York: Random House, 1972.

Halberstam, David. *The Making of A Quagmire.* New York: Random House, 1965.

Halperin, Morton. *Bureaucratic Politics and Foreign Policy.* Washington, D.C.: Brookings, 1974.

Hammer, Ellen. *The Struggle for Indochina.* Stanford, Calif.: Stanford University Press, 1954.

Hammer, Richard. *One Morning in the War: The Tragedy of Son My.* New York: Coward–McCann, 1970.

Hargrove, Erwin. *The Powers of the Modern Presidency.* Philadelphia: Temple University Press, 1974.

Harper, Alan. *The Politics of Loyalty: The White House and the Communist Issue, 1946–52.* Westport, Conn.: Greenwood, 1969.

Harris, Louis and assoc. *The Harris Survey Yearbook of Public Opinion.* Volumes for 1971 and 1973. New York: Louis Harris and Associates, 1975, 1976.

Heath, G. Louis. *Mutiny Does Not Happen Lightly: The Literature of American Resistance to the Vietnam War.* Metuchen, N.J.: Scarecrow Press, 1976.

Herr, Michael. *Dispatches.* New York: Knopf, 1977.

Hersh, Seymour. *My Lai 4: Report on the Massacre and Its Aftermath.* New York: Random House, 1970.

Herz, Martin, ed. *Decline of the West? George Kennan and His Critics.* Washington, D.C.: Ethics and Public Policy Center, Georgetown University, 1978.

Hiller, Dean and David. *John Foster Dulles: Soldier for Peace.* New York: Holt, Rinehart and Winston, 1960.

Hilsman, Roger. *To Move A Nation: The Politics of Foreign Policy in the Administration of John F. Kennedy.* New York: Doubleday, 1967.

Holt, Pat. *The War Powers Resolution: The Role of Congress in U.S. Armed Intervention.* Washington, D.C.: American Enterprise Institute for Public Policy Research, 1968.

Hoopes, Townsend. *The Devil and John Foster Dulles.* Boston: Little, Brown, 1973.

Hoopes, Townsend. *The Limits of Intervention.* New York: David McKay, 1969.

Horowitz, Irving, ed. *The Use and Abuse of Socal Science: Behavioral Research and Policy-Making.* 2d ed. New Brunswick, N.J.: Transaction Books, 1975.

Horowitz, Irving. *Ideology and Utopia in the United States, 1956–1976.* New York: Oxford Univ. Press, 1977.

Huntington, Samuel. *Political Order in Changing Societies.* New Haven, Conn.: Yale University Press, 1968.

Janis, Irving. *Victims of Groupthink.* Boston: Houghton Mifflin, 1972.

Johnson, Chalmers. *Revolutionary Change.* Boston: Little, Brown, 1966.

Johnson, Lyndon Baines. *The Vantage Point: Perspectives of the Presidency, 1963–1969.* New York: Holt, Rinehart and Winston, 1971.

Kahin, George and Lewis, John. *The United States in Vietnam.* New York: Dell, 1969.

Kalb, Marvin and Bernard. *Kissinger.* New York: Dell, 1974.

Kattenburg, Paul. "Moral Dilemmas in U.S. Human Rights Policy." In *The Dynamics of Human Rights in United States Foreign Policy,* ed. Natalie Hevener. New Brunswick, N.J.: Transaction Books, 1980.

Kearns, Doris. *Lyndon Johnson and the American Dream.* New York: Harper & Row, 1976.

Kieffer, John. *Realities of World Power.* New York: David McKay, 1952.

Kinnard, Douglas. *The War Managers.* Hannover, N.H.: University Press of New England, 1977.

Kissinger, Henry. *American Foreign Policy: Three Essays.* New York: Norton, 1969, 1972.

Kissinger, Henry. *The Necessity of Choice: Prospects of American Foreign Policy.* New York: Harper, 1961.

Korb, Lawrence. *The Joint Chiefs of Staff: The First Twenty-Five Years.* Bloomington, Ind.: Indiana University Press, 1976.

Kraslow, David and Loory, Stuart. *The Secret Search for Peace in Vietnam.* New York: Random House Vintage, 1968.

Kreml, William. *The Anti-Authoritarian Personality.* Oxford: Pergammon Press, 1977.

Lacouture, Jean and Devillers, Philippe. *La Fin d'une Guerre: Indochine 1954.* Paris: Editions du Seuil, 1960.

Ladejinsky, Wolf. "Agrarian Reform in the Republic of Vietnam." In *Vietnam: Anatomy of a Conflict,* ed. Wesley Fishel, pp. 517–38. Itasca, Ill.: F.E. Peacock, 1968.

LaFeber, Walter. *America, Russia and the Cold War, 1945–71.* New York: Wiley and Sons, 1972.

Lake, Anthony, ed. *The Vietnam Legacy: The War, American Society, and the Future of American Foreign Policy.* New York: New York University Press, 1976.

Lancaster, Donald. *The Emancipation of French Indochina.* New York: Oxford University Press, 1961.

Landon, Kenneth. *Southeast Asia: Crossroads of Religions.* Chicago: University of Chicago Press, 1949.

Latham, Earl. *The Communist Controversy in Washington: From the New Deal to McCarthy.* Cambridge, Mass.: Harvard University Press, 1966.

Latham, Earl, ed. *The Meaning of McCarthyism.* Boston: D.C. Heath, 1965.

Leach, Richard, ed. *Contemporary Canada.* Durham, N.C.: Duke University Press, 1967.

Lentner, Howard. *Foreign Policy Analysis.* Columbus, Ohio: Chs. Merrill, 1974.

Lewy, Guenter. *America in Vietnam.* New York: Oxford University Press, 1978.

Lord, Donald. *John F. Kennedy: The Politics of Confrontation and Conciliation.* New York: Barron's Educational Series, 1977.

Maxwell, Neville. *India's China War.* New York: Pantheon Books, 1970.

May, Ernest. *Lessons of the Past: The Use and Misuse of History in American Policy.* New York: Oxford University Press, 1973.

McAlister, John and Mus, Paul. *The Vietnamese and Their Revolution.* New York: Harper and Row, 1970.

Mecklin, John. *Mission in Torment.* New York: Doubleday, 1965.

Millet, Allan, ed. *A Short History of the Vietnam War.* Bloomington, Ind.: Indiana University Press, 1978.

Millis, Walter, ed. *The Forrestall Diaries.* New York: Viking Press, 1951.

Montgomery, John. *The Politics of Foreign Aid: American Experience in Southeast Asia.* New York: Praeger, 1962.

Morgenthau, Hans. *A New Foreign Policy for the United States.* New York: Praeger, 1969.

Morgenthau, Hans. *Politics Among Nations: The Struggle for Power and Peace.* New York: Knopf, 1967. (rev. ed.)

Morris, Bernard. "Communist Strategy in India and Southeast Asia." In *Political Change in Underdeveloped Countries: Nationalism and Communism,* ed. John Kautsky. New York: Wiley and Sons, 1962, pp. 293–303.

Nixon, Richard. *The Memoirs of Richard Nixon.* New York: Grosset and Dunlap, 1978.

Oberdorfer, Don. *Tet!* New York: Doubleday, 1971.

O'Donnell, Kenneth and Powers, David. *Johnny, We Hardly Knew Ye: Memories of John Fitzgerald Kennedy.* Boston, Mass.: Little, Brown, 1973.

Osanka, F.M., ed. *Modern Guerrilla Warfare.* New York: Free Press, 1962.

Osgood, Robert. *Ideals and Self-Interest in America's Foreign Relations.* Chicago: University of Chicago Press, 1953.

Pettit, Clyde. *The Experts.* Secaucus, N.J.: Lyle Stuart, 1975.

Pfeffer, Richard, ed. *No More Vietnams? The War and the Future of American Foreign Policy.* New York: Harper and Row, 1968.

Phillips, Cabell. *The Truman Presidency: The History of A Triumphant Succession.* New York: Macmillan, 1966.

Poole, Peter. *The United States and Indochina From F.D.R. to Nixon.* Hinsdale, Ill.: Dryden Press, 1973.

Porter, Gareth. *A Peace Denied: The United States, Vietnam, and the Paris Agreements.* Bloomington, Ind.: Indiana University Press, 1975.

Race, Jeffrey. *War Comes to Long An: Revolutionary Conflict in a Vietnamese Province.* Berkeley, Calif.: University of California Press, 1972.

Randle, F. *Geneva 1954: The Settlement of the Indochina War.* Princeton, N.J.: Princeton University Press, 1969.

Ransom, Harry. *The Intelligence Establishment.* Cambridge, Mass.: Harvard University Press, 1970.

Ravenal, Earl. *Never Again: Learning From America's Foreign Policy Failures.* Philadelphia: Temple University Press, 1978.

Reedy, George. *The Twilight of the Presidency.* New York: New American Library, 1971.

Roherty, James. *Decisions of Robert S. McNamara: A Study of the Role of the Secretary of Defense.* Coral Gables, Fla: University of Miami Press, 1970.

Rosenau, James. *The Adaptation of National Societies.* New York: McCaleb-Seiler, 1970.

Rosenau, James. *The Scientific Study of Foreign Policy.* New York: Free Press, 1971.

Rostow, Eugene. *Peace In The Balance: The Future of American Foreign Policy.* New York: Simon and Schuster, 1972.

Rostow, Walt. "Guerrilla Warfare in Underdeveloped Areas." In *The Guerrilla and How To Fight Him,* ed. Lt. Col. T.N. Greene, pp. 54–61. New York: Praeger, 1962.

Rostow, Walt. *The Stages of Economic Growth: A Non-Communist Manifesto.* Cambridge, Mass.: Harvard University Press, 1960, 1971.

Rostow, Walt. *The United States in the World Arena: An Essay in Recent History.* New York: Harper, 1960.

Rowan, Ray. *The Four Days of Mayaguez.* New York: Norton, 1975.

Rubinstein, Alvin, ed. *The Foreign Policy of the Soviet Union.* New York: Random House, 1966.

Sacks, Milton. "Marxism in Vietnam." In *Marxism in Southeast Asia,* ed. Frank Traeger, Stanford, Calif.: Stanford University Press, 1959.

Schandler, Herbert. *The Unmaking of a President: Lyndon Johnson and Vietnam.* Princeton, N.J.: Princeton University Press, 1977.

Schell, Jonathan. *The Time of Illusion.* New York: Random House Vintage, 1975.

Schell, Jonathan. *The Village of Ben Suc.* New York: Random House Vintage, 1967.

Schlesinger, Arthur. *A Thousand Days.* Boston: Houghton Mifflin, 1965.

Schlesinger, Arthur. *The Bitter Heritage: Vietnam and American Democracy 1941-68.* New York: Houghton Mifflin, 1966.

Schoenbrun, David. *Vietnam: How We Got In, How To Get Out.* New York: Atheneum, 1968.

Shaplen, Robert. *A Forest of Tigers.* New York: Knopf, 1956.

Shaplen, Robert. *The Lost Revolution.* New York: Harper and Row, 1955, 1965.

Sharp, Ulysses. *Strategy for Defeat: Vietnam in Retrospect.* San Rafael, Calif.: Presidio Press, 1978.

Shawcross, William. *Sideshow: Kissinger, Nixon, and the Destruction of Cambodia.* New York: Simon and Schuster, 1979.

Sheehan, Neil et. al. *The Pentagon Papers: The Secret History of the Vietnam War As Published by the New York Times.* New York: New York Times Co. (Bantam), 1971.

Simmons, Robert. "The Communist Side: An Exploratory Sketch." In *The Korean War: A Twenty-five Year Perspective,* ed. Francis Heller, pp. 197–208. Lawrence, Kansas: The Regents Press of Kansas, 1977.

Simmons, Robert. *The Strained Alliance: Peking, Pyonyang, Moscow, and the Politics of the Korean Civil War.* New York: Free Press, 1975.

Slater, Jerome. *Intervention and Negotiation: The United States and the Dominican Revolution.* New York: Harper and Row, 1970.

Smith, Joseph B. *Portrait of a Cold Warrior.* New York: Putnam, 1976.

Snepp, Frank. *Decent Interval.* New York: Random House Vintage, 1978.

Sorenson, Theodore. *Kennedy.* New York: Harper and Row, 1965.

Spanier, John. *American Foreign Policy Since World War II.* 7th rev. ed. N.Y.: Praeger, 1977.

Stavins, Ralph; Barnet, Richard; and Raskin, Marcus. *Washington Plans an Aggressive War.* New York: Random House Vintage, 1971.

Stone, I.F. *In A Time of Torment.* New York: Random House, 1964, 1967.

Strausz-Hupe, Robert. *The Balance of Tomorrow: Power and Foreign Policy in the United States.* New York: G.P. Putnam's Sons, 1945.

Szulc, Tad. *The Illusion of Peace: Foreign Policy in the Nixon Years.* New York: Viking Press, 1978.

Tanham, George. *Communist Revolutionary Warfare: The Viet Minh in Indochina.* New York: Praeger, 1961.

Taylor, Jay. *China and Southeast Asia.* New York: Praeger, 1974, 1976.

Taylor, Maxwell. *Swords and Plowshares.* New York: Norton, 1972.

Taylor, Maxwell. *The Uncertain Trumpet.* New York: Harper, 1960.

Taylor, Telford. *Nuremberg and Vietnam: An American Tragedy.* New York: Bantam, 1971.

Thayer, Carlyle. "Southern Vietnamese Revolutionary Organization and the Vietnam Workers' Party: 1954-1974." In *Communism in Indochina: New Perspectives,* eds. Joseph Zasloff and MacAllister Brown, Lexington, Mass.: D.C. Heath, 1975.

Thompson, Robert. *Defeating Communist Insurgency: The Lessons of Malaya and Vietnam.* New York: Praeger, 1967.

Thompson, Robert. *No Exit From Vietnam.* New York: David McKay, 1969.

Thompson, Robert. *Revolutionary War in World Strategy, 1945-69.* New York: Taplinger, 1970.

Thompson, W. Scott and Frizzel, Donaldson, eds. *The Lessons of Vietnam.* New York: Crane, Russak, 1977.

Tillema, Herbert. *Appeal to Force: American Military Intervention in the Era of Containment.* New York: Crowell, 1973.

Tucker, Robert W. *Nation or Empire: The Debate Over American Foreign Policy.* Baltimore: Johns Hopkins University Press, 1968.

Tucker, Robert W. *The Radical Left in American Foreign Policy.* Baltimore: Johns Hopkins University Press, 1971.

Tugwell, Rexford and Cronin, Thomas. *The Presidency Reappraised.* New York: Praeger, 1974.

Ulam, Adam. *The Rivals: America and Russia Since World War II.* New York: Viking Press, 1971.

Walsh, Edmund. *Total Power: A Footnote to History.* New York: Doubleday, 1948.

Walt, Lewis. *Strange War, Strange Strategy: A General's Report on Vietnam.* New York: Funk and Wagnalls, 1970.

Warner, Dennis. *The Last Confucian.* Harmondsworth, England: Penguin Books, 1963.

Westmoreland, William. *A Soldier Reports.* New York: Doubleday, 1976.

White, Ralph. *Nobody Wanted War: Misperception in Vietnam and Other Wars.* Garden City, N.Y.: Doubleday, 1968.

Wicker, Tom. *JFK and LBJ: The Influence of Personality Upon Politics.* Baltimore: Penguin, 1972.

Wilcox, Francis. *Congress, The Executive, and Foreign Policy.* New York: Harper and Row, 1971.

Willis, Roy. *France, Germany, and the New Europe.* New York: Oxford University Press, 1968.

Windchy, Eugene. *Tonkin Gulf.* New York: Doubleday, 1971.

Wolfers, Arnold. *Discord and Collaboration: Essays on International Politics.* Baltimore: Johns Hopkins University Press, 1962.

Yergin, Daniel. *The Shattered Peace: Origins of the Cold War and the National Security State.* Boston: Houghton Mifflin, 1977.

Zagoria, Donald. *Vietnam Triangle: Moscow, Peking, Hanoi.* New York: Pegasus, 1967.

Zinn, Howard. *Vietnam: The Logic of Withdrawal.* Boston: Beacon Press, 1967.

Index

Abrams, Creighton, 136, 139, 143, 156, 198, 204
Abzug, Bella, 279
Acheson, Dean, 98, 138, 185, 222, 228
Action premium in U.S. policy, 166-69
Adams, John, 70
Adams, John Quincy, 70
Adenauer, Konrad, 32
Afghanistan, 25
Africa, 57, 65, 72, 79, 85, 88, 189, 217, 254, 311, 325; front-line states of, 93; Horn of, 168, 234
Agency for International Development (AID), 85, 91, 112, 169, 177, 205, 214; and technocracy, 192
Agnew, Spiro, 251
Aiken, George, 275
Air Force (U.S.), 110
Alaska, 74
Algeria, 78, 84, 86, 101, 108, 140, 253
Alliance doctrine, 94
Allison, Graham, 221-22
Almond, Gabriel, 88, 190
Alsop, Joseph, 244
American Federation of Labor (AFL/CIO), 175
American Friends of Vietnam, 57
Amin, Idi, 292

Analytic process in U.S. policy, 179-83
Angola, 234
Anh, Tran van, 50
Annam, 8
Anti-Americanism, 90
Anti-war movement, 144, 145, 251, 274, 277-79, 281, 298, 315
ANZUS Pact, 7, 64, 92, 94
Apartheid, 292
Ap Bac, Battle of, 113
Appeasement doctrine, 98
Arab-Israeli Wars, 57, 256, 257, 258
Arab oil-producing nations, 311
Arendt, Hannah, 262
ARVN (Army Republic of Vietnam), 112, 118, 128, 134, 136, 139, 143, 163, 175, 176, 177, 201, 204, 205, 247; battle performance of, 144; in coup against Diem, 143, 224; generals in anti-Diem coup, 116-18; in collapse of South Vietnam, 149
Army (U.S.), 110, 111, 112, 116; v. McCarthy Hearings, 40; Special Warfare Training Center, 112; "Never Again Club" in, 46
Associated Press (AP), 263
Associated States of Indochina, 9, 11, 23, 41, 108, 222
Australia, 7, 8, 49, 64; at Manila